989-249-1687

Democracy
for the Few

Democracy for the Few

Seventh Edition

Michael Parenti

Bedford/St. Martin's

Boston ♦ *New York*

For Bedford/St. Martin's

Political Science Editor: Marilea Polk Fried
Developmental Editor: Amy McConathy
Senior Editor, Publishing Services: Douglas Bell
Production Supervisor: Christie Gross
Project Management: Stratford Publishing Services, Inc.
Marketing Manager: Jenna Bookin Barry
Cover Design: Dick Hannus/Hannus Design Associates
Front Cover Photo: Photo by Susan Walsh for AP/Wide World Photos
Back Cover Photo: Photo by June Felter
Composition: Stratford Publishing Services, Inc.
Printing and Binding: Haddon Craftsmen, Inc., an R.R. Donnelley & Sons Company

President: Charles H. Christensen
Editorial Director: Joan E. Feinberg
Publisher — History, Political Science, and Communication: Patricia Rossi
Director of Marketing: Karen R. Melton
Director of Editing, Design, and Production: Marcia Cohen
Manager, Publishing Services: Emily Berleth

Library of Congress Control Number: 2001088049

For information, write: Bedford/St. Martin's, 75 Arlington Street, Boston, MA 02116 (617-399-4000)

ISBN: 0-312-39250-8

Acknowledgments
Acknowledgments and copyrights appear at the back of the book on pages 327 and 328, which constitute an extension of the copyright page.

To Sally Soriano,
because she fights for social justice

Preface

The study of politics is itself a political act, containing little that is neutral. True, we can all agree on certain neutral facts about the structure of government and the like. However, the book that does not venture much beyond these minimal descriptions will offend few readers but also will interest few. Any investigation of how and why things happen draws us into highly controversial areas. Most textbooks pretend to a neutrality they do not really possess. While claiming to be objective, they are merely conventional or evasive, ignoring the darker side of U.S. political life.

For decades, mainstream political scientists and other apologists for the existing social order have tried to recast practically every deficiency in the U.S. political system into a strength. They would have us believe that the millions who are nonvoters are content with present social conditions, that high-powered lobbyists are nothing to worry about because they perform an informational function vital to representative government, and that the growing concentration of executive power is a good thing because the president is democratically responsive to broad national interests rather than special interests. Mainstream apologists have argued that the exclusion of third parties is really for the best because too many parties (that is, more than two) would fractionalize and destabilize our political system, and besides, the major parties eventually incorporate into their platforms the positions raised by minor parties—which is news to any number of socialist and other reformist parties whose views have remained unincorporated for generations.

Reacting to the mainstream tendency to turn every vice into a virtue, some radical critics of the status quo have felt compelled to turn every virtue into a vice. Thus they have argued that electoral struggle is meaningless, that our civil liberties are a charade, that federal programs for the needy are next to worthless, that reforms are mostly sops to the oppressed, and that labor unions are all complacent and collaborationist with management. These critics have been a much needed antidote to the happy pluralists who painted a silver lining around every murky cloud. But they are wrong in seeing no victories, no "real" progress in the democratic struggles fought and won.

Democracy for the Few tries to strike a balance; it tries to explain how democracy is incongruous with modern-day capitalism and is consistently violated by a capitalist social order, and yet how popular forces continue to fight back and sometimes even make gains.

Democracy for the Few offers an interpretation that students are not likely to get in elementary school, high school, or most of their college courses, nor in the mass media or mainstream political literature. There are political scientists who spend their entire lives writing about American government, the presidency, and public policy without ever once mentioning capitalism, a feat of omission that would be judged extraordinary were it not so commonplace. In this book I talk about that forbidden subject, capitalism, the better to comprehend the underpinnings of the political system we are studying. It may come as a surprise to some academics, but there is a marked relationship between economic power and political power.

I have attempted to blend several approaches. Attention is given to traditional political institutions such as the Congress, the presidency, the bureaucracy, the Supreme Court, political parties, elections, and the law enforcement system. But these formal features of American government are placed in an overall framework that relates them to the realities of class power and interest.

In addition, this book devotes attention to the *foundations and historical development* of American politics, particularly in regard to the making of the Constitution, the growing role of government, and the political culture. The major eras of reform are investigated with the intent of developing a more critical understanding of the class dimension in American politics, the struggle waged by democratic forces, and the difficulties of reform.

Herein we will critically investigate not only who governs, but also who gets what — in other words, the outputs of the system. Instead of concentrating solely on the process of government, as do many texts, I also give attention to the content of actual government practices. Thus a major emphasis is placed throughout the book on the *political economy* of public policy. The significance of government, after all, lies not in its abstracted structure as such, but in what it does and how its policies affect people at home and abroad. I have included a good deal of public-policy information of a kind not ordinarily found in standard texts, first, because students and citizens in general tend to be poorly informed about politico-economic issues, and second, because it makes little sense to talk about the "policy process" as something abstracted from actual issues and content, divorced from questions of power and interest. This descriptive information, however, is presented with the intent of drawing the reader to an analysis and an overall synthesis of U.S. political reality.

This book takes what some would call a "structural" approach. Rather than treating political developments as the result of happenstance or the contrivances of particular personalities or idiosyncratic events, I try to show that most (but not necessarily all) of what occurs is the outcome of broader configurations of power, wealth, class, and institution as structured into the dominant political organizations, the economy, and the society itself.

Unfortunately there are some individuals who believe that a structural analysis demands that we treat conspiracies as imaginary things and conscious human efforts as of no great consequence. They go so far as to argue that we are all now divided into two camps, which they call "structuralists" and "conspiracists." In this book I consider conspiracies (by which most people seem to mean secret, consciously planned programs by persons in high places) to be part of the arsenal of structural rule. No structure and no system exists without human agency. Ruling elements must consciously strive to maintain and advance the conditions of their hegemonic rule. The larger social formation and broader forces do not operate like mystical abstracted entities. They are directed by people who deliberately pursue certain goals, using all sorts of methods of power, including propaganda, persuasion, elections, fraud, lies, fear, incitements, coercion, concessions, and sometimes even secrecy and concerted violence and other criminal ploys. Watergate and Iran-contra are only two of the better publicized instances of this kind of criminal conspiracy in high places — undertaken in the service of structural interests. Rather than seeing conspiracy and structure as mutually exclusive, we might consider how the former is one of the instruments of the latter. Some conspiracies are imagined, some are real. And some of the real ones are part of the existing political structure, not exceptions to it.

This seventh edition contains a new chapter on U.S. global domination; an entirely new section on "free trade" agreements, the World Trade Organization (WTO), and the threat posed to our democratic sovereignty; a newly developed discussion on the controversy around Social Security; and additional materials on health care, the environment, the death penalty, criminal justice, the national security state and the drug trade, and the irregularities of the 2000 election. In addition, almost every page of this edition has been revised and updated with the intent of deepening the book's informative function and advancing its analysis. My hope is that this book, in its new edition, continues to prove useful to students and lay readers.

A number of professors who have used this book in their courses offered helpful suggestions for this new edition: Michelle Brophy-Baermann of the University of Wisconsin, Stevens Point; Kathryn Edwards of Ashland Community College, Kentucky; Dennis Hart, Kent State University; Christopher Leu, California State University, Northridge; Shellie Levine, Johnson State College, Vermont; Richard Stahler-Sholk, Eastern Michigan University; and William Stewart, California State University, Chico. Molly Hudgens, Beth Garber, Sarah Olsen, and Peggy Karp helped organize and file some portions of the mountainous materials I had accumulated for this edition. Alex Calabrese, Lauren Coodley, Sally Soriano, Kamela Wolf, Susan McCallister, and Kathy Lipscomb provided me with useful data. My editors at Bedford/St. Martin's, Marilea Polk Fried and Amy McConathy, offered valuable support and assistance. I wish to express my gratitude to all these fine people.

Michael Parenti

Contents

For Further Reference   *inside front cover*

Preface   *vii*

1 Partisan Politics   1

Beyond Textbooks   1
The Politico-Economic System   3

2 Wealth and Want in the United States   6

Capital and Labor   6
Accumulation and Expansion   8
Who Owns America?   9
Corporate Concentration   11
Monopoly Farming   13
Downsizing and Downgrading   14
Profit-Price Inflation   15
Market Demand and Human Need   16
Productivity: A Mixed Blessing   17
"Desirable" Unemployment   19
The Hardships of Working America   20
The Human Costs of Economic Injustice   23

3 The Plutocratic Culture: Institutions and Ideologies   28

Rule by Corporate Plutocracy   28
Promoting Ideological Orthodoxy   29
Right, Left, and Center   33
Public Opinion: Which Direction?   37
Democracy: Form and Content   39

4 A Constitution for the Few   42

Class Power in Early America   42
Containing the Spread of Democracy   44
Fragmenting Majority Power   47
Plotters or Patriots?   49
Democratic Concessions   52

5 Rise of the Corporate State   55

Serving Business: The Early Years   55
The War against Labor   56
Law in the Service of Business   58
The Not-So-Progressive Era   59
War and Red Scares   60
The New Deal: Hard Times and Tough Reforms   61

6 Politics: Who Gets What?   67

Welfare for the Rich   67
Federal Bailouts, State and Local Handouts   70
Taxes: Helping the Rich in Their Time of Greed   72
Unkind Cuts, Unfair Rates   74
Deficit Spending and the National Debt   76
Some Hidden Deficits   77

7 Military Empire and Global Domination   80

A Global Kill Capacity   80
Military Waste and Fraud   82
Pentagon Profits   83
The Military's Hidden Diseconomies   85
Economic Imperialism   85
The Terror State   88

8 Health, Environment, and Human Services: Sacrificial Lambs   95

The Poor Get Less (and Less)   95
Social Insecurity: Privatizing Everything   97

How Much Health Can You Afford? 98
Buyers Beware, and Workers Too 101
Creating Crises: Schools and Housing 102
"Mess Transit": What's Good for General Motors 104
Toxifying the Earth 106
Eco-Apocalypse 108
Government for the Despoilers 110

9 Unequal before the Law 118

Crime in the Suites 118
Class Law 122
The "Tough on Crime" Craze 123
The Crime of Prisons 125
The Guilty Innocent 126
Sexist Justice 128
The Victimization of Children 130
Bedroom Police 131
Racist Law Enforcement 132

10 Political Repression and National Insecurity 139

The Repression of Dissent 139
Political Prisoners, USA 142
Political Murder, USA 147
Cozy with Right-Wing Violence 149
The National Security Autocracy 151
CIA: Capitalism's International Army or Cocaine
    Import Agency? 155
Watergate and Iran-Contra 157

11 Who Governs? Elites, Labor, and Globalization 164

The Ruling Class 164
Labor Besieged 168
Unions and the Good Fight 170
Globalization, WTO, and the End of Democracy 171

12 Mass Media: For the Many, by the Few 178

He Who Pays the Piper 178
The Ideological Monopoly 182
Official Manipulation 184
Political Entertainment 187
Room for Alternatives? 189

13 Elections, Parties, and Voters 194

Republicrats and Demopublicans 194
The Two-Party Monopoly 197
Proportional Representation: Making Every
  Vote Count 198
Rigging the Game 200
Money: A Necessary Condition 203
The Struggle to Vote 207
Voter "Apathy" and Participation 211
Democratic Input 214

14 Congress: The Pocketing of Power 218

A Congress for the Money 218
Lobbyists: The Other Lawmakers 221
Grassroots Lobbying 224
Helping Themselves: The Varieties of Corruption 225
A Special-Interest Committee System 228
Security, Secrecy, and Fast Track 230
The Legislative Labyrinth 232
Term Limits 235
A Touch of Democracy 237

15 The President: Guardian of the System 241

Salesman of the System 241
The Two Faces of the President 244
The President's Systemic Role 248
A Loaded Electoral College 250
The "New Federalism" Ploy 252
The Growth of Presidential Power 252

The Would-Be King   254
The Conservative Context   257

16 The Political Economy of Bureaucracy   262

The Myth and Reality of Inefficiency   262
Deregulation and Privatization   265
Secrecy, Deception, and Corruption   269
Bureaucratic Action and Inaction   272
Serving the "Regulated"   274
Public Authority in Private Hands   277
Monopoly Regulation versus Public-Service Regulation   279

17 The Supremely Political Court   283

Who Judges?   283
Conservative Judicial Activism   286
Circumventing the First Amendment   289
Freedom for Revolutionaries?   290
As the Court Turns   292
Influence of the Court   300

18 Democracy for the Few   306

Pluralism for the Few   306
The Limits of Reform   309
Democracy as Class Struggle   311
The Roles of the State   314
What Is to Be Done?   316
The Reality of Public Production   321

Index   329

1

Partisan Politics

How does the U.S. political system work? What are the major forces shaping political life? Who governs in the United States? Who gets what, when, how, and why? Who pays and in what ways? These are the questions pursued in this book.

Beyond Textbooks

Many of us were taught a somewhat idealized version of American government, which might be summarized as follows:

1. The United States was founded upon a Constitution fashioned to limit political authority and check abuses of power. Over the generations it has proven to be a "living document," which, through reinterpretation and amendment, has served us well.

2. The people's desires are registered through elections, political parties, and a free press. Government decision makers are kept in check by each other's power and by their need to satisfy the electorate in order to remain in office. The people do not rule directly but they select those who do. Thus, government decisions are grounded in majority rule — subject to the restraints imposed by the Constitution for the protection of minority rights.

3. The United States is a free and pluralistic nation of manifold social and economic groups. The role of government is to mediate the conflicting demands of these groups. Although most policy decisions are compromises that seldom satisfy all interested parties, they usually allow for a working consensus. Hence, every significant group has a say and no one group chronically dominates.

1

4. These institutional arrangements have given us a government of laws and not of individuals, which, while far from perfect, allows for a fairly high degree of liberty and popular participation.

This view of the United States as a happy, pluralistic polity assumes that existing political institutions operate with benign effect; that power is not highly concentrated nor heavily skewed toward those who control vast wealth; and that the state is a neutral entity with no special linkage to those who own the land, technology, and capital of this and other societies. These assumptions will be challenged in the pages ahead.

The theme of this book is that our government more often represents the privileged few rather than the general public, and that elections and the activities of political parties are insufficient defenses against the influences of corporate wealth. It will be argued that the laws of our polity are written principally to advance the interests of the haves at the expense of the rest of us. Even when equitable as written, the law usually is enforced in highly discriminatory ways. This "democracy for the few" is a product not only of the venality of particular officeholders but a reflection of the entire politico-economic system, the way the resources of power are distributed.

The American people are not always passive victims (or willing accomplices) to all of this. The mass of ordinary people have made important political and economic gains, usually after long and bitter contests that have extended beyond the electoral process. This democratic struggle is an important part of the story that will be treated in the pages ahead.

This book tries to demonstrate that just about every part of the politico-economic system, be it the media, lobbying, criminal justice, overseas intervention, or environmental policy, reflects the nature of the whole, and in its particular way serves to maintain the overall system — especially the system's basic class interests. Therefore, seemingly distinct issues and social problems are often interrelated.

The political system comprises the various branches of government along with the political parties, laws, lobbyists, and private interest groups that affect public policy. By public policy I mean the decisions made by government. Policy decisions are seldom neutral. They usually benefit some interests more than others, entailing social costs that are rarely distributed equally. The shaping of a budget, the passage of a law, and the development of an administrative program are all policy decisions, all *political* decisions, and there is no way to execute them with neutral effect. If the wants of all persons could be automatically satisfied, there would be no need to set priorities and give some interests precedence over others; indeed, there would be no need for policies or politics.

Politics extends beyond election campaigns and the actions of government. Decisions that keep certain matters within "private" systems of power — such as leaving rental costs or health care to the private market —

are highly political even if seldom recognized as such. Power in the private realm is generally inequitable and undemocratic and often the source of conflicts that spill over into the public arena, for instance, management-labor disputes and racial and gender discrimination.

Someone once defined a politician as a person who receives votes from the poor and money from the rich on the promise of protecting each from the other. And President Jimmy Carter observed: "Politics is the world's second oldest profession, closely related to the first." Many people share this view. For them, politics is little more than the art of manipulating appearances in order to sell oneself, with the politician acting as a kind of prostitute. While not denying the measure of truth in such observations, I take a broader view. Politics is more than just something politicians do. It is the process of struggle over conflicting interests carried into the public arena. It also involves muting and suppressing conflicting interests. Politics involves not only the competition among groups within the system but the struggle to change the system itself, not only the desire to achieve predefined ends but the struggle to redefine ends and pose alternatives to the existing politico-economic structure.

The Politico-Economic System

Politics today covers every kind of issue, from abortion to school prayer, but the bulk of public policy is concerned with economic matters, which is why some writers refer to the "politico-economic system." The most important document the government produces each year is the budget. Probably the most vital functions of government are taxing and spending. Certainly they are necessary for everything else it does, from delivering the mail to making war. The very organization of the federal government reflects its close involvement with the economy: thus, one finds the departments of Commerce, Labor, Agriculture, Interior, Transportation, and Treasury, and the Federal Trade Commission, the National Labor Relations Board, the Interstate Commerce Commission, the Securities and Exchange Commission, and numerous other agencies involved in the economy. Likewise, most of the committees in Congress can be identified according to their economic functions, the most important having to do with taxation and appropriations.

Politics and economics are two sides of the same coin. Economics is concerned with the allocation of scarce resources, involving conflicts between social classes and among groups and individuals within classes. Much of politics is a carryover of this struggle. Both politics and economics deal with the survival and material well-being of millions of people; both deal with the fundamental conditions of social life itself.

This close relationship between politics and economics is neither neutral nor coincidental. Governments evolve through history in order to protect accumulations of property and wealth. In nomadic and hunting societies, where there is little surplus wealth, governance is rudimentary and usually communal. In societies where wealth and property are controlled by a select class of persons, a state develops to protect the interests of the haves from the have-nots. As wrote John Locke in 1689: "The great and chief end . . . of Men's uniting into Commonwealths, and putting themselves under Government, is the Preservation of their Property." And Adam Smith, the premier exponent of early capitalism, wrote in 1776: "The necessity of civil government grows up with the acquisition of valuable property." And "Till there be property there can be no government, the very end of which is to secure wealth, and to defend the rich from the poor."[1]

Many political scientists manage to ignore the relationship between government and wealth, treating the corporate giants, if at all, as if they were but one of a number of interest groups. They label as "Marxist" any approach that links class, wealth, and capitalism to politics. To be sure, Karl Marx saw such a relationship, but so did more conservative theorists like Thomas Hobbes, John Locke, Adam Smith, and, in America, Alexander Hamilton and James Madison. Indeed, just about every theorist and practitioner of politics in the seventeenth, eighteenth, and early nineteenth centuries saw the link between political organization and economic interest, and between state and class, as not only important but desirable and essential to the well-being of the polity. "The people who own the country ought to govern it," declared John Jay. A permanent check over the populace should be exercised by "the rich and the well-born," urged Alexander Hamilton. Unlike most theorists before him, Marx was one of the first in the modern era to see the existing relationship between property and power as undesirable and exploitative, and this was his unforgivable sin. The tendency to avoid critical analysis of corporate capitalism persists to this day among business people, journalists, and most academics.[2]

Power is no less political because it is economic. By "power" I mean the ability to get what one wants, either by having one's interests prevail in conflicts with others or by preventing others from raising their demands. Power presumes the ability to manipulate the social environment to one's advantage. Power belongs to those who possess the resources that enable them to shape the political agenda and control the actions and beliefs of others, resources such as jobs, organization, technology, publicity, media, social legitimacy, expertise, essential goods and services, organized force, and — the ingredient that often determines the availability of these things — money.

Some people say our politico-economic system does not work and should be changed or overthrown; others say it does work or, in any case, we can't fight it and should work within it. Some argue that the existing system is "the only one we have" and moreover the only one we ever *could* have. They fear that a breakdown in this system's social order would mean a breakdown in all social order or a creation of something far worse. These fearful notions keep many people not only from entertaining ideas about new social arrangements but also from taking a critical look at existing ones. Sometimes the complaint is made: "You're good at criticizing the system, but what would you put in its place?" implying that unless you have a finished blueprint for a better society, you should refrain from pointing out existing deficiencies and injustices. This book is predicated on the notion that it is desirable and necessary for democratic citizens to examine the society in which they live, possibly as a step toward making fundamental improvements. It is unreasonable to demand that we refrain from making a diagnosis of an illness until we have perfected a cure. For how can we hope to find solutions unless we really understand the problem? In any case, an abundant number of solutions and fundamental changes are offered in the closing chapter and in other parts of this book.

Political life is replete with deceit, corruption, and plunder. Small wonder that many people seek to remove themselves from it. But whether we like it or not, politics and government play a crucial role in determining the conditions of our lives. People can leave political life alone, but it will not leave them alone. They can escape its noise and nonsense but not its effects. One ignores the doings of the state only at one's own risk.

If the picture that emerges in the pages ahead is not pretty, this *should not be taken as an attack on the United States,* for this country and its people are greater than the abuses perpetrated upon them by those who live for power and profit. *To expose these abuses is not to denigrate the nation that is a victim of them.* The greatness of a country is to be measured by something more than its rulers, its military budget, its instruments of dominance and destruction, and its profiteering giant corporations. A nation's greatness can be measured by the democratic nature of its institutions, by its ability to create a society free of poverty, racism, sexism, imperialism, and environmental devastation. Albert Camus once said, "I would like to love my country and justice too." In fact, there is no better way to love one's country, and strive for the fulfillment of its greatness, than to entertain critical ideas that enable us to pursue social justice at home and abroad.

Notes

1. John Locke, *Treatise of Civil Government* (New York: Appleton-Century-Croft, 1937), 82; Adam Smith, *An Inquiry into the Nature and Causes of the Wealth of Nations* (Chicago: Encyclopaedia Britannica, 1952), 309 and 311.

2. See William Appleman Williams, *The Great Evasion* (Chicago: Quadrangle, 1964), for an analysis of the way Marxist thought has been stigmatized or ignored by American intellectuals and those who pay their salaries.

2

Wealth and Want
in the United States

Most people who talk and write about the U.S. political system never mention capitalism. But the capitalist economy has an overbearing impact upon political and social life, and so it deserves our critical attention.

Capital and Labor

One should distinguish between those who own the wealth of society and those who must work for a living. The very rich families and individuals whom we might call "the owning class" live mostly on investments: stocks bonds, rents, and other property income. The "employee class" or "working class" live mostly on wages, salaries, fees, and pensions. The latter includes not only blue-collar workers but everyone else who is not independently wealthy. The distinction between owners and employees is blurred somewhat by the range of affluence within both classes. "Owners" refers both to the fabulously wealthy stockholders of giant corporations and to the struggling proprietors of small stores. But the latter control a relatively small portion of the wealth and hardly qualify as part of the *corporate* owning class. Among the victims of big business is small business. Glorified as the purveyors of the entrepreneurial spirit, small businesses are just so many squirrels dancing among the elephants. Every year about seventy thousand or more of them are driven out of business as markets decline or bigger competitors move in.

Among the employee class are professionals and mid-level executives who in income, education, and lifestyle tend to be identified as "middle" or "upper-middle" class. Then there are some corporate lawyers, doctors, entertainment and sports figures, and top business executives who accumulate enough surplus wealth to live off the unearned income of their investments, thereby becoming in effect members of the owning class.

You are a member of the owning class when your income is very large and comes mostly from the labor of other people — that is, when others work for you, either in a company you own or by creating the wealth that allows your investments to increase in value. Hard work seldom makes anyone rich. The secret to wealth is to have others work hard for you. This explains why workers who spend their lives toiling in factories or offices retire with little or no wealth to speak of, while the stockholding owners of these businesses, who do not work in them and usually have never visited them, can amass considerable fortunes.

Wealth is created by the labor power of workers. As Adam Smith noted in 1776, "Labor . . . is alone the ultimate and real standard by which the value of all commodities can at all times and places be estimated and compared. It is their real price; money is their nominal price only."[1] What transforms a tree into a profitable commodity such as paper or furniture is the labor that goes into harvesting the timber, cutting the lumber, and manufacturing, shipping, advertising, and selling the commodity. In addition, there is the labor that goes into making the tools and whatever else needed for production and distribution.

Workers' wages represent only a portion of the wealth created by their labor. The unpaid portion is pocketed by the owners. Today, a private-sector employee is likely to work two hours for herself or himself (the value created and paid back in wages) and six or more hours for the boss (the value realized and pocketed by owners after expenses). The latter portion is what Marx described as "surplus value," the source of the owner's wealth. Capitalists themselves have a similar concept: "value added in manufacture." For example, in 1995, management estimated that the average General Motors autoworker added $150,000 to the value of products for which he or she was paid $38,000, or one-fourth of the value created. Workers employed by Intel and Exxon received only about one-ninth of the value they created, and in industries such as tobacco and pharmaceuticals, the worker's share was a mere one-twentieth of the value added. Between 1954 and 1994, the overall average rate of value added (the portion going to the owner) in the United States increased from 162 percent to 425 percent, far above the exploitation rate in other Western industrialized countries.[2]

Workers endure an exploitation of their labor as certainly as do slaves and serfs. The slave or serf obviously toils for the enrichment of the master and receives only a bare subsistence. (James Madison told a visitor shortly after the American Revolution that he made $257 a year on every slave he owned and spent only $12 or $13 for the slave's keep.) Sharecroppers who must give a third or half their crop to the landowner are also obviously exploited. Under capitalism, however, the portion taken from the worker is not visible. Workers are simply paid substantially less than the value they create. Indeed, the only reason they are hired is to make money from their labor. If wages did represent the total value created by labor (after expenses and improvements), there would be no surplus value, no profits for the owner, no great fortunes for those who do not labor.

Company managers and executives are employees of the firm who represent the interests of the owner. Their task is to extract more performance from workers. Income from ownership is apart from workers' wages or even executives' salaries; it consists of profits — the money one makes *when not working*. The author of a book, for instance, does not make "profits" on his book; he earns an income (fancily misnamed "royalties") from the labor of writing it. Likewise, editors, proofreaders, printers, and salespersons all contribute labor that adds to the value of the book. Profits on the book go to those who own the publishing house and who contribute nothing to the book's marketable value. The sums going to owners are aptly called *unearned* income on tax accounts.

While corporations are often called "producers," the truth is they produce nothing. They are organizational devices for the exploitation of labor and accumulation of capital. The real producers are those who apply their brawn, brains, and talents to the creation of goods and services. The primacy of labor was noted 140 years ago by President Abraham Lincoln in a message to Congress: "Labor is prior to and independent of capital. Capital is only the fruit of labor and could not have existed had not labor first existed. Labor is the superior of capital and deserves much the higher consideration." Lincoln's words went unheeded. The dominance of the moneyed class over labor remains the essence of the U.S. economic system.

Accumulation and Expansion

Capitalists like to say they are "putting their money to work," but money as such cannot create more wealth. What they really mean is that they are putting more human labor to work, paying workers less in wages than they produce in value, thereby siphoning off more profit for themselves. That's how money "grows." Under capitalism, capital annexes living labor in order to convert itself into goods and services that will produce still more capital.[3] All of Rockefeller's capital could not build a house or a machine or even a toothpick; only human labor can do that. Of itself, capital cannot produce anything. It is the thing that is produced by labor.

The ultimate purpose of a corporation is not to perform public services or produce goods but to make as large a profit as possible for the investor. Steel magnate David Roderick once said that his company "is not in the business of making steel. We're in the business of making profits."[4] The social uses of the product and its effects upon human well-being and the natural environment win consideration in capitalist production, if at all, only to the extent that they do not violate the profit goals of the corporation.

This relentless pursuit of profit arises from something more than just greed — although there is plenty of that. Under capitalism, enterprises must expand in order to survive. To stand still amidst growth is to decline, not only relatively but absolutely. A slow-growth firm is less able to move into new markets, hold onto old ones, command investment capital, and control suppliers. Hence, even the biggest corporations are beset by a ceaseless drive to expand, to find new ways of making money.

Who Owns America?

Contrary to a widely propagated myth, this country's wealth does not belong to a broad middle class. The top 10 percent of American households own 98 percent of the tax-exempt state and local bonds, 94 percent of business assets, and 95 percent of the value of all trusts. The richest 1 percent own 60 percent of all corporate stock and all business assets. True, some 40 percent of families own some stocks or bonds, but almost all of these have total holdings of less than $2,000. Taking into account their debts and mortgages, 90 percent of American families have little or no net assets.[5]

The greatest source of individual wealth is inheritance. If you are not rich, it is probably because you lacked the foresight to pick the right parents at birth. Studies show that rags-to-riches is a rare exception. Most people die in the class to which they were born. A large majority of the "self-made" Forbes 400 superrich inherited fortunes or received crucial start-up capital from a family member.[6]

The trend has been toward greater economic inequality. In the mid-1990s, corporate profits more than doubled; income from investments has been growing two to three times faster than income from work. Between 1980 and 1992, the five hundred largest U.S. industrial corporations more than doubled their assets, from $1.8 trillion to $2.7 trillion, while shedding over five million jobs. And the years that followed brought "the highest level of corporate profitability in the post-war era, and probably since the latter stages of the Bronze Age," according to the *Wall Street Journal*.[7] During the last three decades, the richest 1 percent saw their average after-tax incomes soar by 115 percent — while the incomes of the bottom fifth declined by almost 10 percent.[8]

U.S. Census Bureau income studies refer to the "richest 20 percent" who earn thirteen times more than the poorest 20 percent. But dealing with quintiles greatly understates the real chasm between rich and poor. To be in the richest 20 percent, you need earn only $65,000 or more. In fact, the top 20 percent are not rich but mostly upper-middle class, if that. The

"The Duke and Duchess of A. T. & T., the Count and Countess of Citicorp, the Earl of Exxon, and the Marchioness of Avco. The Duke of Warnaco . . ."

very richest stratum consists of not more than a tiny fraction of 1 percent of the population. It controls most of the wealth and is not thirteen times but thousands of times richer than the poorest quintile.[9] Few of the people who study income distribution seem to realize how rich the rich really are.

At the end of the twentieth century, sales of high-priced goods — luxury cars and condominiums, works of art, antiques, precious gems, yachts, and private jets — continued to boom. Income and wealth disparities were greater than at any time over the previous sixty years. As one economist put it: "If we made an income pyramid out of a child's blocks, with each layer portraying $1,000 of income, the peak would be far higher than the Eiffel Tower, but almost all of us would be within a yard of the ground."[10]

Enormous wealth translates into enormous power. The power of the business class is like that of no other group in our society. The giant corporations control the rate of technological development, the availability of livelihoods, and standards of consumption and popular taste. They decide which labor markets to explore and which to abandon, sometimes relegating whole communities to destitution. They devour environmental resources, stripping our forests and toxifying the land, water, and air. They command an enormous surplus wealth while helping to create and perpetuate conditions of scarcity for millions of people at home and abroad. And as we shall see in subsequent chapters, they enjoy a predominant voice in the highest councils of government.

Corporate Concentration

We are taught that the economy consists of a wide array of independent producers who compete with each other for consumer markets. In fact, a small number of giant corporations control most of the private sector. And the trend is toward ever greater concentrations as giant companies are swallowed up by super-giants in industries such as oil, automotive, pharmaceuticals, telecommunications, media, publishing, health insurance, weapons manufacturing, and banking. Mergers and acquisitions are fueled by deregulation, low interest rates, and a booming stock market. In the financial industry alone, during the first half of 1998, there were almost 1,500 mergers, the biggest ones being Banc One Corp.'s acquisition of First Chicago for about $30 billion, and NationsBank's $62.4 billion buyout of Bank of America. In 2000, two banking powerhouses, Chase Manhattan and J. P. Morgan, entered into a $35.2 billion merger.[11]

Mergers are justified as strengthening the competitive capacity of a firm. But merged companies seldom display improved performance. The many billions spent on acquisitions absorb money that could have been better spent on new technologies and production. The mergers benefit the big shareholders, creditors, and top executives who walk away with megaprofits from the sale — while consumers and workers pay the costs. Numerous corporations treat worker pension funds as part of the firm's assets. If and when the corporation merges with another or is bought out, the fund is absorbed by the takeover and the workers often never see a penny of the money they paid into it.[12]

Corporate consolidations lead to bigger corporate debts. Taken together, big business expends about half its earnings just on interest payments to banks and other creditors (all of which is tax deductible). A corporation has to procure large sums to buy a dominant share of its own stock if it wishes to ward off a hostile takeover by corporate raiders. If it is trying to acquire another company, it needs money to buy up that firm's stock. In either case, cash reserves are seldom sufficient and companies must borrow heavily from banks. To meet its debt obligations, the firm reduces wages and benefits, sells off productive plants for quick cash, lays off workers, and enforces speedups. Thus after merging with NationsBank, Bank of America reduced its workforce (through firings and attrition) by 31,000. Sometimes the merged corporation moves to a cheaper labor market abroad. In the last decade, U.S.-based transnational companies created 345,000 jobs abroad while cutting 783,000 jobs in the United States.[13]

A handful of giant business conglomerates, controlled by the Mellons, Morgans, DuPonts, Rockefellers, and a few others, dominate the U.S. economy. The DuPonts control ten corporations, each worth billions of dollars, including General Motors, Coca-Cola, and United Brands, along with many smaller firms. The DuPonts serve as trustees of dozens of colleges. They own about forty manorial estates and private museums in Delaware alone and have set up thirty-one tax-exempt foundations. The DuPonts are frequently the largest contributor to Republican presidential campaigns and various right-wing and anti-labor causes.

Another powerful financial empire, that of the Rockefellers, extends into just about every industry in every state of the Union and every nation of the world. The Rockefellers control five of the world's twelve largest oil companies and four of the biggest banks. At one time or another, they or their close associates have occupied the offices of the president, vice-president, secretaries of state, commerce, defense, and other cabinet posts, the governorships of several states, and key positions in the Federal Reserve Board, the Central Intelligence Agency (CIA), the Council on Foreign Relations, and in the U.S. Senate and House.

Far from being neutral technocrats devoted to the public welfare, top corporate executives are self-enriching members of the owning class. Over the past fifteen years the salaries of chief executive officers (CEOs) of corporations rose an average 500 percent. In 1998, Disney CEO Michael Eisner pocketed $575 million, Gap CEO Millard Drexler took home $495 million, Yahoo CEO Timothy Koogle pulled in $476 million, while IBM CEO Louis Gerstner made off with $336 million. That same year, the nation's top five hundred companies handed out $10.4 *billion* in stock options, mostly to CEOs.[14] At the top of this heap was Microsoft owner Bill Gates, whose net worth slumped from $85 billion to $63 billion, still leaving him the richest person in the United States as of 2000. One corporate chief, Richard Munro, admitted: "Corporate managers lead just about the most privileged lives in our society."[15] Still, it should be remembered that the CEO's salary and bonuses represent but a tiny portion — usually not more than 3 or 4 percent — of the profits distributed to the corporation's super-rich stockholders. In other words, there are others among the superrich who don't work and are far more privileged than the CEOs.

Monopoly Farming

We treat farmers as an interest group apart from business, at a time when a handful of agribusiness firms,[16] big banks, and commercial corporations control most of our food supply and farmlands. Thus, R. J. Reynolds, with vast holdings in cigarettes, transportation, and petroleum, owns Del Monte — itself a transnational agribusiness. Five giant corporations dominate the domestic and world grain market. Just 1 percent of all food corporations control 80 percent of the food industry's assets and close to 90 percent of the profits.[17]

Independent family farms are being driven deeper into debt or completely out of business because the price that agribusiness distributors pay them for their perishable crops is often below the costs of machinery, seeds, and fertilizers. Today, the combined farm debt is many times greater than net farm income. Only 2 or 3 percent of the cost of a farm commodity goes to the farmer, the rest to the corporate distributors. Of the less than two million existing farm families (down from six million in 1940), most survive by finding additional work off the farm.[18]

Contrary to popular belief, large commercial agribusiness farms do not produce more efficiently than small farms, especially when real costs are taken into account. The shift from family farm to corporate agribusiness has brought numerous diseconomies. The family farm uses less pesticides and herbicides, does not resort to genetic engineering, and is concerned about farm waste disposal and preserving the cleanliness of its ground water, which it uses for its own living purposes. Family farms treat their livestock in a healthier more humane way, are more economical in their use of fuel and topsoil, and, because they supply primarily local markets, they have lower transportation costs.

With the growth of corporate agribusiness, regional self-sufficiency in food has virtually vanished. The Northeast, for instance, imports more than 70 percent of its food from other regions. For every two dollars spent growing food in the United States, another dollar is spent transporting it. Giant agribusiness farms rely on intensive row crop planting and heavy use of toxic spraying and artificial fertilizers, causing millions of acres of topsoil to be blown away each year. The nation's ability to feed itself is being jeopardized, as more and more land is eroded or toxified by large-scale, quick-profit, biotechnological, commercial farming, not to mention the damage to people's health resulting from the consumption of foods produced by these chemicalized methods.[19]

On the big commercial agribusiness farms, the plight of the nation's two million landless farm laborers has gone from bad to worse. The pesticides and herbicides they are exposed to and their poor living conditions constitute serious health hazards. Their real wages (accounting for inflation) have dropped 20 percent or more over the last twenty years.[20]

Downsizing and Downgrading

Corporations are hailed by some as great job providers. If anything, many corporate measures are designed to eliminate jobs. The top two hundred corporations account for more than a quarter of the world's economic activity while employing less than one-hundredth of one percent (0.01) of the world's people. As one writer notes, "Today, the more people a company fires, the more Wall Street loves it, and the higher its stock price goes."[21]

The capitalist seeks to raise profitability by downsizing (laying off workers), speedups (making the diminished workforce toil faster and harder), downgrading (reclassifying jobs to lower-wage categories), and using more and more part-time and "contract" labor (hiring people who receive no benefits, seniority, or steady employment). Hundreds of thousands of better-paying manufacturing jobs have been eliminated, while some 80 percent of new jobs created have been in low-paying retail trade, restaurant, clerical, health, and temporary services. In recent downsizing, the ranks of managers and supervisors have been thinned along with workers — but much more slowly, so that a proportionately larger share of the national income goes to supervisors at the expense of production workers.[22]

As a cost of production, wages must be kept down; as a source of consumer spending, wages must be kept up. By holding down wages, employers reduce the buying power of the very public that buys their products, thus creating a chronic tendency toward overproduction and recession. For the big capitalists, economic downturns are not unmitigated gloom. Weaker competitors are weeded out, unions are weakened and often broken, strike activity declines, a reserve supply of unemployed workers helps to depress wages, and profits rise faster than wages. The idea that all Americans are in the same boat, experiencing good and bad times together, should be put to rest. Even as the economy declines, the rich grow richer by grabbing a still bigger slice of whatever exists. Thus, during the 1992 recession, corporate profits grew to record levels, as companies squeezed more output from each employee while paying less in wages and benefits.[23]

Former Secretary of the Treasury Nicholas Brady once remarked that recessions are "not the end of the world" and "no big deal." Certainly not for Brady, who rests comfortably on a handsome fortune, and certainly not for his wealthy associates, who welcome the gratifying opportunity to acquire bankrupted holdings at depressed prices.[24] Brady and friends understand that the comfort and prosperity of the rich require an abundant supply of those who, spurred by the lash of necessity, tend the country club grounds, serve the banquet luncheons, work the mines, mills, fields, and offices, performing a hundred thankless — and sometimes health damaging — tasks for relatively paltry wages.

Wealth and poverty are not just juxtaposed, they are in a close dynamic relationship. Wealth creates poverty and relies on it for its own continued existence. Without slaves and serfs, how would the master and lord live in the style to which they are accustomed? Without the working poor, how would the leisured rich make do? With no underprivileged, who would be privileged?

Profit-Price Inflation

A common problem of modern capitalism is inflation. Inflation occurs when the total supply of money and credit expands at a faster rate than the available goods and services, resulting in a continual rise in prices, or when big companies achieve near monopoly control over a market and jack up prices to maximize their profits. Even a modest inflation rate of 3 or 4 percent substantially reduces within a few years the buying power of wage earners and persons on fixed incomes. Corporate leaders maintain that inflation is caused by wage demands. Generally, however, prices and profits have risen faster than wages. The four essentials, food, fuel, housing, and health care, which together devour 70 percent of the average family income, are among the most inflationary of all. Yet the share going to labor in those four industries has been dropping. The skyrocketing costs of housing in states like California cannot be blamed on construction workers, who have actually suffered wage cutbacks. The rise in food prices is not caused by indebted family farmers or impoverished farm laborers or minimum-wage servers at McDonald's. And the astronomical costs of health care cannot be blamed on the low wages paid to health-care workers.

In most industries the portion of production costs going to workers has been shrinking, while the share taken by executives, shareholders, and interest payments to bankers has risen dramatically. As former Secretary of Labor Robert B. Reich said, "[T]here is no inflation push from wages."[25] The "wage-price" spiral is usually a profit-price spiral, with the worker more the victim than the cause of inflation. (This is not to deny that by depressing wages, business is sometimes able to maintain a slower inflation creep while pocketing big profits. But that is not the same as arguing that wages cause inflation.)

As financial power is concentrated in fewer hands, prices are more easily manipulated. Instead of lowering prices when sales drop, the big monopoly firms often raise them to compensate for sales losses. The same is true with agribusiness: whether crops are poor or plentiful, food prices at the consumer level tend only to rise. Prices are pushed up by limiting production, as when the petroleum cartels create artificial oil and gasoline scarcities that mysteriously disappear after the companies raise their prices.

Massive military expenditures "happen to be a particularly inflation-producing type of federal spending," admits the *Wall Street Journal*.[26] The Civil War, World Wars I and II, the Korean War, and the Vietnam War all produced inflationary periods. Even during peacetime, huge defense outlays consume vast amounts of labor power and material resources, the military being the largest single consumer of fuel in the United States. Military spending creates jobs and consumer buying power while producing no goods and services. The resulting increase in buying power generates an upward pressure on prices, especially since the defense budget is funded partly through deficit spending — that is, by the government's spending more than it collects in taxes.

Market Demand and Human Need

Those who say that private enterprise can answer our needs seem to overlook the fact that private enterprise has no such interest, its function being to produce the biggest profits possible. People may need food, but they offer no market until their need (or want) is coupled with buying power to become a market *demand*. When asked what they were doing about the widespread hunger in the United States, one food manufacturer responded with refreshing candor: "If we saw evidence of profitability, we might look into this."[27]

The difference between need and demand shows up in the international market also. When the free market rather than human need determines how resources are used, poor nations feed rich ones. Beef, fish, and other protein products from Peru, Mexico, Panama, India, and other Third World countries find their way to profitable U.S. markets rather than being used to feed the hungry children in those countries. The children need food, but they lack the money; hence, there is no demand. The free market is anything but free. Money is invested only where money is to be made. Under capitalism, there is a glut of nonessential goods and services for those with money and a shortage of essential ones for those without money. Stores groan with unsold items while millions of people live in acute deprivation.

The human value of productivity rests in its social purpose. Is the purpose to plunder the land without regard to ecological needs, fabricate endless consumer desires, produce shoddy goods designed to wear out quickly, pander to snobbism and acquisitiveness, squeeze as much compulsive toil as possible out of workers while paying them as little as possible, create artificial scarcities in order to inflate prices — all in order to grab ever bigger profits for the few? Or is productivity geared to satisfying essential communal needs first and superfluous desires last, caring for the natural environment and the public's health and well-being? Does it expand educational opportunities and cultural life? Capitalist productivity-for-profit gives little consideration to the latter set of goals.

Productivity: A Mixed Blessing

Capitalism's defenders claim that corporate productivity creates prosperity for all. But productivity should not be treated apart from its social effects. For example, the coal-mining companies in Appalachia were highly productive and profitable while swindling the Appalachians out of their land, forcing them to work under dangerous conditions, destroying their countryside with strip mining, and refusing to pay any of the resulting social costs.

The fruits of corporate productivity are not likely to be shared in a fair manner, if at all. Between 1973 and 1997, worker productivity (output per hour of work) increased by over 20 percent, while real wages (adjusted for inflation) *declined* by 22.6 percent.[28] An increase in productivity, as measured by the gross domestic product or GDP (the total cost of all goods and services in a given year), is no sure measure of society's well-being. Important nonmarket services like housework and child rearing go uncounted, while many things of negative social value are tabulated. Thus, crime and highway accidents, which lead to increased insurance, hospital, and police costs, add quite a bit to the GDP but take a lot out of life. What is called productivity, as measured quantitatively, may actually represent a deterioration in the quality of life.

It is argued that the accumulation of great fortunes is a necessary condition for economic growth, for only the wealthy can provide the huge sums needed for the capitalization of new enterprises. Yet in many industries, such as railroads, aeronautics, nuclear energy, and computers, much of the initial funding came from the government (that is, from the taxpayers). It is one thing to say that large-scale production requires capital accumulation but something else to presume that the source of accumulation must be the purses of the rich.

Giant corporations are subsidized by government for much of their research. And they leave a good deal of the pioneering research to smaller businesses and individual entrepreneurs. The inventiveness record of the biggest oil companies, Exxon and Shell, is strikingly undistinguished. Referring to electric appliances, one General Electric vice president noted: "I know of no original product invention, not even electric shavers or heating pads, made by any of the giant laboratories or corporations. . . . The record of the giants is one of moving in, buying out, and absorbing the small creators."[29] The same can be said of recent advances in the software industry.

Defenders of the free market claim that big production units are needed for the modern age. However, bigness is less the result of technological necessity and more the outcome of profit-driven acquisitions and mergers, as when the same corporation has holdings in manufacturing, insurance, utilities, amusement parks, broadcast media, and publishing.

When times are good, the capitalists sing praise to the wonders of their free-market system. When times are bad, they blame labor for capitalism's

ills. Workers must learn to toil harder for less in order to stay competitive in the global economy, they say; then business would not move to cheaper labor markets in Third World countries. But workers who take wage and benefit cuts "in order to remain competitive" often end up seeing their jobs exported overseas anyway.

One cause of low productivity is technological obsolescence. Unwilling to spend their own money to modernize their plants, big companies cry poverty and call for federal funds to finance technological innovation — supposedly to help them compete against foreign firms. Yet, these same companies might then produce huge cash reserves for mergers. For example, after laying off twenty thousand workers, refusing to modernize its aging plants, and milking the government of hundreds of millions of dollars in subsidies and tax write-offs, U.S. Steel came up with $6.2 billion to purchase Marathon Oil in 1981.

"Desirable" Unemployment

During 1997–2000, inflation was slowing down, unemployment was at its lowest level in years, the federal budget showed a surplus for the first time in decades, corporate coffers were brimming with profits, and the stock market was soaring into the stratosphere. It was called the "Clinton prosperity." But a closer look revealed that real wages were below 1973 levels, consumer debt and personal bankruptcies were at record highs, and the gap between the rich and most other people was wider than at any time since the 1920s. "A rising tide lifts all yachts," as one wag put it. Low-income workers did not share in the prosperity and had yet to recover from the sharp erosion of earnings they had suffered over the previous two decades. The "Clinton prosperity" still left 32.2 million U.S. residents living below the poverty level, with a record number of people requiring the support of charitable food banks.[30]

In capitalist societies, if people cannot find work, that is their misfortune. No free-market economy has ever come close to full employment. If anything, unemployment is useful to capitalism. Without a reserve army of unemployed to compete for jobs and deflate wages, labor would cut more deeply into profits. In recent years the official unemployment count has ranged around 5 to 7 percent, or over nine million people. But this figure does not include an estimated four to five million "discouraged" workers who have exhausted their unemployment compensation and left the rolls, millions of part-timers or reduced-time workers who want full-time jobs, nor the many forced into early retirement, those who join the armed forces because they cannot find work (and who are thereby listed as "employed"), and prison inmates who would have been listed as unemployed but for incarceration.[31]

The number of underemployed part-time workers jumped from 12.6 million to 27.8 million between 1965 and 1995. (Of course, some people on the job market prefer part-time work because of school or family obligations. But they do not make up the bulk of the part-time and some-time employees.) The median hourly wage of part-timers was about one-third less than full-time employees in the same occupations. The number of workers who found it necessary to hold down two jobs climbed from 3.7 million to

8 million between 1975 and 1995. Among the part-timers are millions of "contract workers," who are paid only for hours put in, without promise of regular employment. About one-fifth of them, more than a million, have returned to their previous employers, working at the same jobs but now at lower wages, without health insurance, paid vacations, pension fund, seniority, or hope of advancement. U.S. Labor Department statistics show that only about 35 percent of laid-off full-time workers end up with equally remunerative or better-paying jobs.[32]

Some people say there is plenty of work available; unemployment results because individuals are just lazy. But when unemployment jumps by a half-million or more during an economic slump, is it really because a mass of people suddenly found work too irksome and preferred to lose their income, homes, cars, medical coverage, and pensions? When decent jobs do open up, vast numbers of the "lazy" line up for them. To give a few examples from the 1997–98 "boom years": At a John Deere plant in Ottumwa, Iowa, 4,000 people applied for 53 jobs. In Eleanor, West Virginia, 27,500 applied for 250 openings at a new Toyota plant. And in New York City, 4,000 people lined up for 700 relatively low-paying hotel jobs.

Technological advances and automation can expand worker productivity without bringing a commensurate gain in jobs. For example, Chrysler once announced an investment of $225 million for a new line of Dodge trucks that created only seventy jobs; at the same time Chrysler continued to lay off workers. Another cause of decline in better-paying jobs is the runaway shop: U.S. firms move to cheaper Third World labor markets, supposedly to maintain their competitiveness in the global economy. As one corporate executive put it, "Until we get real wages down much closer to those of the Brazils and South Koreas, we cannot pass along productivity gains to wages and still be competitive."[33] In other words, working people will share in the growing profits only after they join the race to the bottom and are reduced to desperate Third World poverty-wage levels.

The Hardships of Working America

We hear that the United States is a middle-class nation, but actually most Americans are working-class. Their income source is hourly wages and their labor is manual, unskilled, or semiskilled. Even among white-collar service employees, the great majority are nonmanagerial and low-wage.[34] Compared to twenty years ago, U.S. workers put in an annual average of 180 additional hours on the job — the equivalent of six more weeks of toil. They have more forced overtime, fewer paid days off, fewer benefits, less sick leave, shorter vacations, and less discretionary income. Middle-class families are deeper in debt. People are working harder for relatively less in order to generate sufficient income for themselves and their dependents, a necessity that has become more urgent as wages stagnate, higher-paying jobs disappear, and government income supplements are reduced.[35]

One survey found that 70 percent of respondents felt less secure in their jobs and 73 percent reported greater stress on the job in recent years. Another showed that one hundred million U.S. residents are worried that their total family income is not enough to meet expenses.[36] Even conservative business leader Mortimer Zuckerman allowed that "fewer than one job in five pays enough today to support a family of four."[37]

By the end of the twentieth century, the Census Bureau reported 12.7 percent of the U.S. population, or 34.4 million, living below the poverty level. This estimate understates the problem by excluding many undocumented workers and other poor people who go uncounted in the census. Almost two-thirds of the families below the government's official poverty line have a member who is fully employed. They work for a living but not for a living wage. At the height of the "Clinton prosperity," about 5.6 million *full-time* workers were living in poverty.[38]

Among the "working poor" can be numbered the thousands of janitors around the country who launched concerted struggles for a living wage in 2000. In Los Angeles, the 26-percent wage increase that striking janitors won would still leave them with an annual wage of only $19,000 by 2003, in an area where rents often run far higher than their total income.[39] Then there are the farm laborers who toil for meager sums while working and living under distressing conditions, and the growing numbers of sweatshop employees who put in long hours for below minimum wages, plus the immigrant female domestics in affluent households who work twelve-to-fifteen-hour shifts, six days a week, for wages sometimes amounting to as little as two dollars an hour.[40]

An additional twenty-five million people in the United States live just above the official poverty line in dire straits. They have no medical insurance, are often unable to pay utility bills or keep up car payments, and some even lack sufficient funds for food during certain times in the month.[41] It is not laziness that keeps these people down, but the low wages their bosses pay them and the high prices, exorbitant rents, and heavy taxes they must pay others.

As of 2000, the Census Bureau's poverty line for a family of four was $17,050. The poverty level is purportedly adjusted regularly by the Consumer Price Index (CPI) to account for inflation. However, for those of modest means, a larger proportion of their income goes to basic necessities such as rent, food, fuel, and medical care than to other items. The cost of these necessities rose much more rapidly than the general price index, but the Census Bureau has failed to adjust for this, thereby grossly underestimating the nation's poor.[42]

Americans have been taught that they are the most prosperous people in the world. The truth is, of twenty major industrial countries, the United

States ranks fifteenth in life expectancy and has the highest poverty rate, the highest infant mortality rate, and the highest rate of youth deaths due to accidents, homicide, and other violence.[43]

The poor pay more for most things: 30 percent interest on auto loans for unreliable used cars, exorbitant rents in run-down unsafe buildings that slumlords refuse to repair, and installment sales that charge interest rates of 200 to 300 percent. Unregulated and extremely lucrative fringe "banks" and check cashing companies make billions of dollars annually by charging low-income people fees of up to 10 percent to cash their paychecks or welfare and Social Security checks. Others make short-term loans to people who run short of cash between paychecks, a business that made an estimated $2 billion in 2000. Calculated on an annual base, the loan fees can be 500 percent or higher. Many of these storefront usury shops are owned or funded by major banks and corporations, including Chase Manhattan, NationsBank, Ford, and American Express. Their growth has been fueled by a decline in the number of households with bank accounts and an increase in low-income population.[44]

. Especially hard hit are African Americans and Latinos, who are disproportionately concentrated in low-paying jobs, and endure unemployment and poverty rates about twice as high as that of Whites.[45] For all the talk about affirmative action and favoritism to non-Whites, in fact, people of color continue to suffer racial discrimination in employment and other areas of life. One investigation demonstrated that when Whites and African Americans, who were deliberately matched in qualifications, applied for the same jobs, the Whites were three times more likely to be hired, and less likely to encounter discouragement and slighting treatment.[46] Ethnic minorities are still turned down more often than Whites for home mortgages, regardless of income.[47] There does exist a widespread unofficial "affirmative action," but it operates on behalf of middle- and upper-class Whites.

Women also number among the superexploited. Of the more than fifty-eight million females who work, a disproportionately high number are concentrated in low-paying secretarial and service jobs. In the mid-1960s women averaged 69 cents for every dollar men made. After thirty years of struggle and hard work, they now earn 76 cents for every dollar men receive. At that rate, women will need another hundred years of sacrifice and struggle to achieve wage parity. Although twenty million mothers are working, 44 percent of single mothers remain below the poverty level. Two out of three adults in poverty are women.[48]

The Human Costs of Economic Injustice

In 2000, thirteen million of the nation's children lived in poverty, a higher rate than twenty years before. Elected officials and children's advocates across the country cited low wages and high living costs as primary factors in the prevalence of child poverty. Children in poverty are more likely to be born at a low birth weight, die in infancy or early childhood, and contract serious ailments, including diseases associated with malnutrition. They are more likely to experience hunger, suffer from untreated illnesses, be exposed to environmental toxins and domestic and neighborhood violence, and suffer lethargy and delays in learning development.[49] A Surgeon General's report found that young and elderly poor suffer a "silent epidemic of oral disease," from tooth decay to mouth cancer, due largely to poor overall health and inability to pay for dental care or dental insurance.[50]

By the end of the 1990s, during one of the longest economic booms in U.S. history, almost one in ten households (some 30 million people, up from 25 million in 1985) reported not getting enough to eat during some part of the month. Food banks and soup kitchens were busier than ever. Hunger or near-hunger levels were highest in New Mexico, Mississippi, Texas, Arizona, and Louisiana, in that order; and lowest in North Dakota, Massachusetts, South Dakota, Delaware, and Minnesota. Anti-hunger workers note that increasing numbers of families, especially single working mothers, line up for food baskets to supplement their insufficient earnings.[51]

In major cities and small towns, indigents pick food out of garbage cans and dumps. As one columnist noted, "If the president on his visit to China had witnessed Chinese peasants eating from garbage cans, he almost certainly would have cited it as proof that communism doesn't work. What does it prove when it happens in the capitalist success called America?"[52]

One of every five U.S. adults is functionally illiterate, including most unwed mothers. One of four inhabit substandard housing without adequate plumbing or heat. Housing is the largest single expenditure for many low-income families, consuming 60 to 70 percent of their income. Due to realty speculations, gentrification, condominium conversions, unemployment, low wages, and abolition of rent control, people of modest means have been squeezed out of the housing market in greater numbers than ever. Over two million affordable housing units have vanished during the last twenty years, forcing more and more families to double and triple up, imposing hardships and severe strains on domestic relations.[53]

Estimates of homelessness vary from one to three million, almost a third of whom are families with children. Homelessness offers a life of hunger, filth, destitution, loneliness, mental depression, and unattended illness. One study found that many persons who stayed in homeless shelters or makeshift street shelters held full-time jobs. With rents so high and pay so low, they could not afford a place to live.[54] Even among the housed, there are millions who are only a paycheck away from the streets.

Despite all the talk about the affluent elderly, almost half of the people who live in poverty are over sixty-five. Five million of them regularly experience the threat of hunger or do not get enough food to eat. Despite Medicare assistance, the elderly face the highest out-of-pocket health-care costs. Millions are finding that Social Security, pensions, and savings are insufficient. Almost half of all seniors have returned to work or are looking for work.[55]

It is difficult for those who have never known serious economic want to imagine the misery and social pathology it can cause. Studies indicate that drops in income and even modest jumps in unemployment rates bring discernible increases in illness, emotional distress, substance addictions, suicide, crime, and early visits to the grave.[56]

Over 30 percent of Americans have experienced some form of mental "disorder" such as serious depression. Tens of millions are addicted to alcohol, nicotine, or some other drug. Millions more are addicted to medical drugs such as amphetamines and barbiturates. The pushers are the doctors; the suppliers are the drug industry; the profits are stupendous.[57]

Each year, 30,000 Americans on average take their own lives. Another 17,000 or so are murdered. The number of young people who kill themselves has tripled since the 1950s.[58] Millions of U.S. women are battered by men; almost five million sustain serious injury each year.[59] Over two million children — predominantly but not exclusively from lower-income families — are battered, abused, abandoned, or seriously neglected each year.[60] Many elderly also are subjected to serious abuse which, like child abuse, increases dramatically when economic conditions worsen.

In sum, the story of the United States' great "affluence" has a grimmer side. The free market is very good for winners, offering all the rewards that money can buy, but it is exceedingly harsh on millions of others. It is not enough to denounce the inequities that exist between the wealthy and the majority of the population; it is also necessary to understand the connection between them. By its very nature, the capitalist system squanders our natural resources, exploits and underpays our labor, creates privation and desperate social needs, serving the few at great cost to the many.

If we love our country, then we should also care for the people who inhabit it and not want to see them victimized. The data presented in this chapter are an attack not on the United States but on the untrammeled market system that victimizes our nation's people.

Notes

1. Adam Smith, *An Inquiry into the Nature and Causes of the Wealth of Nations* (New York: Modern Library, 1937, originally 1776), 33.
2. The late Victor Perlo wrote frequently on this subject; see his columns in *People's Weekly World*, April 26, 1997; May 31, 1997; and August 1, 1998.
3. For the classic statement on the nature of capitalism, see Karl Marx, *Capital*, vol. 1, available in various editions. For introductory treatments, see Marx's *Wages, Price, and Profit* (various editions), and his *A Contribution to the Critique of Political Economy* (New York: International, 1970).
4. Quoted in Pat Barile, "Where Production Benefits Workers," *Daily World*, September 20, 1984.
5. Internal Revenue Service, *Statistics of Income Bulletin*, 1999–2000; Chuck Collins and Felice Yeskel, *Economic Apartheid in America* (New York: New Press, 2000).
6. "Forbes 400 World Series," *Nation*, October 20, 1997.
7. *Wall Street Journal* quoted in Richard Grossman, "Corporations Must Not Supplant 'We the People,'" *Maine Telegram*, February 4, 1996.
8. John Miller, "A Rising Tide Fails to Lift All Boats," *Dollars and Sense*, May/June 2000.
9. For details on how the Census Bureau fudges the picture, see Michael Parenti, "Economy in Numbers: The Super Rich Are Out of Sight," *Dollars and Sense*, May/June 1998; also available on <http://www.michaelparenti.org>.
10. Paul Samuelson quoted in Sam Pizzigati, *The Maximum Wage* (New York: Apex, 1992); see also Chuck Collins, Chris Hartman, and Holly Sklar, *Divided Decade: Economic Disparity at the Century's Turn* (Boston: United for a Fair Economy, 2000); Stephen Rose, *Social Stratification in the United States 2000* (New York: New Press, 2000).
11. *New York Times*, January 13, 1999; Jake Lewis, "The Making of the Banking Behemoths," *Multinational Monitor*, June 1996; Associated Press report, September 14, 2000.
12. On the "golden parachutes" for top executives, see Victoria Colliver, "The Softest Landing," *San Francisco Examiner*, August 14, 1998; and "Pensions," *Solidarity*, United Auto Workers, May 1966.
13. *San Francisco Chronicle*, July 29, 2000; *Union*, Service Employees International Union, Spring 1996.

14. Sarah Anderson, John Cavanaugh, Chuck Collins, Ralph Estes, and Chris Hartman, *A Decade of Executive Excess: Sixth Annual Executive Compensation Survey* (Boston and Washington, D.C.: United for a Fair Economy and Institute for Policy Studies, 1999); Holly Sklar, "CEO Gravy Train Keeps on Rolling," Z *Magazine*, June 2000.

15. *Washington Post*, February 11, 1982.

16. An agribusiness is a giant corporation that specializes in large-scale commercial farming, usually with a heavy reliance on mechanized farming, monoculture crops, pesticides, herbicides, and government subsidies.

17. "Stand with the Farmers," *People's Weekly World*, December 18, 1999; A. V. Krebs, *The Corporate Reapers* (Washington, D.C.: Essential, 1992).

18. Donald Gruber, "Unfair Prices — Why Family Farmers Go Broke,"*People's Weekly World*, March 8, 1997; "Save the Family Farms and Communities," *People's Weekly World*, March 18, 2000; and Krebs, *The Corporate Reapers.*

19. Marc Lappé and Britt Bailey, *Against the Grain: Biotechnology and the Corporate Takeover of Your Food* (Monroe, Maine: Common Courage, 1998); and Krebs, *The Corporate Reapers,* 75–97 and passim.

20. *New York Times*, March 31, 1997.

21. Allan Sloan, "Corporate Killers," *Newsweek*, February 26, 1996; see also Doug Henwood, *Wall Street: How It Works and For Whom* (New York and London: Verso, 1997).

22. Steven Greenhouse, "Low-Paid Jobs Lead Advance in Employment," *New York Times*, October 1, 2000; National Priorities Project and Jobs with Justice, *Working Hard, Earning Less* (Washington, D.C.: National Priorities Project and Jobs with Justice, 1998); and David Gordon, *Fat and Mean: The Corporate Squeeze of Working Americans and the Myth of Managerial "Downsizing"* (New York: Martin Kessler/Free Press, 1996).

23. *San Francisco Chronicle*, August 8, 1992.

24. Lewis H. Lapham, "Notebook," *Harper's*, April 1991, 11.

25. Reich quoted in *New York Times*, April 26, 1995.

26. *Wall Street Journal*, August 30, 1978.

27. Quoted in *Hunger, U.S.A.*, a report by the Citizens Board of Inquiry into Hunger and Malnutrition in the United States (Boston: Beacon, 1968), 46.

28. As reported by Arthur MacEwan in *Dollars and Sense*, May/June 1998.

29. Quoted in Paul Baran and Paul Sweezy, *Monopoly Capital* (New York: Monthly Review, 1966), 49.

30. Conference Board report summarized in Jacob Schlesinger, "Despite Economic Boom, More Americans Are Likely to Fall Below the Poverty Line," *Wall Street Journal*, June 29, 2000; Associated Press report, September 27, 2000.

31. Edward Herman, "The U.S. Jobs Miracle," Z *Magazine*, July/August 1998; Louis Uchitelle, "Despite Drop, Rate of Layoffs Remains High," *New York Times*, August 23, 1996.

32. See U.S. Bureau of Labor Statistics, Daily Labor Report over the last two years; also *New York Times*, March 3, May 5, and December 8, 1996.

33. Stanley Mihelick, Goodyear Rubber, quoted in *New York Times*, December 12, 1989.

34. Vicente Navarro, "The Middle Class — A Useful Myth," *Nation*, March 23, 1992.

35. *The State of Working America* (Washington, D.C.: Economic Policy Institute, 2000); Peter Meiksins, "Confronting the Time Bind: Work, Family and Capitalism," *Monthly Review*, February 1998.

36. "Counterspin," Pacifica Radio, November 24, 1997; and Bob Herbert's column, *New York Times*, February 10, 1996.

37. Zuckerman in *U.S. News and World Report*, April 3, 1995.

38. *The State of Working America; New York Times*, October 4, 1999.

39. *San Francisco Chronicle*, April 27, 2000.

40. Don Terry, "A Union Vote Sows Bitterness in Calfornia Strawberry Fields," *New York Times*, July 31, 1998; Charles Clark, "A Surge in Sweatshops," *San Francisco Examiner*, Sep-

tember 1, 1996; and Doreen Carvajal, "For Immigrant Maids, Not a Job but Servitude," *New York Times*, February 25, 1996.

41. John Schwarz and Thomas Volgy, "Above the Poverty Line — But Poor," *Nation*, February 15, 1993, 191–92.

42. Schwarz and Volgy, "Above the Poverty Line — But Poor."

43. See the United Nations annual report on human development; and recent reports by UNICEF, 1999; and T. M. Smeeding and L. Rainwater, "Young Child Poverty in a Comparative Perspective," unpublished paper, Maxwell School of Citizenship and Public Affairs, 1996.

44. Michael Hudson (ed.), *Merchants of Misery: How Corporate America Profits from Poverty* (Monroe, Maine: Common Courage, 1996); and *Oakland Tribune*, August 8, 2000.

45. See Urban League's annual report, *The State of Black America, 2000;* Department of Commerce findings cited in *Los Angeles Times*, September 25, 1998.

46. Michael Fix, Raymond Struyk, and Marjorie Turner, *Oppportunities Denied, Opportunities Diminished* (Washington, D.C.: Urban Institute, 1991).

47. *Oakland Tribune*, August 9, 2000.

48. *Washington Post*, June 10, 2000; and survey in *Working Woman*, January 1996.

49. Kathryn Porter and Wendell Primus, *Recent Changes in the Impact of the Safety Net on Child Poverty* (Washington, D.C.: Center on Budget and Priorities, 1999); and study by National Center for Children in Poverty (Columbia University), reported in *New York Times*, August 11, 2000; *Los Angeles Times*, July 1, 1999; and "Shredding the Safety Net," *Backgrounder*, Institute for Food and Development Policy, Winter 1998.

50. *New York Times*, May 26, 2000.

51. U.S. Department of Agriculture state-by-state study reported in *USA Today*, October 15, 1999; and study by Center on Hunger, Poverty, and Nutrition Policy, Tufts University, reported in *San Francisco Bay Guardian*, June 17, 1998, 16; *USA Today*, October 15, 1999.

52. William Raspberry, "Garbage Eaters," *Washington Post*, May 2, 1984; see also Carolyne Zinko, "Going Hungry in Good Times," *San Francisco Chronicle*, March 11, 1998.

53. Report by National Jewish Coalition for Literacy, *USA Today*, November 29, 2000; Michael Janofsky, "Shortage of Housing for Poor Grows in U.S.," *New York Times*, April 28, 1998.

54. For more detailed statistics on homelessness, contact National Coalition for the Homeless and National Law Center on Homelessness and Poverty.

55. Trudy Lieberman, "Hunger in America," *Nation*, March 30, 1998; National Institute on Aging, *Older Americans 2000: Key Indicators of Well-Being* (Washington, D.C.: National Institute on Aging, 2000).

56. Richard Shweder, "It's Called Poor Health for a Reason," *New York Times*, March 9, 1997; M. Harvey Brenner, *Economy, Society and Health* (Washington, D.C.: Economic Policy Institute, 1992); Mary Merva and Richard Fowles, *Effect of Diminished Opportunities on Social Stress* (Washington, D.C.: Economic Policy Institute, 1992).

57. "National Household Survey on Drug Abuse," Department of Health and Human Services, September 1996; see annual reports from National Institute of Mental Health, Center for Disease Control and Prevention, and National Center for Chronic Disease Prevention and Health Promotion, 1998–2000.

58. Kay Redfield Jamison, *Night Falls Fast: Understanding Suicide* (New York: Knopf, 1999); National Center for Health Statistics, *National Vital Statistics Report* (Washington D.C.: National Center for Health Statistics, 1999).

59. Congressional Caucus for Women's Issues, *Violence Against Women* (Washington, D.C.: Government Printing Office, 1992).

60. See report of U.S. Department of Health and Human Services, noted in *USA Today*, June 16, 2000.

3

The Plutocratic Culture: Institutions and Ideologies

In trying to understand the political system we would do well to look at the wider social context in which it operates: the predominant social institutions, values, and ideologies of U.S. society.

Rule by Corporate Plutocracy

American capitalism is more than just an economic system; it is an entire cultural and social order, a *plutocracy*, a system of rule that is mostly by and for the rich. Most universities, publishing houses, mass circulation magazines, newspapers, television and radio stations, professional sports teams, foundations, churches, private museums, charity organizations, and hospitals are organized as corporations, ruled by boards of directors (or they may be called "trustees" or "regents") composed overwhelmingly of affluent business people. These boards exercise final judgment over all institutional matters.[1]

Consider the university. Private and public institutions of higher education are corporations run by boards of trustees with authority over all matters of capital funding and budget; curriculum and tuition; hiring, firing, and promotion of faculty and staff; degree awards and student fees. Daily governance is delegated to administrators, but decision-making power can be easily recalled by the trustees when they choose. Most trustees are successful business people who have no administrative or scholarly experience in higher education. Their decisions are covered by insurance paid out of the university budget, and on most fiduciary questions they rely on accountants. In short, they take no financial risks and offer no special expertise. Why then are they allocated so much power? Their main function seems to be to exercise oligarchic, ideological control over the institution.

The corporate culture increasingly permeates higher education. While serving as the $245,000-a-year president of the University of California, Jack Peltason reportedly received more than $100,000 from seven corporations for serving on their boards as a director.[2] Nor is that an unusual example. The salaries of top college administrators are skyrocketing while library budgets, scholarships, and remedial services are being cut back. Corporate logos are appearing in classrooms and student union buildings. More than ever, private industry is creating endowed professorships, funding think tanks and research centers, sponsoring grants, and influencing who is hired and what is researched and taught.[3]

A fact of real significance in any understanding of political power in America is that almost all "our" cultural institutions are under plutocratic control, linked to the business system, ruled by nonelected, self-perpetuating groups of affluent corporate representatives who are answerable to no one but themselves. We the people have no vote, no portion of the ownership, and no legal decision-making power within these institutions.

Promoting Ideological Orthodoxy

We are taught to think that capitalism is an inherent part of democracy. Little is said about how capitalism also flourishes under the most brutally repressive regimes. Transnational corporate interests have supported the overthrow of democracies in numerous Third World countries and the installation of right-wing dictators who make their lands safe for corporate investments. The private enterprise system, it is said, creates equality of opportunity, rewards those who show ability and initiative, relegates the parasitic and slothful to the bottom of the ladder, provides a national prosperity that is the envy of other lands, and safeguards (through unspecified means) personal liberties and political freedom.

The private enterprise system places a great deal of emphasis on commercial worth: how to sell, compete, and get ahead. As Ralph Nader notes, the free market "only stimulates one value in society — the acquisitive, materialistic, profit value." What about the values relating to justice, health, occupational and consumer safety, regard for future generations, and accountability in government?[4]

Among the institutions of plutocratic culture is our educational system. From grade school to graduate school, students are instructed to believe in America's global virtue and moral superiority and to hold a rather uncritical view of U.S. politico-economic institutions. Surveys show that

most youngsters believe that our political leaders are benevolent and know best. Teachers tend to concentrate on the formal aspects of representative government and accord scant attention to the influences that wealthy, powerful groups exercise over political life. Instructors who wish to introduce critiques of U.S. politico-economic institutions do so often at the risk of their careers. Students who attempt to explore controversial issues in student newspapers have frequently been overruled by administrators and threatened with disciplinary action.[5]

' School texts seldom give more than passing mention to the history of labor struggle and the corporate exploitation of working people at home and abroad. Almost nothing is said of the struggles of First Nation People (also known as Native Americans or "Indians"), indentured servants, small farmers, and Latino, Asian, and European immigrants. The history of resistance to slavery, racism, and U.S. expansionist wars is largely untaught in our schools.[6]

Schools are inundated with printed materials, films, and tapes provided free by the Pentagon and large corporations to promote a glorified view of the military and to argue for deregulation of industry.[7] Business propaganda boosting the wonders of the free market are also widely distributed in schools and communities. Conservative think tanks and academic centers have proliferated, along with conservative journals, conferences, and endowed chairs, all generously funded by corporations and right-wing foundations.

While sometimes portrayed as being above worldly partisan concerns, the average American university performs a wide range of research and training services that are essential to military and corporate interests. The "neutral" university also has a direct investment link to the corporate structure in the form of a substantial stock portfolio.

Economic sanctions are used to punish dissent and reward political conformity. In academia, politically outspoken faculty and even students have suffered negative evaluations and loss of stipends, grants, and jobs. Likewise, journalists, managers, bureaucrats, and most other professionals who wish to advance in their careers learn to go along with things as they are and avoid expressing views that conflict with the dominant economic interests of capitalist society.

Another agent of political socialization is the government itself. Hardly a week passes without the president or some other official feeding us reassuring pronouncements about the economy and alarming assertions about enemies who threaten us from abroad. Helping them in their efforts are the news media, whose performance as an agency of political indoctrination has earned an entire chapter later in this book.

Although we are often admonished to think for ourselves, we might wonder if the American socialization process allows us to do so. Ideological orthodoxy so permeates the plutocratic culture, masquerading as "pluralism," "democracy," and the "open society," that it is often not felt as indoctrination. The worst forms of tyranny are those so deeply ingrained, so thoroughly controlling as not even to be consciously experienced.

In a capitalist society, business tries to get people to consume as much as they can — and sometimes more than they can afford. Mass advertising sells not only particular products but a whole way of life, a glorification of consumer acquisitiveness. Born of a market economy, the capitalist culture is essentially a market culture, one that minimizes cooperative efforts and human interdependence and keeps us busily competing as workers and consumers.

We are admonished to "get ahead." Ahead of whom and what? Of others and of one's present material status. This kind of "individualism" is not to be mistaken for the freedom to choose alternative political and economic practices. People are expected to operate individually but in more or less similar directions. Everyone competes against everyone else but for the same things. "Individualism" in this corporate-dominated culture refers to privatized ownership and consumption. We are expected to get what we can for ourselves and not be too troubled by the problems faced by others. This attitude, considered inhuman in some societies, is labeled approvingly as "ambition" in our own and is treated as a quality of great social value.

Whether or not this "individualism" allows one to have control over one's own life is another story. Most of us do not make the decisions about the quality of the food we eat, the goods we buy, the air we breathe, the prices we pay, the wages we earn, the way work tasks are divided, the modes of transportation available to us, and the images we are fed by the media.

People who occupy privileged positions within the social hierarchy become committed to the hierarchy's preservation and hostile toward demands for a more equitable social system. According to one study, upper-income people were most opposed to equality of political power for all groups, while lower-income respondents were the firmest supporters of equality.[8] Economically deprived groups are seen as a threat because they want more, and more for the have-nots might mean less for the haves.

Along with racism and sexism, there is *class* bigotry, one of the most widely held forms of prejudice in American society and the least challenged. Since material success is treated as a measure of one's worth, then the poor are not worth much and society's resources should not be squandered on them.[9] In capitalist society, the poor in general are condemned as personally deficient and lacking in proper values, the authors of their own straitened circumstances. Rarely are they seen as the victims of poverty-creating economic forces: high rents, underemployment, low wages, unattended illnesses, disabilities, and other such blessings of the free-market paradise. To paraphrase the American humorist Will Rogers, it is no crime to be poor, but it might as well be.

With job downsizing, wage cuts, inflation, and growing tax burdens, many people have been working still harder just to stay in the same place. In a society where money is the overriding determinant of one's life chances, the competitive drive for material success is not merely a symptom of a greed-driven culture but a factor in one's very survival. Rather than grasping for fanciful luxuries, most Americans are still struggling to provide for basic necessities. If they need more money than was essential in earlier days, this is largely because essentials cost so much more.

Because human services in America are based on ability to pay, money becomes a matter of life and death. To have a low or modest income is to run a higher risk of insufficient medical care and job insecurity, and to have less opportunity for education, recreation, travel, and comfort. The desire to "make it," even at the expense of others, is not merely a wrong-headed attitude but a reflection of the material conditions of capitalist society wherein no one is ever really economically secure except the superrich, and even they forever seek to augment and secure their fortunes.

For those who enjoy the best of everything, the existing politico-economic system is a smashing success. For those who are its hapless victims, or who are concerned about the well-being of all and not just themselves, the system is something of a failure. Those in between are not sure. Dreading the decline in earning power and living standards that has afflicted so many, they are absorbed with the struggle to maintain a decent and manageable standard of living within the existing social order.

Right, Left, and Center

Political ideologies traditionally have been categorized as rightist, centrist, and leftist. Here I will try to draw the broad outlines of the three tendencies, without doing justice to all their shadings and ambiguities. What is called the political right consists of conservative and reactionary individuals, including most corporate elites and many persons of high income and wealth, who advocate "free market" capitalism and defend business as the primary mainstay of the good society. Conservative ideology preaches the virtues of private initiative and self-reliance. It says that rich and poor pretty much get what they deserve, that people are poor not because of inadequate wages and lack of economic opportunity but because they are lazy, spendthrift, or incapable. The conservative keystone to individual rights is the enjoyment of property rights, especially the right to make a profit from other people's labor and enjoy the privileged conditions of a favored class.

Conservatives blame the nation's troubles on what billionaire Steve Forbes called the "arrogance, insularity, the government-knows-best mentality" in Washington, D.C. Everything works better in the private sector, they maintain. Most conservatives oppose government regulation of business, including environmental and consumer protections, minimum wage laws, unemployment compensation, job safety regulations, and injury compensation laws. Rich conservative presidents like Ronald Reagan and George Bush have assured us that private charity can take care of needy and hungry people, and that there is no need for government handouts. Ironically, the superrich themselves donate a smaller proportion of their income to private charities than the rest of us.[10]

In practice, conservatives are for or against government handouts depending on whose hand is out. They want to cut spending on human services and aid to lower-income groups, but vigorously support all sorts of government subsidies and bailouts for large corporate enterprises. Conservatives treat economic recession as just part of a natural cycle. They admonish American workers to work harder for less, and have not a harsh word about the devastating effects of corporate mergers and buyouts, the capital flight to cheap labor markets abroad, and the increase in economic hardship for working people.

Conservatives are not really advocates of laissez-faire government. They support strong government measures to restrict dissent and regulate our private lives and personal morals. Most of them avidly support the military, large defense budgets, and the global U.S. empire. But some rightists managed to avoid military service themselves, preferring to let others do the fighting and dying. Such was the case with editor Norman Podhoretz,

"Religious freedom is my immediate goal, but my long-range plan is to go into real estate."

columnist Robert Novak, former Congressman Newt Gingrich, Vice President Dick Cheney, and former Vice President Dan Quayle.

Not all conservatives are affluent. People of rather modest means who oppose big government because they do not see it doing anything for them often call themselves conservatives for want of an alternative. Many are conservative about "cultural issues." They want government to deny equal rights to homosexuals, impose the death penalty more vigorously, and take stronger measures against crime. As one newspaper columnist writes, they think that government has a prime responsibility to protect "their right to kill themselves with guns, booze, and tobacco" but a "minimal responsibility to protect their right to a job, a home, an education or a meal."[11]

Some conservatives who want government to "stop trying to run our lives" also want government to outlaw safe and legal abortions because they believe a fertilized ovum is a human being. They want government to require prayers in our schools and subsidize religious education. They blame the country's ills on decadent morality, homosexuality, feminism, and the loss of family values. Thus television evangelist and erstwhile Republican presidential hopeful Pat Robertson charged that feminism "encourages women to leave their husbands, kill their children, practice witchcraft, destroy capitalism and become lesbians."[12] The religious right supports conservative candidates and causes. In turn, rich conservatives — including heads of corporations like Coors, Pepsico, Mobil Oil, Amoco, Heinz, Marriott, and former heads of RCA and Chase Manhattan Bank — have financed the religious right.[13]

To the extreme right of conservatives are former Nazi collaborators, neofascists, and anti-Semitic and racist activists, many of whom have found a home in the Republican party. These include David Duke, former member of the American Nazi Party and Ku Klux Klan, who ran for governor of Louisiana on the Republican ticket and in the 1992 GOP presidential primaries.[14] Although GOP leaders refused to endorse him, Duke maintained correctly that his program (large military budget, cutbacks in welfare, abolition of affirmative action, and support for big business) was no different from a mainstream Republican one.

More toward the center and left-center of the political spectrum are the "moderates" and liberals, who might be lumped together. Like the conservatives, they accept the capitalist system and its basic values but they think social problems should be rectified by relatively minor reforms and better regulatory policies. Liberal centrists support "free trade" and globalization, thinking it will benefit not just corporations but everyone. They sometimes disapprove of the violent overseas interventionist policies of the United States but they view such actions as irrational mistakes, not as rational functions in the service of a global capitalist order. They back interventions in the Third World if convinced that the White House is waging a moral crusade against some newly defined "evil" and advancing the cause of peace and democracy — as with their support of the North Atlantic Treaty Organization's (NATO's) massive bombing of women, children, and men in Yugoslavia in 1999.

Centrist moderates and liberals see a need for spending more money on public services and environmental protections, and usually support minimum wage laws, unemployment insurance, and other wage supports, along with Social Security, nutritional aid for needy children, occupational safety, and the like. Some of them also advocate huge military budgets and subsidies and tax breaks for business. They are for protection of individual rights against government surveillance and suppression, yet in Congress (where most of them are affiliated with the Democratic party), they support intelligence and surveillance agencies, and sometimes have gone along with cuts in human services for the needy.

On the political left are the progressives and socialists. They want to replace or substantially modify the corporate capitalist system with a system of public ownership, in which many of the large corporations are nationalized, and smaller businesses are under cooperative ownership or at least better regulated for the common interest. Some progressives will settle for a social democracy, with strong labor unions and effective controls on the powers and privileges of business. They argue that untrammeled free-market capitalism uses the land, labor, resources, and technology of society for no goal other than the accumulation of capital, and concentrates economic wealth and political influence in the hands of a privileged few, while creating poverty for millions at home and abroad.

A democratically responsive government, progressives insist, has an important role to play in protecting the environment, advancing education, and providing jobs for everyone able to work, occupational safety protections, secure retirement and disability pensions, and affordable medical care, education, and housing.

Most leftists and progressives reject the now defunct communist societies as models for U.S. socialism, pointing out that countries such as the Soviet Union come from a different tradition, a history of serfdom and poverty, hostile capitalist encirclement, and foreign invasion. Yet some progressives note that whatever the faults, past crimes, and social problems of communist societies, their citizens did have a guaranteed right to a job; were free from hunger and homelessness; had free medical care and free education to the highest level of their ability; and enjoyed such things as subsidized utilities and transportation, free cultural events, and a guaranteed pension after retirement — entitlements that were taken away from them soon after their countries turned to free-market "democratic capitalism."

Most other U.S. leftists and social democrats refrain from uttering a positive word about the former state socialist societies or revolutionary communism in general. Instead, they take pains to display their devotion to anticommunism, denouncing "Stalinism," an exercise that fails to win them additional credibility in the eyes of conservatives or the mainstream media. Many of them seem less worried about global capitalism, the system that has the world in its self-serving grip, than about fighting "Stalinism," a phenomenon that remains conveniently undefined, and is seen as lurking everywhere on the left.

Socialists are distinguished from liberal reformers in their belief that our social problems cannot be solved within the very system that is creating them. They do not believe that every human problem is caused by capitalism but that many of the most important ones are, and that capitalism propagates conditions that perpetuate poverty, racism, sexism, and exploitative social relations at home and abroad. Socialists believe that U.S. corporate and military expansionism abroad is not the result of "wrong thinking" but the natural outgrowth of profit-oriented capitalism. To the socialist, U.S. foreign policy is not beset by folly and irrationality, it unfortunately has been quite successful in maintaining the interests of multinational corporations, crushing social change in many countries, and establishing a U.S. financial and military presence throughout much of the world.

Public Opinion: Which Direction?

Over the last several decades media pundits have tirelessly announced that the U.S. public is in a "conservative mood." In fact, most Americans have positions on issues that are decidedly more progressive than the ones usually enunciated by political leaders and media commentators. Surveys show substantial majorities strongly favoring public funding for Social Security, nursing home care, and subsidized prescription drugs for the elderly. Substantial majorities support unemployment insurance, public assistance, job retraining, child care, price supports for family farms, and food stamps for the needy, while opposing tax cuts for the rich and privatization of social services. New York Times/CBS News polls in the mid- and late 1990s found that large majorities wanted improvements in managed health care, and by nearly three to one rejected the GOP's proposed tax cuts if it also meant cuts in Medicare and Social Security. And most Americans supported the idea of balancing the budget by cutting military spending rather than cutting human services.[15]

Large majorities feel that the gap between rich and poor is growing, that the economic system is "inherently unfair," that government has a responsibility to try to do away with poverty, that labor unions are helpful for workers, that more women should be serving in Congress, and that laws against racial discrimination should be supported, along with special education programs and job training for minorities (but not minority preferences in hiring and promotion).[16]

In sum, on almost every important issue, a majority seems to hold positions contrary to those maintained by conservative politico-economic elites (and closer to the ones enunciated in this book). Opinion polls are only part of the picture. There is the whole history of democratic struggle that continues to this day and remains largely untaught in the schools and unreported in the media. It is expressed in mass demonstrations, strikes, boycotts, civil-disobedience actions, and thousands of arrests — targeting such things as poverty; unemployment; unsafe nuclear reactors; nuclear missile sites; Klan rallies; the training of repressive foreign military personnel at the School of the Americas; U.S.-inspired wars in Central America, the Middle East, and Yugoslavia; the attacks on democratic sovereignty by the World Trade Organization (WTO); and the financial aggressions of the International Monetary Fund (IMF) and World Bank. There have been mass mobilizations in support of legalized abortion, women's rights, gay and lesbian rights, and environmental protections. There have been organized housing takeovers for the homeless, demonstrations and riots against police brutality, and noncompliance with draft registration. The Selective Service System admitted that in the last few decades some 800,000 young men have refused to register (the actual number is probably higher).[17] At the same time, major strikes have occurred in a wide range of industries, showing that labor militancy is not a thing of the past.

This is not to deny that there remain millions of Americans, including many of relatively modest means, who are racist, sexist, and homophobic; who dislike labor unions and look down on the poor; who swallow the conservative line that government is the enemy (not the powerful interests it serves); and who are readily whipped into jingoistic fervor when their leaders go to war against vastly weaker nations. Nor can it be denied that hate crimes against African Americans, Asians, Latinos, immigrants, Jews, and gays continue, and that advocates of compulsory pregnancy have committed many acts of violence against abortion clinics and abortion doctors.[18]

This society does not produce large numbers of conservative activists. There are no mass demonstrations demanding tax cuts for big business, more environmental devastation, more wars, more privileges for the rich, or more corporate devastation. But the system does produce millions who are uninformed about and turned off by politics, who have been made apolitical by the insipid nature of much public discourse, disheartened by the seemingly insuperable obstacles to change, and distracted by the idiocies of entertainment media. Socialization in the United States is largely apolitical and this itself has political significance.

Yet despite the endless distractions of a mind-numbing mass culture, despite news shows and commentators who give more attention to superficial questions and image manipulation than to substantive policies, and despite all the propaganda and indoctrination by plutocratic institutions, Americans still have some real concerns about the conditions of their lives. The disparities between what the ruling interests profess and what they practice remain apparent to large numbers of people. There is a limit to how effectively the sugar-coated nostrums of capitalist culture can keep our citizens from tasting the bitter realities of economic life.

In addition, political socialization often produces contradictory and unexpected spin-offs. When opinion makers indoctrinate us with the notion that we are a free and prosperous people, we, in fact, begin to demand the right to be free and prosperous. The old trick of using democratic rhetoric to cloak an undemocratic class order can backfire when people begin to take the rhetoric seriously and translate it into democratic demands.

Furthermore, there are people who love justice more than they love money or narrow professional success, and who long not for more things for themselves but for a better quality of life for all. It is not that they are without self-interest, but that they define their interests in a way that conflicts with the interests of the privileged and the powerful. In general, if Americans were given more truthful information and if they could see a way to change things, they would be more likely to move in a progressive direction on most economic policies — and, indeed, they show signs of wanting to do just that.

Democracy: Form and Content

Americans of all political persuasions profess a dedication to "democracy" but they tend to mean different things by the term. In this book, democracy refers to a system of governance that represents both in form and content the interests of the broad populace. Decision makers are to govern for the benefit of the many, not for the advantages of the privileged few. The people hold their representatives accountable by subjecting them to open criticism, the periodic check of elections, and, if necessary, recall and removal from office. Democratic government is limited government, the antithesis of despotic absolutism.

But a democratic people should be able to enjoy freedom from economic, as well as political, oppression. In a real democracy, the material conditions of people's lives should be humane and not insufferable and grossly unequal. Some writers would disagree, arguing that democracy is simply a system of rules for playing the political game, with the Constitution and the laws as a kind of rule book; we should not try to impose particular economic agendas on this open-ended game. This approach certainly does reduce democracy to a game. It presumes that formal rules can exist in a meaningful way independently of substantive realities.

The law in its majestic equality, French novelist Anatole France once observed, prohibits rich and poor alike from stealing bread and begging in the streets. And in so doing the law becomes something of a farce, a fiction that allows us to speak of "the rights of all" divorced from the class conditions that often place the rich above the law and the poor below it. In the absence of certain material conditions, formal rights are of little value to millions who lack the means to make a reality of their rights.

Take the "right of every citizen to be heard." In its majestic equality, the law allows both the rich and the poor to raise high their political voices: both are free to hire the best-placed lobbyists and Washington lawyers to pressure public officeholders. Both are free to shape public opinion by owning a newspaper or television station. And both rich and poor have the right to engage in multimillion-dollar election campaigns to win office for themselves or their political favorites. But again, this formal equality is something of a fiction. Of what good are the rules for those millions who are excluded from the game?

For conservatives, liberals, and most others on the right and center, capitalism and democracy go together. The free market supposedly creates a pluralistic society of manifold groups, a "civic society" that acts independently of the state and provides the basis for political freedom. In fact, many capitalist societies — from Nazi Germany to today's Third World dictatorships — have private enterprise systems but no political freedom. In such systems, economic freedom means the freedom to exploit the labor of the poor and get endlessly rich, and little more than that. Transnational corporate capitalism is no guarantee of political democracy and is often a barrier to it. Big business is concerned with maximizing private profits for the benefit of relatively few, while shifting many of its diseconomies onto the shoulders of the public. Thus, unemployment, poverty, environmental devastation, and occupational injuries are all largely "externalities," that is, by-products of the private economy.

When it works with any efficacy, democracy is dedicated to protecting the well-being of the many and rolling back the economic oppressions and privileges that serve the few. Democracy attributes equal value to all individuals and seeks to ensure that even those who are not advantaged by wealth or special talent can earn a decent living. The contradictory nature of "capitalist democracy" is that it professes egalitarian political principles while generating enormous disparities in material well-being and political influence.

Some people think that if you are free to say what you like, you are living in a democracy. But freedom of speech is not the sum total of democracy, only one of its necessary conditions. Too often we are free to say what we want, while those of wealth and power are free to do what they want to us regardless of what we say. Democracy is not a seminar but a system of power, like any other form of governance. Freedom of speech, like freedom of assembly and freedom of political organization, is meaningful only if the free speech is heard and if it keeps those in power responsible to those over whom power is exercised.

Nor are elections and party competitions a sure test of democracy. Some two-party or multiparty systems are so thoroughly controlled by well-financed like-minded elites that they discourage broad participation and offer policies that serve establishment interests no matter who is elected. In the chapters ahead, we will take a critical look at our own political system and measure it not by its undoubted ability to hold elections but by its ability to serve democratic ends. It will be argued that whether a political system is democratic or not depends not only on its procedures but on its substantive outputs, the actual material benefits it distributes and the social justice or injustice it propagates. A government that pursues policies that by design or neglect are so inequitable as to deny people the very conditions of life is not democratic no matter how many elections it holds.

Again, it should be emphasized that when we criticize the lack of democratic substance in the United States, we are not attacking or being disloyal to our nation itself. Quite the contrary. A democratic citizenry should not succumb to uncritical state idolatry but should remain critical of the privileged powers that work against the democratic interests of our nation and its people.

Notes

1. On the ruling class, see Chapter 11; see also my book *Land of Idols: Political Mythology in America* (New York: St. Martin's, 1994), especially chapter 7, "Monopoly Culture," for a discussion of how social and cultural institutions are linked to corporate power.

2. *San Francisco Examiner,* November 20, 1994, and October 21, 1996.

3. Geoffry White with Flannery Hauck (eds.) *Campus, Inc.: Corporate Power in the Ivory Tower* (Amherst, N.Y.: Prometheus, 2000); Lawrence Soley, *Leasing the Ivory Tower: The Corporate Takeover of Academia* (Boston: South End, 1997); and Michael Yates, "Laboring in the Academic Factory," *Monthly Review,* January 2000.

4. Nader quoted in *Home and Gardens,* August 1991, 144.

5. A survey of five hundred high-school newspapers found widespread censorship: *Washington Post,* December 30, 1981; see also Michael Parenti, *Dirty Truths* (San Francisco: City Lights, 1996), 235–52.

6. On the biases of textbooks, see the studies cited in Michael Parenti, *History as Mystery* (San Francisco: City Lights, 1999), 11–21.

7. Linda Rocawich, "Education Infiltration: The Pentagon Targets High Schools," *Progressive,* March 1994.

8. William Form and Joan Rytina, "Ideological Beliefs on the Distribution of Power in the United States," *American Sociological Review* 34, February 1969, 19–31; and Robert Coles, *Privileged Ones: The Well-Off and the Rich in America* (Boston: Little, Brown, 1977).

9. Jacqueline Jones, *The Dispossessed: America's Underclasses from the Civil War to the Present* (New York: Basic, 1992); and Jonathan Kozol, *Savage Inequalities* (New York: Crown, 1991).

10. *New York Times,* August 22, 1996.

11. Frank Scott, editorial in *Coastal Post* (Marin County, California), February 1, 1996.

12. Robertson quoted in *Nation,* January 10–17, 2000, 49.

13. On the dangers posed by the radical right, see Sara Diamond, *Facing the Wrath* (Monroe, Maine: Common Courage, 1996).

14. On the GOP's ties with Hitler collaborators, see Russ Bellant, *Old Nazis: The New Right and the Reagan Administration* (Cambridge, Mass.: Political Research Associates, 1988).

15. Harris poll, *Business Week,* November 20, 1995; Anthony Lewis in *New York Times,* January 9, 1996; *New York Times,* October 26, 1995, and October 15, 1998.

16. Surveys reported in *New York Times,* December 14, 1997; *Washington Post,* November 3 and December 4, 1991; *Z Magazine,* November 1992; and survey by the Center for the Study of Policy Alternatives, December 1994.

17. Stephen Kohn, *The History of American Draft Law Violations 1658–1985* (Westport, Conn.: Greenwood, 1986).

18. Jack Levin and Jack McDevitt, *Hate Crimes: The Rising Tide of Bigotry and Bloodshed* (New York: Plenum, 1993).

4

A Constitution for the Few

To understand the U.S. political system, it would help to investigate its origins and fundamental structure, beginning with the Constitution. The men who gathered in Philadelphia in 1787 strove to erect a strong central government. They agreed with Adam Smith that government was "instituted for the defense of the rich against the poor" and "grows up with the acquisition of valuable property."

Class Power in Early America

Early American society has been described as egalitarian, free from the extremes of want and wealth that characterized Europe. In fact, from colonial times onward, men of influence received vast land grants from the crown and presided over estates that bespoke an impressive munificence. By 1700, three-fourths of the acreage in New York belonged to fewer than a dozen persons. In the interior of Virginia, seven individuals owned over 1.7 million acres. By 1760, fewer than five hundred men in five colonial cities controlled most of the commerce, shipping, banking, mining, and manufacturing on the eastern seaboard. In the period from the American Revolution to the Constitutional Convention (1776–1787), the big landowners, merchants, and bankers exercised a strong influence over politico-economic life, often dominating "the local newspapers which voiced the ideas and interests of commerce."[1]

In twelve of the thirteen states (Pennsylvania excepted), only property-owning White males could vote, probably not more than 10 percent of the total adult population. Excluded were all indigenous First Nation People ("Indians"), persons of African descent, women, indentured servants, and White males lacking sufficient property. Property qualifications for holding office were so steep as to exclude even most of the White males who could vote. A member of the New Jersey legislature had to be worth at least £1,000. South Carolina state senators had to possess estates worth at least £7,000 clear of debt (equivalent to about a million dollars today). In Maryland, a candidate for governor had to own property worth at least £5,000. In addition, the absence of a secret ballot and of a real choice among candidates and programs led to widespread voter apathy.[2]

Not long before the Constitutional Convention, the French chargé d'affaires wrote to his government:

> Although there are no nobles in America, there is a class of men denominated "gentlemen." . . . Almost all of them dread the efforts of the people to despoil them of their possessions, and, moreover, they are creditors, and therefore interested in strengthening the government and watching over the execution of the law. . . . The majority of them being merchants, it is for their interest to establish the credit of the United States in Europe on a solid foundation by the exact payment of debts, and to grant to Congress powers extensive enough to compel the people to contribute for this purpose.[3]

In 1787, it was just such wealthy and powerful "gentlemen," our "founding fathers," many interlinked by kinship, marriage, and business dealings, who congregated in Philadelphia for the professed purpose of revising the Articles of Confederation and strengthening the central government.[4] Under the Articles, "the United States in Congress" wielded a broad range of exclusive and binding powers over treaties, trade, currency, disputes among the various states, war, and national defense. But these and other actions, including those relating to borrowing money and making appropriations, required the assent of at least nine states.[5] The Congress also had no power to tax, which left it dependent upon levies agreed to by the states. It was unable to compel the people to contribute to the full payment of the public debt, most of which was owed to wealthy private creditors.

The delegates to Philadelphia wanted a stronger central power that would (a) resolve problems among the thirteen states regarding trade and duties, (b) protect overseas commercial and diplomatic interests, (c) effectively propagate the financial and commercial interests of the affluent class, and (d) defend the wealthy from the competing claims of other classes within the society. Most historians usually ignore or deny (c) and (d).[6]

Most troublesome to the framers of the Constitution was the insurgent spirit evidenced among the people. In 1787, George Washington wrote to a former comrade-in-arms, "There are combustibles in every State, to which a spark might set fire." Even plutocrats like Gouverneur Morris, who shortly before the Constitutional Convention had opposed strong federation, now "realizing that a political alliance with conservatives from other states would be a safeguard if the radicals should capture the state government . . . gave up 'state rights' for 'nationalism' without hesitation."[7] Their newly found devotion to nation-building did not possess them as a sudden inspiration. As their private communications show, it was a practical response to immediate material conditions, born of a common class interest.

The working populace of that day has been portrayed as parochial spendthrifts who never paid their debts and who advocated inflated paper money. Most historians say little about the plight of the common people. Most of the population consisted of poor freeholders, tenants, and indentured hands (the latter trapped in servitude for many years). A study of Delaware farms at about the time of the Constitutional Convention found that the typical farm family might have a large plot of land but little else, surviving in a one-room house or log cabin, no barns, sheds, draft animals, or machinery. The farmer and his family pulled the plow.[8]

Small farmers were burdened by heavy rents, ruinous taxes, and low incomes. To survive, they frequently had to borrow money at high interest rates. To meet their debts, they mortgaged their future crops and went still deeper into debt, caught in that cycle of rural indebtedness that today is still the common fate of agrarian peoples in this and other countries.[9] Interest rates on debts ranged from 25 to 40 percent, and taxes fell most heavily on those of modest means. No property was exempt from seizure, save the clothes on a debtor's back.[10]

Throughout this period, newspapers complained of the increasing numbers of young beggars in the streets. Economic prisoners crowded the jails, incarcerated for debts or nonpayment of taxes.[11] Among the people there grew the feeling that the revolution against the English crown had been fought for naught. Angry armed crowds in several states began blocking foreclosures and forcibly freeing debtors from jail. In the winter of 1787, debtor farmers in western Massachusetts led by Daniel Shays took up arms. But their rebellion was forcibly put down by the state militia after several skirmishes that left eleven men dead and scores wounded.[12]

Containing the Spread of Democracy

The specter of Shays' Rebellion hovered over the delegates who gathered in Philadelphia three months later, confirming their worst fears. They were determined that persons of birth and fortune should control the affairs of the nation and check the "leveling impulses" of the propertyless multitude who composed "the majority faction." "To secure the public good and private rights against the danger of such a faction," wrote James Madison in *Federalist* No. 10, "and at the same time preserve the spirit and form of popular government is then the great object to which our inquiries are directed." Here Madison touched the heart of the matter: how to keep the "form" and appearance of popular government with only a minimum of the substance; how to construct a government that would win some popular support but would not tamper with the existing class structure, a government strong enough to serve the growing needs of an entrepreneurial class while withstanding the democratic egalitarian demands of the popular class.

The framers of the Constitution could agree with Madison when he wrote also in *Federalist* No. 10 that "the most common and durable source of faction has been the various and unequal distribution of property. Those who hold and those who are without property have ever formed distinct interests in society" and that "the first object of government" is "the protection of different and unequal faculties of acquiring property" (that is, wealth).

The framers were of the opinion that democracy was "the worst of all political evils," as Elbridge Gerry put it. For Edmund Randolph, the country's problems were caused by "the turbulence and follies of democracy." Roger Sherman concurred: "The people should have as little to do as may be about the Government." According to Alexander Hamilton, "All communities divide themselves into the few and the many. The first are the rich and the wellborn, the other the mass of the people. . . . The people are turbulent and changing; they seldom judge or determine right." He recommended a strong centralized state power to "check the imprudence of democracy." And George Washington, the presiding officer at the Philadelphia convention, urged the delegates not to produce a document merely to "please the people."[13]

There was not much danger of that. The delegates spent many weeks debating and defending their interests, but these were the differences of merchants, slaveholders, and manufacturers, a debate of haves versus haves in which each group sought safeguards in the new Constitution for its particular concerns. Added to this were disagreements about constitutional structure: How might the legislature be organized? How much representation should the large and small states have? How should the executive be selected? What length of tenure should exist for the different officeholders?

The founders decided on a bicameral legislation, consisting of a House of Representatives elected every two years in its entirety, and a Senate with six-year staggered terms (a third of the Senate to be elected every two years). It was decided that seats in the House would be allocated among the states according to population; while each state, regardless of population, would have two seats in the Senate.

Major questions, relating to the new government's ability to protect the interests of property, were agreed upon with surprisingly little debate. On these issues, there were no poor farmers, artisans, indentured servants, or slaves attending the convention to proffer an opposing viewpoint. Ordinary working people could not take off four months to go to Philadelphia and write a constitution. The debate between haves and have-nots never occurred.

Not surprisingly, Article 1, Section 8, that most consequential portion of the Constitution, which gives the federal government the power to support and regulate commerce and protect the interests of property, was adopted within a few days with little debate. Congress was to regulate commerce among the states and with foreign nations and "Indian tribes," lay and collect taxes and excises (the power that makes all other government functions possible), impose duties and tariffs on imports but not on commercial exports, "Pay the Debts and provide for the common Defence and general Welfare of the United States," establish a national currency and regulate its value, borrow money, fix the standard of weights and measures necessary for trade, protect the value of securities and currency against counterfeiting, and establish uniform bankruptcy laws throughout the country — all measures of primary concern to investors, merchants, and creditors.

Some of the delegates were land speculators who invested in western holdings. Accordingly, Congress was given the "Power to dispose of and make all needful Rules and Regulations respecting the Territory or other Property belonging to the United States." Most of the delegates speculated in highly inflated Confederation securities, nearly worthless paper scrip that the earlier Confederation had issued to pay soldiers and small suppliers. Wealthy speculators bought up huge amounts of this scrip for a trifle from the impoverished holders. Under Article 6, all debts incurred by the Confederation were valid against the new government, a provision that allowed the speculators to make enormous profits when their securities were fully honored at face value.[14]

By assuming this debt, the federal government — under the policies of the first secretary of the treasury, Alexander Hamilton — used the public treasury to create by government fiat a vast amount of private capital and credit for big investors, based on the government's newly established ability to tax the general population. The payment of the debt came out of the pockets of the general public and went into the pockets of a moneyed class. Financing this assumed debt consumed nearly 80 percent of the annual federal revenue during the 1790s.[15] This process of using the taxing power to gather money from the working populace in order to bolster private investment continues to this day, as we shall see in the chapters ahead.

In the interest of merchants and creditors, the states were prohibited from issuing paper money or imposing duties on imports and exports or interfering with the payment of debts by passing any "Law impairing the Obligation of Contracts." The Constitution guaranteed "Full Faith and Credit" in each state "to the Acts, Records, and judicial Proceedings" of other states, thus allowing creditors to pursue their debtors across state lines.

Slavery — a major form of property — was afforded special accommodation in the Constitution. Three-fifths of the slave population in each state were to be counted when calculating the state's representation in the lower house, giving the slave states disproportionately more seats in the House beyond their actual voting population. The Constitution never abolished the slave trade. Indeed, the importation of slaves was explicitly guaranteed for another twenty years until 1808, after which there was the option but no requirement that it be abolished. Many slaveholders assumed they would have enough political clout to keep the trade going beyond that year. Slaves who escaped from one state to another had to be delivered up to the original owner upon claim, a provision that was unanimously adopted at the Convention.[16]

The framers believed the states acted with insufficient force against popular uprisings, so Congress was given the task of "organizing, arming, and disciplining the Militia" and calling it forth to "suppress Insurrections." The federal government was empowered to protect the states "against domestic Violence." Provision was made for "the Erection of Forts, Magazines, Arsenals, dock-Yards and other needful Buildings" and for the maintenance of an army and navy for both national defense and to establish an armed federal presence within the potentially insurrectionary states — a measure that was to prove a godsend to the industrial barons a century later when the U.S. Army was used repeatedly to break strikes by miners and railroad and factory workers.

Fragmenting Majority Power

In keeping with their desire to contain the majority, the founders inserted what Madison called "auxiliary precautions," designed to fragment power without democratizing it. By separating the executive, legislative, and judicial functions and then providing a system of checks and balances among the various branches, including staggered elections, executive veto, Senate confirmation of appointments and ratification of treaties, and a bicameral legislature, they hoped to dilute the impact of popular sentiments. They contrived an elaborate and difficult process for amending the Constitution, requiring proposal by two-thirds of both the Senate and the House, and ratification by three-fourths of the state legislatures.[17] To the extent that it existed at all, the majoritarian principle was tightly locked into a system of minority vetoes, making swift and sweeping popular action less likely.

The propertyless majority, as Madison pointed out in *Federalist* No. 10, must not be allowed to concert in common cause against the propertied class and its established social order. The larger the nation, the greater the "variety of parties and interests" and the more difficult it would be for a mass majority to act in unison. As Madison argued, "A rage for paper money, for an abolition of debts, for an equal division of property, or for any other wicked project will be less apt to pervade the whole body of the Union than a particular member of it." An uprising of impoverished farmers may threaten Massachusetts at one time and Rhode Island at another, but a national government will be large and varied enough to contain each of these and insulate the rest of the nation from the contamination of rebellion.

Second, not only must the majority be prevented from finding horizontal cohesion, but its vertical force, its upward thrust upon government, should be blunted by interjecting indirect forms of representation. Thus, the senators from each state were to be elected by their respective state legislatures rather than directly by the voters. The chief executive was to be selected by an electoral college voted by the people but, as anticipated by the framers, composed of political leaders and men of substance who months later would gather in their various states and choose a president of their own liking. It was believed that they would usually be unable to muster a majority for any one candidate, and that the final selection would be left to the House, with each state delegation therein having only one vote.

The electoral college is still in operation. Its main function has been to create artificial majorities out of slim pluralities. Thirteen times since 1838, a candidate with a plurality (the largest percentage of votes of all the various candidates but still short of a majority) was elected president with a substantial majority of the electoral college. This happens because a candidate might have, say, 47 percent of the vote in a particular state (with the other 53 percent divided among several other candidates), but wins 100 percent of the winner-take-all electoral college vote, thus greatly inflating the winning tally.

The undemocratic effects of the electoral college were felt more than two hundred years after the Constitutional Convention in the 2000 presidential election. Vice President Al Gore won the popular vote by almost 540,000 ballots, but Texas governor George W. Bush won a larger number of smaller states with their padded electoral votes, thereby gleaning a majority of the electoral college. A highly dubious count of votes in Florida tilted the electoral college to Bush, and when that count was challenged in the courts, the Republican-controlled Florida legislature declared its intent to brush aside all challenges and summarily accept the list of pro-Bush electors that the Florida secretary of state, an active member of the Bush campaign, had certified as the winning slate. The Florida lawmakers were within their legal (if not moral) rights, for Article 2, Section 1 of the Constitution states that the electors in each state shall be appointed "in such manner as the Legislature thereof may direct," demonstrating yet another undemocratic feature of the electoral system.[18]

The Supreme Court was to be elected by no one, its justices being appointed to life tenure by the president, with confirmation by the Senate. Senators were elected by their various state legislators. Direct popular election of the Senate was achieved when the Seventeenth Amendment was adopted in 1913 — a mere 126 years after the Philadelphia convention — demonstrating that the Constitution is sometimes modifiable in a democratic direction, though it does seem to take awhile.

Originally, the only portion of government directly elected by the people was the House of Representatives. Many of the delegates would have preferred excluding the public entirely from direct representation. They were concerned that demagogues would ride into office on a populist tide only to pillage the treasury and wreak havoc on the wealthy class. John Mercer observed that he found nothing in the proposed Constitution more objectionable than "the mode of election by the people." And Gouverneur Morris warned, "The time is not distant, when this Country will abound with mechanics [artisans] and manufacturers [factory and mill workers] who will receive their bread from their employers. Will such men be the secure and faithful Guardians of liberty? . . . The ignorant and dependent [read, poor and propertyless] can be . . . little trusted with the public interest."[19]

When the delegates finally agreed to having "the people" elect the lower house, as noted earlier, they were referring to a select portion of the population that excluded all those without property: all females, Native Americans, and indentured servants. Also excluded were slaves, who constituted almost one-fourth of the entire population. Even among those African Americans who had gained their freedom, in both the North and South, few were allowed to vote.

Plotters or Patriots?

In a groundbreaking book published in 1913, Charles Beard argued that the framers were guided by the interests of their class. Disputing Beard are those who say that the framers were concerned with higher things than just lining their purses. True, they were moneyed men who profited directly from policies initiated under the new Constitution, but they were motivated by a concern for nation building that went beyond their particular class interests. To quote Justice Holmes, "High-mindedness is not impossible to man."

That is exactly the point: high-mindedness is a common attribute among people even when, or especially when, they are pursuing their personal and class interests. The fallacy is to presume that there is a dichotomy between the desire to build a strong nation and the desire to protect wealth and that the framers could not have been motivated by both. In fact, like most other people, they believed that what was good for themselves was ultimately good for their country. Their nation-building values and class interests went hand in hand, and to discover the existence of the "higher" sentiment does not eliminate the self-interested one.

Most persons believe in their own virtue. The founders never doubted the nobility of their effort and its importance for the generations to come. Just as many of them could feel dedicated to the principle of "liberty for all" while owning slaves, so could they serve both their nation and their estates. The point is not that they were devoid of the grander sentiments of nation building but that there was nothing in their concept of nation that worked against their class interest and a great deal that worked for it.

The framers may not have been solely concerned with getting their own hands in the till, although enough of them did, but they were admittedly preoccupied with defending the interests of the wealthy few from the laboring

many. "The Constitution," as Staughton Lynd noted, "was the settlement of a revolution. What was at stake for Hamilton, Livingston, and their opponents, was more than speculative windfalls in securities; it was the question, what kind of society would emerge from the revolution when the dust had settled, and on which class the political center of gravity would come to rest."[20]

The small farmers and debtors, who opposed a central government that would be even farther beyond their reach than the local and state governments, have been described as motivated by self-serving, parochial interests — unlike the supposedly high-minded statesmen who journeyed to Philadelphia.[21] How and why the wealthy became visionary nation builders is never explained. Not too long before, many of them had been proponents of laissez-faire and had opposed a strong central government. In truth, it was not their minds that were so much broader but their economic interests. Their motives were no higher than those of any other social group struggling for place and power in the United States of 1787. But possessing more time, money, information, and organization, they enjoyed superior results.

Though supposedly dedicated to selfless and high-minded goals, the delegates nevertheless bound themselves to the strictest secrecy. Proceedings were conducted behind locked doors and shuttered windows (despite the sweltering heat). Madison's notes, which recorded most of the actual deliberations, were published, at his insistence, only after all participants were dead, fifty-three years later, most likely to avoid political embarrassment to them.[22]

Those who argue that the founders were motivated primarily by high-minded objectives consistently overlook the fact that they themselves repeatedly stated their intention to erect a government strong enough to protect the haves from the have-nots. Deliberating in secrecy, they gave voice to the crassest class prejudices and most disparaging opinions about popular involvement. At no time did they deny the fact — as have their latter-day apologists — that their concern was to diminish popular control and resist all tendencies toward class equalization (or "leveling," as it was called). Their dedication to their class interests was so unabashedly avowed as to cause one delegate, James Wilson of Pennsylvania, to complain of hearing too much about how the sole or primary object of government was property. The cultivation and improvement of the human mind, he maintained, was the most noble object — a fine sentiment that evoked no opposition from his colleagues as they continued about their business.

If the founders sought to restrain power through a system of "checks and balances," they seemed chiefly concerned with restraining mass power, while assuring the perpetuation of their own class power. They supposedly had a "realistic" opinion of the rapacious nature of human beings — readily evidenced when they talked about the common people — yet they held a remarkably sanguine view of the self-interested impulses of their own class, which they saw as inhabited largely by virtuous men of "principle and property." According to Madison, wealthy men (the "minority faction") would be unable to sacrifice the rights of other citizens, nor jeopardize the institution of property and wealth and the untrammeled uses thereof, which in the eyes of the framers constituted the essence of "liberty."[23]

In sum, the Constitution was consciously designed as a conservative document, elaborately equipped with a system of minority checks in order to resist the pressure of popular tides. It furnished special provisions for the slaveholding class. It provided ample power to build the state services and protections needed by a rising bourgeoisie. For the founders, liberty meant something different from democracy. It meant liberty to invest, speculate, trade, and accumulate wealth and without encroachment by the common populace.

The civil liberties designed to give all individuals the right to engage in public affairs won little support from the delegates. When Colonel Mason recommended that a committee be formed to draft "a Bill of Rights," a task that could be accomplished "in a few hours," the other convention members offered little discussion on the motion and voted almost unanimously against it.

If the Constitution was so blatantly elitist, how did it manage to win ratification? It was strongly opposed in most of the states, but the same superiority of wealth, organization, and control of political office and press that allowed the rich to monopolize the Philadelphia convention enabled them to orchestrate a successful ratification campaign. The Federalists also used bribes, intimidation, and fraud against their opponents. What is more, the Constitution never was submitted to a popular vote. Ratification was by state convention composed of delegates drawn mostly from the same affluent stratum as the framers. Those who voted for these delegates were themselves usually subjected to property qualifications.[24]

Democratic Concessions

For all its undemocratic aspects, the Constitution was not without its historically progressive features. Consider the following:[25]

- The very existence of a written constitution with specifically limited powers represented an advance over more autocratic forms of government.
- No property qualifications were required for any federal officeholder, unlike in England and most of the states. And salaries were provided for all officials, thus rejecting the common practice of treating public office as a voluntary service that only the rich could afford.
- The president and legislators were elected for limited terms. No one could claim a life tenure on any elective office.
- Article 6 reads: "no religious Test shall ever be required as a Qualification to any Office or public Trust under the United States," a feature that represented a distinct advance over a number of state constitutions that banned Catholics, Jews, and nonbelievers from holding office.
- Bills of attainder, the practice of declaring by legislative fiat a specific person or group of people guilty of an offense, without benefit of a trial, were made unconstitutional. Also outlawed were ex post facto laws, the practice of declaring some act to be a crime, then punishing those who had committed it *before* it was made unlawful.
- Supporters of the new Constitution recognized their tactical error in failing to include a Bill of Rights and pledged the swift adoption of such a bill as a condition for ratification. So, in the first session of Congress, the first ten amendments were swiftly passed and then adopted by the states; these rights included freedom of speech and religion; freedom to assemble peaceably and to petition for redress of grievances; the right to keep arms; freedom from unreasonable searches and seizures; freedom from self-incrimination, double jeopardy, cruel and unusual punishment, and excessive bail and fines; the right to a fair and impartial trial; and other forms of due process.
- The Bill of Rights also prohibited Congress from giving state support to any religion. Religion was to be something apart from government, supported only by its own devotees and not by the taxpayer — a stricture that often has been violated in practice.

The Constitution represented a consolidation of national independence, a victory of republicanism over British imperialism. It guaranteed a republican form of government and explicitly repudiated monarchy and aristocracy; hence, Article 1, Section 9 states: "No title of Nobility shall be granted by the United States." According to James McHenry, a delegate from Maryland, at least twenty-one of the fifty-five delegates favored some form of monarchy. Yet few dared venture in that direction out of fear of popular opposition. Furthermore, delegates like Madison believed that stability for their class order was best assured by a republican form of government. The time had come for the bourgeoisie to rule directly without the baneful intrusions of kings and nobles.

On a number of occasions during the Philadelphia convention, this assemblage of men who feared and loathed democracy found it necessary to show some regard for popular sentiment (as with the direct election of the lower house). If the Constitution were going to be accepted by the states and if the new government were to have any stability, it had to gain some measure of popular acceptance. While the delegates and their class dominated the events of 1787–1789, they were far from omnipotent. The class system they sought to preserve was itself the cause of marked restiveness among the people.

Land seizures by the poor, food riots, and other violent disturbances occurred throughout the eighteenth century in just about every state and erstwhile colony. This popular ferment spurred the framers in their effort to erect a strong central government but it also set a limit on what they could do. The delegates "gave" nothing to popular interests, rather — as with the Bill of Rights — they reluctantly made democratic concessions under the threat of popular rebellion. They kept what they could and grudgingly relinquished what they felt they had to, driven not by a love of democracy but by a fear of it, not by a love of the people but by a prudent desire to avoid riot and insurgency. The Constitution, then, was a product not only of class privilege but of class struggle — a struggle that continued and intensified as the corporate economy and the government grew.

Notes

1. Sidney Aronson, *Status and Kinship in the Higher Civil Service* (Cambridge, Mass.: Harvard University Press, 1964), 35; and Daniel M. Friedenberg, *Life, Liberty, and the Pursuit of Land: The Plunder of Early America* (Amherst, N.Y.: Prometheus, 1992); Merrill Jensen, *The New Nation* (New York: Random House, 1950), 178.

2. Aronson, *Status and Kinship,* 49; A. E. McKinley, *The Suffrage Franchise in the Thirteen English Colonies in America* (Philadelphia: B. Franklin, 1969, originally 1905).

3. Quoted in Herbert Aptheker, *Early Years of the Republic* (New York: International, 1976), 41.

4. On the class interests of the framers, see Charles Beard, *An Economic Interpretation of the Constitution of the United States* (New York: Macmillan, 1936, originally 1913). Even Forrest McDonald, a conservative critic of Beard's interpretation, documents the opulent

background of fifty-three of the fifty-five delegates; see his *We, the People: The Economic Origins of the Constitution* (Chicago: University of Chicago Press, 1958), chapter 2.

5. Articles of Confederation, in *National Documents* (New York: Unit, 1905), 59–71.

6. For instance, see most of the articles in Robert Goldwin and William Schambra (eds.), *How Democratic Is the Constitution?* (Washington, D.C.: American Enterprise Institute, 1980).

7. Merrill Jensen, *The Articles of Confederation* (Madison: University of Wisconsin Press, 1948), 30.

8. Bernard Herman, *The Stolen House* (Charlottesville: University Press of Virginia, 1992).

9. Jensen, *The Articles of Confederation,* 9–10; and Beard, *An Economic Interpretation,* 28.

10. Aptheker, *Early Years of the Republic,* 33–36. Historians like Robert Brown, who attack Beard's view, assert that little poverty existed in post-Revolutionary America. They ignore the large debtor class, poorhouses, and crowded debtor jails. They also ignore studies like Clifford Lindsey Alderman, *Colonists for Sale: The Story of Indentured Servants in America* (New York: Macmillan, 1975).

11. Aptheker, *Early Years of the Republic,* 137, 144–145.

12. David Szatmary, *Shays' Rebellion: The Making of an Agrarian Insurrection* (Amherst: University of Massachusetts Press, 1980).

13. For these and other unflattering comments by the delegates regarding the common people and democracy, see Max Farrand (ed.), *Records of the Federal Convention of 1787* (New Haven, Conn.: Yale University Press, 1937, 1966), vols. 1–3, passim.

14. Beard, *An Economic Interpretation,* passim. Enormous profits accrued to holders of public securities.

15. Aptheker, *Early Years of the Republic,* 114.

16. For an excellent study of the enormous influence wielded at the founding by the slaveholding class, see Paul Finkelman, *Slavery and the Founders* (Armonk, N.Y., and London: M. E. Sharpe, 1996).

17. Amendments could also be proposed through a constitutional convention called by Congress on application of two-thirds of the state legislatures and ratified by conventions in three-fourths of the states. This method has yet to be tried. For a general discussion of the Madisonian Constitutional legacy, see Jennifer Nedelsky, *Private Property and the Limits of American Constitutionalism* (Chicago: University of Chicago Press, 1994).

18. For further discussion of the 2000 election and the controversy in Florida, see Chapter 13.

19. Farrand, *Records of the Federal Convention,* vol. 2, 200 ff.

20. Staughton Lynd, *Class Conflict, Slavery and the United States Constitution* (Indianapolis: Bobbs-Merrill, 1967). For discussions of the class interests behind the American Revolution, see Alfred Young (ed.), *The American Revolution: Explorations in the History of American Radicalism* (DeKalb: Northern Illinois University Press, 1977); and Edward Countryman, *A People in Revolution* (Baltimore: Johns Hopkins Press, 1982).

21. For examples of those who confuse the founders' broad class interests with the national interest, See David G. Smith, *The Convention and the Constitution* (New York: St. Martin's, 1965); see also several of the essays in Goldwin and Schambra (eds.), *How Democratic Is the Constitution?*

22. Farrand, *Records of the Federal Convention,* vol. 1, xii–xv. Sparser notes on proceedings, delegation votes, and other matters were published in 1819 and 1824.

23. *Federalist No. 10.*

24. Jackson Turner Main, *The Antifederalists* (Chapel Hill: University of North Carolina Press, 1961). For a state-by-state account, see Michael Gillespie and Michael Lienesch (eds.), *Ratifying the Constitution* (Lawrence: University Press of Kansas, 1989). Probably not more than 20 percent of the adult White males voted for delegates to the ratifying conventions, if that many.

25. This section on the Constitution's progressive features is drawn mostly from Aptheker, *Early Years of the Republic,* 71 ff. and passim.

5

Rise of the
Corporate State

It is commonly taught that the United States government has
been a neutral arbiter presiding over a polity free of the class antagonisms
that beset other societies. The truth is, our history has been marked by intense and often violent class struggles, and government has played a partisan role in these conflicts, mostly on the side of big business.

Serving Business: The Early Years

The upper-class dominance of public life so characteristic of the founding
fathers' generation continued throughout the nineteenth century. As early
as 1816, Thomas Jefferson complained of an "aristocracy of our monied corporations which . . . bid defiance to the laws of our country."[1] In the 1830s,
the period of "Jacksonian democracy," supposedly the "era of the common
man," a financial aristocracy exercised a predominant influence over the nation. President Andrew Jackson's key appointments were drawn overwhelmingly from the ranks of the rich, and his policies regarding trade, finances,
and the use of government lands reflected the interests of that class.[2]

In 1845 in New York, Baltimore, New Orleans, St. Louis, and other
urban centers, the richest 1 percent owned the lion's share of the wealth,
while a third of the population lived in utter destitution. Poverty and overcrowding brought repeated cholera and typhoid epidemics during which
the wealthy fled the cities, while the poor stayed and died. Many of the impoverished were addicted to alcohol and drugs (mostly opium). Some communities reportedly had more drug addicts than alcoholics. Adolescent girls

labored from six in the morning until midnight for paltry wages. Children as young as nine and ten toiled fourteen-hour shifts, falling asleep beside the machines they tended, suffering from malnutrition and sickness.[3] In an address before "the Mechanics and Working Classes" in 1827, a worker lamented: "We find ourselves oppressed on every hand — we labor hard in producing all the comforts of life for the enjoyment of others, while we ourselves obtain but a scanty portion."[4]

During these industrial conflicts, First Nation People ("Indians") struggled valiantly against the expropriation of their lands and the slaughter of their nations, a process that began with the earliest seventeenth-century European settlements, and continued full force with the massacre of Sioux men, women, and children by the U.S. Army in 1890 at Wounded Knee.

The War against Labor

Contrary to the view that the nation was free of class conflict, class struggles in nineteenth-century America "were as fierce as any known in the industrial world."[5] After the sporadic uprisings and strikes of the early decades, there came the railroad strikes of the 1870s, followed by the farmers' rebellions and the great industrial strikes of the 1880s and 1890s. Involving hundreds of thousands of people, these struggles were highly organized and sometimes even revolutionary in tone.

In the battle between labor and capital, civil authorities intervened almost invariably on the side of the owning class, using police, state militia, and federal troops to quell disturbances and crush strikes. As early as 1805, when eight shoemakers were indicted in Philadelphia for "a combination and conspiracy to raise wages," employers used the courts to brand labor unions as conspiracies against property and the Constitution.[6]

Repeatedly throughout the nineteenth century and well into the twentieth, police, militia, company thugs, and federal troops attacked industrial workers, strikers, and other protestors, killing hundreds, and beating, wounding, and jailing thousands more. In 1886, police in Chicago's Haymarket Square killed at least twenty demonstrators and wounded some two hundred in response to a bomb thrown into their ranks (killing seven police). Four anarchist leaders — none of whom had been on the scene — were tried and hanged for inciting the incident. That same year, thirty striking African-American sugar workers were massacred in Thibodaux, Louisiana, by a militia group composed of the town's affluent citizens. The two strike leaders were dragged from jail and lynched. In 1892, Pinkerton gun thugs hired by a steel company killed nine striking steel workers in Homestead, Pennsylvania. The strike was eventually broken by the National Guard. In 1894, U.S. Army troops killed thirty-four railroad workers who were on strike against the Pullman company. Over the next few years, scores of striking coal miners were murdered.

In the infamous Ludlow Massacre of 1914, Colorado National Guardsmen fired into a tent colony of miners who were on strike against a Rockefeller-owned company, killing forty, including two women and eleven children. In Arkansas in 1919, over one hundred striking cotton pickers were massacred by U.S. troops and an armed group of the town's most prosperous citizens. In 1915, sheriff's deputies in Everette, Washington, killed eleven and wounded twenty-seven members of the Industrial Workers of the World (IWW) who were protesting restrictions on free speech. In 1932, Henry Ford's private police fired upon unemployed factory workers, killing four and wounding twenty-four. In 1937, the Chicago police fired upon a peaceful crowd of striking steel workers, killing ten and wounding over forty.[7]

As even this incomplete list might suggest, there is no reason to believe that the United States was saved from the civil strife that plagued other capitalist nations. From the local sheriff and magistrate to the President and Supreme Court, the forces of "law and order" were utilized to suppress "labor combinations" (unions). The industrial barons regularly called soldiers to their assistance. Armories were erected in the principal cities for that purpose.[8] Short of having the regular army permanently garrisoned in industrial areas, as was the desire of some owners, government officials took steps "to establish an effective antiradical National Guard."[9]

Law in the Service of Business

The same federal government that remained immobilized while violence was perpetrated against abolitionists, and was unable to stop the illegal slave trade that continued right up until the Civil War, was able to comb the land with bands of federal marshals to capture fugitive slaves and return them to their masters. The same government that could not find the constitutional means to eliminate contaminated foods and befouled water supplies could use federal troops to break strikes, shoot hundreds of workers, and slaughter thousands of First Nation People. The same government that had not a dollar for the indigent (poverty being a matter best left to private charity) gave twenty-one million acres of land and $51 million in government bonds to a few railroad magnates. Statutes intended to outlaw monopolies and conspiracies in restraint of trade were rarely used in the nineteenth century except against labor unions.

While insisting that the free market worked for all, most business people showed little inclination to deliver themselves to the stern treatment of an untrammeled free market. Instead they resorted to such government protections and supports as tariffs, public subsidies, land grants, government loans, contracts, and corporate charters.

The Constitution makes no mention of corporations. And for the first few decades of the new nation, corporate charters were issued sparingly for specific purposes and fixed periods, usually of twenty or thirty years. Corporations could not own stock in other corporations or any land beyond what they needed for their business. Corporate records were open to public scrutiny, and state legislatures limited the rates that corporations could charge. In time, with the growing power of the business class, all such democratic controls were eliminated.[10]

In the first half of the nineteenth century, using the law of "eminent domain," the government took land from farmers and gave it to canal and railroad companies. The idea of a fair price was replaced with the doctrine of *caveat emptor* (let the buyer beware). When workers were killed or maimed in unsafe work conditions, employers were not held liable.[11] In the late nineteenth century, still more of the commonwealth was transformed into private wealth. Millions of dollars collected by the government "from the consuming population, and above all from the . . . poor wage earners and farmers," constituting an enormous budget surplus, were doled out to big investors.[12] Likewise, a billion acres of land in the public domain, almost half the present area of the continental United States, was put into private hands.

> This benevolent government handed over to its friends or to astute first comers, . . . all those treasures of coal and oil, of copper and gold and iron, the land grants, the terminal sites, the perpetual rights of way — an act of largesse which is still one of the wonders of history. The Tariff Act of 1864 was in itself a shel-

tering wall of subsidies; and to aid further the new heavy industries and manufactures, an Immigration Act allowing contract labor to be imported freely was quickly enacted; a national banking system was perfected.[13]

Though strenuously supportive of business needs, the government remained laissez-faire in regard to the needs of the common people, giving little attention to poverty, unemployment, unsafe work conditions, child labor, and the spoliation of natural resources. Yet democratic struggle persisted throughout the nineteenth century. A women's suffrage movement gathered strength. And labor unions repeatedly regrouped their shattered ranks to fight pitched battles against the industrial moguls.

One important victory that came with the Civil War was the defeat of the Southern slavocracy and the abolition of legalized slavery. The Reconstruction period in the former Confederate states was one of the few times the power of the federal government — backed by troops and the participation of poor Whites and former slaves organized into leagues and self-defense militias — was used to decree equal rights, enfranchisement for all males regardless of income, popular assemblies, fairer taxes, schools for the poor, and some very limited land reform. But once the Northern capitalists put an end to Reconstruction and allied themselves with the Southern oligarchs, the better to face their struggles against labor and western farmers, most of the democratic gains of Reconstruction were rolled back, not to be regained until well into the next century — if then.[14]

The Not-So-Progressive Era

In the twentieth century, wealthy interests continued to look to the federal government to do for them what they could not do for themselves: repress democratic forces and bolster the process of capital accumulation. During the 1900–1916 period, known as the Progressive Era, federal price and market regulations in meat packing, food and drugs, banking, timber, and mining were initiated at the insistence of the strongest companies within these industries. The overall effect was to raise profits for the larger producers, tighten their control over markets, and weed out smaller competitors.[15]

The individuals who occupied the presidency during the Progressive Era were faithful collaborators of big business. Teddy Roosevelt, for one, was hailed as a "trust buster" because of his occasional verbal attacks against the "malefactors of great wealth," yet his major proposals reflected the corporate agenda. He was hostile toward unionists and reformers, derisively dubbing the latter "muckrakers," and invited business magnates into his administration. Neither William Howard Taft nor Woodrow Wilson, the other two White House occupants of that period, saw any serious conflict between their political goals and those of big business.[16] Wilson, a Democrat, railed against big trusts but his campaign funds came from a few rich contributors, and he worked as closely with associates of Morgan and Rockefeller as any Republican. "Progressivism was not the triumph of small business over the trusts, as has often been suggested, but the victory of big businesses in achieving the rationalization of the economy that only the federal government could provide."[17]

The period is called the Progressive Era because of the much publicized but largely ineffectual legislation to control monopolies; the Sixteenth Amendment allowing for a graduated income tax; the Seventeenth Amendment providing for the direct election of U.S. senators; and such dubious electoral reforms as the long ballot and nonpartisan elections. By 1915, many states had passed laws limiting the length of the work day and providing worker's compensation for industrial accidents. Several states had passed minimum wage laws and thirty-eight states had enacted child labor laws restricting the age at which children could be employed and the hours they could work. In a few industries, workers won an eight-hour day and time-and-a-half overtime pay.

These enactments represented longstanding demands by workers, going back over a century. They were wrested from a fiercely resistant owning class after bitter and often bloody struggle. Even so, the conditions of labor remained far from good, and much of the reform legislation went unenforced. The workers' "real wages — that is, their ability to buy back the goods and services they produced — were lower in 1914 than during the 1890s."[18] Millions worked twelve- and fourteen-hour days, usually six or seven days a week, and two million children, according to government figures, were still forced to work in order to supplement the family income.

War and Red Scares

World War I brought industry and government even closer. Sectors of the economy were converted to war production along lines proposed by business leaders — many of whom now headed government agencies in charge of defense mobilization.[19] As of 1916, millions worked for wages that could not adequately feed a family. Each year 35,000 were killed on the job, mostly because of unsafe work conditions, while 700,000 suffered injury, illness, blindness, and other work-related disabilities.[20]

The war helped quell class conflict at home by focusing people's attention on the menace of the "barbarian Huns" of Germany. Americans were exhorted to make sacrifices for the war effort. Strikes were now treated as seditious interference with war production. Federal troops raided and ransacked IWW headquarters and imprisoned large numbers of workers suspected of radical sympathies. In 1918, as the war was winding down, Congress passed the Sedition Act, which mandated a twenty-year prison sentence for any "disloyal" opinion and any contemptuous reference to the U.S. government, flag, or Constitution. Harsh sentences were dealt out to labor organizers, socialists, and anarchists. Later that year, Attorney General Thomas Gregory proudly told Congress: "Never in its history has this country been so thoroughly policed."[21]

During the postwar "Red scare" of 1919–1921, the federal government continued to suppress radical publications, issue injunctions against strikes, violently mistreat strikers, and inflict mass arrests, deportations, political trials, and congressional investigations on political dissidents. The public was treated to lurid stories of how the Bolsheviks (Russian communists) were about to invade the United States, and how they were murdering anyone in their own country who could read or write or who wore a white collar.[22] Bourgeois leaders around the world greeted the Russian Revolution of 1917 as a nightmare come true: the workers and peasants had overthrown not only the autocratic czar but the capitalist class that owned the factories, mineral resources, and most of the lands of the czarist empire. As Secretary of State Robert Lansing noted, this revolution was a bad example to the common people in other nations, including the United States.[23] Along with England, France, and eleven other capitalist nations, the United States invaded Soviet Russia in 1917 in a bloody but unsuccessful three-year attempt to overthrow the revolutionary government, a chapter of history that most Americans have never heard about.

The "Jazz Age" of the 1920s (the "roaring twenties") was supposedly a prosperous era. Stock speculations and other get-rich-quick schemes abounded. But the bulk of the population lived under conditions of severe want, often lacking basic necessities. In 1928, Congressman Fiorello La Guardia reported on his tour of the poorer districts of New York: "I confess I was not prepared for what I actually saw. It seemed almost incredible that such conditions of poverty could really exist."[24] On top of this, the stock market crash of 1929 signaled a major collapse of productive forces, ushering in the Great Depression.

The New Deal: Hard Times and Tough Reforms

The Great Depression of the 1930s brought an increase in hunger, destitution, and unemployment. In its first four years, fifteen million workers lost their jobs and millions lost their retirement savings. There was no national system of unemployment insurance and very few pension plans, only charity and soup lines. Those lucky enough to have jobs faced increasingly oppressive work conditions:

> Speed-up, reduced work hours, reduced salaries, the firing of high-salaried employees and the employing of those willing to work for much less, exposure to deteriorated and dangerous machinery and a general reduction of safety

standards, thought and speech control so intense in some plants that workers never spoke except to ask or give instructions, inability to question deductions from paychecks, beatings by strikebreaking Pinkertons and thugs, and compelled acquiescence to the searches of their homes by company men looking for stolen articles.[25]

Senator Hugo Black (D-Ala.) observed in 1932: "Labor has been underpaid and capital overpaid. This is one of the chief contributing causes of the present depression. . . . You cannot starve men employed in industry and depend upon them to purchase."[26] Even banker Frank Vanderlip admitted: "Capital kept too much and labor did not have enough to buy its share of things."[27] But most members of the plutocracy blamed the depression on its victims. Thus, millionaire Henry Ford said the crisis came because "the average man won't really do a day's work. . . . There is plenty of work to do if people would do it." A few weeks later Ford laid off seventy-five thousand workers.[28]

With a third of the nation ill-fed, ill-clothed, and ill-housed, and easily another third just managing to get by, a torrent of strikes swept the nation, involving hundreds of thousands of workers. Between 1936 and 1940, the newly formed Congress of Industrial Organizations (CIO) organized millions of workers and won significant gains in wages and work conditions. These victories were achieved only after protracted struggles in which many thousands occupied factories in sitdowns, or were locked out, fired, blacklisted, beaten, and arrested; hundreds more were wounded or killed by police, soldiers, and company thugs.[29] The gains were real but they came at a high price.

The first two terms of President Franklin Roosevelt's administration have been called the New Deal, an era commonly believed to have brought great transformations on behalf of "the forgotten man." Actually, the New Deal's central dedication was to business recovery rather than social reform. First came the National Recovery Administration (NRA), which set up "code authorities," usually composed of the leading corporate representatives in each industry, to restrict production and set minimum price requirements — with results that were more beneficial to big corporations than to smaller competitors.[30] In attempting to spur production, the Reconstruction Finance Corporation alone lent $15 billion to big business.

The federal housing program stimulated private construction, with subsidies to construction firms and protection for mortgage bankers through the loan insurance program — all of little benefit to the many millions of ill-housed. Likewise, the New Deal's efforts in agriculture primarily benefited the large producers through a series of price supports and production cutbacks. Many tenant farmers and sharecroppers were evicted when federal acreage rental programs took land out of cultivation.[31]

Faced with mass unrest, the federal government created a relief program that eased some of the privation. But as the New Deal moved toward measures that threatened to compete with private enterprises and undermine low wage structures, business withdrew its support and became openly hostile. While infuriating Roosevelt, who saw himself as trying to rescue the capitalist system, business opposition enhanced his reformist image in the public mind.

The disparity between the New Deal's popular image and its actual accomplishments remains one of the unappreciated aspects of the Roosevelt era. For instance, the Civilian Conservation Corps (CCC) provided jobs at subsistence wages for only three million of the fifteen million unemployed. At its peak, the Works Progress Administration (WPA) employed almost nine million people but often for unstable duration and grossly inadequate wages. Of twelve million workers who were earning less than 40 cents an hour, only about half a million were reached by the minimum wage law. The Social Security Act of 1935, covering but half the population, provided paltry monthly payments and no medical insurance or protection against illness before retirement. Similarly, unemployment insurance covered only those who had enjoyed sustained employment in select occupations. Implementation was left to the states, which were free to set whatever restrictive conditions they chose.[32]

While government programs were markedly inadequate for the needs of the destitute, they achieved a high visibility and helped dilute public discontent. Once the threat of political unrest subsided, federal relief was slashed, and large numbers of destitute people were thrust onto a labor market already glutted with the unemployed.[33]

The Roosevelt administration's tax policy was virtually a continuation of former President Hoover's program, with its generous loopholes for business. When taxes were increased to pay for military spending in World War II, the major burden was taken up by middle- and low-income classes, who had never before been subjected to income taxes.[34]

All this is not to deny that, in response to enormous popular agitation and the threat of widespread radicalization, the Roosevelt administration produced real democratic gains, including some long-overdue social welfare legislation, a number of worthwhile conservation and public works projects, a rural electrification program for many impoverished areas, and a reduction in unemployment from 25 to 19 percent. The New Deal created millions of public works jobs for the unemployed, built or improved roads across the country, and built thousands of schools, parks, playgrounds, athletic fields, and airports. The CCC created 52,000 acres of public campgrounds, built over 13,000 foot trails, and restored almost 4,000 historic landmarks or monuments. It stocked waterways with millions of fish, made important contributions to firefighting, rodent and pest control, water conservation, and preventing soil erosion. In addition, the New Deal constructed hundreds of hospitals, post offices, bridges, dams (which were thought to be a good thing in those days), and courthouses. And thousands of unemployed writers, actors, musicians, and painters were given modest support and opportunity to enrich the lives of culturally deprived people.

Before the New Deal, unions were readily broken by court injunctions, heavy fines, and violent repression. The New Deal produced a series of laws to strengthen labor's ability to organize and bargain collectively. The Norris–La Guardia Act greatly limited the use of injunctions and made unenforceable the hated yellow-dog contract, which forced workers to swear they would never join a union. Other legislation banned management-controlled company unions. Probably the most important New Deal labor law was the National Labor Relations Act (1935), which set up the National Labor Relations Board (NLRB) with broad powers to oversee the certification of unions and penalize employers who violated the organizing rights of workers. Workers now had a federal law that guaranteed their right to unionize. Such legislation was both a response and a stimulus to labor's growing organization and militancy.[35]

Yet the New Deal era hardly adds up to a great triumph for the people. They were ready to go a lot further than Roosevelt did, and probably would have accepted a nationalized banking system, a less grudging and more massive job program, and a national health-care system. In regard to desegregation, open housing, fair employment practices, voting rights for Blacks, and anti-lynch laws, the New Deal did nothing. African Americans were excluded from jobs in the CCC, received less than their proportional share of public assistance, and under the NRA were frequently paid wages below the legal minimum.[36]

Industrial plant utilization more than doubled after the United States entered World War II in December 1941. Almost all the 8.7 million unemployed were either drafted into the armed forces or drawn back into the workforce, along with ten million new workers, many of them women. The gross national product, which stood at $88 billion in 1940, mushroomed to $135 billion within a few years. Those who profited most were the industrial tycoons and arms contractors. Only by entering the war and remaining thereafter on a permanent war economy was the United States able to significantly reduce unemployment. The ruling politico-economic elites were willing to make the kind of all-out spending effort to kill people in wartime that they would not make to assist people in peacetime.

In sum, government's growing involvement in economic affairs was not at the contrivance of meddling Washington bureaucrats but was a response to the increasing concentration of production and wealth. Along with the many small labor conflicts handled by local government, there developed large-scale class struggle — which had to be contained by a large state. The growth of federal power, a process initiated by the framers of the Constitution, among other reasons to secure the class interests of the owning class, continued at an accelerated pace through the nineteenth and twentieth centuries. Government provided the regulations, subsidies, services, and protections that business could not provide for itself. The corporate economy needed a corporate state.

While the populace won formal rights to participate as voters, the state with its judges, courts, police, army, and officialdom remained mostly at the disposal of the moneyed class. The law was rewritten and reinterpreted to better serve capital and limit the ability of labor to fight back. However, working people were not without resources of their own, specifically the ability to disrupt and threaten the process of capital accumulation by withholding their labor through strikes, and by engaging in other acts of protest and resistance. Such agitation wrested concessions from the owning class and the state. These victories fell far short of any all-out attack on capitalism but they represented important democratic gains for working people.

Notes

1. Andrew Lipscomb (ed.), *The Writings of Thomas Jefferson* (New York: Putnam, 1897), vol. 15, 112.

2. Edward Pessen, *Riches, Class and Power before the Civil War* (Lexington, Mass.: D. C. Heath, 1973), 278, 304; and Howard Zinn, *A People's History of the United States* (New York: Harper & Row, 1980), 125–29.

3. Edward Pessen, *The Many Faceted Jacksonian Era* (Westport, Conn.: Greenwood, 1977), 7–31; Otto L. Bettmann, *The Good Old Days — They Were Terrible* (New York: Random House, 1974), 152–53.

4. Zinn, *A People's History*, 216; Richard Boyer and Herbert Morais, *Labor's Untold Story* (New York: United Electrical, Radio and Machine Workers, 1971), 25 and passim; John Spargo, *The Bitter Cry of the Children* (Chicago: Quadrangle, 1968, originally 1906).

5. Historian David Montgomery quoted in Boyer and Morais, *Labor's Untold Story*, 221. A comprehensive study is Philip Foner, *History of the Labor Movement in the United States*, vols. 1–6 (New York: International Publishers, 1947, 1955, 1964, 1965, 1980, 1981).

6. Boyer and Morais, *Labor's Untold Story*, 216. See Sidney Fine, *Laissez-Faire and the General-Welfare State* (Ann Arbor: University of Michigan Press, 1964), for a description of capitalist, anti-Marxist orthodoxy in the United States in the late nineteenth century and its control over business, law, economics, university teaching, and religion.

7. For these and other examples of corporate state violence, see Sidney Lens, *Radicalism in America* (New York: Thomas Y. Crowell, 1969); Daniel Fusfeld, *The Rise and Repression of Radical Labor in the United States 1877–1918* (Chicago: Charles H. Kerr, 1985); Foner, *History of the Labor Movement*; Boyer and Morais, *Labor's Untold Story*.

8. Matthew Josephson, *The Robber Barons* (New York: Harcourt, Brace, 1934), 365.

9. William Preston Jr., *Aliens and Dissenters* (Cambridge, Mass.: Harvard University Press, 1963), 24.

10. Richard Grossman and Frank T. Adams, *Taking Care of Business: Citizenship and the Charter of Incorporation* (Cambridge, Mass.: Charter Ink., 1993); and *Why Do Corporations Have More Rights Than You?* (Arcata, Calif.: Democracy Unlimited, n.d.).

11. Morton Horowitz, *The Transformation of American Law 1780–1860* (Cambridge, Mass.: Harvard University Press, 1977).

12. Josephson, *The Robber Barons*, 395.

13. Josephson, *The Robber Barons*, 52.

14. James S. Allen, *Reconstruction: The Battle for Democracy, 1865–1876* (New York: International, 1937); Eric Foner, *Reconstruction* (New York: Harper & Row, 1988).

15. Gabriel Kolko, *The Triumph of Conservatism* (Chicago: Quadrangle, 1967), chapters 1 and 2.

16. Kolko, *The Triumph of Conservatism*, 281.

17. Kolko, *The Triumph of Conservatism*, 283–84; see also Frank Harris Blighton, *Woodrow Wilson and Co.* (New York: Fox Printing House, 1916).

18. Boyer and Morais, *Labor's Untold Story*, 180–81.

19. Paul Koistinen, "The 'Industrial-Military Complex' in Historical Perspective," *Journal of American History* 56, March 1970, reprinted in Irwin Unger (ed.), *Beyond Liberalism* (Waltham, Mass.: Xerox College Publishing, 1971), 228–29.

20. Boyer and Morais, *Labor's Untold Story*, 184 and passim.

21. John Higham, *Strangers in the Land* (Piscataway, N.J.: Rutgers University Press, 1988), 212 and passim.

22. Robert Murray, *Red Scare* (New York: McGraw-Hill, 1955), 95–98; Christopher May, *In the Name of War* (Cambridge, Mass.: Harvard University Press, 1989).

23. William Appleman Williams, "American Intervention in Russia: 1917–1920," in David Horowitz (ed.), *Containment and Revolution* (Boston: Beacon, 1967), 38.

24. Zinn, *A People's History*, 376; and the Brookings Institution study cited in Boyer and Morais, *Labor's Untold Story*, 237.

25. Charles Eckert, "Shirley Temple and the House of Rockefeller," in Donald Lazare (ed.), *American Media and Mass Culture* (Berkeley: University of California Press, 1987), 174.

26. Rhonda Levine, *Class Struggle and the New Deal* (Lawrence: University Press of Kansas, 1988), 70.

27. Boyer and Morais, *Labor's Untold Story*, 249.

28. Quoted in Zinn, *A People's History*, 378.

29. Irving Bernstein, *Turbulent Years: A History of the American Worker 1933–1941* (Boston: Houghton Mifflin, 1970); and Boyer and Morais, *Labor's Untold Story*, passim.

30. Barton Bernstein, "The New Deal," in Barton Bernstein (ed.), *Toward a New Past* (New York: Pantheon, 1963), 269; Levine, *Class Struggle and the New Deal*, chapters 1 and 4.

31. Frances Fox Piven and Richard Cloward, *Regulating the Poor* (New York: Pantheon, 1971), 76; also Bernstein, "The New Deal," 269–70.

32. Piven and Cloward, *Regulating the Poor*, chapters 2 and 3; Paul Conkin, *The New Deal* (New York: Crowell, 1967).

33. Piven and Cloward, *Regulating the Poor*, 46.

34. Gabriel Kolko, *Wealth and Power in America* (New York: Praeger, 1962), 31; and Conkin, *The New Deal*, 67.

35. Michael Goldfield, "Worker Insurgency, Radical Organization, and New Deal Labor Legislation," *American Political Science Review* 83, December 1989, 1258; Art Preis, *Labor's Giant Step* (New York: Pioneer, 1964); Roger Keeran, *The Communist Party and the Auto Workers' Union* (New York: International Publishers, 1981).

36. Bernstein, "The New Deal," 278–79.

6

Politics:
Who Gets What?

With the advent of World War II, business and government became ever more entwined. Occupying top government posts, business leaders were able to set the terms of war production, freezing wages and letting profits soar.[1] Immediately after World War II, thousands of government-owned facilities were sold off as "war surplus" for a pittance of their actual value, representing a major transfer of public capital to private business. From the 1950s to today, successive Democratic and Republican administrations have supported the corporate business system with subsidies, tax favors, and military spending programs that transformed the United States into a permanent war economy. Rather than a laissez-faire government that allowed the breakdown of business during the Great Depression, we have a corporate state that plays an increasingly active role in sustaining the capital accumulation process.

Welfare for the Rich

In the 1950s, the Eisenhower administration sought to undo what conservatives called the "creeping socialism" of the New Deal by handing over to private corporations some $50 billion (or $200 billion in today's dollars) worth of offshore oil reserves, government-owned synthetic rubber factories, public lands, and public power and atomic installations. During this period, the federal government also built a multibillion-dollar interstate highway system that provided the infrastructure for the trucking and automotive industries.

The pattern of using the public's money and resources to subsidize private enterprise continues to this day. Every year, the federal government doles out anywhere from $125 billion to $167 billion (estimates vary) in corporate welfare, in the form of tax exclusions, tax credits, reduced tax assessments, excessive depreciation write-offs, price supports, loan guarantees, payments in kind, research and development grants, subsidized insurance rates, marketing services, export subsidies, irrigation and reclamation programs, and research and development grants.[2]

The government leases or sells — at a mere fraction of market value — billions of dollars worth of oil, coal, and mineral reserves. It fails to collect hundreds of millions of dollars in royalties, interest, and penalties from giant oil companies. It pays out huge sums in unnecessarily high interest rates. It permits billions in public funds to remain on deposit in private banks without collecting interest. The federal government lends out billions at below-market interest rates. It tolerates overcharging by firms with whom it does business, and it provides long-term credits and tariff protections to large companies. It pays out billions to reimburse big corporate defense contractors for the costs of their mergers. The government gave away the entire broadcasting spectrum valued at $37 billion — instead of leasing or auctioning it off — representing nearly five times the broadcasting space that the big networks previously controlled.[3]

Every year, the federal government loses tens of millions of dollars charging ranchers below-cost grazing rates on over twenty million acres of public lands; these "ranchers" include a number of billionaires, big oil companies, and insurance conglomerates. Over the past five decades, at least $100 billion in public subsidies have gone to the nuclear industry and many billions worth of federally funded research and development has passed straight into corporate hands without the government's collecting a cent in royalties. Companies mine valuable minerals and metals from federal lands without paying royalties, sometimes with the right to purchase the land title for a nominal fee.[4]

The U.S. Forest Service has built almost 400,000 miles of access roads through national forests — eight times the size of the entire federal interstate highway system. Used for the logging operations of timber companies, these roads can cause massive mudslides that contaminate water supplies, ruin spawning streams, and kill people. After the timber companies clear-cut an area, the government then replants trees, costing the taxpayers additional millions annually.

The U.S. government's Agency for International Development (AID) spent $1 billion in taxpayer money over the past decade to help companies move U.S. jobs to cheaper labor markets abroad. AID provided low-interest loans, tax exemptions, travel and training funds, and advertising. AID also furnished blacklists to help companies weed out union sympathizers from their workforces in various countries.

"SOME OF THOSE PEOPLE ON WELFARE AREN'T EVEN INCORPORATED"

In any one year, subsidies totaling between $5 and $6 billion go to agribusiness producers of feed grain, wheat, cotton, rice, soy, dairy, wool, tobacco, peanuts, and wine, with relatively little going to small agrarian producers. Subsidies to big commercial farms encourage wasteful water practices and increased toxic runoffs into rivers and bays from pesticides, herbicides, and chemical fertilizers. The General Accounting Office (GAO) estimates that agribusiness enterprises that use legal loopholes to circumvent subsidy limits yearly collect more than $2 billion in unjustified farm program payments.[5]

The federal government has subsidized exporters of iron, steel, textiles, tobacco, paper, and other products, along with the railroad, shipping, and airline industries. The government paid 92 percent of the $3.7 billion invested in expanding the airline industry from 1940 to 1944.[6] It doles out huge amounts in grants and tax "incentives" to the big companies to encourage oil exploration. Several major petroleum companies leased acreage in Alaska for oil exploration, paying $900 million for lands that were expected to yield $50 billion.

Whole new technologies are developed at public expense — nuclear energy, electronics, aeronautics, space communications, mineral exploration, computer systems, biomedical genetics, and others — only to be handed over to industry for private gain. Thus, AT&T managed to have the entire satellite communications system put under its control in 1962 after U.S. taxpayers had put up the initial $20 billion to develop it. The costs are socialized; the profits are privatized.

Under corporate-state capitalism the ordinary citizen pays twice for most things: first, as a taxpayer who provides the subsidies and supports, then as a consumer who buys the high-priced commodities and services. Numerous medications marketed by the pharmaceutical industry have been paid for in whole or part by taxpayers — who often then cannot afford the high prices charged, even though the drug may not have been all that expensive to produce.

Federal Bailouts, State and Local Handouts

Billions of taxpayers' dollars go to bail out giant companies like Chrysler and Lockheed, while small businesses are left to sink or swim on their own. When one of the nation's largest banks, Continental Illinois, was on the brink of failure, it received $7.5 billion in federal aid. Another $8 billion went to the International Monetary Fund (IMF) to offset the losses incurred by U.S. banks in bad loans to Third World nations. The government spent billions to "rescue the Mexican peso" — really a bailout for wealthy Wall Street firms and banks that made bad investments in Mexican bonds.[7]

In the late 1980s and early 1990s, the government put over $500 billion into bailing out the savings and loan (S&L) associations. Under the deregulated thrift market adopted during the Reagan years, S&Ls could take any investment risk they wanted with depositors' money, often at great profit to themselves, with the understanding that failures and bad debts would be picked up by the government. In many instances, thrift industry heads funneled deposits directly into personal accounts, executive salaries, or fraudulent deals — sometimes involving organized crime and the Central Intelligence Agency (CIA).[8] When hundreds of thrifts failed, the government compensated depositors, 90 percent of whom held accounts of $100,000 or more, in what amounted to the biggest bailout and financial scandal in human history. The people hurt the most are the ordinary taxpayers who are paying $101 billion a year for the S&L bailout, and will continue to pay that amount for another twenty-five years or so.

The government spent billions bailing out hedge funds — at a time when Congress was tightening bankruptcy rules for ordinary citizens. Hedge funds allow the wealthy to evade all regulation while putting their money in the riskiest investments (which because they are risky offer high returns). When the investments fail, the hedge fund falls into a federal safety net. Once more, fat cats walk away fully compensated and the taxpayers are stuck with the bill.[9]

State and local governments also let big business feed at the public trough. They compete with each other in attracting new businesses and keeping old ones from leaving. In 1999 Pennsylvania gave $307 million to a Norwegian engineering firm to open a shipyard in Philadelphia; Alabama gave $253 million to Mercedes-Benz (now Mercedes-Benz/Chrysler) to build an assembly plant, including a $30 million training school — in an area where public schools were underfinanced and overcrowded. North Carolina annually gives tens of millions of dollars to the insurance and banking industries. California has handed out billions in tax-exempt bond-financing to Shell, Mobil, Chevron, PG&E, and other transnational corporations, while New York City gave huge tax breaks to General Motors, Merrill Lynch, Disney, and dozens of other rich companies. In cities across the country, taxpayers were being made to pay hundreds of millions for new sports stadiums, while the wealthy owners of professional teams pocketed record profits.[10]

State and local governments also provide business with low-interest loans, tax-free investment opportunities, special zoning privileges, and below-market land sales. They regularly waive environmental regulations to attract business. Eugene, Oregon, provided $12 million for a corporation to cut down an impressive stand of historic giant trees and build a parking garage and apartments. Such expenditures are justified as necessary to create new jobs. Yet new jobs rarely materialize in any appreciable numbers. For example, Baton Rouge, Louisiana, gave Exxon a $14-million tax break in exchange for a net gain of one job (by Exxon's own estimate). Michigan gave a company $81 million to build a mill that created only thirty-four permanent jobs — at $2.3 million per job.[11]

Several hundred thousand firms illegally retain billions of dollars each year in Social Security and withholding taxes from their employees' paychecks. Relatively few of them have been prosecuted.[12] Over one hundred of the largest private utilities annually collect taxes on their monthly billings to customers, but by taking advantage of write-offs and loopholes, they are able to pocket most of what they collect. In various states, state legislatures have approved multibillion-dollar bond sales that force taxpayers to bail out utility companies for bad investments made in nuclear power plants.[13]

In sum, free-market advocates, who constantly admonish the poor to lift themselves by their own bootstraps, are the first to turn to governments at all levels for handouts, bailouts, special services, and privileged protections.

Taxes: Helping the Rich in Their Time of Greed

The capitalist state uses taxation as well as public spending to redistribute income in an upward direction. Taking into account all taxes at the federal, state, and local levels, as well as Social Security payments, we find that lower-income people pay a higher average percentage of their earnings (12.5 percent) than do the richest (7.9 percent).[14] The higher the income, the greater are the opportunities to enjoy lightly taxed or tax-free income, including tax-free state and municipal bonds and tailor-made write-offs.

In the last two decades, income from property ownership (dividends, interest, rents) has risen three times faster than income from work. The rich have grown richer, while their tax burden has grown lighter. The Internal Revenue Service (IRS) reports that thousands of U.S. residents in the highest bracket pay less than 5 percent of their income in taxes. Almost 2,400 paid no taxes at all in the mid-1990s, and the number has been growing since then.[15] In 1991, billionaire presidential contender Ross Perot pocketed $285 million from his investments and paid $15 million in federal taxes, quite a large sum, yet it represents only about 6 percent of his earnings. Meanwhile, a schoolteacher who makes $35,000 might pay only $6,500 in federal income tax, much less than Perot; yet that sum represents upwards of 20 percent of her modest salary, and does not count the regressive sales and excise taxes and state income tax she also must pay. Still, the regressive principle seems to hold: the higher the bracket, the lower the actual *rate* of tax payment after deductions and write-offs.

Each year a dozen or more billionaires give up their U.S. citizenship and move to the Bahamas or other offshore tax havens, thereby saving millions on income and estate taxes.[16] (They are still allowed to spend 124 days a year in the United States.) Many of the superrich employ various stratagems to evade capital gains taxes (the federal tax on profits from the sale of stock, land, or other assets). Most capital gains taxes are now paid by smaller investors who own mutual funds.[17]

Corporations too are making more money and paying less in taxes. The proportion of federal revenues coming from corporate taxes has dropped from 50 percent in 1945 to less than 8 percent today. The resultant revenue loss is made up by an increase in taxes on the middle and working classes and greater government borrowing. Corporations can deduct for production costs, overhead, wages, marketing expenses, advertising, business conferences, and moving costs. They can write off business meals, travel and entertainment, investment incentives, operational losses, interest payments, and depreciation. They shift profits to overseas branches in low-tax countries. They indulge in tax shelters so complex that government auditors sometimes cannot properly trace them. They incur merger and acquisition costs that are then written off as deductions. And they dispatch lobbyists to

Washington to pressure Congress for still more tax breaks. The result is that, in 1998, a company like General Motors, the largest corporation in the United States, while reporting $4.61 *billion* in profits, paid the IRS less than 1 percent in taxes.[18] If employees' stock options in a company go up in value, the company can treat those gains as a deduction. This enabled Cisco Systems, the producer of Internet-switching gear, to make $2.67 billion in profits in 2000 and pay almost no federal income tax. Microsoft also got a huge stock option deduction.[19]

Media tycoon Rupert Murdoch avoids paying taxes on his U.S. holdings, though they account for the greater part of his immense fortune. In any one year, he siphons off many millions in state-side profits to his subsidiary in the Netherlands Antilles, a place that has virtually no income taxes. In addition, the $1.8 billion he paid to acquire U.S. television stations is written off against profits, further reducing his taxable income.[20] In effect, Uncle Sam helps to pay for Murdoch's growing media empire.

Under the Internal Revenue Code, over five hundred firms operating in Puerto Rico bring the profits back to their U.S. parent companies tax-free. (Puerto Rico is a U.S. colony where nearly two-thirds of the population live in poverty.) American-owned shipping companies incorporated in foreign countries are exempted from U.S. income taxes. Corporate overseas profits that are not repatriated are tax-exempted. Oil and mineral royalties that firms pay abroad can be treated as tax credits at home. A tax *credit* is even better than a tax deduction. A $5,000 *deduction* means that $5,000 of your income can be treated as nontaxable, saving you $1,550 (at a 31-percent tax rate). But a $5,000 tax *credit* allows you to subtract that amount from the actual taxes you have to pay, saving you $5,000. The royalties that Exxon and Mobil give to Saudi Arabia for the oil they extract from that country are treated as a tax credit, directly subtracted from the taxes the companies would have paid to the U.S. government.

A working mother with two children earning $15,000 pays more taxes in a year than any number of giant transnational corporations. Even as they brag to stockholders of record profits, over 60 percent of U.S. corporations pay no income taxes, according to a report from the General Accounting Office (GAO), the investigative agency of the U.S. Congress.[21]

It has been argued that taxing the wealthy more heavily would make no appreciable difference in federal revenue since they are relatively few in number. In fact, if rich individuals and corporations paid a graduated progressive tax of 70 percent, as they did twenty years ago, with no loopholes or shelters, hundreds of billions of additional dollars would be collected yearly and the national debt could be swiftly and substantially reduced. Just the deductions that corporations claim for the interest on their business loans costs the government nearly $100 billion a year in lost revenue. These are not trifling sums.

Responding to pressure from conservative lawmakers in Congress, the IRS has increased its focus on the poorest Americans and smallest businesses while paying less attention to richer people and larger companies. Among taxpayers making $100,000 or more, only 1.1 percent were audited in 1999, down from 11.4 percent five years earlier. Most working people have their taxes deducted from their paychecks and thereby are deprived of any opportunity to fudge their tax bill. Reduced IRS surveillance creates greater opportunities for evasion principally for those who enjoy a business income and who can resort to creative deductions and imaginative bookkeeping. This includes some of the biggest companies in the world. Yet the IRS reduced corporate audits substantially.[22] One reason the rich are paying so much less is the drop in auditing imposed on them.

Unkind Cuts, Unfair Rates

Most of the "tax reforms" produced by Congress are paraded as relief for the besieged middle class when actually they mostly benefit the higher-income brackets. Thus, for every dollar in tax cuts accorded the bottom 80 percent, the Taxpayer Relief Act of 1997 gave $1,189 to the wealthiest 1 percent. In fact, the poorest 60 percent received next to nothing in relief.[23] To help pay for these upper-income tax breaks, Congress slashed the modest allocation slated for rebuilding rundown schools.[24] Likewise the "middle-class tax plan" before Congress in 2000 offered the lion's share of cuts to the very richest.[25]

There are several ways people can be taxed. A *progressive* income tax imposes a substantially higher effective tax rate on the rich, based on the principle that taxes should fall most heavily on those who have the greatest ability to pay. Thus, in 1980 the very richest paid a 70-percent tax rate and the poorest only 18 percent. That rate is not as severe as it sounds, for it did not apply to one's entire income. The tax was graduated so that the rich paid the 70-percent rate only on the uppermost portion of their income. In addition, they continued to enjoy various deductions.

A *proportionate* income tax, or "flat tax," imposes the same rate on everyone, regardless of ability to pay. Its proponents argue that a flat tax brings simplicity and clarity to the tax code. Instead of the rich paying 70 percent and the poor paying 15 percent, which is supposedly all too complicated for us to grasp, we would *all* pay 17 percent or whatever; this way we ordinary folks would be less confused. A flat tax would lower the taxes on wealthier Americans and raise taxes on just about everyone else.

Those who advocate a progressive tax consider the flat tax to be unfair, for while everyone is paying the same rate, and the richer person is paying more dollars, the poorer person is being cut closer to the bone. If both rich and poor pay, say, 20 percent of their income, then a person who earns

$10,000 pays $2,000 in taxes and has only $8,000 to live on, while one who makes $1 million pays $200,000 but still has $800,000. A dollar taken from someone of modest means has a greater deprivation impact than even a thousand dollars taken from the super rich. Furthermore, most flat-tax proposals would tax wages and pensions but not dividends, interest, capital gains, corporate profits, and large inheritances.[26]

A *regressive* tax is even more unfair than a flat tax, for it imposes the highest effective tax rate upon those who have the least. Instead of paying the same rate as in a flat tax, rich and poor pay the very same amount. When both a janitor and a top executive pay the exact same tax on a gallon of gas, the janitor is sacrificing a far greater portion of income than the executive. Sales and excise taxes are highly regressive.[27]

Some conservatives advocate a *national sales tax* to replace the income tax. This would be most regressive of all. To raise as much as does the current income tax, we would have to pay an estimated 30 percent sales tax on most products, a regressive burden that would cost 90 percent of families vastly larger portions of their disposable income. As Senator Richard Lugar (R-Ind.) conceded when proposing a national sales tax: "I admit that if the point of taxation is progressivity or so-called fairness and redistribution, then my plan will not be your cup of tea."[28]

Some lawmakers advocate a *value added tax*, which is just a more covert and complicated version of a national sales tax. Taxes would be added at every stage of production and distribution (leaving businesses with about as much paperwork as they have now), with the consumer paying the full tab at the end of the line.

Then there is the estate tax or inheritance tax, which is very progressive, since it applies only to inheritances of over $1 million. In the decade ahead, scions of the wealthiest families in the United States, the top 1 percent or so, stand to inherit at least several *trillion* dollars. In 2000, a Republican-led Congress voted to repeal the estate tax, which if it had not been vetoed by Clinton would have given the superrich an extra $105 billion in the first ten years as the tax was phased out and then $750 billion in the decade after the tax is repealed, most of which would have gone to the top one-tenth of 1 percent of the population.[29]

Taxes are even more regressive at the state and local levels. In forty-five of fifty states, the poorest 20 percent of the population pay higher state and local rates than the richest 1 percent. For example, in Washington State, the poor pay 17.4 percent in state and local taxes, while the rich pay only 3.4 percent; in Texas, the difference is 17.1 to 3.1; and in Connecticut, 11.9 to 4.2.[30] In the early 1990s, state sales and excise taxes, which hit low-income people proportionately harder, were raised almost $12 billion. By mid-decade the states began cutting state income taxes, making state tax systems still more regressive.

Deficit Spending and the National Debt

When government expends more than it collects in revenues, this is known as deficit spending. To meet its yearly deficits, it borrows from wealthy individuals and financial institutions in the United States and abroad. The accumulation of these yearly deficits constitutes the national debt.

By 1940, given the deficit spending of the New Deal, the national debt had grown to $43 billion. The cost of World War II brought it to $259 billion. By 1981, it had climbed to $908 billion. Conservative leaders who sing hymns to a balanced budget have been among the wildest deficit spenders. The Reagan administration in eight years (1981–1988) tripled the national debt to $2.7 trillion. During the next four years, the Bush administration brought the debt to $4.5 trillion. By early 2000, it had climbed to over $5.7 trillion — the amount that today's taxpayers (and future generations) owe to rich bondholders and financial institutions.

In 1993, the federal government's yearly payouts on the national debt came to $210 billion. By the end of the decade, payments had climbed to about $350 billion. Several things have contributed to the growing national debt:

First, the billions of dollars in tax cuts to wealthy individuals and corporations represent lost revenue that is made up increasingly by borrowing. The government borrows furiously from the moneyed interests it should be taxing.

Second, there is the budget-busting impact of immense military spending. In twelve years, the Reagan-Bush expenditures on the military came to $3.7 trillion. In eight years, Bill Clinton spent over $2 trillion on the military.

Third, the national debt itself contributes to debt accumulation, growing at an increasing rate, so that the interest paid on the national debt has been expanding faster than the economy and twice as fast as the budget. Every year, a higher portion of debt payment has been for interest alone, with less and less for retirement of the principle, the debt itself. By 1990, over 80 percent of all government borrowing went to pay for interest on money previously borrowed. Thus, the debt becomes its own self-feeding force. The interest paid on the federal debt each year is the second largest item in the budget (after military spending).

To borrow money, the government sells treasury bonds. These bonds are promissory notes that are repaid in full after a period of years. Who gets the hundreds of billions in yearly interest on these bonds? Mostly the individuals, investment firms, banks, and foreign investors with money enough to buy them. Who pays the interest? Mostly ordinary U.S. taxpayers. Interest payments on the federal debt constitute an upward redistribution of wealth from those who work to those who live on personal wealth. Moneyed creditors lend their surplus capital to the U.S. government and watch it grow risk-free at public expense, backed by the "full faith and credit" of the U.S. government, just as the framers of the Constitution intended. We the people will be servicing this astronomical debt for generations to come. As Karl Marx wrote, "The only part of the so-called national wealth that actually enters into collective possessions of modern peoples — is their national debt."[31]

The debt serves the capitalist class well. Instead of investing their accumulated wealth in new production that would glut the market and remain unsold, capitalists invest in U.S. Treasury bonds to accumulate interest. Lending money to the government becomes a relatively risk-free but profitable investment at a time when investment opportunities are lagging because of stagnant consumer demand or are increasingly chancy because of a volatile stock market.

By 2000, the economic boom had brought about a budget surplus for the first time. Rather than demanding that the surplus be used to reduce the debt, GOP leaders in Congress called for additional cuts in taxes for the wealthy. To justify such tax breaks they predicted unbridled growth and enormous budget surpluses in the decade ahead, conveniently overlooking the possibility of sudden economic downturns.

Some Hidden Deficits

Predictions of large budget surpluses also overlook the additional but hidden deficits that exist. First, there is the "off-budget" deficit, an accounting gimmick that allows the government to borrow additional billions outside the regular budget. A government-created (but nominally "private") corporation is set up to borrow money in its own name. For instance, monies to subsidize agricultural loans are raised by the Farm Credit System, a network of off-budget banks, instead of being provided by the Agriculture Department through the regular budget. Congress also created an off-budget agency known as the Financing Corporation to borrow the hundreds of billions needed for the savings-and-loan bailout, instead of using the Treasury Department. These sums are taken out of the general revenue, compliments of the U.S. taxpayer.

Another hidden deficit is in trade. As we consume more than we produce and import and borrow from abroad more than we export, the U.S. debt to foreign creditors increases. Interest payments on these hundreds of billions borrowed from abroad have to be met by U.S. taxpayers.

Social Security also is used to disguise the real deficit. The Social Security payroll deduction — a regressive tax — soared during the Reagan years, and today produces a yearly surplus of over $120 billion. By 1991, 38 percent of U.S. taxpayers were paying more in Social Security tax than in

"There, there it is again — the invisible hand of the marketplace giving us the finger."

federal income tax. Many Americans willingly accept these payroll deductions because they think the monies are being saved for their retirement. In fact, Social Security taxes are used to offset deficits in the regular budget, paying for White House limousines, jet bombers, corporate subsidies, and interest on the debt.

U.S. political leaders have assiduously ignored the surest remedies for reducing the astronomical national debt: (a) sharply reduce individual and corporate tax credits and deductions, (b) reintroduce a progressive income tax that would bring in hundreds of billions more in revenues, and (c) greatly reduce the bloated military budget and redirect spending toward more productive and socially useful sectors of the economy.

To summarize the main points of this chapter: In almost every enterprise, government has provided business with opportunities for private gain at public expense. Government nurtures private capital accumulation through a process of subsidies, supports, and deficit spending and an inequitable tax system. From ranchers to resort owners, from brokers to bankers, from automakers to missile makers, there prevails a welfarism for the rich of such stupendous magnitude as to make us marvel at the corporate leaders' audacity in preaching the virtues of self-reliance whenever lesser forms of public assistance threaten to reach hands other than their own.

Notes

1. Richard Boyer and Herbert Morais, *Labor's Untold Story* (New York: United Electrical, Radio and Machine Workers, 1972), 331–32, 339.

2. Mark Zepezauer and Arthur Naiman, *Take the Rich off Welfare* (Tucson, Ariz.: Odonian, 1996); Donald Bartlett and James Steele, "Corporate Welfare," *Time*, November 9, 16, and 23, 1998; Janice Shields, *Corporate Welfare and Foreign Policy* (Washington, D.C.: Interhemispheric Resource Center, 1999).

3. Zepezauer and Naiman, *Take the Rich off Welfare*, 75–77; "Department of Interior Looks the Other Way," *Project on Government Oversight Reports*, April 1995; and "The Airwaves: Al Gore's Amazing Gift," *Nation*, March 10, 1997.

4. Ralph Nader, *Cutting Corporate Welfare* (New York: Seven Stories, 2000); John Canham-Clyne, "Cut Corporate Welfare," *Public Citizen*, July/August 1995, 1, 9–11; Jonathan Dushoff, "Gold Plated Giveaways," *Multinational Monitor*, January/February 1993, 16–20.

5. Zepezauer and Naiman, *Take the Rich off Welfare* , 56–68.

6. Frank Kofsky, *Harry S Truman and the War Scare of 1948* (New York: St. Martin's, 1994).

7. "$62 Billion Bank Bailout in Mexico Incites Outrage as Critics Say It Helps the Rich," *New York Times*, July 31, 1998.

8. Peter Brewton, *The Mafia, CIA & George Bush* (New York: Shapolsky, 1992); *Washington Post*, September 2, 1988, and May 27, 1990.

9. "Crony Capitalism," *Nation*, October 19, 1998, 3.

10. Bartlett and Steele, "Corporate Welfare"; survey of thirty cities by the U.S. Conference of Mayors, reported in *San Francisco Bay Guardian*, October 6, 1999; Joanna Cagan and Neil deMause, *Field of Schemes: How the Great Stadium Swindle Turns Public Money into Private Profit* (Monroe, Maine: Common Courage Press, 1998).

11. Zepezauer and Naiman, *Take the Rich off Welfare*, 115–16.

12. *Washington Post*, March 3, 1988.

13. Savannah Blackwell, "You Lose," *San Francisco Bay Guardian*, August 13, 1997.

14. Michael Haddigan, "Rockefeller Foundation Will Weigh in During Tax Debate," *Arkansas Times*, December 13, 1996.

15. *New York Times*, April 18, 1997.

16. Ken Silverstein, "Trillion-Dollar Hideaway," *Mother Jones*, December 2000.

17. *New York Times*, December 1, 1996.

18. Michael Phillips, "Taking Shelter," *Wall Street Journal*, August 4, 1999.

19. *Wall Street Journal*, October 10, 2000.

20. *New York Times*, July 29, 1996.

21. GAO report, *San Francisco Examiner*, April 15, 1999; Paul Sweeny, "Profiting from Tax-Proof Companies," *New York Times*, April 5, 1998.

22. "IRS Shifts Audit Focus from Rich to Poor," Associated Press report, April 16, 2000; David Cay Johnston's reports in *New York Times*, April 13 and 18, 1997.

23. Congressional Budget Office statistics reported in *New York Times*, April 5, 1998.

24. "Money for Nothing," *Nation*, September 1, 1997, 5.

25. *CTJ News*, Citizens for Tax Justice, Washington, D.C., July 1999.

26. *CTJ Update*, Citizens for Tax Justice, November 1997.

27. A sales tax is a fixed rate imposed on a wide range of products and services uniformly. An excise tax is imposed on a specific product at a specific rate: the gasoline tax and the cigarette tax are excise taxes.

28. Quoted in *Tax Notes*, July 31, 1995.

29. *New York Times*, September 1, 2000; and *CTJ Update*, April 2000.

30. "Who Pays? A Distributional Analysis of the Tax Systems in All 50 States," Citizens for Tax Justice, June 2000: <http://www.ctj.org>.

31. Karl Marx, *Capital*, vol. 1 (Harmondsworth, Middlesex, England: Penguin, 1976), 919.

7

Military Empire and Global Domination

The United States is said to be a democracy, but it is also the world's only superpower and foremost militaristic state as measured by the destructive capacity of its armed forces and the frequency of its direct and indirect interventions abroad against weaker nations.

A Global Kill Capacity

During the Reagan-Bush years, the United States deployed thousands of nuclear weapons and hundreds of thousands of military personnel at over 350 major bases and hundreds of minor installations that span the entire globe. This massive military apparatus was supposedly needed to contain a relentlessly expansionist Soviet Union — although evidence indicates that the Soviets were never as strong or eager to pursue the arms race as our Cold War policymakers claimed.[1] Despite the overthrow of the USSR and other Eastern European Communist nations in 1990–1991, U.S. military allocations continue at the budget-busting stratospheric level, and U.S. overseas military strength remains deployed in much the same pattern as before. At the same time, the U.S. maintains its Cold War nuclear weapons triad of Inter-Continental Ballistic Missiles (ICBMs), Sea-Launched Ballistic Missiles, and long-range bombers armed with nuclear bombs — all aimed at the former Soviet Union, an enemy that no longer exists. Between 1995 and 2000, the list of sites targeted by U.S. nuclear weapons grew by 20 percent, including targets in Russia, Belarus, Ukraine, Kazakstan, China, Iran, Iraq, and North Korea.[2]

President Clinton failed to cancel any of the weapons systems begun during the Cold War and added a variety of new ones during his administration (1993–2000). His military budgets were higher than the arms-race budgets of the 1970s, even after adjusting for inflation. Before leaving office, Clinton projected military budgets totaling $1.87 trillion for the years 2000 to 2005.[3]

In contrast, other nations have been cutting back on military spending. In 1999, while Congress expended about $289 billion on the military, Russia, the second largest spender, allocated only $55 billion, followed by Japan with $41 billion, China with $37.5 billion, and the United Kingdom with $34.6 billion. The United States is also the world's largest arms merchant, with $53.4 billion in weapons exports in 1999, twice as much as its nearest competitor, the United Kingdom. It costs U.S. taxpayers over $7 billion a year to subsidize these arms sales. The federal government spends another $26 million annually promoting U.S. weaponry to foreign leaders and at international trade shows. All the profits from these subsidized overseas sales go to the corporate defense contractors.[4]

If along with direct military spending we also take into account (a) veterans' benefits, (b) the military's share of federal debt payments — an annual $150 billion or so, (c) the 70 percent of federal research and development funds that goes to the military, (d) space programs that have a military function, and (e) other overlooked defense expenses picked up by nonmilitary agencies including the Energy Department's nuclear weapons programs, which consumes more than half the department's entire budget, then actual annual military spending has averaged well over $500 billion a year in recent times, or more than one-third the entire federal budget.

The federal budget is composed of *discretionary spending* (the monies that the president and Congress allocate and spend each year), and *mandatory spending* (the monies that must be allotted in compliance with already existing authorizations, such as payments on the national debt or Social Security). In the discretionary budget we spend more on the military than on all domestic programs combined.

The Clinton administration dedicated $7 billion to revive the Reagan plan to extend U.S. destructive capacity to an outerspace missile system that promises to be unworkable and immensely expensive, having already cost $55 billion. This "Son of Star Wars" project will supposedly intercept all land-based nuclear missile attacks. If successful, it will make the nuclear arsenals of other nations obsolete and deprive them of any deterrence against U.S. missiles. This in turn will encourage them to spend more updating their own nuclear attack systems.[5] Joseph Ashy, commander-in-chief of the U.S. Space Command declared: "We're going to fight from space and we're going to fight into space. We will engage terrestrial targets someday — ships, airplanes, land targets — from space."[6]

The Pentagon intends to deploy anti-satellite weapons that will enable the U.S. to knock out competitors' "eyes in the sky." The professed goal of

U.S. Space Command is to dominate "the space dimension of military operations to *protect U.S. interests and investments.*"[7] Such projects are in violation of the Outer Space Treaty, signed by ninety-one nations including the United States, which bans weapons of mass destruction in space.

The military can now beam powerful electromagnetic or pulsed radio-frequency radiation transmissions back to earth, seriously impairing the mental capacity of whole populations. As the U.S. Air Force describes it, the transmissions can cause "severe physiological disruption or perceptual disorientation" for an extended period, against which there would be no defense. Here are sinister weapons in the hands of elite interests unrestrained by any countervailing power.[8]

Military Waste and Fraud

The Department of Defense (also named "the Pentagon" after its enormous five-sided headquarters) has a procurement program that is rife with fraud and profiteering. The General Accounting Office (GAO), the investigative agency of Congress, found that the military budget was regularly padded with billions of dollars to ensure against congressional cuts. The Pentagon's own inspector general admitted that accounts often are so chaotic as to defy auditing. By most expert estimates, $15 to $40 billion disappears every year and is never recovered or adequately accounted for.[9] Such sums do not just evaporate; they find their way into somebody's pockets.

Waste, fraud, and duplication seem to be part of the military's modus operandi. The GAO reported that the Pentagon was storing $41 billion in excess supplies and equipment gathering dust or rusting away.[10] The U.S. Army allocated $1.5 billion to develop a heavy-lift helicopter, even though it already had heavy-lift helicopters and the U.S. Navy was building an almost identical one. The U.S. Air Force spent $64 billion to build the F-22 fighter plane with estimated cost overruns of $6 to $15 billion — all to replace the F-16, which was already by far the world's most advanced fighter. Meanwhile the navy was spending $80 billion to purchase one thousand new FA-18 fighter planes. Congress voted for additional ships the navy did not need, and C-130 cargo planes the air force did not want, while President Clinton pushed for Sea Wolf submarines and extra B-2 bombers that the Pentagon never requested.[11]

Defense contractors routinely charge unjustifiably huge consultation fees. They have been known to make out duplicate bills to different military agencies, getting paid twice for the same service. Tests have been rigged and data falsified to make weapons appear more effective than they actually are. Many of the top defense contractors have been under criminal investigation, but most fraud goes unpunished.[12]

The public purse is pilfered on small items too. The military paid $511 for lightbulbs that cost ninety cents and $640 for toilet seats that cost $12. After paying Boeing Aircraft $5,096 for two pliers, the tough Pentagon procurers renegotiated the price down to $1,496 — a real bargain. And a C-17 door hinge that should cost $31 was billed at $2,187 by McDonnell Douglas.[13]

Billions are spent on military pensions that go mostly to upper-income senior officers. Vast sums have been expended at military bases for golf courses, polo fields, restaurants, and officers' clubs — complete with gold-plated chandeliers, oak paneling, and marble fixtures. There is a Pentagon-leased luxury hotel outside Disney World in Florida that requires an annual federal subsidy of $27.2 million. Two golf courses at Andrews Air Force Base in Maryland were not enough, so a third one costing $5.1 million was built. And in the midst of intense budget cutting of human services, Congress found $1 billion for seven luxury aircrafts to service the Pentagon's top commanders.[14]

Pentagon Profits

From the taxpayer's point of view, much defense spending is wasteful. But for the giant corporate contractors, defense spending is wonderful, allowing them a return on their investments that is easily two or three times higher than what their nonmilitary ventures yield. Consider the following:

- There are almost no risks. Unlike automobile manufacturers, who must worry about selling the cars they produce, the weapons dealer has a guaranteed contracted market.
- Almost all contracts are awarded without competitive bidding at whatever price a corporation sets. Many large military contracts have cost overruns of 100 to 700 percent. To cite a notorious example, the C-5A transport plane had a $4-billion cost overrun (and its wings kept falling off).[15]
- The Pentagon directly subsidizes private business with free research and development, public lands, buildings, renovations, and yearly cash subsidies totaling about $7 billion.[16]
- In a capitalist economy the overproduction of consumer products can lead to a glutted market, but defense spending provides an area of demand and investment that does not compete with the consumer market and is virtually limitless. There are always more advanced weapons of destruction to develop.

Military spending is much preferred by the business community to many other forms of government expenditure. Public monies invested in occupational safety, environmental protection, drug rehabilitation, public schools, and other human services provide for human needs and create jobs and buying power. But such programs expand the *nonprofit* public sector, bringing no direct returns to business — if anything, shifting demand away from the private market. In contrast, a weapons contract injects huge amounts of public funds directly into the private corporate sector at an unusually high rate of profit.

U.S. leaders say that military spending creates jobs. So do pornography and prostitution, but there are more worthwhile ways of spending money and creating employment. In any case, civilian spending generates more jobs than military spending. For example, $1 billion (1990 value) of military procurement creates an average of 25,000 jobs, but the same amount would create 36,000 jobs if spent on housing, 41,000 jobs in education, and 47,000 in health care.[17] GAO auditors report that billions could be saved by closing unneeded military bases. This supposedly would cause too much hardship for the communities that serve these bases. Not so, according to these same auditors, who note that communities that already have lost base facilities are rebounding economically, though some are faring better than others.[18]

The total annual expenses of the legislative and judiciary branches and all the regulatory commissions combined constitute less than 1 percent of what the Pentagon spends. The $800 million that Congress saved in 1997 by cutting Supplementary Security Income for 150,000 disabled children amounts to less than one-third the cost of building and maintaining one B-2 bomber.[19] The hundreds of billions spent on new fighter planes in the last few years could finance the construction of modern mass transit systems for most of our major cities. What the people of an average U.S. city give in a few weeks in taxes to the Pentagon would be enough to wipe out their municipal debts. Pensions for the top military brass (senior officers only) amount to more than the total costs of federal welfare, the school lunch program, and all other child nutrition expenditures combined. The $5.5 trillion spent for nuclear weapons over the last half-century exceeded the combined federal spending on education, social services, job programs, the environment, general sciences, energy production, agriculture, law enforcement, and community and regional development.[20]

To keep America on its arms-spending binge, the corporate defense contractors propagate the military's cause with campaign contributions, lobbying, and mass advertising. The Department of Defense spends hundreds of millions on exhibitions, films, publications, and a flood of press releases to boost various weapons systems. It finances military-related research projects in the sciences and social sciences at many institutions of higher learning. In hundreds of conferences and thousands of brochures, articles, and books written by "independent scholars" in the pay of the Pentagon, the military viewpoint is lent an appearance of academic respectability.

The Military's Hidden Diseconomies

The military inflicts numerous hidden costs upon the environment and human life. The armed services use millions of acres of land at home and abroad in bombing runs and maneuvers, causing long-lasting damage to vegetation, wildlife, and public health. The Puerto Rican island of Vieques, having been used as a bombing range by the U.S. military for a half-century despite vigorous protests, has been heavily contaminated with uranium and other carcinogenic heavy metals, leaving a cancer rate among the island's inhabitants several hundred times higher than in any normal population. The same terrible health and environmental effects can be found at U.S. bombing sites in South Korea.[21]

The military uses millions of tons of ozone-destroying materials. It contaminates the air, soil, and groundwater with depleted uranium, plutonium, tritium, lead, fuel, and other toxic wastes, while amassing vast stockpiles of lethal chemical and biological agents. Populations at home and abroad have been contaminated by nuclear bomb tests. After decades of denial, the government is conceding that American workers who helped make nuclear weapons were exposed to radiation and chemicals that produced cancer and early death. The Department of Energy admits that it will cost more than $200 billion and take decades to clean up the contamination generated by nuclear arms production and testing. Yet it is spending $40 billion on nine new plants capable of designing additional nuclear weapons.[22]

The military is also a danger to its own ranks. Enlisted personnel are regularly killed in firing exercises, practice flights, maneuvers, and other readiness preparations — resulting in an average 2,534 *noncombat* deaths a year.[23] Tens of thousands of veterans have been sickened or have died from exposure to atomic testing during the 1950s or from toxic herbicides used in the Vietnam War. And more than 200,000 Gulf War veterans may have been exposed to depleted uranium or other highly hazardous materials, including anthrax inoculations that are suspected of causing serious illness. The anthrax supposedly immunizes soldiers from bacteriological warfare. When Congress asked that the vaccine be discontinued until more research could determine whether it was safe, the Pentagon refused. As of 2000, soldiers could still be court-martialed for refusing anthrax shots.[24]

Economic Imperialism

In recent decades, U.S. industries and banks have invested heavily in the "Third World" (Asia, Africa, and Latin America), attracted by the high return that comes with underpaid labor and the near absence of taxes, environmental regulations, and safety and consumer protections. The U.S. government has subsidized this overseas flight of capital and jobs by paying some of the relocation expenses. The government also grants tax concessions on overseas corporate investments, along with compensations for losses due to war or confiscation by a foreign government. As a matter of policy, Washington refuses aid to any country that nationalizes, without full compensation, assets owned by U.S. firms.

U.S. corporate investments do little to improve and much to diminish the lot of Third World peoples. This helps explain why the number of the world's poor is growing at a faster rate than the world's population. The transnationals push out local businesses and preempt their markets. Agribusiness cartels expropriate the best land for cash-crop exports, usually monoculture crops requiring large amounts of pesticides, leaving less acreage for the hundreds of varieties of organically grown foods that feed the local populations.[25]

By displacing local populations from their lands and robbing them of their self-sufficiency, corporations create overcrowded labor markets of desperate people who are forced to toil for poverty wages, often in violation of their countries' minimum wage laws. In Haiti, for instance, workers are paid 11 cents an hour by corporate giants such as Disney, Wal-Mart, J. C. Penny, and Sears.[26] The United States is one of the few countries that has refused to sign an international convention for the abolition of child labor and forced labor. This position stems from the child labor practices of U.S. corporations throughout the Third World and in the United States itself, where children as young as twelve suffer high rates of injuries and fatalities, and are often paid less than the minimum wage.[27]

The savings that corporations reap from cheap labor at home and abroad are not passed on in lower prices to their customers. Corporations do not go to far-off low-wage regions in order to save money for U.S. consumers but to increase their margin of profit. Thus, shoes made by Indonesian children working eighty-hour weeks for 13 cents an hour sold for $80 or more in the United States (1990 prices); labor accounted for only about $2.60 of the total cost.[28]

Since World War II, more than $230 billion in U.S. military aid has been given to some eighty-five nations. The U.S. has trained and equipped over two million foreign troops and police, the purpose being not to defend these countries from outside invasion but to protect capital investments and the ruling oligarchs from their own restive populations.[29]

U.S. aid money also subsidizes the infrastructure needed by private corporate investors in other countries: ports, highways, communications, and the like. U.S. nonmilitary aid to foreign nations comes with strings attached. It often must be spent on U.S. products, and the recipient nation is required to give investment preferences to U.S. companies, shifting consumption away from home-produced foods and commodities in favor of imported ones, creating more dependency, hunger, and debt.[30] Much aid money

never sees the light of day, going directly into the personal coffers of sticky-fingered officials and financial speculators in the recipient countries.

Aid also comes from other sources. In 1944, at a conference in Bretton Woods, New Hampshire, the United Nations created the World Bank and the International Monetary Fund (IMF). Voting power in both organizations is determined by a country's financial contribution. As the largest "donor," the United States has a dominant voice, followed by Germany, Japan, France, and Great Britain. Though funded by the taxpayers of these nations, the IMF operates in secrecy with a select group of bankers and staffs drawn mostly from the finance ministries of the rich nations.

The World Bank and IMF are supposed to assist nations in their development. What actually happens is another story. A poor country borrows from the World Bank to build up some aspect of its economy. Should it be unable to pay back the heavy interest because of declining export sales or some other reason, it must borrow again, this time from the IMF. But the IMF imposes a "structural adjustment program" (SAP), requiring debtor countries to grant tax breaks to the transnational corporations, reduce wages, and make no attempt to protect local enterprises from foreign imports and foreign takeovers. The debtor nations are pressured to privatize their economies, selling at scandalously low prices their state-owned mines, railroads, and utilities to private corporations. They are forced to open their forests to clear-cutting and their lands to strip-mining, without regard to the ecological damage done. The debtor nations also must cut back on subsidies for health, education, transportation, and food, consuming less in order to have more money to meet debt payments. Required to grow cash crops for export earnings, they become even less able to feed their own populations.

Here then we have explained a "mystery": why as aid and investment increased abroad over the last half-century, so has poverty.

Throughout the Third World, real wages have declined, and national debts have soared to the point where debt payments absorb almost all of the poorer countries' export earnings.[31] Some critics conclude that IMF and World Bank structural adjustments do not work; the end result is *less* self-sufficiency and more poverty for the recipient nations. Why then do the rich member states continue to fund the IMF and World Bank? It is because foreign loan programs *do* work. Their intent is not to uplift the masses in other countries but to serve the interests of global finance, to take over the lands and local economies of Third World peoples, indenture their labor with enormous debts, privatize public services, and eliminate the trade competition these countries might have posed had they ever really been allowed to develop. In these respects, foreign loans and structural adjustments work very well indeed.

The Terror State

To make the world safe for capitalism, the U.S. government suppresses insurgent peasant and worker movements and reformist governments around the world. But such a policy is coated with patriotic appearances. We are told that U.S. interventionism is needed to fight terrorism, stop drug trafficking, and thwart aggressive autocrats. Closer examination shows that U.S. leaders mainly have been defending the capitalist world from social change — even when the change has been peaceful and democratic. So they overthrew reformist governments in Iran (1953), Guatemala (1954), the Congo (1961), the Dominican Republic (1962), Brazil (1964), and Chile and Uruguay (1973).[32] Similarly, in Greece, the Philippines, Indonesia, East Timor, and at least ten Latin American nations, military oligarchs — largely trained and financed by the Pentagon and the CIA — overthrew popular governments that pursued egalitarian policies for the benefit of the destitute classes. And in each instance, the United States was instrumental in instituting right-wing regimes that were unresponsive to popular needs and more accommodating to U.S. investors.[33]

Throughout the 1980s and early 1990s, U.S. leaders continued their violent interventions against reformist governments. In Nicaragua, a U.S.-backed mercenary force killed over 30,000 people, orphaned more than 9,000 children and destroyed over $3 billion worth of homes, schools, health clinics, crops, and other facilities. In Angola and Mozambique, wars waged by CIA-backed forces left several million dead and millions more homeless and destitute. In East Timor, the U.S.-funded Indonesian military slaughtered some 200,000 people, more than one-third the population.[34]

The United States invaded Grenada in 1983 and Panama in 1989 to overthrow populist reformist governments, replacing both with free-market regimes propped up by U.S. force, bringing U.S.-financed elections, along with higher unemployment, lower wages, cutbacks in education and human services, and a dramatic increase in crime, drugs, and poverty.[35] What Nicaragua, Angola, Mozambique, East Timor, Grenada, and Panama had in common were governments that were redirecting some portion of their countries' labor and resources toward the needs of the people, putting them very much out of step with the rigors of free-market globalization.

In 1990–1991, Iraq refused to go along with oil quotas that boosted prices and favored the giant petroleum companies. In retaliation for the slant drilling of its oil fields by the feudal rulers of Kuwait, Iraqi dictator Saddam Hussein (a former CIA client) invaded Kuwait, providing the excuse needed by President Bush to launch massive bombing attacks that contaminated Iraq's fertile agricultural lands with depleted uranium and killed, by Pentagon estimates, 200,000 people.[36] Due to the U.S.-led economic blockade over the ensuing decade, water and sanitation systems deteriorated in Iraq, and as of 2000, some 1,200,000 Iraqis (including 800,000 children) had perished.[37]

As of September 2000, innocent Iraqi civilians routinely continued to be killed by U.S. and British airstrikes. Iraq, which once had the highest standard of living in the Middle East, with free education and medical care, has been reduced to an utterly destitute Third World country, kept down by sanctions. With its own oil kept off the international market, it is unable to infringe upon oil cartel profits.[38]

Also targeted was Yugoslavia, a fairly large and prosperous country that still retained some socialist features even after the overthrow of all the Eastern European communist countries. Some 75 percent of its economy was in the public sector. Yugoslavia was one nation that showed no interest in joining the North Atlantic Treaty Organization (NATO) or the European Union (EU), and its people, especially in the Serbian Republic, resisted the push to complete privatization (despite having opened themselves to IMF loans and free-market structural adjustment programs).

A series of Western-financed secessionist wars helped break Yugoslavia into a cluster of weak republics under Western suzerainty. These republics were ethnically cleansed of Serbs, who were the strongest proponents of a federal system. The Serbs were accused by Western leaders and Western media of being mass rapists and practitioners of genocide. What remained of Yugoslavia continued to resist, waging a civil war in Kosovo against Albanian rebels that took fewer lives in its entirety than any one major battle of the U.S. Civil War, and fewer lives than the dictatorial regimes of U.S. client states like Guatemala, Indonesia, and Turkey.[39]

For its attempts at resisting dismemberment, Yugoslavia was charged with "genocide" and "ethnic cleansing" by President Clinton and his associates, and subjected in 1999 to a massive bombing campaign by U.S.–led NATO forces that killed or wounded thousands and devastated the country's industry, infrastructure, and ecology, in what amounted to a forced and violent Third Worldization of a once prosperous nation.[40]

Subsequent reports by Western agencies themselves demonstrated that there had been no systematic mass rape and mass atrocity policy by the Serbs, though atrocities of a sporadic and local nature had been committed by all sides in the Yugoslav wars. Likewise, the reports of mass graves in Kosovo containing thousands of bodies failed to materialize once NATO forces occupied that province.[41] The greatest atrocity was the repeated bombings by Western forces of Yugoslavia, causing a degree of death and destruction entirely out of proportion to the war crimes charges leveled against Yugoslav leaders.

In 1998, when officials from thirty nations voted to establish the International Criminal Court to try crimes against humanity, the United States and China were the only nations to reject it. And in 2000, when the United Nations planned the establishment of a permanent international criminal court aimed at punishing those responsible for war crimes and human rights abuses, the United States sought a blanket exemption for all U.S. military personnel. Apparently defenders of the Free (market) World should not be held to the same standards demanded from others.[42]

U.S. leaders, both Democratic and Republican, have supported brutal wars of attrition against popular insurgencies in Guatemala (1962–1996), with estimated deaths of over 200,000; El Salvador (1980–1994), with over 75,000 deaths; Haiti (1987–1994); Thailand (1965–1973); and in Indochina against Vietnam (1945–1973), Cambodia (1955–1973) and Laos (1957–1973). In all these instances, torture and death squad terror killings were common methods of "counterinsurgency."[43] It is no accident that U.S. companies lead the world in the manufacturing of torture devices, including electroshock weapons, for domestic use and export.[44]

In 1999, President Clinton apologized for past U.S. support of rightwing governments in Guatemala that killed massive numbers of people. Such involvement "in violence and widespread repression was wrong"; it was a "mistake," and must never happen again, said the president, even as he continued to support repressive interventions against Iraq, Yugoslavia, Haiti, and other countries.[45]

In Vietnam, U.S. forces dropped almost 8 million tons of bombs, 18 million gallons of chemical defoliants, and nearly 400,000 tons of napalm. Over 40 percent of Vietnam's plantations and orchards were destroyed by chemical herbicides, as were over 40 percent of its forest lands and much of its fish and sea resources. Several million Vietnamese, Laotians, and Cambodians were killed; millions more were maimed or contaminated by toxic chemicals; almost ten million were left homeless. Some 58,000 Americans lost their lives and hundreds of thousands more were wounded or permanently disabled. But the war did benefit the top ten military contractors (including DuPont, ITT, and Dow Chemical), who grossed $11.6 billion (in 1973 dollars).[46] The U.S. intervention so shattered and impoverished Indochina as to make impossible its independent development. From 1979 into the 1990s,

U.S. leaders aided the genocidal, maniacal Khmer Rouge in Cambodia in order to destabilize the socialist-leaning government of that country, prolonging a civil war that took tens of thousands of lives.[47]

U.S. leaders have supported repressive governments that remain faithful to the dictates of free-market global finance. When the Mexican government was challenged by an insurgent movement in Chiapas, the U.S. national security state helped the Mexican military carry out a campaign of assassinating protest leaders, torturing suspects, burning crops, and displacing peasants.[48]

Colombia is another country that has a history of U.S.-financed repression, including the systematic murder of workers, students, farmers, and clergy who try to organize for social betterment. Through much of the 1990s about 35,000 lives were taken annually in Colombia. U.S. spokespersons blamed the violence on drug trafficking. But the Andean Commission of Jurists estimated that less than 2 percent of the killings had anything to do with drugs, while "70 percent is the work of Colombia's army, police and paramilitary death squads." From 1986 to 1994 more than 1,500 union members in Colombia were assassinated by CIA-supported death squads. Along with weaponry and helicopters, the U.S. military also provides defoliation chemicals that are wreaking havoc on Colombia's environment and people. In 2000, Congress voted $1.3 billion ostensibly to fight the Colombian narcotics traffic, though it was conceded that the funds would also be applied to the war against the revolutionary guerrillas (and the poor populations that support them).[49]

U.S. corporations sometimes have been directly involved in the human rights abuses perpetrated to make the world safe for global investments. In countries like Indonesia, Nigeria, India, Burma, and Colombia, big corporations have paid police and military to beat, arrest, and in some cases kill local residents who organize against the ecological damage or community displacement caused by the corporation's enterprise.[50]

For all their talk about "human rights," U.S. government leaders have propped up "pro-Western" regimes throughout the world that have used assassination squads, torture, and terror against their own populations. Strikes have been outlawed, unions destroyed, wages cut, and dissidents murdered.[51] At times, elections are manipulated with the use of enormous sums, dishonest counts, and well-directed terror, as happened in Jamaica (1980), Chile (1964), El Salvador (1984), and elsewhere.[52] But if election outcomes are not satisfactory to U.S. leaders, they are declared "rigged" and "fraudulent," (regardless of what international supervisors might say) as happened in revolutionary Nicaragua in the 1980s, in Yugoslavia in the 1990s and 2000, and in Haiti in 2000.

If we define "imperialism" as that relationship in which the ruling interests of one country dominate, through use of economic and military power, the land, labor, resources, finances, and politics of another country, then the

United States is the greatest imperialist power in history. The American empire is of a magnitude never before seen, with military bases that ring the entire globe, a nuclear overkill capacity of over 8,000 strategic weapons and 22,000 tactical ones, ground and air forces ready to strike anywhere, and a fleet larger in total tonnage and firepower than all the other navies of the world combined. With only 5 percent of the earth's population, the United States expends one-third of the world's military funds.

This U.S. global expansionism is designed to protect and advance the opportunities for global finance, and prevent the emergence of social orders that are revolutionary or reformist or even conservative nationalist (as in Iraq); ones that might utilize their wealth and labor in ways that cut into the profits or challenge the dominance of a corporate global economic empire. The profits of this empire flow into the hands of the privileged few, while the growing costs are largely borne by the common people at home and throughout the world.

Notes

1. Tom Gervasi, *The Myth of Soviet Military Supremacy* (New York: Harper & Row, 1986); Fred Kaplan, *Dubious Specter: A Skeptical Look at the Soviet Nuclear Threat* (Washington, D.C.: Institute for Policy Studies, 1980).

2. *Defense Monitor* (publication of the Center for Defense Information, Washington, D.C.), no. 5, 2000.

3. *Defense Monitor*, no. 2, 2000.

4. "Last of the Big Time Spenders," *Defense Monitor*, no. 8, 1999, 3; Martha Honey, "Guns 'R' Us," *In These Times*, August 11, 1997; and David McGowan, *Derailing Democracy* (Monroe, Maine: Common Courage, 2000), 95.

5. Christopher Hitchens, "Political Defense System," *Nation*, February 1, 1999; Josef Joffe, "A Warning from Putin and Schröder," *New York Times*, June 20, 2000; "U.S. Missile Defense Project May Spur China Nuke Buildup," *Oakland Tribune*, August 10, 2000.

6. Quoted in Karl Grossman, "U.S. Violates World Law to Militarize Space," *Earth Island Journal*, Winter/Spring 1999.

7. U.S. Space Command, *Vision for 2020*, 1998, quoted in McGowan, *Derailing Democracy*, 196 (emphasis added); see also Bruce Gagnon, "Pyramids to the Heavens: The Coming Battle for Control and Exploitation of Space," *Toward Freedom*, September/October 1999; and George and Meredith Friedman, *The Future of War: Power, Technology & American World Dominance in the 21st Century* (New York: St. Martin's, 1998).

8. Gar Smith and Clare Zichuhr, "Project HAARP: The Military's Plan to Alter the Ionosphere," *Earth Island Journal*, Fall 1994; and Nick Begich and Jeane Manning, "Vandalism in the Sky," *Nexus*, December 1995/January 1996.

9. Center for Defense Information Newsletter, May 2000; David Hackworth, "The Pentagon's Missing $33 Billion," *San Francisco Examiner*, April 17, 1995.

10. "Pentagon or Bust," *Nation*, March 24, 1997; General Accounting Office, *Financial Integrity Act Report* (Washington, D.C.: Government Printing Office, January 1990).

11. Edward Herman, "Privileged Dependency and Waste," *Z Magazine*, November 1997; "An Arms Race with Ourselves," Business Leaders for Sensible Priorities, New York, n.d. <http://www.businessleaders.org>; Graham Usher, "Military Monopoly," *Nation*, January 13/20, 1997, 6–7; *San Francisco Examiner*, November 23, 1997.

12. General Accounting Office, Financial Management: Billion Dollar Decisions Made Using Inaccurate and Unreliable Air Force Data, February 1990; *San Francisco Chronicle,* February 26, 1997.

13. *The Pentagon Follies* (Washington, D.C.: Council for a Livable World and Taxpayers for Common Sense, 1996); *Washington Post,* July 13, 1990.

14. See *The Pentagon Follies;* and *New York Times,* August 6, 1990, April 1, 1996, and October 8, 1999.

15. For a recent cost overrun involving a laser used for hydrogen bomb research, see *New York Times,* May 26, 2000.

16. Lora Lumpe, "Costly Giveaways," *Bulletin of Atomic Scientists,* October 1996.

17. "Why We Overfeed the Sacred Cow," *Defense Monitor,* no. 2, 1996.

18. *San Francisco Examiner,* November 19, 1998.

19. Robert Scheer, "Our Rained-Out Bomber," *Nation,* September 22, 1997.

20. *Atomic Audit: 1940–1996* (Washington, D.C.: Brookings Institution, n.d.); and *The U.S. Nuclear Weapons Cost Study Project* (Washington, D.C.: Brookings Institution, 2000).

21. Jim Creaven, "On the Ground in Puerto Rico," *Veterans for Peace,* Spring 2000; and <http://www.viequeslibre.org>; and Karen Talbot, "Korea: The Anatomy of a War and Prospects for Reunification" <http://www.covertaction.org.>, October 2000.

22. Seth Shulman, *The Threat at Home: Confronting the Toxic Legacy of the U.S. Military* (Boston: Beacon, 1992); Jeffrey St. Clair, "30 Years After: The Legacy of America's Largest Nuclear Test," *In These Times,* August 8, 1999; *Status Report on "Paths to Closure"* (Washington, D.C.: U.S. Department of Energy, March 2000); *New York Times,* January 29, 2000.

23. Department of Defense, *Worldwide U.S. Military Active Duty Military Personnel Casualties,* Directorate for Information Operations and Reports booklet M07.

24. Tod Ensign, "Guinea Pigs & Disposable GIs," *CovertAction Quarterly,* Winter 1992–1993; Kathleen Sullivan, "Gulf War Map a Clue to Vet Ills?" *San Francisco Examiner,* January 24, 1999; Hank Roth, "Anthrax and Other Small Favors," *North Coast Xpress,* Spring 2000.

25. See "Feeding Dependency, Starving Democracy," report by Grassroots International, Somerville, Mass., 1997; and Richard Jolly et al., *Human Development Report* (New York: Oxford University Press, 1996).

26. Eric Verhoogen, "The U.S. in Haiti: How to Get Rich on 11 Cents an Hour," *Crossroads,* April/May 1996.

27. Terry Collingsworth, "Child Labor in the Global Economy," policy brief by the Interhemispheric Resource Center and the Institute for Policy Studies, Washington, D.C., 1997; *Fingers to the Bone: United States Failure to Protect Child Farmworkers,* report by Children's Rights Division of Human Rights Watch, June 2000, <http://www.hrw.org/campaigns/crp/farmchild/index.htm>.

28. *New York Times,* March 16, 1996.

29. For instance, William Hartung and Bridget Moix, "Deadly Legacy: U.S. Arms to Africa and the Congo War" <http://www.worldpolicy.org/projects/arms/reports/congo.htm>.

30. Graham Hancock, *Lords of Poverty: The Power, Prestige, and Corruption of the International Aid Business* (New York: Atlantic Monthly, 1989).

31. "IMF/World Bank Watch," *Asheville Global Report,* February 24–March 1, 2000; Susan George and Fabrizio Sabelli, *Faith and Credit: The World Bank's Secular Empire* (Boulder, Colo.: Westview, 1994); William Greider, "Time to Rein in Global Finance," *Nation,* April 24, 2000; and "IMF to the Rescue (of Bankers)," *Labor Party Press,* May 1998.

32. For the first time, the CIA acknowledged in 2000 that it "dealt with" those who plotted the coup in Chile, including false propagandists and assassins: Associated Press, September 20, 2000. But the agency still denies it was involved in any human rights abuses.

33. William Blum, *Rogue State* (Monroe, Maine: Common Courage, 2000), 125–67.

34. Reed Brody, *Contra Terror in Nicaragua* (Boston: South End, 1985); Holly Sklar, *Washington's War on Nicaragua* (Boston: South End, 1985); United Church of Christ

Commission for Racial Justice, "Why Is the U.S. Prolonging War in Angola?" *Washington Post*, October 5, 1989; Augustus Richard Norton, "The Renamo Menace: Hunger and Carnage in Mozambique," *New Leader*, November 16, 1987; Blum, "East Timor, 1975–99," *Rogue State*, 146–47.

35. On how reporting on Grenada and Panama have been distorted, see Michael Parenti, *Inventing Reality: The Politics of News Media*, 2nd ed. (New York: St. Martin's, 1993), 148–51, 159–63.

36. London *Times*, March 3, 1991.

37. Ramsey Clark et al., *Challenge to Genocide* (New York and San Francisco: International Action Center, 2000).

38. *Washington Post*, June 23, 2000.

39. On Turkey, see Ertugrul Kurkeu, "Trapped in a Web of Covert Killers," *CovertAction Quarterly*, Summer 1997.

40. Michael Parenti, *To Kill a Nation: The Attack on Yugoslavia* (New York and London: Verso, 2000).

41. Parenti, *To Kill a Nation*.

42. John Hooper, "US Plans to Thwart War Crimes Court," *Guardian Weekly* (U.K.), July 26, 1998; "U.S. Seeking Immunity for Troops from New War Crimes Court," *San Francisco Chronicle*, June 12, 2000.

43. *New York Times*, August 5 and December 30, 1996, and February 26, 1999; Dana Priest, "Army Instructed Latins on Executions, Torture," *Washington Post*, September 21, 1996; David Kirsh, "Death Squads in El Salvador: A Pattern of U.S. Complicity," *CovertAction Quarterly*, Summer 1990.

44. *Chicago Tribune*, March 4, 1997; *Washington Times*, March 4, 1997.

45. *New York Times*, March 11, 1999.

46. William Hoffman, "Vietnam: The Bloody Get-Rich-Quick Business of War," *Gallery*, November 1978; also Marvin Gettleman et al. (eds.), *Vietnam and America* (New York: Grove, 1985), which despite its sloppy editing contains pertinent data.

47. Ben Kiernan (ed.), *Genocide and Democracy in Cambodia*, Yale University/Southeast Asia Students monograph series, no. 41, 1993; John Pilger, "Pol Pot: The Monster We Created," *Guardian Weekly* (U.K.), April 26, 1998.

48. *Nonviolent Activist* (publication of War Resisters League), May/June 2000.

49. Javier Giraldo, S.J., *Colombia: The Genocidal Democracy* (Monroe, Maine: Common Courage, 1996); "Colombia and the Drug War Fraud," *Focus*, Office of the Americas, July 1997; and *Columbia Update*, Colombia Human Rights Network, Fall 1997/Winter 1998; "Defoliation in Colombia," International Action Center <http://www.iacenter.org>; and *New York Times*, June 25, 2000.

50. Arvind Ganesan, "Corporation Crackdowns, Business Backs Brutality," *Dollars and Sense*, May/June 1999.

51. Edward Herman, *The Real Terror Network* (Boston: South End, 1985); Michael Parenti, *Against Empire* (San Francisco: City Lights, 1995); Blum, *Rogue State*, 92 ff.

52. Edward Herman, *Demonstration Elections* (Boston: South End, c. 1984); Parenti, *Against Empire*, 125–29; *New York Times*, March 8, 1997.

8

Health, Environment, and Human Services: Sacrificial Lambs

The plutocracy rules but not always in the way it would like. From time to time, those of wealth and power must make concessions, giving a little in order to keep a lot, taking care that the worst abuses of capitalism do not cause people to agitate against the system itself. After the important gains won during the Great Depression of the 1930s, democratic forces continued to press their fight against economic and social injustice. In response, the federal government initiated a series of human services that helped many but failed to reach millions, including many of those most in need. In recent years even these inadequate but important gains have come under serious attack.

The Poor Get Less (and Less)

Public funds ostensibly intended for the needy often end up in the wrong hands. In 1965, the government declared "war on poverty" in Appalachia, an impoverished hilly strip that runs from New York to Mississippi. For the next thirty-five years, more than $16 billion was invested by federal, state, and local governments in Appalachia, but the spending chiefly benefited merchants, bankers, coal companies, and contractors rather than the poor.

Federal programs frequently fail to reach those in need. The Special Supplemental Food Program for Women, Infants, and Children (WIC) assists only about half of the eligible. In 1996, a law supported by President

Clinton phased out Aid to Families with Dependent Children (AFDC or "welfare"). More than half of the subsequent $54 billion in welfare cuts were taken out of the food stamps such families received. Another $3 billion was cut from child nutrition programs. Food stamps were completely eliminated for an estimated 650,000 legal immigrants, including many elderly who were ejected from private nursing homes once their federal checks stopped coming in. Clinton's cutback of welfare "hit hardest those who couldn't afford to feed themselves and their families."[1]

The great majority of former food stamp recipients include those who are not readily employable because of mental or physical impairments or advanced age. They have been left to go hungry or search out private soup kitchens and food banks run by churches and other charities. These organizations are unable to keep up with the increasing numbers of hungry people.[2]

During the Reagan-Bush-Clinton era (1981–2000), billions of dollars were slashed from college scholarships, legal services for the poor, remedial education, school breakfast programs, maternal and child health care, and assistance to the aged, blind, and disabled. Programs employing hundreds of thousands of people — mostly women — to staff day-care centers and libraries and offer services to the disabled and aged were abolished. A study by the U.S. Department of Health and Human Services shows that, because of lack of funds, only 15 percent of the low- and moderate-income children eligible for government-funded child care are getting it.[3]

The Reagan Administration cut Supplemental Security Income (SSI), the "safety net" for low-income aged, blind, or disabled persons. Clinton's welfare "reform" included removing nearly 100,000 disabled children (mostly mentally impaired) from SSI.[4] By 2000, at least one-third of those needing SSI were no longer being reached. These cuts in federal services have meant more hunger and malnutrition, more isolation and unattended illness, more homelessness and suffering for those with the fewest economic resources and the least political clout.

The picture is no brighter at the municipal, county, and state levels, where federal grants have been slashed by as much as 40 to 60 percent, causing many states to cut their welfare programs. Of the fourteen million recipients of family assistance, almost all have been single mothers and children with no other means of support. Less than 1 percent are able-bodied men. Contrary to prevailing myths, most welfare recipients are White (although African Americans and Hispanics are disproportionately represented); and most stay on welfare for not more than two years and have only one or two offspring. Welfare recipients do not live in luxury. Their combined food, rent, and clothing allotments are far below the poverty level. With inflation, cutbacks, and tightened eligibility, real welfare benefits have fallen nearly 40 percent in the past twenty years.[5]

It has been charged that welfare is rife with fraud. In fact, investigations show that AFDC was among the most strictly supervised federal programs with only a negligible number of fraudulent claims.[6] The real fraud has come with privatization. Private corporations have been picking up many publicly funded contracts to perform tasks that were once the government's responsibility, such as screening welfare applicants, and administering benefits and job placement. Many state officials who arrange such contracts with private companies later end up on the company's payroll. As services are handed over to corporations, welfare is more about reaping profits than helping people to survive. The companies withhold benefits, discourage people from applying, and render inferior service to children in foster care or clients with special (and costly) needs. The more funds they can withhold, the more they pocket for themselves.[7]

Money that might have helped the needy pay their rent or buy food now goes into the pockets of company executives. Multimillion dollar job-training programs bring in lots of profits for the companies handling them but end up placing relatively few unemployed people.[8] Public assistance is hardly an adequate solution to the problems inflicted upon the poor by a capitalist economy. But eliminating aid or handing services over to profiteering companies are even worse solutions.

Social Insecurity: Privatizing Everything

Plutocrats do not lightly tolerate a viable public sector that creates jobs and fulfills human wants while engendering no profits for corporate America. So the owning class constantly advocates *privatization* of public services and resources, both within the United States and throughout the world. Among the things targeted for privatization are utilities, schools, pension funds, transportation, housing, libraries, prisons, health services, and state-owned media.

In recent years, Social Security has come under intense fire from the privateers. A little over half the $500 billion or so that annually goes into Social Security comes out of employees' paychecks; the rest must come from employers, which is a major reason why employers so dislike the program. Opponents of Social Security predict that the retirement fund will go broke three decades from now because of the growing number of seniors. They recommend that employees should be allowed to invest their Social Security payments in the stock market where it will grow at a greater rate, leaving everyone with ample fortunes when they retire.[9]

The reality is something else. If retirement funds were transferred into millions of private accounts on the stock market, Wall Street brokerage firms would make billions in fees every year, but Social Security as a pooled system of payments, a collective safety net, would come to an end. The stock market is not a pension program; it is a form of gambling that could prove risky to many unpracticed retirees (and even to many practiced investors).

Stock markets can crash without quickly bouncing back. After the crash of the Great Depression, stocks did not regain their 1929 highs until 1954.

When calculating the bountiful returns that retirees allegedly would get from stock investments, privateers use rosy projections about a continually booming market. But when predicting bankruptcy for Social Security, they switch to pessimistic projections of a low-growth economy with abnormally low payments into the fund. Rather than being a drain on the budget, Social Security has been producing immense surpluses. By 2008, the fund will have an estimated accumulated surplus of $1.5 trillion, which should allow for payments in full through 2032, according to the 1998 Report of the Social Security Trustees. Actually, the fund should be able to meet payments indefinitely. Should there be a shortfall thirty years hence, it could easily be met by a slight rise in the tax rate or by extending the Social Security tax to income earnings above $76,200, which was the cap as of 2000.[10]

Social Security is not merely a retirement fund; it is a three-pronged *insurance* program, consisting of (a) pensions for over thirty million seniors and their spouses; (b) survivor's insurance for over three-and-a-half million children of deceased or disabled workers; (c) support for four million persons of all ages who suffer disabling injuries or other serious impairments. Privatization schemes have little to say about providing for survivor and disability insurance.

Social Security protects disabled and retired persons from the worst effects of inflation by annual cost-of-living increases, something private accounts cannot do. By providing over 60 percent of income for average older Americans, it is the most effective antipoverty program in the country, without which fourteen million more seniors and disabled people would sink below the poverty level.[11]

While free-market opponents maintain that Social Security doesn't work, what really bothers them is that it does. It is one of the most successful human services programs in U.S. history. In over six decades, it has never missed a payment. Its administrative costs are only about one percent of annual payouts. By comparison, administrative costs for private insurance are about 13 percent. Social Security helps the many instead of the few, redistributing billions of dollars in a more egalitarian not-for-profit fashion. This is why the privileged few demand that it be "reformed."

How Much Health Can You Afford?

There prevails a wide health gap between economic classes. Too often the first examination patients receive in an emergency room is of their wallets. Many seriously injured are refused emergency care at for-profit hospitals because they cannot show proof of ability to pay. Meanwhile, public hospitals are closing down for lack of funding. Patients are ejected in the midst of

ETTA ©1995 FORT WORTH STAR-TELEGRAM
HULME

*"We both think you need surgery, but we
have to get a third opinion from an accountant."*

an illness when they run out of money. People with prolonged illnesses are bankrupted by medical bills despite supposedly "comprehensive" insurance coverage. To maximize profits, hospital staffs are cut and overworked, sometimes to the point of being unable to give proper care.[12]

A report by the National Institute of Medicine reveals that medical errors and iatrogenic illness (sickness caused by the treatment itself) kill up to 98,000 persons every year in U.S. hospitals, about one of every 500 patients. Contrary to the myth that "private enterprise can do it better," death rates and patient expenses are higher at for-profit hospitals than at nonprofit facilities.[13]

The number of Americans without health insurance has risen to over forty-four million, of whom eleven million are children. Cuts in employer insurance programs have been a major cause.[14] Employers reduce benefits, and even cancel coverage for employees who get seriously ill. Millions who *are* insured pay monthly premiums that place a crushing burden on family finances. The care people are receiving is not getting better, only more expensive.

Top corporate executives and other wealthy individuals experience a different kind of health system from ordinary folks. CEOs generally are provided with complete health coverage by their companies. They pay no deductibles and virtually no premiums for medical visits and hospitalization, and they enjoy state-of-the-art treatment at the very best private hospitals in luxury suites with gourmet menus.[15]

Since Congress and the states began cutting back on welfare in 1996, nearly a million low-income people have lost Medicaid coverage. Medicaid is the federal program that provides treatment for the poor. Millions of poverty-level adults and children are not receiving medical and dental care covered by Medicaid, usually because they have difficulty finding doctors and dentists who want to bother treating them.[16]

Medicaid treats the poor, while Medicare treats the aged and disabled, serving as a popular insurance program for millions. Unfortunately, Medicare is far from perfect. Among its prime beneficiaries have been hospitals and doctors who fraudulently overcharge the government billions of dollars a year, while rendering substandard care. The General Accounting Office discovered that around the country criminal groups had formed scores of phony medical companies in order to bilk Medicaid and Medicare of hundreds of millions of dollars for services and equipment that were never rendered.[17]

Nursing homes care for nearly two million elderly and disabled, ringing up $87 billion in business each year, with more than 75 cents of every dollar picked up by the taxpayer through Medicaid and Medicare. The less the nursing home spends on patient care, the more it keeps for itself and its shareholders. Profit-driven nursing homes have become the shame of the nation, with their insufficient and poorly trained staffs, filthy conditions, and neglect and abuse of patients.[18]

Canada's "single-payer" health-care program and Britain's nationalized system are portrayed in the U.S. corporate-owned press as providing poor service. Critics focus on the long waits, failing to mention that the waits are a direct result of universal coverage and reduced government funding. Even so, there is no waiting list for emergency operations and little wait for non-cosmetic surgery in Canada or Britain. On a per capita basis, Americans spend considerably more than Canada, Germany, or France on health care, yet these nations, and a number of others, provide affordable medical care for *all* their citizens. The Canadian and Western European public health systems have more physicians and hospital beds per person, lower infant mortality rates, and healthier average populations with higher life expectancies.[19]

The medical industry is one of the United States' largest businesses, with an annual health bill of $1 trillion, or 14 percent of the gross domestic product. The industry's greatest beneficiaries are big insurance companies and Health Maintenance Organizations (HMOs). An HMO is a group of physicians, or an insurance company contracting with a group of physicians, who provide private health care for individuals who can afford the monthly premiums. The goal of HMO managers and owners is to maximize profits. They achieve this in three ways: first, by charging premiums that take an inordinately large chunk out of family budgets; second, by requiring doctors to spend less time with each patient, withholding costly — even if necessary — treatment; third, by subjecting the entire staff to salary squeezes and speedups. Most HMOs pay doctors only a small fixed yearly fee per patient, no matter how many visits, operations, or hospitalizations are needed. Doctors, whose reputation for compassion and excellence attract a large share of the sickest (and costliest) patients, are feeling increasingly demoralized because they cannot make a living on fixed HMO fees while trying to treat those who need extensive care.[20]

This nation has fifteen hundred different health insurance programs. Together they spend over $100 billion a year on promotional and administrative costs and fat executive salaries. That sum would be enough to provide long-term care for millions of uninsured people. Private health insurance companies spend 12 percent of premiums on administrative and overhead costs, compared to 3.2 percent spent for Medicaid and Medicare, or 0.9 percent for Canada's single-payer system — which got rid of health insurance companies over two decades ago. Insurance companies and HMOs exclude applicants who are likely to need expensive care.[21] Many HMOs claim a nonprofit status, ostensibly because they are engaged in a "public service mission" — even though they are high profit-making corporations. As "nonprofit" organizations, they avoid paying income taxes and property taxes.[22]

Medicines are often drastically overpriced. Pharmaceutical companies claim they need high prices to support innovative research. But they spend three times more on sales promotions and advertising than on research, and enjoy astronomical profits. Furthermore, pharmaceutical research is financed by the government to the tune of over $15 billion annually.[23] The government also finances the development of "orphan drugs," which treat rare diseases. They earned that name because, given their limited market, pharmaceutical companies refused to develop them. So Congress passed the Orphan Drug Act of 1983, giving drug companies that developed medications for relatively "rare" diseases (under 200,000 afflicted) a seven-year market protection against any losses plus generous tax breaks.[24] Once again, the private sector will serve a public need only if generously bribed by the public sector.

Buyers Beware, and Workers Too

The Food and Drug Administration (FDA) tests only about 1 percent of the drugs and foods marketed. Toothpaste, shampoo, sunscreen, body lotion, body talc, cosmetics, and hair dye are often contaminated with carcinogenic by-products, yet the FDA has done little about it.[25] Of the drugs it approves, half of them cause serious adverse reactions. It is estimated that adverse reactions to medical drugs, aside from medical error as such, may cause the death of more than 100,000 people a year. Some drug companies conceal data and fail to publicize the potential dangers of their products.[26]

When Monsanto (recently purchased by DuPont) introduced bovine growth hormone (BGH) to induce dairy cows to produce abnormally high amounts of milk, the FDA approved the biotech "wonder drug" even though consumer and environmental groups questioned its unknown effects on children and adults. Cows injected with BGH suffer from illness and malnutrition, making it necessary to augment their already high intake of antibiotics. The increased milk production costs taxpayers additional federal surplus milk purchases, mostly benefiting a few giant dairy producers.[27]

"Factory farms" around the country cruelly confine livestock in crates and cages for the entire duration of their lives, where they are fed ground-up animal parts and even sewage sludge among other things. Antibiotics are regularly pumped into these unfortunate creatures to keep them from sickening, and to promote "feed efficiency" by increasing their weight through water retention. But antibiotics also create virulently resistant strains of bacteria that infect humans through the meat, milk, and eggs they consume, and for which there is no treatment. Hundreds have suffered prolonged illness, and over nine thousand deaths occur each year in the United States due to E. coli and other food-borne illnesses.[28]

One cannot talk about the health of America without mentioning occupational safety. Every year over 10,000 die from on-the-job injuries and another 50,000 from occupational diseases. An additional 50,000 to 60,000 sustain permanent disability, and millions more suffer from work-related illnesses.[29] Industrial work always carries some risk, but the present carnage is mostly due to inadequate safety standards and lax enforcement of codes.

Organized labor has long fought for safer work conditions. In 1970 Congress finally created the Occupational Safety and Health Administration (OSHA). With only 2,300 inspectors to cover 6.7 million workplaces, OSHA's resources remain sadly insufficient. Employers file OSHA reports of injuries and fatalities on a purely voluntary basis, making existing statistics unreliable.[30] When cited for violations, corporations sometimes find it less expensive to pay the relatively light fines — often renegotiated and greatly reduced — than to sustain the production costs to improve safety conditions.

Worker-compensation laws usually place the burden of proof on the injured employee, provide no penalties when industry withholds or destroys evidence, and impose a statute of limitations that makes it difficult to collect on work-related diseases that have a long latency period. Only about 10 percent of the millions of workers injured actually win any benefits. And those who do then forfeit their right to sue a negligent employer. Thus, to some extent, the government compensation program actually shields industry from liability.

Creating Crises: Schools and Housing

Economic inequality extends into the field of education. Because states rely heavily on property taxes to fund public schools, wealthy districts expend as much as ten times more per pupil than poor districts. Poorer schools suffer from overcrowding and underfunding.[31] Various lawmakers and commentators say, "We can't solve the public school problem by just throwing money at it." Strange to hear this from people who never tire of throwing titanic sums at the Pentagon in order to improve the kill capacity of the U.S. military. A Rand Corporation study shows that smaller class sizes, more preschool enrollment, better classroom materials for teachers to use, and additional money for remedial services does indeed improve the morale and performance of children from low-income families.[32] While not the only consideration, money — or the lack of it — *is* a core problem. Some critics are seeking to privatize public education by giving parents money vouchers which they could spend on any private school of their choice, including parochial ones. The schools and teachers would not be certified and there would be no performance or quality control. Anybody could start a school to make some quick bucks from the vouchers. This is supposed to represent a step forward.

Dramatic funding disparities exist in higher education as well. What we have is affirmative action for the affluent. Federal aid tends to favor the already rich elite universities rather than needy community colleges and evening schools, making it ever more difficult for low-income persons to get a quality education. Federal aid also goes to medical schools and graduate and postgraduate science programs. Through the 1980s and 1990s, tuition costs rose dramatically in both public and private institutions, while federal grants for low-income college students were less than half what they were in the 1970s.[33]

So with housing. The bulk of federal housing assistance goes not to poor households but to affluent ones. Middle- and upper-income homeowners receive property tax exemptions, tax deductions for the interest paid on their mortgages, and capital gains deferrals on housing sales, all of which costs the government $100 billion in revenues each year. This is several times more than what the Department of Housing and Urban Development (HUD) is allocated for low-income housing.[34]

Upper-income people who own beachfront homes receive federally subsidized insurance that leaves the government liable for billions of dollars in claims. One such beneficiary was multimillionaire ex-president George Bush, who regularly preached free-market self-reliance while benefiting from federal insurance that covered most of the $300,000 to $400,000 storm damage to his Maine estate.[35]

Private housing developments built with federal assistance are often rented to low-income people for a year or two to qualify for federal funds, then sold to other private owners who, not held to the original contract, evict the tenants and turn the units into high-priced rentals or condominiums. Every year, hundreds of thousands of low-income housing units are lost to demolition, gentrification, and sales to private investors. In communities where rent control laws have been rolled back, landlords can raise rents at will or evict tenants without cause.

The government has two programs for low-income tenants. The first is public housing, which accommodates about 1.3 million families, half of whom collect some form of public assistance.[36] Public housing projects plagued by drugs and gang crime have received a lot of media attention. But the many housing projects, including ones for the elderly, that work fairly well receive little press notice.

The other government housing program consists of Section 8 vouchers, which provide 1.5 million low-income families with rent subsidies. The family pays the landlord 30 percent of its income and the government pays the landlord the rest. Again, the public sector subsidizes the private-profit sector. About half of the million or so low-income households that receive rent vouchers return them unused because affordable apartments are unavailable. Only one-quarter of poor U.S. households receive any kind of housing subsidy — the lowest level of any industrialized nation.[37]

The reduction in public housing funds during the 1980s was the major cause of homelessness. The fastest growing group of homeless are families.[38] As the supply of affordable housing has shrunk, rents have soared far above incomes in many parts of the country. Millions of Americans not classified as homeless double up, or pay more than they can comfortably afford for cramped, substandard quarters.

Many cities are criminalizing homelessness, passing ordinances that make it a crime to sit or lie in a public place with sleeping bag or shopping cart. Homeless people are harassed, roughed up, and arrested, driven from one town to another, their few possessions confiscated and destroyed, their campgrounds and other sleeping spaces sealed off.[39] Homeless people have become so commonplace since the 1980s cutbacks in public housing that they are now perceived as a regular part of the urban landscape by a whole generation of young Americans who have no idea that they were once considered a rarity and a social outrage.

"Mess Transit": What's Good for General Motors

The transportation system provides another example of how private profit takes precedence over public need. Until the 1920s the transporting of passengers and goods was done mostly by electric car and railroad. Mass transit rails use only a fraction of the fuel consumed by cars and trucks. But these very efficiencies are what make them so undesirable to the oil and auto industries.

Consider the fate of Los Angeles. In 1935 that city was served by one of the largest rail systems in the world, covering a 75-mile radius with quiet, pollution-free electric trains that carried 80 million passengers a year. But General Motors and Standard Oil, using dummy corporations as fronts, purchased the system, and replaced the electric cars with GM buses fueled by Standard Oil. By 1955, the corporations had replaced electric streetcar networks with gas-guzzling high-emission buses in over one hundred cities across the nation. Then they cut back on city and suburban bus services to encourage mass dependency on cars. In 1949, General Motors was found guilty of conspiracy in these activities and fined the grand sum of $5,000.[40]

Motor vehicles extract a staggering social cost. Each year in the United States about 47,000 people are killed in motor vehicle accidents and two million are injured, many of them seriously incapacitated for the remainder of their lives. More than three million Americans have perished on the roads, twice the number killed in all the wars fought in the nation's history. This figure does not include deaths that occur several days or weeks after accidents or the estimated 30,000 yearly deaths caused by automotive emissions. Motor vehicles also kill over one million animals *each day*. More deer are slaughtered by cars than by hunters.[41]

More than half the land in U.S. cities is taken up by the movement, parking, and servicing of vehicles. Whole neighborhoods are razed to make way for highways and more roads — which eventually create only more congestion. The automobile requires communities to spread out to make room for it, causing higher per capita costs for sewage construction, road maintenance, and other services, and higher food transportation costs as farms on the metropolitan fringe are displaced by suburban sprawl.

Federal, state, and local governments spend over $300 billion annually to subsidize automotive use through road construction and maintenance, highway patrols, ambulance and hospital services, and realty tax losses as more land is converted to roads and highways. The automobile is the single greatest cause of air pollution in urban areas throughout the world. Rubber tire and oil slick runoffs and the tons of salt poured on winter roads damage bays and rivers and cause trees and vegetation to wither. Medical costs for auto victims are enormous, as are the costs of a court system that spends so much time litigating vehicular injuries. As much as one-fifth of the average household's income is expended on car payments, auto insurance, gasoline, and other auto-related costs. Urban sprawl and population growth increase the hours we spend stuck in traffic. Those who are unable to drive — the elderly, the disabled, and the young — are frequently isolated by a car-dominated transport system.

A good part of mass transit money goes for metrorails that benefit the affluent suburbanites who commute to downtown business centers. Municipal transit systems are funded in part by deficit spending, with tax-free bonds sold to wealthy individuals and banks. To meet payments of these bonds, transit systems raise fares and cut services, which means fewer riders, less revenue, and more debt. The more mass transit pays for debt, the less is spent on actual service. During his administration, Clinton slashed funds for mass transit, further deepening America's transportation problems.

Toxifying the Earth

Like sin, environmental pollution is regularly denounced but vigorously practiced. Every year industry dumps over a billion pounds of toxins, including sulfur dioxide, nitrogen dioxide, carbon dioxide, selenium, mercury, lead, asbestos, and hundreds of other noxious substances into our environment. Industry introduces about a thousand new chemicals into the marketplace annually, often with unreliable information about their effects. Each year some ten thousand spills from pipelines and tankers spread millions of gallons of oil into our coastal waters, taking a dreadful toll as the oil works its way through fish-spawning and animal-breeding cycles.[42]

Strip mining and deforestation by coal and timber companies continue to bring ruination to wildlife and watersheds. Rain forests throughout the world, with their precious stock of flora and fauna, are being turned into wastelands. Only 20 percent of the world's original forest cover remains today, mostly in Russia, Canada, and Brazil, almost all of it threatened by rapacious clear-cutters.[43]

In the United States, more than 96 percent of the ancient redwood forests have been obliterated. As the trees disappear so do the spawning streams and distinctive menagerie of life.[44] Heavy metals and other poisons leach from mines into groundwaters. Sediments from denuded lands pour into waterways and irrigation systems, ruining food production and fisheries. The U.S. Department of Agriculture (USDA) estimates that every year up to 400,000 acres of wetlands in the United States are obliterated by commercial farming and developers. Tons of nitrogen and phosphorus excess running off from farms and city sewers, and from airborne nitrates from automobiles and power plants, cause massive algae blooms that create huge "dead zones" of oxygenless water in our bays, estuaries, and seas.[45]

The industrial production of livestock for meat consumption fouls large areas of land and waterways with waste runoff, and preempts millions of acres for grazing and growing livestock feed. According to one report, meat consumption is the most environmentally harmful activity consumers can engage in, except for operating a gas-driven car.[46]

Another environmentally harmful activity is excessive procreation. As the world's population climbs beyond six billion, there is more toxic effusion, ecological disruption, and extinction of other species. Food sources are not keeping up with population growth, either on land or sea. Large commercial fleets are driving out small-scale fishermen (much as agribusiness is driving out the family farmer), and by overfishing they are wiping out the world's fish supply.

Many chemicals widely used in industry and commercial agriculture are endocrine disrupters and hormone mimickers. Working their way into the food chain, they undermine the health and genetic viability of humans (as well as hundreds of other species). Toxic waste dumps and incinerators are situated predominantly in or near low-income African-American, Latino,

"IT IS ILLEGAL FOR AN INDIVIDUAL TO RELIEVE HIM OR HERSELF IN A STREAM, BUT NOT FOR A CORPORATION."

—RALPH NADER

and Native American communities, contributing to inordinately high cancer rates among these populations. Unusually high levels of leukemia and brain and testicular tumors have been found among children who live near utility power plants and toxic sites.[47]

More than forty-five million Americans are drinking and bathing in water that is polluted with parasites, pesticides, and toxic chemicals.[48] Excess lead levels have been found in the drinking water of one of every five Americans, contributing to hypertension, strokes, heart ailments, and learning disabilities.

An estimated 50,000 to 100,000 deaths each year in the United States are caused by air pollution. Over the past two decades, asthma cases increased by 75 percent among children, as air quality continued to deteriorate.[49] Not without cause do some ecologists conclude that the air we breathe, the water we drink, and the food we eat are the leading causes of death in the United States.

Six million acres of topsoil are eroded yearly by chemical farming. The use of toxic herbicides and pesticides has doubled over the last few decades, approaching three billion pounds a year, causing increasing rates of birth defects, liver and kidney diseases, and cancer.[50] Brainwashed by TV commercials, homeowners drench their yards and lawns with three to six times more herbicides and insecticides per acre than even farmers use, causing serious harm to themselves, while killing many useful insects that aerate the soil and pollinate plants. High levels of pesticide are found in foods and drinking water, at levels exceeding federal safety standards, creating risks of cancer and long-term damage to the brain and nervous system. Some $8 billion a year in hidden costs are associated with pesticide use, including groundwater contamination, injuries to health, and loss of fish, birds, and trees.[51]

The more chemicals poured into the environment, the more needed. For example, forest and lawn pesticides kill the songbirds that eat bugs, thereby removing a natural pest control and causing greater insect infestation — which in turn creates a greater reliance on pesticides. Pesticides produce generations of insects more resistant to chemical controls — which calls for more potently toxic chemicals. The result is that over a thirty-five-year period, pesticide use has increased tenfold, yet crop losses to insects and other pests have almost doubled.[52]

A national media campaign devised by right-wing think tanks and funded by corporate polluters is dedicated to attacking independent environmental education. They agree with former President George Bush who insisted that ecological safeguards have to be "consistent with economic growth and free market principles."[53] In fact, environmental regulation has *not* led to any appreciable job loss and in some cases has created more jobs while keeping U.S. companies competitive.[54] Meanwhile, fast-buck exploitation of the planet's resources, along with population explosion, has brought an annual extinction rate of 17,500 species of plants and animals. Chemical fertilizers, used so abundantly in the United States and elsewhere, now do little to raise output. Since 1984, the production of the world grain staples that most of humanity survives on has been falling behind population growth.[55]

Eco-Apocalypse

The life support systems of the entire ecosphere — the planet's thin skin of air, water, and topsoil — are threatened by global warming, ozone depletion, and overpopulation. Global warming is caused by tropical deforestation, motor vehicle exhaust, power plants, and other fossil fuel emissions that create a "greenhouse effect," trapping heat close to the earth's surface. International panels of scientific experts have voiced their alarm at the accelerated rate of destabilizing climatic changes. Despite urgings from the scientific community, Republicans in Congress along with some Democrats have rejected efforts to curb industrial emissions linked to global warming.[56]

Senator Steve Symms (R-Idaho) once said that if he had to choose between capitalism and ecology, he would choose capitalism. The senator doesn't get it. Without a viable ecology, there will be no "ism" of any kind to choose.

The 1990s was the warmest decade on record, with 1997 the warmest year of the twentieth century — until 1998, which in turn was surpassed by 1999 and then 2000.[57] Carbon dioxide, the most common of greenhouse gases, has increased by about 25 percent since the mid-1800s. These buildups are altering the climatic patterns on which we depend for our rainfall — resulting in meteorological aberrations across much of the planet, including record hurricanes and windstorms. Global warming is causing the Arctic ice caps to melt, effecting a rise in sea levels that are already beginning to inundate shorelines and small islands, and bring severe floods and droughts, disrupting natural ecosystems.[58] In northern climes as well as warmer ones, rising temperatures have diminished soil moisture, thereby disrupting the ability of forests to renew themselves, while contributing to more forest fires.[59]

Global warming is playing havoc with the breeding habits of wildlife, and threatening species with extinction through the release of new viruses and increased vulnerability to disease. Global warming also puts humans at risk by bringing more heat stress, air pollution, infectious disease, and droughts.[60] Unless we can move away from fossil fuels and toward wind and solar power, the compounding effects of global warming are likely to bring utter disaster to the entire planet.

Another potential catastrophe is the shrinkage of the ozone layer that shields us from the sun's deadliest rays. About 2.6 billion pounds of ozone-depleting chemicals, chiefly chlorofluorocarbons (CFCs), are emitted into the earth's atmosphere every year. The top five CFC polluters in the United States are corporate military contractors. U.S. space shuttles also have disastrously damaging effects on the ozone layer, yet the space program goes on and on.[61] The worst batches of CFCs, released over the last two decades, have yet to reach the ozone. So the dangers will increase in the years ahead regardless of any improvements that might be attempted now.

First detected over Antarctica, the ozone hole has since appeared over wide areas of the Northern Hemisphere. Excessive ultraviolet radiation has begun to damage trees, crops, coral reefs, and fish, and is destroying the ocean's phytoplankton — source of about half of this planet's oxygen. If the oceans die, so do we. Ultraviolet radiation also disrupts the DNA of plants and humans, and depresses the human immune system.[62]

Capitalism's modus operandi is to produce and sell at an ever expanding rate, treating the world's resources as limitlessly expendable. But the earth is finite, as is its water supply, oxygen, topsoil, and ability to absorb toxins and heat from energy consumption. An infinitely expanding capitalism and a fragile, finite ecology appear to be on a calamitous collision course.

Government for the Despoilers

With the fate of the planet at stake, the U.S. government's response has been less than encouraging. The Safe Drinking Water Act remains largely unenforced. The Clean Air Act became a bonanza bailout for coal producers who were given billions of dollars to clean up their act. And the Endangered Species Act, one of the world's toughest wildlife preservation laws, has proven ineffectual over the last two decades, with the failures mounting faster than the successes. A 1958 law that did not tolerate even a trace of pesticides in processed foods was repealed by Congress; the new law, signed by Clinton, creates a much weaker standard of "no perceivable harm." The Clinton administration also did little to cut back on the pollution tied to global warming.[63]

Studies in the United States and Europe of people living near cell phone towers and microwave transmitters reveal alarming rates of cancers, cardiovascular ailments, and genetic mutations.[64] Nuclear power is another major menace. People exposed to atmospheric nuclear tests and the contaminating clouds vented from underground tests have suffered a variety of tragic illnesses. Serious nuclear mishaps have occurred at reactors in a dozen states. In the area around Three Mile Island, Pennsylvania, livestock aborted and died prematurely, and households experienced what amounts to an epidemic of cancer, birth defects, and premature deaths.[65] Nuclear plants are so hazardous that insurance companies refuse to cover them.

There are some twenty thousand radioactive and toxic chemical sites at military bases and nuclear weapons plants and laboratories across the United States. Many of these have repeatedly released radioactive wastes and poisonous chemicals into the air and waterways, including millions of gallons dumped illegally into makeshift evaporation ponds, pits, and seepage basins, causing a contamination that will require tens of billions of dollars in cleanup costs. In fact, the government now admits that most of them will never be cleaned up, and will need "permanent stewardship" for generations to come.[66] The Department of Energy has no known safe method of disposing of radioactive waste.

For decades the government knowingly let uranium and other lethal substances leak into the groundwater and drinking wells. And it has allowed private industry and the military to deposit radioactive nuclear wastes into ocean dumps and prime fishing beds along the east and west coasts of the United States.[67]

We were told that nuclear power would be clean and inexpensive. In fact, the construction of nuclear plants has involved cost overruns of 400 to 1,000 percent, bringing higher rather than lower electric rates. The nuclear industry has no long-term technology for the entombment or decontamination of old plant sites. Thousands of tons of "slightly" radioactive metal from nuclear reactors and laboratories are being considered for recycling, to be used in such common items as zippers, food cans, and silverware. Nuclear

industry representatives say the effect of such radioactive commodities on human health would be "negligible."[68]

The U.S. Coast Guard, responsible for policing our waterways, has dumped over 100,000 used batteries containing lead, mercury, and other chemicals into rivers and lakes. The U.S. military is a major polluter, using vast amounts of ozone-depleting materials, and generating 500,000 tons of toxins yearly. The Pentagon admitted to Congress that some 17,500 military sites violate federal environmental laws.[69]

Profits are higher when corporations can dump their diseconomies onto the public. The costs of industrial effluents (which compose 40 to 60 percent of the loads treated by municipal sewage plants), and the costs of developing new water sources (while industry and agribusiness consume 80 percent of the nation's daily water supply), are passed on to the public. So are the costs of cleaning up radioactive sites, and tending to the sickness and disease caused by pollution; likewise the costs of floods and droughts, inefficient and wasteful energy usage, and the loss of topsoil, farmlands, wetlands, fisheries, and aquifers.

Toxic heavy metals, chemicals, and radioactive wastes are being recycled as fertilizer, spread over farmers' fields and grazing lands nationwide. Nor are they listed as ingredients since, unlike many other industrial nations, the United States does not regulate fertilizers. The use of industrial waste — including lead, arsenic, cadmium, and dioxin — as fertilizer is a growing national phenomenon.[70]

Corporate polluters are more often rewarded than punished. The Department of Defense has paid private defense contractors upwards of $1 billion to clean up pollution from their own operations. Again the public sector must generously bribe the private-profit sector to get it to show a shred of social responsibility. When the Department of Energy imposes cash penalties on contractors who violate its safety rules, the companies are allowed to bill the government for the fines! Private contractors virtually took over the Superfund toxic waste cleanup program, raking in profits as high as 940 percent for often inadequate work. The leading Superfund polluter is General Electric, with eighty-six sites. Under the Superfund program only a small number of the thousands of toxic sites have been cleaned up — for a runaway cost of about $9 billion.[71]

The federal government's Environmental Protection Agency (EPA) has conducted almost no basic research on the long-term health effects of pollution. The EPA monitors only about 1 percent of the seventy thousand different synthetic chemicals and metals in commercial use.[72] Every year hundreds of new contaminants and chemicals, including many known carcinogens, are released into the environment, pumping new vigor into our cancer epidemics, yet most violations go unreported by the EPA. State and federal officials take action in less than 2 percent of the thousands of annual complaints, and usually only after prolonged public agitation forces them to do what they are being paid to do. Urged on by major industries, various state governments have adopted legislation that allows corporate polluters to monitor themselves, without having to tell authorities or the public the results.[73]

The government not only fails to stop environmental damage, it actively contributes to it. In 1992, the Department of the Interior announced it would open millions of acres of national parks and forests to strip-mining. The Army Corps of Engineers opened 60 million acres of wetlands to private developers. The corps has spent more than $25 billion in this century building dams and levees that have left a bleak legacy of ecologically ravaged rivers, silted lakes thick with dead fish, and destruction of wildlife and plant habitats. Levees also prevent the surrounding wetlands and other flood plains from performing one of their most important natural functions: controlling floods by absorbing overflow. Containing rivers in narrowly corseted waterways only intensifies the velocity and frequency of floods.[74]

In some states, agribusiness companies have succeeded in passing "food disparagement laws" that allow them to sue anyone who questions the safety of their products. Whether they win or not, such litigious threats have a chilling effect on investigators.[75] The transnational corporation Monsanto has spent hundreds of millions of dollars to develop "biotech engineered" or genetically modified corn, beets, rice, and soybeans to make the crops resistant to Monsanto's own herbicide, Roundup. In this way still more herbicide can be poured around crops without killing them. By 2000, Monsanto was spraying over twenty-six million pounds of herbicide worldwide annually. The genetically modified seeds are supposedly resistant to pests because they have pesticide built into them. Despite corporate claims, the USDA reports that farmers using genetically modified crops are getting the same yields as those raising traditional crops, and still have to use about the same amount of pesticide.

Bioengineering also allows Monsanto to exercise monopoly control over crops by use of sterile "terminator seeds." With sterile seeds, farmers in the United States and around the world are required to buy new seeds from Monsanto for each year's planting, rather than setting aside their own seed stock. In any case, no one knows what long-term effects such modified foods will have upon human health and ecology. Genetically modified "Frankenfood" (as opponents call it) constitutes a massive experiment that treats our health and environment as guinea pigs — without our permission. Monsanto even opposes labeling, so consumers will not know when they are eating genetically engineered foods. Under the Clinton Administration, the FDA, EPA, and Department of Agriculture resisted all calls for mandatory labeling or safety testing of genetically modified food.[76]

Far more effective than cleaning up pollution is preventing it before it occurs. There are hopeful developments, if not within official circles, then among growing numbers of people who have been developing organic agriculture and environmentally sustainable energy sources. Today there are hundreds of thousands of people in this country and around the world already relying on solar heating devices. Wind and solar power plants in California provide power for nearly a million people. They can be built faster and cheaper than nuclear or fossil-fuel plants and have no toxic emissions. Renewable nonpolluting energy provides about 7.5 percent of this country's energy production. Twelve states in the Great Plains have a wind energy potential greater than the electric use of our entire nation.[77] However, the Reagan, Bush, and Clinton administrations have done next to nothing to develop these alternative sources.

Alternative energy is far more cost efficient, especially if one takes into account all the hidden costs of fossil fuels, including the damage done to our health and property by global warming, acid rain, soil erosion, oil spills, and air and water pollution. Solar and wind sources would be readily accessible if government and corporations devoted more resources to the technological development and distribution of these alternative sources. A new generation of high-efficiency windmill turbines are becoming the fastest-growing energy source in parts of Europe, Latin America, and India. But inexpensive and renewable wind and solar energy sources undermine the profit structure of the private utilities and the petrochemical industry, so they have been largely ignored or declared "not cost efficient."

For the same reason, auto companies do little to develop zero emission vehicles (ZEVs). They say there is insufficient demand. But investigations show that fleet managers and the general public have been complaining that they cannot get ZEVs when they want them and that the auto manufacturers have been putting roadblocks on ZEV sales.[78]

Thousands of farmers have abandoned chemical farming and have turned to organic methods, achieving larger yields at less cost by using crop rotation, natural pest control, and nonchemical fertilizers, methods that revitalize the soil. One study found that chicken farmers in Denmark did just as well or better after eliminating the use of antibiotics in feed. Likewise, tomato farmers in Florida who switched from methyl bromide (a soil fumigator and pesticide banned by Congress) to bahia grass pasture earned much higher profits per acre. But organic farming means no profits for Monsanto and other big chemical companies. Alternative agriculture has developed with no assistance from the Department of Agriculture, which is wedded to corporate agribusiness. Less than one-tenth of 1 percent of the USDA's research budget is devoted to studying organic farming; the rest serves agribusiness and chemical farming.[79]

In sum, serious contradictions exist between our human needs and the corporate profit-driven economic system. The "natural capital" of land, mineral resources, and water is treated as a free and limitless resource, never put in the balance sheet when reckoning the costs of capitalism. Corporations foul the environment and leave it to government to incur the enormous cleanup expenses. Things work best for big business when costs are socialized and profits are privatized. Government is an insufficient bulwark against the baneful effects of giant corporate capitalism and often a willing handmaiden. Why that is so will be examined in chapters ahead.

Notes

1. Anuradha Mittal, "Hungry and Poor in a Rich Nation," *San Francisco Chronicle,* November 25, 1998; and "Shredding the Safety Net," *Backgrounder,* Institute for Food and Development Policy, Winter 1998.
2. Trudy Lieberman, "Hunger in America," *Nation,* March 30, 1998.
3. *San Francisco Chronicle,* October 20, 1999.
4. "Thousands of Kids Lose Disability Aid," *San Francisco Chronicle,* August 15, 1997.
5. *Welfare Myths,* report by Center on Social Welfare Policy and Law, New York, May 1996; Myriam Marquez, "Debunking AFDC Mythology," *San Francisco Examiner,* March 7, 1997.
6. *New York Times,* September 29, 1995.
7. Mark Dunlea, "The Poverty Profiteers Privatize Welfare," *CovertAction Quarterly,* Winter 1996–97; Adam Fifield, "Corporate Caseworkers," *In These Times,* June 1997; Christopher Cook's report in *Christian Science Monitor,* March 1997.
8. Lucia Hwang, "Training in Vain," *San Francisco Bay Guardian,* October 6, 1999.
9. "The Case for Killing Social Security," *Time,* May 20, 1995.
10. Doug Henwood, "The Myth of Social Security's Imminent Collapse," *Extra!* July/August 1995; "If Politics Got Real," *Nation,* May 1, 2000.
11. "Ten Excellent Reasons to Strengthen Social Security and Oppose Privatization," *Solidarity,* July/August 2000.

12. Lawrence J. O'Brien, *Bad Medicine: How the American Medical Establishment Is Ruining Our Healthcare System* (Amherst, N.Y.: Prometheus, 1999).

13. *To Err is Human: Building a Safer Health System* (Washington, D.C.: National Institute of Medicine, 1999); David Himmelstein and Steffie Woolhandler, *Bleeding the Patient Dry: The Consequences of Corporate Healthcare* (Monroe, Maine: Common Courage, 2000).

14. *New York Times*, October 4, 1999.

15. Allen Myerson, "A Double Standard in Health Coverage," *New York Times*, March 17, 1996; "Hospital for the Rich," *Solidarity*, January/February 1997.

16. *New York Times*, June 29, 1999, and June 20, 2000; *San Francisco Chronicle*, July 30, 1998, and May 25, 2000.

17. L. J. Davis, "Medscam," *Mother Jones*, March/April 1995; *New York Times*, July 17, August 8, and December 14, 1997; *New York Times*, November 4, 1999; Investigation by Inspector General's Office of the Department of Health and Human Services and the General Accounting Office, reported in *Los Angeles Times*, July 28, 1997.

18. Eric Bates, "The Shame of Our Nursing Homes," *Nation*, March 29, 1999.

19. Phil Benjamin, "The Nation's Health," *People's Weekly World*, February 26, 2000; "The Canadian Health Care System," *Economic Notes*, July/August 1991; Craig Whitney, "Medical Care in Germany," *New York Times*, January 23, 1993.

20. Michael Makover, *Mismanaged Care: How Corporate Medicine Jeopardizes Your Health* (Amherst, N.Y.: Prometheus, 1998); Charles Andrews, *Profit Fever: The Drive to Corporatize Health Care and How to Stop It* (Monroe, Maine: Common Courage, 1995); Ron Adler, "Why Your Doctor Isn't Happy to See You," *San Francisco Chronicle*, April, 7, 2000.

21. "HMOs to Drop 934,000 on Medicare," *San Francisco Examiner*, July 23, 2000; Laura McClure, "Just Healthcare," *Labor Party Press*, November 1998.

22. Lisa Davis, "Sutter's Giant Sucking Sound," *San Francisco Weekly*, January 21–27, 1998.

23. Ken Silverstein, "Millions for Viagra, Pennies for Diseases of the Poor," *Nation*, July 19, 1999; Don Sloan, "Profit and Loss in Medical Research," *People's Weekly World*, November 21, 1998.

24. *Baltimore Sun*, October 19, 1996.

25. Joel Bleifuss, "Take a Powder," *In These Times*, March 3, 1997.

26. *FDA Drug Review Disapproval Risk*, General Accounting Office, Washington, D.C., May 1990; "Free-Market Medicine," *Progressive*, March 1992; *New York Times*, March 20, 1996, and April 15, 1998.

27. *New York Times*, February 21, 1994; Hilary Varner, "Milking the Public," *Chicago Life Magazine*, October 1995.

28. *The Use of Drugs in Food Animals: Benefits and Risks*, National Research Council, 1998; Margaret Mellon, "Prescription for Trouble," *Nucleus*, Winter 1998–99; "FACT Calls for End to Farm Drug Abuse," annual report of Food Animal Concerns Trust, Chicago, Winter 1999; Humane Society statement: *New York Times*, February 27, 1998.

29. See <http://www.osha.gov/oshstats/work.html>; and <http://www.osha-slc.gov/OshDoc/toc_FatalFacts.html>; also Joseph Kinney et al., *Ending Legalized Workplace Homicide* (Chicago: National Safe Workplace Institute, 1988); and *Race and the Risk of Fatal Injury at Work*, study by the Department of Epidemiology, University of North Carolina, 1998.

30. Christopher Cook, "Losing Life and Limb on the Job," *Progressive*, February 2000.

31. Jonathan Kozol, *Savage Inequalities* (New York: Crown, 1991); Neil Christopher, "Property Taxes Fund Education Inequity," *People's Weekly World*, July 1, 2000.

32. *New York Times*, July 27, 2000.

33. "Cost of College Shutting Students Out," *San Francisco Chronicle*, November 18, 1998.

34. "Naked Cities," *Nation*, January 6, 1997.

35. *Los Angeles Times*, April 18, 1992.

36. Christopher Jencks, "Half-Right on Public Housing," *New York Times*, May 20, 1997.

37. Michael Winerip, "Doors Shut to Poor Seeking Homes," *New York Times*, July 22, 1996; Study by Center on Budget and Policy Priorities, reported in *New York Times*, April 22, 1996.

38. U.S. House of Representatives task force report in *Washington Post*, December 26, 1987; Joel Blau, *The Visible Poor, Homelessness in the United States* (New York: Oxford University Press, 1992).

39. See annual reports on homelessness by the National Law Center on Homelessness and Poverty, Washington, D.C.; and Becky Johnson and Robert Norse, "Mean Sweeps," *Street Spirit* (Bay Area, Calif.), June 1997.

40. Jane Holtz Kay, *Asphalt Nation: How the Automobile Took over America, and How We Can Take It Back* (New York: Crown, 1997).

41. *Washington Post*, September 3, 1989; Kay, *Asphalt Nation*.

42. For recent examples of industrial pollution, see *New York Times*, March 16, 1997; Associated Press report, January 25, 1999; *Diluth News-Tribune*, May 2, 1999; Pratap Chatterjee, "Who Is Stealing Our Future," *CovertAction Quarterly*, Fall 1996; Lois Marie Gibbs and Citizens Clearing House for Hazardous Waste, *Dying from Dioxin* (Boston: South End, 1995).

43. "Brazil of the North," *Briarpatch* (Saskatchewan, Canada), July/August 1997.

44. "Cutting the Heart Out of the Ancient Redwoods," *Greenpeace Quarterly*, Spring 1997.

45. *San Francisco Chronicle*, October 26, 1998.

46. Michael Brower and Leon Warren, *The Consumer's Guide to Effective Environmental Choices* (New York: Three Rivers, 1999).

47. Theodore Colborn, Dianne Dumanoski, and John Peterson Meyers, *Our Stolen Future* (New York: Dutton, 1996); Ron Nixon, "Toxic Gumbo," *Southern Exposure*, Summer/Fall 1998; *New York Times*, July 17, 1995; Ulla Lehtinen, "Nuclear Waste and Native Land," *Oregon PeaceWorker*, September 1998; *San Francisco Examiner*, March 23, 1998.

48. According to a study by Natural Resources Defense Council, Environmental Working Group, and Environmental Information Center, May 9, 1996.

49. *Nucleus*, Union of Concerned Scientists, Spring 1998; *Greenpeace Magazine*, Fall 1997; Marian Hetherly, "Worth Noting," *Humanist*, March/April 2000.

50. Sandra Steingraber, *Living Downstream: An Ecologist Looks at Cancer and the Environment* (Reading, Mass.: Addison-Wesley, 1997).

51. On pesticides and related health issues, see *Our Children at Risk* (Washington, D.C.: Natural Resources Defense Council, 1997); reports by Consumers' Union: <http://www.consumersunion.org/food/food.htm>; studies by Environmental Working Group, Washington D.C.: <http://www.ewg.org/pesticides>; and *Environmental Health Perspectives*, March 1999; and *Bioscience*, November 1992.

52. Robert Van Den Bosch, *The Pesticide Conspiracy* (Garden City, N.Y.: Doubleday, 1978).

53. Bush quoted in *Los Angeles Times*, February 6, 1990; see also Jed Greer amd Kenny Bruno, *Greenwash: The Reality behind Corporate Environmentalism* (New York: Apex, 1997); and *Endangered Education: How Corporate Polluters Are Attacking Environmental Education* (Oakland, Calif.: Center for Commercial Free Public Education, 1997).

54. Eban Goodstein, "Does Preserving Earth Threaten Jobs?" *Dollars and Sense*, May 1997.

55. Lester Brown, "Natural Limits," *New York Times*, July 24, 1993; Zero Population Growth newsletter, Washington, D.C., June 1993.

56. Ross Gelbspan, "Putting the Globe at Risk," *Nation*, November 30, 1998; *Nucleus* (publication of Union of Concerned Scientists), Summer 1997; David Corn, "White House vs. Greenhouse," *Nation*, October 13, 1997.

57. *Los Angeles Times*, January 9, 1998; Greenpeace newsletter, July 2000; *San Francisco Chronicle*, March 11, 2000.

58. *New York Times*, November 3, 1997.

59. Ross Gelbspan, *The Heat Is On: The Climate Crisis, the Cover-Up and the Prescription* (Reading, Mass.: Perseus, 1998); *Washington Post,* June 12, 2000.

60. Robert Gould, "The Greenhouse Effect on Health," *San Francisco Examiner,* October 27, 1997.

61. Christian Parenti, "NASA's Assault on the Ozone Layer," *Lies of Our Times,* September 1993. For updates on the ozone, see <http://www.newscientist.com/dailynews/news .jsp?id=ns999961>.

62. Richard McKenzie et al., "Increased Summertime UV Radiation in New Zealand in Response to Ozone Loss," *Science,* September 10, 1999; Janet Wagner, "Double Exposure," *Nucleus,* Winter 1995–96.

63. For these several examples, see *San Francisco Examiner,* May 15, 1997; *Los Angeles Times,* August 3, 1996; and *New York Times,* October 10, 1997.

64. Chellis Glendinning, "Cell-Phone Towers' Effects Under Wraps," *Santa Fe New Mexican,* April 15, 2000.

65. Karl Grossman, "Three Mile Island: They Say Nothing Happened," *Extra!,* July/ August 1993.

66. Greenpeace newsletter, April 1997; "Feds Say Nuke Sites Will Never Be 'Clean,'" *Oakland Tribune,* August 8, 2000.

67. Carole Gallagher, *American Ground Zero* (Cambridge, Mass.: MIT Press, 1993); *Washington Post,* September 6, 1989, and September 22, 1991.

68. *San Francisco Examiner,* September 19, 1999.

69. *New York Times,* September 2, 1998; Tyrone Savage, "The Pentagon Assaults the Environment," *Nonviolent Activist,* July/August 2000.

70. San Francisco Chronicle, July 7, 1997.

71. *Los Angeles Times,* July 7, 1992; Daniel Rosenberg, *Super Polluters: The Top 25 Superfund Polluters and Their Toxic Waste Sites* (Washington, D.C.: Public Interest Research Groups, 1998); and *The PIRG's Campaign against Toxics,* Executive Summary, Public Interest Research Groups, August 1998.

72. Chatterjee, "Who Is Stealing Our Future."

73. *New York Times,* January 30, 1997.

74. Marc Reisner, *Cadillac Desert: The American West and Its Disappearing Water,* rev. ed. (New York: Penguin, 1993).

75. Sheldon Rampton and John Stauber, "Shut Up and Eat: The Lessons of the Oprah Trial," *Nation,* February 16, 1998; Helen Cordes, "Watch Your Mouth," *Utne Reader,* January 2, 1996.

76. Marc Lappé and Britt Bailey, *Against the Grain: Biotechnology and the Corporate Takeover of Your Food* (Monroe, Maine: Common Courage, 1998); Kirkpatrick Sale, "Monsanto: Playing God," *Nation,* March 8, 1999; "Food Safety," *San Francisco Bay Guardian,* August 9, 2000.

77. *Building Economic Alternatives* (publication of Co-Op America), Winter 1990; *Cool Energy, The Renewable Solution to Global Warming* (publication of the Union of Concerned Scientists), Cambridge, Mass., 1990.

78. "Ground Zero for Zero Emission Vehicles," *California Today* (publication of Planning and Conservation League), June 2000.

79. Margaret Mellon, "Wholesome Harvest," *Nucleus,* Winter 1997–98; *San Francisco Examiner,* September 28, 1999; *Organic Gardening,* May/June 2000.

9

Unequal before the Law

Behind the government's democratic facade, there stand the police, courts, prisons, and various agencies of the national security state, all prepared to defend the existing politico-economic order. Although we have been taught to think of the law as a neutral instrument serving the entire community, it is often written and enforced in the most tawdry class-biased ways, favoring the rich over the rest of us. The very definition of what is lawful contains a class bias. The theft of merchandise from a neighborhood store is unlawful, but the theft of the store itself and the entire surrounding neighborhood in an "urban renewal" program instigated by speculators and public officials is hailed as an act of civic development.

Crime in the Suites

People fear street crime more than the white-collar variety because of the immediacy of its violence and its vivid portrayal in movies and television shows. But white-collar corporate crime inflicts far greater monetary, environmental, and human costs. Handguns cause 15,000 deaths a year, while unsafe working conditions and occupational disease result in more than 60,000 annual deaths. Burglary and robbery cost the public about $4 billion a year, while corporate fraud costs at least $200 billion a year.[1] Every year the Federal Bureau of Investigation (FBI) and the Justice Department issue national crime reports on murder, robbery, and other street crimes — without a mention of corporate crimes. Crime is thereby officially defined as "crime in the streets" not "crime in the suites."

118

One of the more egregious instances of corporate malfeasance involved DuPont, Ford, General Motors, ITT, and other companies whose factories in Germany produced tanks, bombers, synthetic fuels, and synthetic rubber for the Nazi war machine during World War II. After the war, rather than being prosecuted for aiding and abetting the enemy, ITT collected $27 million from the U.S. government for damages inflicted on its German plants by Allied bombings. General Motors received over $33 million for damages. U.S. plants usually were spared from Allied bombing. Thus while the German city of Cologne was leveled, its Ford factory — providing armed vehicles that the Nazi military used to kill American troops — was untouched; indeed, it was used by German civilians as an air-raid shelter. At least fifty U.S. transnational corporations operated in Germany from 1933 to 1945, the years the Nazis were in power. Before the war, as the *New York Times* reported on its front page, Boeing was arming Nazi Germany with a "mighty" air fleet, for which the company waxed rich in profits. Faced with class-action law suits in 1999–2000, growing numbers of corporations now admit having used and profited greatly from unpaid slave labor supplied from Nazi concentration camps.[2] No U.S. corporate head was ever prosecuted for complicity in these war crimes.

Corporate crime is not a rarity but a regularity. The Department of Justice found that 60 percent of the 582 largest U.S. companies have been guilty of one or more criminal actions, be it tax evasion, price-fixing, illegal kickbacks, bribes to public officials, consumer fraud, or violations of labor codes, workplace safety, and environmental laws. The Department of Labor found that corporations have filched hundreds of billions of dollars from worker pension funds.[3] Top banks routinely blur the line between crime and capital by accepting and laundering money from shady operations. The global trend toward privatization of state assets and diminished government supervision promotes illicit activities.[4]

Many companies are repeat offenders. Over the years, General Electric has been convicted of 282 counts of contract fraud and fined $20 million. In 1999, charged with 216 violations involving toxic substances, MCI World-Com was fined $625,000. The Federal Communications Commission found that regional Bell telephone companies could not locate $5 billion worth of equipment that they claimed on their accounts, lending support to allegations by consumer groups that phone companies routinely inflate their cost reports in order to justify higher rates for consumers and bigger tax write-offs for themselves. The Interior Department reported that over a sixteen-year period major oil firms may have shortchanged the federal government by nearly $856 million in royalties by understating the value of the oil they pumped from federal lands.[5] Not one of the executives involved in these various violations went to jail.

The four thousand or so people on death rows in the United States killed only a few more than their own number. Had they used lethal industrial

chemicals, unsafe pharmaceutical drugs, or dangerously defective products, or had they illegally dumped toxic wastes or maintained unsafe work conditions, they could have killed and crippled tens of thousands more without ever going to prison. Over the years, Honeywell ignored defects in gas heaters resulting in twenty-two deaths and seventy-seven crippling injuries, for which it was fined $800,000. Johns-Manville Corporation suppressed information about the asbestos poisoning of its workers; when ordered to pay damages in civil court it declared bankruptcy to avoid payment. SmithKline Beckman refrained from telling the Food and Drug Administration that hundreds of users of one of its drugs had suffered kidney and liver damages and thirty-six had died. General Motors produced a pickup truck with a dangerously faulty gas tank design. Three hundred people reportedly died in GM pickup fires before the vehicles were finally recalled. In none of these cases did anyone go to prison.[6]

An executive of Eli Lilly pleaded no contest for failing to inform the government about the effects of Oraflex, a drug suspected of causing forty-nine deaths in the United States and several hundred abroad. He was fined $15,000. W. R. Grace pleaded guilty to having lied to the Environmental Protection Agency about dumping toxic chemicals into well water subsequently linked to eight leukemia deaths. Grace was fined $10,000. After being charged with unlawfully burning toxic wastes into the atmosphere for twenty years, Potomac Electric Power Co. of Washington, D.C., was fined all of $500. When Firestone pleaded guilty to filing false tax returns concealing $12.6 million in income and conspiring to obstruct legal audits of its accounts, it was fined $10,000, and no one went to jail. Over seven hundred people a year go to jail for tax evasion, almost all of them for sums smaller than the amount Firestone concealed.[7]

Even when the fine is more substantial, it usually represents a fraction of company profits and fails to compensate for the damage wreaked. Rockwell International agreed to pay a seemingly hefty $18.5 million after pleading guilty to five felonies for radioactive and chemical contamination at the Rocky Flats nuclear bomb plant — but the actual cleanup will cost the government billions of dollars. Over several years Food Lion cheated its employees of at least $200 million by forcing them to work "off the clock," but in a court settlement the company paid back only $13 million.[8] Who says crime does not pay?

Penalties often are uncollected or suspended. The General Accounting Office (GAO) discovered that the Justice Department had not collected some $7 billion in fines and restitution from 37,000 individuals and corporations convicted of felonies. Over one hundred savings and loan (S&L) plea-bargainers, who escaped long prison terms by promising to make penalty repayments of $133.8 million, repaid less than 1 percent of that amount.[9] In 1989 an Exxon tanker spilled eleven million gallons of oil over one thousand miles of Alaskan shoreline, bringing ruination to marine life, wildlife, and the fishing industry. U.S. taxpayers picked up most of the cleanup costs. Of the $5.3 billion in compensatory damages awarded by a jury, Exxon had not paid a penny ten years later.[10]

Prominent public personages seldom go to jail even when caught red-handed. James Watt, Interior Secretary under the Reagan administration, helped rich clients secure millions of dollars in low-income housing funds that they never used to build low-income housing. Watt was able to sidestep eighteen felony charges of perjury and plead guilty to a misdemeanor, for which he was sentenced to five years probation and a $5,000 fine.[11] On the relatively rare occasions that white-collar criminals are given prison terms, the sentence is usually light and sometimes not even served. The S&L defendants convicted for having stolen hundreds of millions of dollars spent fewer months behind bars on average than car thieves — and at relatively comfortable minimum security prisons. The average jail sentences for white-collar criminals was five months in 1994, upped to eleven months in 1996.[12]

Wall Street investor Michael Milken pleaded guilty to six securities violations and was sentenced to ten years — reduced to twenty-two months, most of which was spent out of jail doing community service. White-collar criminals sentenced to community service seldom do but a small portion of it, if any. Milken had to pay back $1.1 billion to settle criminal and civil charges but retained a vast fortune of $1.2 billion from his dealings. Likewise, Ivan Boesky walked off with $25 million after paying his fine for insider trading and doing a brief spell behind bars. "Every major participant in these [Wall Street investment] crimes emerged from the experience as a wealthy man."[13] Again, who says crime does not pay?

Many corporate crimes are not even prosecuted. Claiming it did not have enough lawyers and investigators, the government failed to pursue more than one thousand fraud and embezzlement cases involving S&L associations and banks, amounting to billions of dollars in losses to U.S. taxpayers. Well-funded corporate lawyers are able to pursue litigation and appeals for years in order to exhaust the plaintiffs.[14]

Corporations have been using SLAPP suits (Strategic Lawsuit against Public Participation) against consumer and environmental groups as a way of silencing public criticism about corporate products or practices. The meat industry sued Oprah Winfrey for "product disparagement," after she commented on her television show that hamburgers were not safe to eat. Winfrey won the case but it cost her some stress and money — and she has done no more shows on the meat industry. Consumer Union spent $10 million and eight years defending itself against a lawsuit by Isuzu Motors because it ruled one of Isuzu's cars as unsafe. In West Virginia, an environmental activist was sued for $200,000 for charging that a coal company was poisoning a local river. Win or lose, such lawsuits have a chilling effect on critics of corporate wrongdoing, many of whom lack the financial resources and emotional stamina to sustain a prolonged defense. As one New York Supreme Court judge remarked about SLAPP suits: "Short of a gun to the head, a greater threat to First Amendment expression can scarcely be imagined."[15]

Of the more than fifty thousand federal criminal indictments the U.S. Justice Department hands down, only a few hundred involve violations of the nation's environmental, occupational safety, and consumer safety laws. Given the well-documented record of widespread and repeated violations by corporations, the small number of federal charges hardly supports the corporate view of business as the victim of a merciless federal government run amok. More often than not, government lawyers are outspent and outdone.[16]

Class Law

Supreme Court Justice Hugo Black once noted that there "can be no equal justice where the kind of trial a man gets depends on the amount of money he has."[17] Whether the legal system treats a person as prince or pariah rests largely on one's financial resources. The corporate executive with deep pockets and a team of high-powered attorneys experiences different treatment from the law than the poor person with an underpaid court-appointed lawyer who sees the defendant for the first time on the day of the trial.[18]

Poor and working-class persons, the uneducated, and members of racial minorities are more likely to be arrested, denied bail, induced to plead guilty, and do without a pretrial hearing or adequate representation. They are less likely to have a jury trial if tried; more likely to be convicted and receive a harsh sentence — including the death penalty; less able to launch extended appeals; and less likely to receive probation or a suspended sentence than are mobsters, business executives, and more affluent people in general. As has been said, the rich have little reason to fear the legal system and the poor have little reason to respect it.

Working people engaged in labor struggles have cause for complaint. In recent years, police have attacked striking farm laborers, truckers, miners, meatpackers, janitors, and factory and construction workers, arresting and injuring hundreds. Private security forces beat up striking workers and break picket lines with acts of violence that go unchallenged by police and prosecutors. Workers have been imprisoned for resisting court injunctions against strikes and pickets, and even for shouting at scab workers or daring to talk back to police while on picket lines. In Elmwood, Indiana, seven strikers were shot by company goons. A striking coal miner in Harlan County, Kentucky, was shot dead by a gun thug, as was another miner in McDowell County, West Virginia, and a farmworker in Texas. In none of these cases did police apprehend anyone — despite eyewitness evidence of the identity of the killers.[19]

The "Tough on Crime" Craze

This society is not "soft on crime," at least not in regard to the street crimes of the poor. A Norfolk, Virginia, man got ten years for stealing 87 cents; a youth in Louisiana received fifty years for selling a few ounces of marijuana; a Houston youth was sentenced to fifty years for robbing two people of $1; a five-time petty offender in Dallas was sentenced to one thousand years in prison for stealing $73; a man caught trying to break into a house in Florida, thus violating his probation for shoplifting, was sentenced to life in prison; in Texas a man was sentenced to thirty years for possession of a small amount of heroin.[20]

Lawmakers of both mainstream political parties have vied in their efforts to be "tough on crime." Imitating his two White House predecessors, President Clinton called for a $23-billion crime bill to establish a national police force, build more prisons, and provide severer sentences including life without parole for three-time felony offenders (known as "three strikes and you're out"). Between 1980 and 2000, prison sentences doubled in length, while prison and jail populations tripled. In California, the inmate population mushroomed from 19,600 to 159,000 in about two decades, and in New York State it climbed from 12,000 to 71,000. Many states are now spending more on prisons than on education. By early 2000, more than two million U.S. residents were behind bars, giving the United States the highest incarceration rate in the world. About five and a half million — three of every one hundred U.S. adults — were either incarcerated or on parole or probation.[21]

Some people maintain that the tougher lock-'em-up policy has brought a lower crime rate. But there are states and municipalities with low incarceration rates that also show a drop in crime, sometimes more dramatic decreases than locales with high incarceration rates.[22] States that have imposed a draconian "three strikes and you're out" law show no greater drop in violent crime than states without it. In 85 percent of such cases in California, the third strike has often been for relatively minor or nonviolent offenses committed by persons who were otherwise mending their lives.[23]

The "war on drugs" is most responsible for the prison population explosion. Playing upon public fears about narcotics, lawmakers throughout the country outdid themselves in passing harsh mandatory drug sentences. The result is that three-fourths of our federal and state inmate population consists of mostly young petty drug offenders serving astronomical prison sentences. Many first offenders in nonviolent drug cases are averaging more jail time than felons with long records, including mobsters, murderers, child molesters, and rapists.[24]

Not all narcotics violations are treated severely. Close relatives of U.S. senators and representatives have received suspended sentences or have had charges dropped. For example, the son of Representative Dan Burton (R-Ind.) was arrested for transporting nearly eight pounds of marijuana in Louisiana, then arrested again for possession of thirty marijuana plants in Indiana. Federal authorities declined to prosecute; Indiana prosecutors recommended dismissal of the charges; and a Louisiana judge sentenced young Burton to community service.[25]

While treating most small-time dealers and users with severity, the "war on drugs" hardly touches the big narcotic cartels. Legislation to stop the laundering of drug money through legitimate financial institutions remains virtually unenforced. When Richard Held resigned as head of the FBI's San Francisco office, he remarked: "There's never been any war on drugs," just much manipulation of appearances "to give the public the impression something is being done."[26]

We hear that over six million violent crimes are committed in the United States in an average year. What we do not hear is that only 1 percent of the victims are hurt seriously enough to require hospitalization. The FBI cooks its crime statistics by failing to distinguish between habitual petty offenders and more vicious felons. Under federal law, even drug trafficking and prostitution are counted as violent crimes. All this feeds public fears and lends support for still larger law enforcement budgets and more repressive police-state measures. To be sure, violent crime is a serious problem, but a more accurate description of its scope would help calm fears and encourage a more rational and just approach to enforcement.[27]

The Crime of Prisons

Of the people in prison, over 90 percent are men, 41 percent are White, 51 percent are African American, and about 14 percent are classified as of Latino origin (including some whites and African Americans). The typical inmate "is a young, poorly educated male who was unemployed at the time of arrest." As already noted, the majority are nonviolent offenders charged with selling or possessing drugs.[28]

Prisons are anything but "correctional institutions." Most of them remain breeding grounds for disease and violence. Prisoners are sometimes forced by authorities to take powerful body-racking, mind-altering drugs. Those who protest such treatment risk being subjected to harsh retribution. As many as one in five male prisoners are raped, or tens of thousands every day. Prison rape can be a death sentence because of AIDS. Rape victims sometimes commit suicide. One tragic illustration: Rodney Hulin was arrested for starting a fire in a dumpster. Despite a long history of mental illness, the teenager was sentenced as an adult to ten years in a Texas prison, where he was repeatedly beaten and gang-raped. He ended his torment by hanging himself.[29]

Thirty-six states and the federal correctional system now have super-maximum security facilities that are little better than "high-tech dungeons." Prisoners in such special control units never see daylight. They live under constant electronic monitoring, isolated in bare concrete cells sealed off by solid steel doors cutting off sound and visual contact with others. They are denied reading material, television, radio, counseling, and religious services. They must eat in their cells, and are repeatedly harassed, taunted, and severely beaten for trivial infractions of inconsistent rules. Some suffer serious physical or psychological deterioration and retreat into madness, only to be put on psychiatric medication and subjected to a still greater degree of abuse.[30]

Amnesty International reports on the electroshock weapons, including stun belts, that some U.S. prisoners are made to wear. Activated by remote control, the belts deliver a 50,000 volt shock that lasts eight seconds, causing severe pain and instant incapacitation. Minors "are not exempt from being made to wear the stun belt." Amnesty notes the horrific conditions in some U.S. jails, including "overflowing toilets" and "prisoners forced to sleep on filthy floors without mattresses, [and] cells infested with vermin and lacking ventilation."[31]

In jails and prisons around the country, inmates have died under suspicious circumstances, often murdered by other prisoners or dying from the torture and beatings administered by guards. Prisoners have perished after being strapped for days in "The Chair," a steel-framed restraint that shackles inmates' legs and hands behind them. Some have been fatally shot by guards during prison yard "gladiator" fights staged by the guards themselves. Disabled inmates who are unable to care for themselves often suffer terrible neglect and are most at risk.[32] To make matters worse, Congress passed and President Clinton signed the Prison Litigation Reform Act and other bills that reduced the inmates' already limited legal protections against custodial brutality.[33]

There is endemic waste and pilfering in prisons. A great deal of food is left to spoil, incorrectly stored, or thrown away rather than donated to the needy. Guards steal food, equipment, office supplies, sporting gear, and whatever else to supplement their usually generous pay and benefits. Millions of dollars are lost each year because of unauthorized telephone calls by prison staff. As they spend more, they get more. To quote one guard: "If there's any money in the prison's operating budget at the end of the year, the administration orders it spent. They're afraid the politicians won't increase next year's budget if money is left over."[34]

New five-hundred-bed prisons continue to be opened almost every week, and more and more bodies are being corralled to fill them, usually from the most vulnerable communities. More and more state and federal prisons are being built and run by private firms in what has been termed "the prison-industrial complex." The private company often extracts free acreage, plus tax abatements, and then gets the state or federal government to pay the maintenance costs and provide the equipment. To be profitable, private prisons cut back on benefits for prison staff, skimp on food and medical care for prisoners, and ensure that the prisons are kept filled. A 90- to 95-percent capacity is needed "to guarantee the hefty rates of return needed to lure investors."[35] When these ventures prove insufficiently profitable, companies lease back the prisons to government for a profit — the same government that subsidized the original construction — thereby obliging the taxpayer to pay twice over.

The Guilty Innocent

The criminal justice system is not only unjust, it is highly fallible. In hundreds of documented cases, the wrong person is apprehended and convicted. For example, in 1986, Roy Criner, who worked at a logging camp, was arrested for the rape and murder of a teenage girl in a nearby town. No physical evidence linked him to the crime and a guard said Criner had never left the camp. At his trial his lawyer put on no defense, believing the jury would not convict because of the total lack of evidence. Yet Criner was found guilty and sentenced to ninety-nine years in prison. It took eight years of appeals and a DNA test demonstrating his innocence to finally bring about his release.[36] Hayes Williams spent *thirty years* in prison for a murder he did not commit; he was finally freed in 1997. The actual perpetrators had been freed years before him (after serving for other crimes).[37]

A wrongful conviction creates the additional injustice of allowing the real culprits to go free. For eighteen years three perpetrators got away with a gang rape and double murder in Chicago for which four innocent African-American males were convicted: two were given life sentences and two were sent to death row. Their eventual release came when DNA tests showed that none of the four could have committed the rape. This proved to some observers that "the system works." In fact, it was the system that imprisoned them. They were freed thanks to the energetic efforts of a Northwestern University journalism professor and his student investigators.[38]

The criminal justice system has become more inhospitable to self-correction. In a series of rulings since 1991, a conservative Supreme Court has drastically restricted the rights of death-row prisoners — including the wrongfully convicted — to appeal their convictions. In 1996, Congress passed and President Clinton signed the Anti-Terrorism and Effective Death Penalty Act, which severely limits the rights of prisoners to appeal in federal courts.

Some argue that the death penalty acts as a deterrent to capital crimes. The evidence does not support this view. States that do not have the death penalty do not have higher crime rates. States that adopt the death penalty do not experience any discernible drop in capital crime rates over the years. Homicide rates have risen and fallen along roughly symmetrical paths in states with and without the death penalty, suggesting that the threat of the death penalty rarely deters criminals.[39]

A compelling argument against capital punishment is that it assumes the infallibility of a very fallible enforcement process, tainted by coerced confessions, mistaken identifications, perjurious testimony, suppression of troublesome evidence by overzealous police and prosecutors, incompetent defense attorneys, and the rampant class and racial prejudices of judges and juries.

Of the people on death row, the great majority are low-income; some are mentally ill or retarded; 10 percent are without counsel; and virtually all had court-appointed lawyers. Prosecutors are far more likely to seek the death penalty if the *victim* was White. Almost all inmates on death row (whether Black or White) are there for murdering a White person. African Americans are almost four times more likely to receive the death penalty and significantly less likely to have it commuted than similarly situated Caucasians.[40] In some states the racial disparity is even more pronounced.

Over the past century hundreds of innocent persons in the United States have been wrongly convicted of capital crimes; many of them have been executed.[41] Even demonstrable evidence may not be enough to save the wrongly convicted: Leonel Torres Herrera was executed in 1992 in Texas even though there was clear evidence of his innocence, acknowledged by the very court that refused to stay his execution — because the evidence was submitted too late for an appeal.[42]

In Illinois in 2000, Governor George Ryan, a Republican and advocate of the death penalty, called a moratorium on executions after thirteen of the twenty-seven inmates on death row in his state were released because new evidence (often DNA tests) proved them innocent. The Nebraska legislature

"Ahem! Uh . . . er . . . ah . . . hmm . . . (shuffle shuffle) . . . we, ah, made a couple of big mistakes in your death penalty trial."

passed a similar moratorium the year before. As of mid-2000, across the country, eighty-seven wrongly convicted persons had been released from death row, roughly one exoneration for every seven executions.[43] If they had been rushed to the death chamber, there would have been no opportunity to reopen their cases.

The United States is one of the few nations that still allows execution of minors (under eighteen years old), along with Saudi Arabia, Yemen, Pakistan, and Nigeria. During the 1990s, eight juvenile offenders were executed in the United States, more than in any other country.[44]

Sexist Justice

It is no crime to be against crime. Effective law enforcement is needed to protect the public from corporate felons, organized mobsters, murderers, rapists, muggers, child abusers, spouse batterers, hate-crime perpetrators, and others. But the law frequently fails those most in need of its protection. For instance, every year an estimated two to four million women are assaulted by their male partners. Domestic violence is the single largest cause of injury to women in the United States. Most female murder victims die at the hands of current or former husbands or boyfriends. A woman is beaten every twelve seconds in the United States, but we can be sure that a man is not arrested every twelve seconds for these assaults. Only a small percentage of male batterers are ever incarcerated. But women who kill their abusers usually receive severe sentences even if the battering had become life-threatening.[45]

For many poor women, welfare and family assistance is their primary means of escape, enabling them to leave their batterers by providing alternative support for them and their children. Cutbacks in welfare have caused a dramatic drop in the number who attempt to leave abusive relationships.[46]

The legal system is often a generator of sexism rather than a safeguard against it. Child support and alimony frequently are set unfairly low. Female victims of domestic violence find their complaints trivialized by unsympathetic judges. Only a small fraction of rapists are ever prosecuted or incarcerated for any appreciable time. Rape victims are too often treated as if they brought it on themselves. In many law schools, rape is treated from the viewpoint of the accused rather than the victim.[47]

After years of struggle, working women have made important gains, moving into professions and occupations previously deemed "unsuitable" for females. Feminist organizations also have had some limited success in getting law officials to take more active measures against rapists, batterers, and child molesters. But women on average still earn less for doing the same work as men and are more likely to be relegated to lower-paying, dead-end jobs.

Over the last twenty-five years, advocates of compulsory pregnancy — who believe that a fertilized ovum is a human being with rights that take precedence over its human carrier — have perpetrated more than 1,700 arson attacks and bombings against abortion and family planning clinics, along with thousands of bomb threats; death threats; acts of vandalism, intimidation, and harassment; assaults and burglaries; two kidnappings; at least five sniper attacks; and several shootings of doctors who performed legal abortions or shootings of other persons at abortion clinics, three of them fatal. About 85 percent of the nation's counties lack access to abortion providers, yet 1.5 million women still manage to have safe and legal abortions every year, most of them voicing their profound thanks for the service.[48] In societies where abortion is illegal, large numbers of women die from makeshift, unsafe attempts.

Law officers have been notably lax about deterring the compulsory-pregnancy terrorists. Erstwhile FBI director William Webster would not take action against the group of anti-abortionists called "Warriors of God," who perpetrated more than twenty bombings and burnings of family-planning clinics. Webster claimed they did not constitute "a definable group."[49] The FBI still does not classify anti-abortion violence as domestic terrorism. It is hard to imagine such a lackadaisical response if identifiable radical groups had subjected 1,700 *banks* to arson attacks and bombings.

Since 1990, the number of women in prison has almost doubled. Incarcerated women have endured poor medical care, sexual harassment, rape, and forced strip searches by male guards.[50] What kind of women end up in prison? Mostly young, impoverished, single mothers with few marketable job skills, many having left home early because of sexual or physical abuse, many with a drug- or alcohol-related history. Most have been charged with prostitution, shoplifting, robbery, or petty drug dealing. None of them are big-time narcotic traffickers, gangsters, or embezzlers. Few have committed an act of violence, though many have been victims of violence in their lives. Many are charged as accessories to crimes committed by men, sometimes implicated by boyfriends or ex-boyfriends seeking lighter sentences. On the boyfriend's testimony, some women have been given life in prison without parole for conspiracy to distribute drugs — even when the government concedes that they had played only a tangential role and never actually used or sold narcotics.[51]

The Victimization of Children

Children are another oppressed group who have received insufficient protection from federal and state authorities. Family violence or extreme neglect and starvation annually claim the lives of almost 2,000 children, with upwards of 140,000 left seriously injured and thousands permanently impaired. Child abuse is the major cause of death for children under four years. In 1999, there were 1,054,000 confirmed cases of child abuse in the United States, a 34-percent increase since 1985. The actual number is probably greater since some nonaccidental injuries and deaths of children are dismissed by authorities as "accidents." Every year 150,000 children are reported missing, of whom some 50,000 are never found.[52] An estimated 45,000 to 50,000 women and children are brought into the United States every year under false pretenses and forced to work as prostitutes, laborers, or servants. In 2000, Congress approved a law designed to assist states and local governments to fight domestic violence and toughen laws against the trafficking of women and children.[53]

Sensationalized media accounts of high-school shoot-ups and "youth crime waves" cause some people to forget that youngsters are more often *victims* than perpetrators of violence. Statistically, they are safer in school than in their homes. By 1997, overall rates of youth crime actually dropped below 1980 levels, with the downward trend continuing into 1998–1999.[54] Yet federal and state lawmakers continue to initiate more severely punitive measures against minors, trying them as adults, including some as young as twelve years. Perhaps the most outlandish case occurred in Tallahassee,

Florida, in 1998, when Chaquita Doman was arrested and charged as a felon following a minor schoolyard altercation. She was five years old.[55]

Youngsters have been given life sentences without any attempt at rehabilitation. "Tough on Crime" lawmakers have sponsored bills to incarcerate juveniles as young as thirteen with adults, prior to even being convicted of any wrongdoing.[56] More than a million children are kept in orphanages, reformatories, and adult prisons. Most have been arrested for petty transgressions or have committed no crime at all and are jailed without due process. Almost all are from impoverished backgrounds; a majority are of one or another ethnic minority. Minors incarcerated in juvenile correctional facilities are routinely subjected to beatings, sexual assault, torture, prolonged solitary confinement with sensory deprivation, powerful and stupefying psychoactive medications, and, in some cases, psychosurgery.[57]

The use of Ritalin increased by 250 percent among children (including preschoolers) between 1990 and 1995. Little is known about the safety or efficacy of this kind of drug. It can be prescribed for totally nonmedical reasons, as when a child is being fidgety or inattentive, or otherwise incurs the disfavor of institutional custodians.[58]

Parents who dislike their children's lifestyle, friends, dissenting political views, or "bad attitude" can have them confined indefinitely in psychiatric institutions. Millions of adult U.S. residents also have spent time in psychiatric wards at one time or another. It is easier to get committed than one might think, and harder to get out. Some people languish there for decades under terrible conditions with no legal recourse. Some of the worst of these institutions have suspiciously high death tolls.[59] Most hospitals will release mental patients who have no state funding or whose insurance runs out, even if they are in real need of help, a practice referred to as "dumping." In many instances, county jails end up holding mentally ill persons, usually for minor disturbances.[60]

Studies suggest that about one in four women and almost one in six men report having been sexually abused as children by adults, usually by a close family member — criminal offenses that leave lifelong emotional scars on the victims. Only a minute percentage of molesters are ever convicted, with many receiving probation or light sentences. Sometimes, judges grant custody or unsupervised visitation rights to the sexually abusive parent.[61]

Bedroom Police

Homosexuals are another group who have been the target of legal and social oppression. By 1999, twelve states and Puerto Rico still had "antisodomy" laws that made oral and anal sex a "crime against nature" — even between a husband and wife. In Michigan, for example, oral-genital contact carries a penalty of up to fifteen years' hard time. In five other states antisodomy laws specifically target only gays and lesbians.[62]

Thousands of lesbians and gays have been harassed and hounded out of the armed forces or out of civilian jobs because of their sexual orientation. They have been denied custody of their children on the grounds that their sexual proclivities made them unfit parents. In one case, a Florida judge transferred custody of a girl from her devoted lesbian mother to her father, who had served eight years in prison for murdering his first wife.[63] The U.S. Supreme Court ruled that a teacher could be fired for no other reason than being gay and that the Constitution does not protect homosexual relations between consenting adults even in the privacy of their own homes.[64]

Violence against gays and lesbians is on the increase, ranging from physical harassment to murder. The perpetrators too often get off with lenient sentences or acquittals.[65] The organized struggles launched by homosexuals against antigay housing and employment practices and homophobic hate crimes have met with some success. But homophobic attitudes and actions remain a widespread problem — including among law enforcers themselves.

Racist Law Enforcement

For all the talk about favored treatment and quotas, African Americans and other ethnic minorities still confront serious discrimination in job recruitment, housing, medical care, education, and at the hands of the law. The higher crime rates in poverty areas only partially explain why this nation's prison population is disproportionately African American, Latino, low-income, and underemployed. The class and racial biases of the law enforcement system also are major factors in determining who goes to prison.

An attorney who specializes in juvenile cases notes that youngsters from well-to-do families who get into minor scrapes with the law are turned over to their parents with a warning to stay out of trouble. "But when the same incidents happen in the less affluent neighborhoods, children are arrested, charged and brought to court."[66] African-American youths are more likely than their White counterparts to be apprehended, held in jail, put on trial, and convicted. They are less often allowed to plea-bargain their way out of tough mandatory prison sentences and more likely to get longer prison terms than Whites convicted of the same crimes.[67]

In regard to narcotics, five times as many Whites use drugs as African Americans, yet 62 percent of drug offenders sent to state prisons nationwide are African American; in some states it is as high as 90 percent. Almost 60 percent of Blacks in prison are serving time for nonviolent offenses. Several U.S. district court judges have dismissed drug charges after prosecutors refused to turn over records to show whether they selectively prosecuted non-White defendants.[68]

Police have stopped drivers based on their skin color rather than on the way they were driving, in what has been called "racial profiling." On Interstate 95 between Baltimore and Delaware, African Americans drove only 14 percent of the cars but accounted for 73 percent of the stops.[69] Investigations of police departments in numerous locales reveal that incidents of racist brutality are widespread and often tolerated by department commanders. In recent years, Philadelphia and Los Angeles police have been indicted on criminal charges, including illegal searches, planted evidence, falsified reports, unjustified shootings, beatings, thefts, witness intimidation, and perjury. Hundreds of convictions have been overturned, nearly all involving Latino and African-American suspects. Excessive force liability payouts against police departments around the country run into tens of millions of dollars every year. In Los Angeles alone, it was $28 million in one year.[70]

Unarmed African-American and Latino persons have been shot or beaten to death mostly by White police officers in circumstances that are impossible to justify. In 1999, four New York City police officers in plain clothes fired forty-one times at Amadou Diallo, an unarmed man who was standing in the hallway of his house, hitting him nineteen times, including several bullets in the back. In 1998 in Riverside, California, police fired twenty-four rounds at nineteen-year-old Tyisha Miller, who had been asleep in her locked car, but who supposedly reached for a gun on her lap when the police revived her by breaking the driver's window. In 1997 in Queens, New York, five cops from the vice squad rushed into a restaurant and shot the cook, Jose Antonio Sanchez, who was holding a kitchen knife, as cooks often do. In 1998, Los Angeles police shot Michael William Arnold 106 times, claiming he had brandished a weapon — an air gun that miraculously was still in his right hand when his body was examined, even though he had been shot several times in the head and three times in his right hand, oddly with no damage to the gun. In August 1997, Abner Louima was taken to a precinct house in New York, where police sodomized him with the handle of a toilet plunger which punctured his small intestine and injured his bladder.[71]

In 1991 in Irvington, New Jersey, three police officers entered the apartment of Darlene Antoine during a birthday party and began pushing people around. When her brother Max told her to write down the officers' badge numbers, they began beating him. They beat Max again in jail so badly that he was left deaf in one ear, blind in one eye, confined to a wheelchair, paralyzed from the waist down, and bereft of bowel, bladder, and sexual functions.[72] In 1997 in New York, Lebert Folkes was dragged from his sister's car parked in front of his house and shot in the face by a semiautomatic weapon. The next day police apologized for the shooting; his car had been mistakenly identified as stolen. Anthony Baez, a Bronx man, died in an illegal choke hold applied by a police officer who was angry because a football being tossed around by Baez and his friends had accidentally hit his patrol car.[73]

One could go on with hundreds of such examples from all over the country. With few exceptions the police get away with it. Prosecutors are extremely hesitant to bring charges against cops, and White middle-class juries, fed a steady diet of crime shows and crime news, are reluctant to convict. The FBI and Justice Department do not even keep national statistics on killings by police officers. And state and local governments refuse to give out any numbers.[74]

To be sure, many laws enhance public safety and individual security. The police sometimes protect life and limb, direct traffic, administer first aid, assist in times of community emergency, and perform other commendable services. But the police also serve a class-control function, protecting the haves from the have-nots. The police deal with the losers of a competitive corporate society: the ill-fed and ill-housed, the addicted and abused, the angry and desperate. The slums are not the problem, they are the solution: they are the way capitalism deals with the surplus people of a market economy. It is the police's job to sweep protest and poverty under the rug — even if it takes a club or gun. Repressive acts by police are not the aberrant behavior of a few psychotics in uniform but the outgrowth of the kind of class-control function that law officers perform and rulers insist upon — which explains why the police are able to get away with murder. And once they sense that they are not held accountable and are free to get as rough as they want, some of them indulge in excessive and even homicidal force.

Decades ago, while serving as Boston Police Commissioner, Robert DiGrazia noted the class function that police served:

> [T]hose who commit the crime which worries citizens most — violent street crime — are, for the most part, the products of poverty, unemployment, broken homes, rotten education, drug addiction and alcoholism, and other social and economic ills about which the police can do little, if anything.
>
> Rather than speaking up, most of us stand silent and let politicians get away with law and order rhetoric that reinforces the mistaken notion that police — in ever greater numbers and with more gadgetry — can alone control crime. The politicians, of course, end up perpetuating a system by which the rich get richer, the poor get poorer, and crime continues.[75]

A final word about corporate crime and street crime. We should be aware of how they are interrelated. The poor get poorer because the rich get richer. The white-collar corporate plunderers take a terrible toll on society, especially upon those who are least able to defend themselves. They help create the very want, scarcity, injustice, and maldistribution that contribute so much to street crime. If it is true that we need more law and order, more respect for other people's rights, then we should start at the top, vigorously applying the law to those who try to grab everything for themselves regardless of the ruinous effects on others.

Notes

1. W. S. Albrecht et al., *Fraud: Bringing Light to the Dark Side of Business* (New York: McGraw-Hill, 1994).

2. *New York Times,* May 11, 1934; Charles Higham, *Trading with the Enemy* (New York: Dell, 1983); eyewitness report by E. F. Patterson, *Ramparts,* August 1974; *New York Times,* April 29, 2000; and Associated Press report, March 14, 1998.

3. U.S. Department of Labor, Office of the Inspector General, *Changes Are Needed in the ERISA Audit Process to Increase Protections for Employee Benefit Plan Participants,* Report no. 09-90-001-12001, Washington, D.C., 1989.

4. Michel Chossudovsky, "The Business of Crime and the Crimes of Business," *Covert-Action Quarterly,* Fall 1996.

5. *Los Angeles Times,* March 10, 1990; Ashville Global Report, October 21–27, 1999; *San Francisco Chronicle,* August 13, 1998; Internal Report of U.S. Department of Interior Audit, Project on Government Oversight, Washington, D.C., April 13, 1995.

6. *New York Times,* September 12, 1985, and November 9, 1986; *Washington Post,* October 23, 1988; *America's Censored Newsletter,* March 1993.

7. David Friedrichs, *Trusted Criminals: White Collar Crime in Contemporary* Society (Belmont, Calif.: Wadsworth, 1996); also *Washington Post,* June 1, 1988, and March 6, 1991; *Utility Notes,* Bulletin from the Office of the People's Counsel, Washington, D.C., December 30, 1988; *New York Times,* June 2, 1992.

8. Robert Sherrill, "A Year in Corporate Crime," *Nation,* April 7, 1997; *New York Times,* August 22, 1995.

9. General Accounting Office, *Financial Integrity Act Report* (Washington, D.C.: Government Printing Office, January 1990); *San Francisco Examiner,* February 25, 1993.

10. Russell Mokhiber and Robert Weissman, *Corporate Predators* (Monroe, Maine: Common Courage, 1999).

11. *Los Angeles Times,* March 13, 1996.

12. *USA Today,* November 10, 1997.

13. James Stewart, *Den of Thieves* (New York: Touchstone, 1992), 527; see also Benjamin J. Stein, *A License to Steal: The Untold Story of Michael Milken and the Conspiracy to Bilk the Nation* (New York: Simon & Schuster, 1992); *New York Times,* January 30, 1993.

14. Ralph Nader and Wesley Smith, *No Contest: Corporate Lawyers and the Perversion of Justice in America* (New York: Random House, 1996); Michael Waldman, *Who Robbed America* (New York: Random House, 1990).

15. Judge Nicholas Cobella, quoted in Molly Ivins, "Corporations Wielding Cynical Lawsuits against Free Speech," *San Jose Mercury News,* January 23, 2000.

16. David Burnham, *Above the Law* (New York: Scribner, 1996); Nader and Smith, *No Contest.*

17. *Griffin v. Illinois* (1956).

18. James C. Turner and Joyce A. McGee, "Freedom of Legal Information: Increasing Court Access for Americans of Limited Means," *Management Information Exchange Journal,* Summer 1999.

19. *Los Angeles Times,* June 16, 1990; *People's Daily World,* June 14, 1989, January 23, 1990, and October 7, 1995; and documentary film, *Harlan County, USA,* 1978.

20. Jeffrey Toobin, "Women in Black," *New Yorker,* October 30, 2000; *New York Times,* August 5, 1984; *City Paper* (Washington, D.C.), April 21, 1989.

21. Vincent Schiraldi, "Poor Prison Policy," *San Francisco Bay Guardian,* May 5, 1999; Adolph Reed, Jr., *Without Justice for All* (Boulder, Colo.: Westview, 1999); Darrell Gilliard and Allen Beck, *Prison and Jail Inmates,* Bureau of Justice Statistics report, Washington, D.C., 1998; *New York Times,* June 1, 2000.

22. "Crime Drop Not Linked to Arrest Rates," *Prison Focus*, Winter 2000; and *New York Times*, July 5 and August 28, 2000.

23. "The Impact of 'Three Strikes and You're Out' Laws," *Prison Focus*, Winter 1997; and *San Francisco Chronicle*, March 7, 1997.

24. *Behind Bars: Substance Abuse and America's Prison Population,* National Center on Addiction and Substance Abuse, Columbia University, 1998; and various issues of *FAMM-gram,* publication of Families Against Mandatory Minimums Foundation.

25. Eric Schlosser, "More Reefer Madness," *Atlantic Monthly,* April 1997; "Congressional Family Drug Offenders Escape Mandatory Sentences, Get Favorable Treatment," *North Coast Xpress,* Spring 2000.

26. *San Francisco Examiner,* May 24, 1993.

27. Richard Moran, "FBI Scare Tactics," *New York Times,* May 7, 1996.

28. According to the New York Criminal Justice Alliance, see Julia Lutsky, "Torture in America's Prisons," *People's Weekly World,* September 13, 1997.

29. Tom Cahill, "Prisoner Rape: Institutionalized Torture in the U.S.," *Prison Focus,* Winter 2000, and see <http://www.prisons.org>.

30. *United States of America — Rights for All,* report by Amnesty International, October 1998; Corey Weinstein and Eric Cummins, "The Crime of Punishment at Pelican Bay Maximum Security Prison," *CovertAction Quarterly,* Summer 1993.

31. *United States of America — Rights for All,* Amnesty International, October 1998.

32. *United States of America — Rights for All,* Amnesty International, October 1998; Lutsky, "Torture in America's Prisons"; *Prison Legal News,* October 1999; *San Francisco Chronicle,* June 10, 2000; Jean Stewart, "Life, Death and Disability Behind Bars," *New Mobility,* June 1998.

33. Audrey Bomse, "Congress Closes Courthouse Doors to Prison Litigation," *Legal Journal* (National Lawyers Guild Prison Law Project), Winter/Spring 1997.

34. Willie Wisely, "Why Prisons Cost So Much," *North Coast Xpress,* April/May 1995.

35. David McGowan, *Derailing Democracy* (Monroe, Maine: Common Courage, 2000), 136.

36. *Los Angeles Times,* July 29, 2000.

37. *San Francisco Chronicle,* December 1, 1997. For ten other case studies of wrongly convicted people, see Barry Scheck, Peter Neufeld, Jim Dwyer, *Actual Innocence* (Garden City, N.Y.: Doubleday, 1999).

38. *New York Times,* June 15 and July 4, 1996.

39. *New York Times,* September 22, 2000.

40. Richard Dieter, *The Death Penalty in Black and White,* report by Death Penalty Information Center, Philadelphia, June 1998.

41. Michael Radelet, Hugo Adam Bedau, and Constance Putnam, *In Spite of Innocence: The Ordeal of 400 Americans Wrongly Convicted of Crimes Punishable by Death* (Boston: Northeastern University Press, 1992); and Michael Radelet, William Lofquist, and Hugo Adam Bedau, "Death Penalty Symposium: Prisoners Released From Death Rows Since 1970 Because of Doubts about Their Guilt," *Thomas M. Cooley Law Review* 13, 1996.

42. "In Spite of Innocence," newsletter of Campaign to End the Death Penalty, Chicago, 1998.

43. *New York Times,* August 22, 1999, and June 12, 2000.

44. Shirley Dicks (ed.), *Young Blood: Juvenile Justice and the Death Penalty* (Amherst, N.Y.: Prometheus, 1995); and *United States of America — Rights for All,* Amnesty International, October 1998.

45. Lorraine Dusky, *Still Unequal: The Shameful Truth about Women and Justice in America* (New York: Crown, 1996); U.S. Surgeon General's report: *San Francisco Chronicle,* October 2, 1998; *New York Times,* March 17, 1998.

46. Nina Siegal and Martin Espinoza, "No Escape," *San Francisco Bay Guardian,* April 30, 1997; Jennifer Gonnerman, "Welfare's Domestic Violence," *Nation,* March 10, 1997.

47. Karen Winner, *Divorced from Justice* (New York: Regan, 1996); Dusky, *Still Unequal*, passim.

48. Jennifer Gonnerman, "The Anti-Abortion Stealth Campaign," *On the Issues*, Fall 1996; "Crusade of Terror," *Nation*, December 16, 1998.

49. *New York Times* editorial, December 7, 1984.

50. U.S. Department of Justice report cited in McGowan, *Derailing Democracy*, 117; Bobbie Stein, "Life in Prison: Sexual Abuse," *Progressive*, July 1996; Nina Siegal, "Death Behind Bars," *San Francisco Bay Guardian*, February 5, 1997.

51. Nancy Kurshan, "Women and Prison Today," *North Coast Xpress*, February/March 1997; Arianna Huffington's column, *San Francisco Examiner*, June 25, 2000.

52. U.S. Advisory Board on Child Abuse and Neglect, *A Nation's Shame: Fatal Child Abuse and Neglect in the United States* (Washington, D.C.: U.S. Advisory Board on Child Abuse and Neglect, 1995); report by Child Protective Services, *San Francisco Chronicle*, May 9, 1999.

53. *New York Times*, October 7, 2000.

54. Franklin Zimring, *American Youth Violence* (New York: Oxford University Press, 1998); *New York Times*, May 17, 1999.

55. McGowan, *Derailing Democracy*, 57.

56. A. Clay Thompson, "The Lost Boys," *San Francisco Bay Guardian*, January 27, 1999; Vincent Schiraldi in *Christian Science Monitor*, November 1997.

57. Allen Jones, "Crime and Too Much Punishment," *San Francisco Examiner*, June 28, 2000; Dwight Edgar Abbott, *I Cried, You Didn't Listen* (Los Angeles: Feral House, 1991), with Jack Carter's concluding essay, "America's Incarcerated Children Today," 159–71; Louise Armstrong, *And They Call It Help: The Psychiatric Policing of America's Children* (Reading, Mass.: Addison-Wesley, 1993); Thomas Cottle, *Children in Jail* (Boston: Beacon, 1977); Kenneth Wooden, *Weeping in the Playtime of Others* (New York: McGraw-Hill, 1976).

58. Peter Breggin, *Talking Back to Ritalin* (Monroe, Maine: Common Courage, 2000); *New York Times*, February 23, 2000.

59. *San Francisco Bay Guardian*, July 10 and August 14, 1996; *Street Spirit* (San Francisco), July 1996 and August 1996.

60. *New York Times*, March 5, 1998, and May 22, 1999; *San Francisco Examiner*, December 10, 1997.

61. For testimonials regarding incest abuse, see "Childhood Sexual Abuse," special issue of *Central Park* (New York), Spring 1993; also "Incest Statistics," *Witness*, April 1988; John Crewdson, *By Silence Betrayed: Sexual Abuse of Children in America* (Boston: Little, Brown, 1988); Jane Ashley, "When Incest Haunts Love," *Washington Post*, August 27, 1990.

62. *New York Times*, May 10, 1998; Elisabeth Flynn and Chong Choe, "Down by Law," *San Francisco Bay Guardian*, June 26, 1996.

63. *New York Times*, June 1, 2000, and August 31, 1996; Debbie Nathan, "Sodomy for the Masses," *Nation*, April 19, 1999; and the case of Sandy Nelson, newsletter, National Lawyers Guild, Seattle chapter, August 1995.

64. *Gish v. Board of Education of Paramus, N.J.* (1976); *Bowers v. Hardwick* (1986).

65. See the annual reports of the National Gay and Lesbian Task Force, Washington, D.C., and National Coalition of Anti-Violence Programs; *San Francisco Chronicle*, October 13, 1998.

66. *Washington Post*, November 30, 1986.

67. Eileen Poe-Yamagata and Michael A. Jones, *And Justice for Some* (National Council on Crime and Delinquency, 2000).

68. *Punishment and Prejudice: Racial Disparities in the War on Drugs*, Human Rights Watch, 2000; Report by the National Criminal Justice Commission, cited in McGowan, *Derailing Democracy*, 71; *Washington Post*, October 9, 1996.

69. *USA Today*, March 24, 1998.

70. *New York Times*, December 12, 1995, and March 13, 1997; *Los Angeles Times*, January 25, 2000; *San Francisco Bay Guardian*, July 2 and July 9, 1997.

71. McGowan, *Derailing Democracy*, 47–48; and *Los Angeles Times*, June 13 and July 26, 1999; *New York Times*, August 14, 1997, and May 5, 1999; see also Christian Parenti, *Lockdown America: Police and Prisons in the Age of Crisis* (New York and London: Verso, 1999); and Bruce Shapiro, "When Justice Kills," *Nation*, June 9, 1997.

72. *New York Press*, June 15–22, 1999.

73. Bob Herbert, "A Brutal Epidemic," *New York Times*, April 27, 1997.

74. Belinda Griswold, "The Thin Blue Line," *San Francisco Bay Guardian*, October 15, 1997.

75. Quoted in *Parade*, August 22, 1976. However, even in the best of social circumstances there are ruthlessly self-interested people who resort to violent and unlawful means to get what they want. Not all crime is a reaction to deprivation and class inequity.

10

Political Repression and National Insecurity

The capitalist state directs its repressive mechanisms against progressive causes. It is more sincerely dedicated to fighting organized dissent than fighting organized crime. The law often appears ineffective when attempting to implement social reforms that benefit the many. But when mobilized against political heterodoxy, the resources of the law seem boundless, and enforcement is pursued with a punitive vigor that itself becomes lawless.

The Repression of Dissent

One agency used for political harassment is the Internal Revenue Service (IRS), which has gone after civil rights leaders and radical individuals, organizations, and publications. The Communist party had its assets seized and was illegally denied tax exemption for years — while the two major pro-capitalist political parties enjoyed uninterrupted tax exemption. In some of these punitive forays, the IRS has been prodded by the White House, the Central Intelligence Agency (CIA), or members of Congress.[1]

The State Department and the Immigration and Naturalization Service (INS) are two other agencies involved in political repression, excluding anyone from abroad who might be affiliated with communist, anarchist, or "terrorist" groups, or engaged in activities "prejudicial to the public interest." Every year under these sweeping provisos, dozens of prominent writers, artists, scientists, and labor leaders from other countries have been denied the right to visit and address audiences in the United States, including Nobel

Prize winners like Dario Fo, Pablo Neruda, and Gabriel Garcia Marquez. Only after much public outcry have such luminaries been allowed entry.[2]

Under a 1990 change in the law, supposedly no one can be refused a visa because of ideology, yet the State Department and the INS continue to maintain an ideological "lookout list" of some 345,000 individuals. Persons with connections to leftist organizations can be removed from the restrictive list if they recant and demonstrate their anticommunism. Canadian communists must formally denounce their past political beliefs, file their fingerprints with the Federal Bureau of Investigation (FBI) and the Royal Canadian Mounted Police, make "pro-American" vows, and provide proof that they are actively engaged in opposing communism.[3]

In general, rightists — be they officials of procapitalist governments or individuals fleeing left-wing governments — enjoy easy entry into the country. While leftists — be they representatives of governments like Cuba or individuals fleeing repressive procapitalist regimes — are excluded.[4] Not surprisingly so, since the left generally opposes the privileged corporate class order and its attendant inequities, while the right supports them. In fact, that is the major difference between left and right.

The U.S. government signed the Helsinki accords, an international agreement not to impose travel restrictions on its own citizens. Yet thousands of U.S. citizens have been denied passports because the State Department decided that their activities were "contrary to the interests of the United States."

Corporations have fired employees because of their deviant political hues. The courts have ruled that the First Amendment of the Constitution prohibits only government — not private-sector employers — from suppressing speech.[5] People with affiliations to anticapitalist groups have been hounded out of jobs in labor unions, academia, entertainment, and various other fields including government itself by both private employers and federal and state investigators.[6]

There are almost ten million FBI files on organizations and individuals, alive and dead, often containing uncorroborated rumors from anonymous sources concerning personal lives, sexual practices, and political leanings.[7] A secret court created by the Foreign Intelligence Surveillance Act (FISA) of 1978 regularly authorizes thousands of electronic surveillance requests from the FBI and the National Security Agency (NSA). Each of its decisions is reached in secret, with no published opinion or record. The targeted individual or organization is not allowed to see the transcripts or tapes, or contest the surveillance in any manner. In 1995, in violation of the Fourth Amendment's protection against unreasonable search and seizure, President Clinton signed an executive order that greatly expanded the FISA court's mandate. It could now authorize "black bag operations," physical searches as well as electronic ones, without obtaining a warrant in open court, without notifying the target or providing an inventory of items seized.

The target need not be under suspicion of committing a crime but might simply be deemed to have questionable associations that pose a "threat to U.S. national security."[8]

During the 1960s struggle against racial segregation, some activists suffered physical assault and even death at the hands of White vigilantes while state and local police and FBI informants either looked the other way or actually assisted.[9] One police official declared that there were more law officers throughout the country "on political intelligence assignments than are engaged in fighting organized crime."[10] In various cities, secret police units, commonly known as "Red squads" — assisted by state-of-the-art surveillance technology provided by federal authorities — have spied on and harassed lawful advocacy groups, and monitored hundreds of thousands of individuals and organizations.[11] Perhaps one reason authorities cannot win the "war on crime" and the "war on drugs" is that they have been too busy fighting the war on political heterodoxy.

As part of that war, the FBI launched — with White House authorization — a counterintelligence program (Cointelpro) designed to disrupt and subvert progressive groups. Working closely with police Red squads and private right-wing organizations, the FBI used forged documents, illegal break-ins, false charges, intercepted mailings, telephone taps, and undercover provocateurs and informants. The bureau infiltrated various labor unions in attempts to brand them "communist-controlled" and cooperated with management in the surveillance of strikers.[12] As the *New York Times* belatedly acknowledged, "Radical groups in the United States have complained for years that they were being harassed by the Federal Bureau of Investigation and it now turns out that they were right."[13] One FBI agent reminds us, "The [Cointelpro] program is still in operation, but under a different code name."[14] The FBI continues to keep a "security index" of many thousands of names, mostly members of anticapitalist groups, who are slated for arrest and detention in case of a "national emergency" — even though the law authorizing this practice was declared unconstitutional.[15]

As director of the FBI for almost half a century, J. Edgar Hoover kept elaborate dossiers on the private lives of notables — including presidents and their cabinet members, Supreme Court justices, and members of Congress — often threatening exposure of the seamier side of their personal lives. He planted witchhunting stories in the press, collaborated with segregationists, and harassed civil rights leaders like Martin Luther King, Jr. He used FBI funds for his private profit and pleasure and accepted lavish gifts from wealthy friends whom he then protected from criminal investigation. Hoover also cultivated close and corrupt relations with organized crime figures, making no serious effort to move against the mob for more than thirty years.[16]

President Ronald Reagan authorized intelligence agencies to infiltrate and "influence the activities" of organizations — even in the absence of any suspected lawbreaking, in effect legalizing many illegal Cointelpro tactics used in earlier years. So the FBI continued with its break-ins and disruptive infiltrations of anticapitalist parties, antiwar organizations, environmental groups, civil liberties organizations like the National Lawyers Guild, and supporters of political prisoner solidarity groups.[17]

Political Prisoners, USA

The U.S. government maintains that it has no political prisoners. In truth, this country has endured a long history of politically motivated incarcerations. In 1915, radical labor leader Joe Hill was jailed and executed in Utah for a crime most investigators believe he did not commit. The great labor leader Eugene Debs and some six thousand other socialists, pacifists, and radical labor organizers were imprisoned or deported during World War I or immediately after. The Italian anarchists Sacco and Vanzetti were arrested and eventually executed for a crime virtually all investigators say they never committed.

Hundreds of war resisters were arrested during World War II and the Korean War. During World War II, 120,000 law-abiding Japanese Americans were uprooted from their homes, farms, and businesses and sent to internment camps as "security risks." Several hundred West Coast Italian aliens, including elderly grandparents, also had their homes confiscated and were forcibly interned. The Smith Act of 1940 prohibited the mere advocacy of revolutionary ideas and was used to jail scores of American Communists and other anticapitalists, including Gus Hall, a Communist party leader who spent nine years in prison or underground for advocating politically incorrect thoughts. Others spent time behind bars for refusing to cooperate with congressional witchhunts during the McCarthy era. Julius and Ethel Rosenberg were convicted of having stolen "atomic secrets" and executed, on what many critics believe was flimsy or nonexistent evidence. In 1950 and several years after, Congress passed laws requiring "subversive" groups to register with the Attorney General, and persons suspected of subversion to be detained in concentration camps during times of national emergency.[18]

During the Vietnam War, several thousand youths were jailed for refusing to serve in what they felt was an unjust conflict; thousands more chose exile. Almost every antiwar activist who occupied a position of national or even local leadership was arrested at one time or another; many were jailed or went underground.[19]

The Immigration and Naturalization Service is holding about ten thousand asylum seekers in prison under insufferable conditions, some of them for years. Many fled torture and death threats from their right-wing procapitalist governments, and have decried human rights abuses in their home country. For this reason alone they are treated as suspect. In effect, they are political prisoners of the United States.[20]

Numerous African-American leaders involved in progressive community causes and struggles against drug pushers have been railroaded into prison on trumped-up charges. Thus, after police planted heroin in his bookstore, Martin Sostre, an outspoken opponent of the heroin traffic, was sentenced to thirty years for drug dealing, on the word of a convict who later admitted that his testimony had been fabricated. Sostre served nine years, mostly in solitary confinement. After much pressure from progressive groups, New York governor Mario Cuomo granted him amnesty.[21]

Frank Shuford, an African-American activist and anticapitalist in Santa Ana, California, developed a number of community programs and helped people organize against drug dealers and their corrupt police allies. He was arrested for the shooting of two store clerks. Neither clerk identified him as the gunman and no material evidence was presented against him. At his trial, Shuford was branded a "revolutionary troublemaker" by the prosecution. His own lawyer conducted a strangely lackadaisical defense, then was himself appointed a district attorney immediately after Shuford was found guilty by an all-White jury and sentenced to thirty years. In prison, Shuford was drugged, beaten, denied medical care, and scheduled for a lobotomy. Only community pressure on his behalf prevented the operation from taking place. Shuford served over ten years.[22]

The leaders of Black Men's Movement Against Crack, an organization dedicated to fighting the narcotics trade in New York, were imprisoned on trumped-up charges of "illegal possession of weapons, attempted escape, and assault."[23]

In Tchula, Mississippi, Eddie Carthan was elected the first African-American mayor since Reconstruction, and the first to buck the local plutocracy. Carthan refused to appoint cronies of the big planters, declined bribes, and investigated the corruption of previous administrations. He started programs for nutrition, health care, day care, and housing rehabilitation for poor people. The Board of Aldermen, dominated by planter interests, cut his salary to virtually nothing and barred him from his city hall office. The governor had all federal funds to Tchula cut off, ending most of the mayor's programs. When Carthan retook his office with five auxiliary police, he was charged with assault and sentenced to three years, convicted on the testimony of a witness who later recanted. The FBI targeted the mayor, combing through his records and papers, discovering only that Carthan had authorized an assistant to sign his name to a delivery receipt for day-care equipment; for this "fraud" he was given an additional four-year sentence. Then, after a Black alderman was robbed and murdered and the murderer convicted, Carthan was charged with having plotted the murder. He was eventually released only after protest campaigns were launched around the country.[24] The low-income Black voters of Tchula got a lesson in what happens to democratic leaders when they intrude — however modestly — upon an entrenched and wealthy class power.

©1976 HERBLOCK

Community activist and leader of African self-determination, Fred Hampton, Jr. (son of Black Panther leader Fred Hampton, who was murdered by law officers), was tried on a bogus charge of arson in Chicago. During the trial no evidence was produced demonstrating that Hampton was connected to the fires or that they had ever actually happened. Yet he was given eighteen years and later subjected to serious mistreatment in prison for organizing around inmates' rights.[25]

Prisoners who propagate radical political views or who engage in protests regarding prison conditions have been singled out for mind-control programs, subjected to mind-altering drugs, beatings, forced rectal searches, prolonged shackling, isolation, and other tortures. Inmates in U.S. prisons, noted Amnesty International in 1998, "have reportedly been put in supermax units because of their political affiliations."[26]

From 1968 to 1971, over three hundred members of the Black Panther Party were arrested, many held without bail or trial for long durations. At least ten former Panthers, convicted on fabricated evidence and testimony that was subsequently recanted, served thirty years each in prison. Still in prison as of 2000 are three Panthers, Herman Bell, Anthony Bottom, and Albert Washington, whose trial included perjured testimony and evidence suppressed by the prosecution. Panther leader Geronimo Pratt was charged with murdering a woman when he was a UCLA student. The FBI conveniently lost its surveillance records showing that Pratt was actually four hundred miles away attending a Panther meeting in Oakland at the time of the murder. The FBI chose to let the real murderer go free in order to jail a political radical. Pratt finally had his conviction overturned in 1997, and was paid a settlement of $4.5 million.[27]

There is the highly celebrated death-row case of Mumia Abu-Jamal, ex-Panther, radio journalist, and articulate critic of social injustice and police brutality, who had been under police and FBI surveillance for years even though he had no criminal record. He was shot when trying to stop a cop from beating his brother. The officer doing the beating was killed by one of the bullets fired. In a deeply flawed trial, involving an incompetent defense, police perjury, and intimidated witnesses, Abu-Jamal was convicted of murder, even though no ballistic evidence linked him to the shooting, and several eyewitnesses claimed that another man shot the cop and fled the scene.[28]

Also imprisoned were members of the American Indian Movement, including Leonard Peltier, charged with shooting two FBI agents, and convicted on affidavits that the government now concedes were fabricated; Peltier has been incarcerated since 1976.[29] Still behind bars as of 2000 are members of the Black Liberation Army, the Republic of New Afrika (a Black separatist movement), the African Peoples Socialist Party, Chicano and North American anticapitalist revolutionaries, community radical organizers, and peace activists.[30] Puerto Rican nationalists, who claim prisoner-of-war status, were given an average sentence of sixty-seven years for seditious conspiracy, specifically, harboring beliefs about Puerto Rican independence and being members of a group that intended to overthrow the U.S. government and U.S. rule in Puerto Rico.[31] (Sedition is defined as the incitement of resistance to lawful authority.)

The members of Plowshares, a peace group, jackhammered the concrete around a nuclear missile silo in Kansas in 1984. For this protest action, eleven of them were sentenced to eighteen years in prison. Barbara Curzi-Laaman, a White working-class woman once active in antiracist organizing and in an "underground anti-imperialist movement," was given fifteen years for "seditious conspiracy" and threatened with additional sentences of 265 years. Another White woman, Linda Evans, organized so effectively against racism that the Louisiana Ku Klux Klan put her on its death list. To protect herself, she purchased guns using false identification. For this and for harboring a fugitive, Evans has been serving forty-five years in prison. Susan Rosenberg and Tim Blunk, anticapitalist activists, were each given fifty-eight years for weapons possession and false identification. Marilyn Buck, who organized against the Vietnam War and aligned herself with the Black liberation movement, was convicted of conspiracy to oppose government policies through use of violence against government property, and sentenced to a total of eighty years in prison.[32]

Silvia Baraldini, an Italian citizen, was an antiwar activist and sympathizer of Puerto Rican independence and Black liberation. Refusing to testify before a grand jury, she was tried for conspiracy and criminal contempt and sentenced to forty-three years. Along with Susan Rosenberg and Puerto Rican nationalist Alejandrina Torres, Baraldini was held for two years in the high-security unit at Lexington, Kentucky, enduring windowless cells, deprived of fresh air and human contact, and subjected to constant surveillance by a battery of cameras and hostile male guards. In time, their eyesight and health deteriorated. Baraldini underwent two operations for cancer. Torres suffered a heart attack.[33] Neither Curzi-Laaman, Evans, Rosenberg, Blunt, Buck, Baraldini, Torres, nor others like them were ever convicted of harming anyone or anything. They were in prison not for what they had done but for who they were, revolutionary advocates and activists.

In sum, political prisoners receive grossly disproportionate sentences, are routinely denied parole even when qualifying for it, and are subjected to isolation, behavior modification, brutality, and other specially punitive treatments. It is only through the determined efforts of support groups that some of them are eventually released short of serving their entire sentences.

In December 1999, in Seattle, Washington, a major demonstration involving over eighty thousand trade unionists, environmentalists, and progressives of all stripes was launched against a meeting of the World Trade Organization (WTO), the internationalist capitalist organization that fosters free market oligarchy (rule by the elite few) over democratic sovereignty.[34] In early 2000, another major demonstration, this time against the International Monetary Fund (IMF) and World Bank took place in Washington, D.C., followed by large demonstrations that summer in Philadelphia against the Republican presidential nominating convention, and in Los Angeles against the Democratic convention. In each instance, police acted repressively, closing down protest offices on flimsy excuses, beating, gassing, and arresting hundreds of nonviolent protestors without justifiable cause in "preemptive raids." In Philadelphia, one protest leader was held on a million-dollar bail, later reduced to $100,000. Charges against him were eventually dropped for lack of evidence.[35]

Of the Washington protest, a participant noted that the D.C. police force "can't seem to get its act together to fight crime" and responds to citizen calls at a leisurely pace, yet it can turn out in heavily equipped massive numbers to squelch largely peaceful demonstrations, even breaking up training sessions in which protestors teach themselves how to organize legally and effectively. "Where are all those cops the rest of the year when we need them?" he asked.[36] The same might be said of police in other cities. They seem so much more capable and energized when attacking protestors than when confronting mobsters.

Political Murder, USA

During the Vietnam War, antiwar protestors were attacked by police on dozens of campuses throughout the country and in major demonstrations. In Orangeburg, South Carolina, police fired into a peaceful campus demonstration, killing three African-American students and wounding twenty-seven others. Ohio National Guardsmen killed four Caucasian students and maimed two others who were participating in an antiwar protest at Kent State University. Ten days later, at the all-Black Jackson State College in Mississippi, police opened fire into a women's dormitory where protesting students had congregated, killing two and wounding a dozen others.[37] In these and other incidents, law enforcers whose lives were never in danger used lethal force against unarmed protestors. "Impartial investigations" by the very authorities responsible for the killings exonerated the uniformed murderers.

Police attacked the Black Panther Party (a Marxist revolutionary organization) in more than ten cities, wrecking offices, stealing thousands of dollars in funds, and arresting, beating, and shooting occupants in planned operations, coordinated with the FBI. At least thirty-four Panthers were murdered by police by the early 1970s, including Chicago leader Fred Hampton, who was shot while asleep in his bed. A paramilitary "peacekeeping" force, established by the U.S. Bureau of Indian Affairs under FBI direction, carried out a terrorist campaign on the Pine Ridge Reservation that was directly responsible for more than sixty deaths and for hundreds of assaults of supporters of the American Indian Movement.[38]

Three Haitian talk-show hosts in Miami who aired critical commentaries about CIA-supported military repression in Haiti were shot dead between 1991 and 1993.[39] Individuals in the Cuban American community who advocated a more conciliatory policy toward the Cuban communist government were subjected to threats and attacks. An antisocialist Cuban exile terrorist group claimed credit for some twenty-one bombings between 1975 and 1980 and for the murder of a Cuban diplomat in New York; the group escaped arrest in all but two instances. A car bombing in Miami that cost a Cuban radio news director both his legs also remains unsolved. When the Center for Cuban Studies was destroyed by a bomb, police questioned the center's director about leftist radicals, while doing nothing about the Cuban exile group that openly claimed credit for the bombing.[40]

In the United States between 1981 and 1987, there were eleven fatal shootings of Vietnamese publishers, journalists, and activists who had advocated normalized relations with the communist government of Vietnam. In each instance, the U.S.-based "Vietnamese Organization to Exterminate Communists and Restore the Nation" (VOECRN) claimed responsibility. One of VOECRN's victims, a publisher of a Vietnamese-language weekly, survived his shooting and identified the gunman, a leader of a Vietnamese extortion gang. The assailant was convicted but the conviction was reversed at the prosecutor's request because "he had no prior criminal record in this country." The police and FBI repeatedly claimed that such attacks were unrelated and devoid of a political motive — despite VOECRN's communiqués claiming responsibility. In 1987, after a bombing that killed a Vietnamese-language publisher in Garden Grove, California, the FBI belatedly began investigating to determine whether "a pattern [of terrorism] is emerging."[41]

There is the strange case of Professor Edward Cooperman, an American, who was shot in his office at California State University, Fullerton. As founder of an organization advocating scientific cooperation with Vietnam, Cooperman had received death threats. Lam Van Minh, a Vietnamese émigré and Cooperman's former student, admitted witnessing the professor's death and was arrested. As he tells it, Cooperman produced a gun that accidentally discharged and killed him. Minh left in a panic, for some reason taking the gun with him. He then took a female friend to a movie, after which he returned to the office and placed the gun in Cooperman's hand. The office had the appearance of a struggle, which, Minh's attorney argued, resulted from the professor's attempts to get up after being left for dead. The prosecution introduced little to dispute Minh's improbable story. He was convicted of involuntary manslaughter, sentenced to three years and served one. Minh had been previously arrested for possession of stolen property, at which time police found guns in his car and home. His lawyer was procured by a spokesperson for a right-wing Vietnamese organization.[42]

In Chicago, after repeated death threats, Rudy Lozano, a Chicano union organizer and communist, who worked effectively to unite Latinos, African Americans, and Whites around working-class causes, was shot dead in his home by someone who came to his door on the pretense of asking for a drink of water and who stole nothing. According to family members, paramedics who arrived at the scene thought they could save Lozano's life, but police blocked them from getting near him, because "evidence might be destroyed."[43]

Other political murders or suspicious deaths in the United States include those of Manuel De Dios, a reporter and editor who frequently pointed the finger at drug dealers and money launderers; Alan Berg, a popular Denver talk-show host who engaged in impassioned arguments with anti-Semitic and racist callers and who was shot by members of a White supremist group; Don Bolles, who at the time of his murder was involved in an investigation of a far-reaching financial scandal said to implicate some of Arizona's most powerful political and business leaders; Karen Silkwood, who was investigating radiation safety negligence at Kerr-McGee corporation; Danny Casolaro, whose investigation of government and business corruption might have implicated high-ranking U.S. officials; David Nadel, a Berkeley, California, political activist and organizer, whose murderer is known to police and is living untouched at an identifiable location in Mexico; and Marine Colonel James Sabow at Marine Corps Air Service, El Toro (declared a "suicide" even though the back of his head was bashed), who threatened to blow the whistle on corrupt covert operators with links to drug trafficking. Four other specialists and contractors connected with the El Toro operation were all found dead under suspicious circumstances. None of these deaths has been properly investigated.[44]

Cozy with Right-Wing Violence

In contrast to the way they treat the left, federal agents have done little to discourage violent right-wing extremist groups and sometimes have supported their activities. In San Diego, the FBI financed a cryptofascist outfit called the Secret Army Organization, whose operations ranged from burglary and arson to kidnapping and attempted murder.[45] The Senate Intelligence Committee revealed that the FBI organized forty-one Ku Klux Klan chapters in North Carolina. Paid FBI informants in the Klan did nothing to stop Klan members from committing murder and other acts of violence. In some instances, as in the Greensboro (North Carolina) massacre of four members of the Communist Workers Party, they assisted the murderers by procuring weapons for them and directing them to the right location.[46]

From 1969 to 1972, U.S. Military Intelligence and the Chicago police Red squad jointly operated an organization called the Legion of Justice. Its members clubbed and maced protestors and antiwar demonstrators, broke into their headquarters, stole files, vandalized a progressive bookstore, and committed other criminal acts against those who did not adhere to the free-market dedications of the national security state.[47]

In contrast to the astronomical prison terms handed out to antiwar and anticapitalist dissidents, violent rightists usually get off lightly. Consider the ten members of the Vipers, an Arizona-based right-wing militia suspected of planning acts of violence against government buildings and charged with conspiracy to manufacture and possess destructive devices. They were given sentences ranging from one to nine years; some got probation and served no time at all.[48] The same Louisiana district court that sentenced civil rights activist Linda Evans to forty-five years sentenced Don Black, a KKK member who transported illegal weapons and attempted to set up a drug cartel, to three years. He was out in two.

In instances of right-wing violence against the left, police rarely manage to catch the perpetrators. When asked what they intended to do about the fifteen or so right-wing paramilitary terrorist camps within the United States, a Justice Department official said the camps did not appear to be in violation of any federal statute.[49] When two Chicano socialists were killed by bombs planted in their cars, the FBI made no arrests. When a powerful bomb wrecked the offices of several progressive and civil-liberties groups in New York, injuring three people, the police made only a perfunctory investigation. After a series of threats, an antinuclear organizer was shot dead in Houston and an assistant was seriously wounded; police came up with not a clue.[50]

When agents of the Philippine dictator Ferdinand Marcos conducted operations against Filipino dissidents in the United States, the FBI cooperated with them. One known FBI informant admitted to having witnessed the murder of two Filipino union leaders who were prominent in the anti-Marcos movement in the United States. The FBI refused to release hundreds of documents relating to the case.[51]

The FBI also cooperated with El Salvador's security forces, supplying them with the names of Salvadoran refugees who were about to be deported from the United States so that Salvadoran security forces could apprehend them upon their return, some to face certain torture and death. Salvadoran activists in this country have endured assaults, kidnappings, death threats, car smashings, and apartment break-ins. The police hardly bestirred themselves, making no serious attempt to investigate.[52]

The FBI was quick to make arrests when environmentalists Judi Bari and Darryl Cherney were seriously injured by a car bomb in 1990. They arrested Bari and Cherney, calling them "radical activists," charging that the bomb must have belonged to them. Bari, an outspoken advocate of nonviolence and effective organizer, was seriously injured in the blast. Never fully recovering her health, she died of cancer in 1997. The charges were eventually dropped for lack of evidence. The FBI named no other suspects. But Bari's organization has launched a countersuit charging that the FBI was itself involved in the bombing.[53] Across the United States, environmental activists experience violence and intimidation because of their political work. In many cases, law enforcement officials look the other way.[54]

That neo-Nazis, skinheads, and other rightist terrorists repeatedly have been able to commit acts of violence and even publicly claim responsibility without getting caught, means law enforcers have made little effort to monitor and deter their actions, unlike the way they deal with legal, peaceful groups on the left. Again, there is nothing inconsistent about this position. Leftist groups — no matter how nonviolent and lawful — challenge the capitalist system or some aspect of its privileges and abuses, while rightist groups — no matter how violent and unlawful — do the dirty work for that system. Thus there is a community of interest between the rightists and the law agencies and often a community of methods. However, when right-wing extremists engage in counterfeiting and bank robberies and plan attacks against federal targets instead of leftist targets, as with the Oklahoma City bombing of a federal building that claimed 168 lives, including 19 children, in 1995, then law enforcers move against them, albeit sometimes belatedly.

The National Security Autocracy

Within the government there exists what some have called "the national security state," consisting of the president, the secretaries of state and defense, the National Security Council, the Joint Chiefs of Staff, and numerous intelligence agencies. The national security state often operates like an unaccountable sovereign power of its own. Its primary function is to defeat political forces that seek alternatives to free-market globalization or that try to introduce any economically redistributive politics, even within the existing capitalist framework.

Congress has no exact idea how much it allocates for intelligence operations because the total figure is hidden in other budget items — in violation of Article 1, Section 9 of the Constitution, which reads: "No Money shall be drawn from the Treasury, but in Consequence of Appropriations made by Law; and a regular Statement and Account of the Receipts and Expenditures of all public Money shall be published from time to time." Attempts in Congress to require public disclosure of expenditures for intelligence agencies have been voted down. Some insiders do estimate that the entire federal budget for the "intelligence community" is more than total federal outlays for education.[55]

There is the Pentagon's Defense Intelligence Agency, which deals with military espionage and counterintelligence, and the State Department's Bureau of Intelligence and Research. Every echelon within the Pentagon — army, navy, and air force — and every regional command around the world has its own intelligence service.[56] The National Reconnaissance Office (NRO) tends to numerous satellites in orbit, eavesdropping on telephone conversations and diplomatic communications, and photographing potential targets for military action. The NRO reports to both the Central Intelligence Agency (CIA) and the secretary of defense, but not to Congress, which seems to know little about its operations. In the early 1990s, it was revealed that the NRO could not account for $4 billion in secret funds. Its top two NRO managers were ousted, but no one went to jail.[57]

The Pentagon's National Security Agency, created in 1952, breaks codes and monitors nearly all telephone calls and telegrams between the United States and other countries and a great deal of domestic telephone traffic. FBI agents may also be monitoring our email and using all sorts of new biometric and surveillance technologies to track people.[58]

While supposedly protecting us from foreign threats, the various intelligence agencies spend a good deal of time policing the U.S. public. They have admitted to maintaining surveillance on members of Congress, the White

House, the treasury and commerce departments, and on millions of private citizens. They plant operatives of their own throughout the other agencies of government. They plant stories in the U.S. media, secretly enlisting the co-operation of newspaper owners, media network bosses, and hundreds of journalists and editors. The CIA alone has subsidized the publication of hundreds of books and has owned outright more than two hundred wire services, newspapers, magazines, and book publishing complexes. The agency has recruited some five thousand academics from across the country as spies and researchers, secretly financing and censoring their work. CIA agents have infiltrated student, labor, and scientific groups, and have participated in academic conferences. The agency even conducts its own resident-scholar programs, and offers internships to undergraduate and graduate students.[59]

The CIA has infiltrated and subverted dissenting organizations in this country and abroad. In what was code-named "Operation CHAOS," CIA operatives subverted the National Conference for New Politics (NCNP), a progressive coalition that sought to develop a course independent of the major political parties. The NCNP never recovered from the CIA's divisive and disruptive attacks from within.[60]

The CIA admitted to carrying out 149 mind-control projects at over eighty institutions, sometimes on unsuspecting persons, and was responsible for the death of at least one government employee.[61] In violation of the National Security Act of 1947, which states that the CIA "shall have no police, subpoena, law enforcement or internal security functions," the agency has equipped and trained local police forces in the United States. Under an executive order by President Reagan, the CIA was authorized to conduct domestic surveillance and covert operations against U.S. citizens both in the United States and abroad and enter into secret contracts with corporations, academic institutions, other organizations and individuals for the provision of services and goods. The agency also has contacts with about four hundred foreign military and intelligence services in other nations, and recruits persons within those agencies.[62]

U.S. intelligence agencies do more than just gather intelligence; they have perpetrated terrible crimes. One could fill a whole book delineating the CIA's crimes against humanity, and whole books have been written. In countries like Guatemala, Greece, Brazil, Chile, Indonesia, Argentina, Zaire, and the Philippines, U.S. national security forces have used every means to overthrow populist or democratically elected governments, and install reactionary regimes that were totally accommodating to U.S. corporate interests. What a 1968 State Department memorandum had to say about Guatemala could apply to any number of places, namely that the government used indiscriminate "counter-terror" to combat insurgency. "People are killed or disappear on the basis of simple accusations. . . . Interrogations are brutal, torture is used and bodies are mutilated. We [the U.S. government] have condoned counter-terror. . . . We encouraged the Guatemalan Army to do these things."[63]

Countries that achieved popular revolutions, such as Nicaragua, Mozambique, and Angola, promptly had their economies and peoples devastated by the murderous assaults of U.S.-supported mercenary armies. The CIA has disrupted and stolen elections abroad and waged massive disinformation campaigns. It has bribed officials, incited ethnic enmities, and funded and assisted secret armies, paramilitary forces, saboteurs, torture teams, and death squads. It has pursued destabilization and assassination campaigns against labor unions, and peasant, religious, and student organizations in numerous nations.[64] Consider a few examples:

- Over thirty years after the fact, the *New York Times* acknowledged that "Marxist-Leninist" Cheddi Jagan, who led Guyana, a small South American country, to independence and was its first popularly elected prime minister, had been a victim of a CIA "destabilization campaign" that included disinformation, sabotage, and inciting labor unrest and race riots.[65]
- The Intelligence Oversight Board, a presidential panel, charged the CIA with knowingly hiring a number of Guatemalan military officers "suspected of political assassinations, extrajudicial killings, kidnapping and torture."[66]

- A fourteen-month investigation of Honduras by the *Baltimore Sun* revealed that "hundreds of citizens were kidnapped, tortured and killed in the 1980s by a secret army unit trained and supported by the Central Intelligence Agency."[67]
- As of 2000, the CIA continued to supply right-wing rebels in Angola with arms and supplies to pursue their war of attrition after their leader Jonas Savimbi lost the election, a war that has lasted twenty-five years and taken over two million lives. All the while the agency denied to congressional committees that arms were being shipped to the Angolan rebels.[68]
- The former leader of Haiti's most feared right-wing paramilitary group, FRAPH, admitted that he was a paid agent of the CIA. FRAPH has been charged with murdering thousands of democratic activists in Haiti. Another Haitian junta leader, trained by the U.S. military and connected to a CIA-supported security agency in Haiti, Joseph Michel François, supervised death squads and vigilante gangs; he was charged with smuggling tons of cocaine into the United States. A third Haitian leader, Emmanuel Constant, founder of FRAPH and "accused of supervising murders, rapes and torture of supporters of democracy," was released from U.S. custody instead of being deported back to Haiti to face charges, a decision "made for reasons that were primarily political not legal."[69]
- As of late 2000, the new and fragile democracy in Haiti was being destabilized through a wave of murders and robberies by shadowy right-wing death squads. U.S. officials refuse to release some 160,000 government documents they spirited from Haiti to Washington in 1994, containing names and information about the death squads.[70]
- A federal judge ordered a retired Guatemalan general Héctor Gramajo to pay $47.5 million to an American nun who was raped and tortured by troops under his command. Gramajo, who led a scorched-earth military campaign that killed tens of thousands of villagers, claimed close contacts with the CIA when he was on active duty.[71]
- CIA training manuals unearthed by a Freedom of Information lawsuit revealed that the agency taught methods of torture to Central American and other Third World military, such as electric shock; water torture; sleep, food, and sensory deprivation; and psychological torture such as forcing victims to witness the torture of loved ones, including children. Other CIA manuals taught methods of assassination.[72]

Torture has become an American export. In 1991–1993, according to Amnesty International, the U.S. Commerce Department issued over 350 export licenses worth more than $27 million for thumb-screws, leg-irons, shackles, stun guns, and electroshock instruments, "specifically designed implements of torture," along with police equipment, much of it to countries with dismal human rights records.[73]

Released CIA documents disclosed that the agency maintained a clandestine biological warfare program targeting the populations and crops of a number of countries, including North Korea, Vietnam, Laos, Panama, and Cuba. The agency deployed weather modification technology to desecrate Cuba's sugar crops, and a virus that caused African swine fever, the first such infection in the Americas, forcing the slaughter of 500,000 pigs in Cuba to prevent a widespread epidemic among the human population. The CIA is also charged with causing an epidemic of dengue hemorrhagic fever, transmitted by mosquitoes, afflicting some 300,000 people, killing 57 Cuban adults and 101 children, the first major epidemic of dengue in the Western Hemisphere. After a U.S. crop duster plane intruded upon Cuban air space and repeatedly sprayed areas of Matanzas province, an infestation of Thrips palmi karay, an insect never before found in Cuba, inflicted tremendous damage to crops in Matanzas. In 1997, Cuba presented a report to the United Nations charging Washington with "biological aggression."[74]

It has been recently revealed that the U.S. government granted immunity to scientists of the notorious Japanese biological warfare outfit, Unit 731. Part of the Japanese military during World War II, Unit 731 had developed methods of creating plagues, and had conducted frightful human experiments in China and elsewhere, including vivisections (with and without anesthesia). Evidence indicates that the U.S. military very likely used Unit 731 scientists during the Korean War (1950–1953) to create a hemorrhagic-fever epidemic, a disease previously unknown in Korea. Both the North Korean and Chinese governments lodged charges of bacteriological warfare against Washington. The U.S. also used Unit 731 research on dioxin for its defoliation campaign during the Vietnam War.[75]

CIA: Capitalism's International Army or Cocaine Import Agency?

After World War II, U.S. intelligence agencies put thousands of Nazi war criminals and their collaborators on the U.S. payroll, utilizing them in repressive operations against the left in Latin America and elsewhere.[76] A network of Eastern European emigrés, anti-Semites, and former Nazi collaborators found a home in the "ethnic outreach" program of the Republican party.[77] (President Bush had to get rid of some of them when it finally made the national media during the 1992 presidential campaign.) In various Western European countries throughout the 1970s and 1980s, the CIA helped maintain secret paramilitary units to carry out acts of terrorism against anticapitalist organizations.[78] The House Intelligence Committee reported that "several hundred times a day" CIA officers "engage in highly illegal activities" overseas that endanger the freedom and lives of the participating foreign nationals and sometimes even the undercover CIA officer.[79]

In 1978, syndicated columnist Jack Anderson revealed that the CIA had recruited mafia hit men for "international murder missions," and that "for over twenty years, the Justice Department has been winking at crimes committed by employees of the Central Intelligence Agency. Even serious crimes and felonies unrelated to official duties have been ignored."[80] The CIA supplied arms and money to the Italian and Corsican mafias to beat and murder members of communist-led dockworkers' unions in Italy and France in 1947 and 1950. After these unions were broken, the mobsters were given a freer hand transporting tons of heroin from Asia to Western Europe and North America. The CIA buttressed anticommunist druglords in Southeast Asia and Afghanistan, whose opium production and distribution increased tenfold, assisted by the agency itself.[81]

CIA involvement in Central America contributed to the U.S. cocaine epidemic of the 1980s. CIA planes transported guns and supplies down to right-wing mercenary troops in Nicaragua, the "contras," and procapitalist political and military leaders in other Latin countries; the planes then were reloaded with cocaine for the return trip to the United States.[82] The CIA itself admits having known and done nothing about narcotic shipments to inner city populations in this country. Even the usually compliant *New York Times* reported that a CIA "anti-drug unit" was involved in cocaine trafficking at that time.[83] Drug infestation can serve as a useful social control mechanism. National security authorities prefer to have young African-American and Latino males shooting themselves up with needles and each other with guns rather than organizing militant revolutionary groups as in the 1960s.

A former chief of an elite DEA unit observed: "In my 30-year history in the Drug Enforcement Administration and related agencies, the major targets of my investigations almost invariably turned out to be working for the CIA."[84] In November 1993, former director of the DEA Robert Bonner and DEA agent Anabel Grim appeared on a CBS *60 Minutes* segment entitled "The CIA's Cocaine," and detailed the agency's massive theft of cocaine from DEA warehouses. The cocaine was later sold on U.S. streets. Meanwhile, DEA efforts at thwarting the drug outflow from Burma have been stymied by the CIA and State Department, who seem to be in a cozy relationship with Burma's viciously repressive but corporation-loving, drug-running, military dictatorship.[85]

CIA operatives participated with mafia associates and business and political leaders to profit from the multibillion-dollar savings-and-loan swindles. Monies gained from such deals, along with drug money laundered through various banks and other financial institutions, were illegally used to finance CIA covert activities.[86]

A mountain of evidence exists suggesting that elements of the intelligence community, assisted by certain mobsters, were involved in the assassination of President John Kennedy in 1963 and in the subsequent massive cover-up. Kennedy was considered a dangerous liability by the intelligence community because of what were perceived as his "liberal" foreign and domestic policies, including his unwillingness to pursue an all-out ground war in Indochina, and his determination to bring the intelligence community under firm executive control.[87]

In 1982, at the urging of the Reagan administration, Congress passed a law that made it a crime to publish any information that might lead to the disclosure of the identities of present or former intelligence agents and informers, even if the information came from already published sources. Under the law, some journalistic exposés of illegal covert activities themselves became illegal.

It has been argued that a strong intelligence system is needed to gather the information needed by policymakers. But the CIA and other agencies have been unlawfully involved in covert actions that go beyond intelligence gathering: economic and military sabotage, disinformation campaigns directed against the U.S. public itself, drug trafficking, mercenary wars, assassinations, and other terrorist acts.

With the overthrow of the Soviet Union and other communist countries, the spies and militarists of the national security state faced the threat of a lack of threats. How would they justify their enormous size and global crimes if there were no adversaries menacing us? New ones had to be conjured: "rogue nations," "international terrorists," "Islamic extremists," and the like, all of whom apparently just suddenly emerged to pounce upon the United States. Such alarmist stories did little to protect our national security but much to protect the budgets of the national security establishment, and much to keep the repressive global apparatus intact. In addition, the CIA and National Security Agency got themselves an additional role: they began spying on foreign firms, intercepting private communications and gleaning insider information in order to help U.S. corporations compete in the global market. Now the agency works even more directly on behalf of the transnational corporations.[88]

Watergate and Iran-Contra

In June 1972, a group of ex-CIA agents were caught breaking into the Democratic party headquarters in the Watergate building in Washington, D.C. The burglary was part of an extensive campaign directed by members of President Nixon's White House staff, involving electoral sabotage, wiretapping, theft of private records, and illegal use of campaign funds. It was subsequently revealed that Nixon himself was involved in the Watergate skulduggery and its related cover-up activities. Facing impeachment, he resigned from office. Vice-President Gerald Ford succeeded to the presidency and promptly pardoned Nixon for all crimes relating to Watergate, including any that might come to light at some future time. Members of the administration found guilty in the Watergate affair were given relatively light sentences. Nixon never served a day in jail and retired on his presidential pension. Congress and the press treated Watergate as a deviant instance of government lawlessness instead of another of many illicit actions by presidents and their national security operatives.

In 1986, another scandal, known as "Iran-contra," rocked the White House. It was discovered that the Reagan administration had been selling millions of dollars worth of arms to Iran, a country it repeatedly accused of supporting terrorism. As part of a covert operation to bypass Congress, the law, and the Constitution, the funds from these secret sales were funneled to the Nicaraguan mercenaries known as the "contras." Funds also may have been diverted to pay for the television campaign expenses of Republican candidates in the 1986 election. President Reagan admitted full knowledge of the arms sales, but claimed that he had no idea what happened to the money. He asked the public to believe that these operations were conducted by subordinates, including his own National Security Advisor, without being cleared with him. In subsequent statements, his subordinates said that Reagan had played an active role in the entire Iran-contra affair.[89]

Despite abundant evidence of involvement by the White House, the National Security Council, and the CIA, virtually no high officials were undone, and no reforms to rein in secret operations were implemented. A special prosecutor did manage to convict eleven individuals of perjury, destroying government documents, obstructing justice, illegally diverting funds, or other such crimes, nine of whom were given probation and light fines, and only one went to jail for a short spell. Some of the people involved, such as former CIA director and then–Vice President George Bush, were never indicted despite testimony directly implicating them. Once Bush became president in 1989, he pardoned key defendants, including Defense Secretary Caspar Weinberger, before he was to stand trial.[90]

The congressional investigation of this affair produced nothing tangible, except to demonstrate that Congress could not and would not control the intelligence community. It left untouched serious allegations of government-sanctioned drug-running involving White House operatives and the contras.[91]

In sum, under the guise of "fighting communism" or "protecting U.S. interests," or "defending democracy," the purveyors of state power have committed horrendous crimes against the people in this and other countries, violating human rights and the Constitution in order to make the world safe for privilege and profit. The ancient question of political philosophy, *quis custodiet ipsos custodes?* (who guards the guardians?), remains with us. The national security state continues to operate like a state within the state, a law unto itself, though it has come under increasing attack from those who care about democratic accountability.

Notes

1. David Burnham, *A Law Unto Itself: The IRS and the Abuse of Power* (New York: Vintage, 1989), 255–90.

2. Margaret Spillance, "Fo's Last Laugh — II," *Nation*, November 3, 1997.

3. Merrily Weisbord, *The Strangest Dream: Canadian Communists, the Spy Trials, and the Cold War* (Toronto: Lester and Orpen Dennys, 1983), 7.

4. *Bias and Restrictionism Towards Central American Asylum Seekers in North America* (Washington, D.C.: United States Committee for Refugees, 1988).

5. *Lloyd Corporation v. Tanner* (1972).

6. Ellen Schrecker, *Many Are the Crimes: McCarthyism in America* (Princeton, N.J.: Princeton University Press, 1999); Stanley Kutler, *The American Inquisition* (New York: Hill & Wang, 1982); Richard Curry (ed.), *Freedom at Risk: Secrecy, Censorship and Repression in the 1980s* (Philadelphia: Temple University Press, 1988).

7. *New York Times*, August 11, 1996.

8. Philip Colangelo, "The Secret FISA Court," *CovertAction Quarterly*, Summer 1995.

9. James Kirkpatrick Davis, *Assault on the Left: The FBI and the Sixties Antiwar Movement* (New York: Praeger, 1997). On the FBI's longstanding battle against integration, see James Dickerson, *Dixie's Dirty Secret* (Armonk, N.Y.: M. E. Sharpe, 1998); and Kenneth O'Reilly, *Racial Matters: The FBI's Secret File on Black America, 1960–1972* (New York: Free Press, 1989).

10. Quoted in Frank Donner, "The Theory and Practice of American Political Intelligence," *New York Review of Books*, April 22, 1971, 28; also Frank Donner, *The Age of Surveillance* (New York: Knopf, 1980).

11. Mike Rothmiller and Ivan Goldman, *L.A. Secret Police* (New York: Pocket, 1992); Frank Donner, *Protectors of Privilege: Red Squads and Police Repression in Urban America* (Berkeley: University of California Press, 1991).

12. Nelson Blackstock, *COINTELPRO* (New York: Pathfinder, 1988); Ward Churchill and Jim Vander Wall, *COINTELPRO Papers: Documents from the FBI's Secret Wars against Dissent in the United States* (Boston: South End, 1990); M. Wesley Swearingen, *FBI Secrets: An Agent's Exposé* (Boston: South End, 1995).

13. *New York Times*, November 24, 1974.

14. Swearingen, *FBI Secrets*, 105–6.

15. Brian Glick, *War at Home* (Boston: South End, 1989).

16. Anthony Summers, *Official and Confidential: The Secret Life of J. Edgar Hoover* (New York: Putnam, 1993); Herbert Mitgang, *Dangerous Dossiers* (New York: Donald Fine, 1988); Hank Messick, *John Edgar Hoover: A Critical Examination of the Director and of the Continuing Alliance between Crime, Business, and Politics* (New York: David McKay, 1972); Athan Theoharis and John Stuart Cox, *The Boss: J. Edgar Hoover and the Great American Inquisition* (Philadelphia: Temple University Press, 1988); Michael Milan, *The Squad: The Government's Secret Alliance with Organized Crime* (New York: Shapolsky, 1989).

17. Heather Rhoads, "FBI Ups Psychological Warfare against Activists," *Guardian*, August 28, 1991; Ross Gelbspan, *Break-ins, Death Threats, and the FBI* (Boston: South End, 1991).

18. Robert J. Goldstein, *Political Repression in Modern America, from 1870 to the Present* (Boston: Schenkman/Hall, 1978); Schrecker, *Many Are the Crimes*; David Caute, *The Great Fear: The Anti-Communist Purge under Truman and Eisenhower* (New York: Simon & Schuster, 1978).

19. Kenneth Heineman, *Campus Wars: The Peace Movement at American State Universities in the Vietnam Era* (New York: NYU Press, 1993); American Civil Liberties Report edited by Norman Dorsen, *Our Endangered Rights* (New York: Pantheon, 1984); also Michael Parenti, "Struggles in Academe: A Personal Account," in Parenti, *Dirty Truths* (San Francisco: City Lights, 1997).

20. William Blum, "A Day in the Life of a Free Country," unpublished ms., January 1998.

21. Theodore Becker and Vernon Murray (eds.), *Government Lawlessness in America* (New York: Oxford University Press, 1971), 153–57.

22. *Guardian*, September 24, 1975; Shuford Defense Committee Newsletter, January 1978.

23. *Guardian*, August 3, 1988.

24. John Wojcik, "The Incredible Frameup of Mayor Eddie Carthan," *World Magazine*, May 6, 1982.

25. News release, National People's Democratic Uhuru Movement, Chicago, 1997.

26. *United States of America — Rights for All*, Amnesty International, October 1998.

27. "Political Prisoners in the U.S.," *Prison Focus*, Fall 1997/Winter 1998; *Los Angeles Times*, April 26, 2000; Churchill and Wall, *Agents of Repression*.

28. *Philadelphia Inquirer*, May 23, 1996; "The Case for a New Trial," Equal Justice USA, Quixote Center, n.d.; also <http://www.mumia.org>.

29. Newsletter, Leonard Peltier Defense Committee, February 1999; *Nonviolent Activist*, March/April 1996.

30. For a partial listing, see *Can't Jail the Spirit: Political Prisoners in the U.S.* (Chicago: Editorial El Coqui, c. 1990).

31. *Guardian*, May 30, 1990.

32. Sandra Baird and Louise Andrews, "Torture — American Style," *Toward Freedom*, March/April 1998; Legal Services for Prisoners with Children newsletter, San Francisco, January 1999; *Can't Jail the Spirit*, 170–71; William Reuben and Carlos Norman, "The Women of Lexington Prison," *Nation*, June 27, 1987.

33. Mary O'Melveny, "Lexington Prison High Security Unit," *CovertAction Information Bulletin*, Winter 1989; Baird and Andrews, "Torture — American Style."

34. On the World Trade Organization, see Chapter 11.

35. <http://www.cybernaute.com/earthconcert2000/PressCoverUP.htm>; and Barbara Jean Hope, "Massive Arrests from Peaceful GOP Demos," *People's Weekly World*, August 12, 2000.

36. <http://www.indgmedia.org>, April 18, 2000; and <http://www.a16.org/a16_notebook.cfm>, April 25, 2000.

37. Jack Nelson and Jack Bass, *The Orangeburg Massacre* (New York: World, 1969); I. F. Stone, "Fabricated Evidence in the Kent State Killings," *New York Review of Books*, December 3, 1970; Tim Spofford, *Lynch Street: The May 1970 Slayings at Jackson State College* (Kent, Ohio: Kent State University Press, 1988).

38. Churchill and Wall, *Agents of Repression*; Peter Mathiessen, *In the Spirit of Crazy Horse* (New York: Viking, 1983).

39. Their names were Jean-Claude Olivier, Fritz Dor, and Dona St. Plite: *Silenced by Death: Journalists Killed in the United States (1976–1993)* (New York: Committee to Protect Journalists, 1993); *New York Times*, October 26, 1993.

40. Jeff Stein, "Inside Omega 7," *Village Voice*, March 10, 1980; Peter Katel, "A Rash of Media Murders," *Newsweek*, July 5, 1993; *Cuba Update*, Center for Cuban Studies, New York, October 1980.

41. Steve Grossman, "Vietnamese Death Squads in America?" *Asia Insights*, Asia Resource Center, Summer 1986; and Steve Grossman, "Vietnamese Death Squads: Is This the End?" *Indochina Newsletter*, Asia Resource Center, May/June 1988.

42. Grossman, "Vietnamese Death Squads in America."

43. *Daily World*, June 10, 1983.

44. Ace Hayes "Col. Sabow Murder and Cover-up," *Portland Free Press,* July/October 1996.

45. *San Francisco Examiner,* January 11, 1976; Donner, *The Age of Surveillance,* 444–45.

46. *New York Times,* May 12, 1985; Michael Parenti and Carolyn Kazdin, "The Untold Story of the Greensboro Massacre," *Monthly Review,* November 1981.

47. Ken Lawrence, "Klansmen, Nazis, and Skinheads," *CovertAction Information Bulletin,* Winter 1989.

48. *Los Angeles Times,* November 29, 1997.

49. James Ridgeway, "Looney Tune Terrorists," *Village Voice,* July 23, 1985.

50. *Guardian,* February 4, 1981; *New Age,* July 1979.

51. *Guardian,* June 14, 1989.

52. Vince Bielski, Cindy Forster, and Dennis Bernstein, "The Death Squads Hit Home," *Progressive,* October 1987.

53. "COINTELPRO Tactics Target Environmentalists," newsletter of Redwood Summer Justice Project, n.d. <http://www.monitor.net/-bari>; "Who Bombed Judi Bari?" newsletter Redwood Summer Justice Project, April 1997, and October and November 1997 updates; Ward Churchill, "The FBI Targets Judi Bari," *CovertAction Quarterly,* Winter 1993–94.

54. National Radio Project, May 2000: <http://www.radioproject.org>.

55. Russ Baker, "CIA Out of Control," *Utne Reader,* January/February 1992.

56. *Final Report of the Select Committee to Study Governmental Operations with Respect to Intelligence Activities,* Senate Report 755, 94th Congress, 2nd Session, 1976; James Bamford, *The Puzzle Palace: A Report on America's Most Secret Agency* (Boston: Houghton Mifflin, 1982); *Washington Post,* October 9, 1990.

57. David Wise, "The Spies Who Lost $4 Billion," *George,* October 1998; *New York Times,* February 27, 1996.

58. David Banisar, "Big Brother Goes High-Tech," *CovertAction Quarterly,* Spring 1996; John Dillon, "Are the Feds Sniffing Your Re-mail?" *CovertAction Quarterly,* Summer 1996.

59. Angus Mackenzie, *Secrets: The CIA's War at Home* (Berkeley: University of California Press, 1997); Stuart Loory, "The CIA's Use of the Press," *Columbia Journalism Review,* September/October 1974, 9–18; Robert Witanek, "Students, Scholars and Spies: The CIA on Campus," *CovertAction Information Bulletin,* Winter 1989; Sigmund Diamond, *Compromised Campus: The Collaboration of Universities with the Intelligence Community* (New York: Oxford University Press, 1992).

60. William Pepper, *Orders to Kill* (New York: Carroll & Graff, 1995), 9.

61. John Marks, *The Search for the Manchurian Candidate* (New York: Times Books, 1979); *First Principles,* September 1977.

62. *New York Times,* December 5, 1981.

63. Memorandum quoted in McGowan, *Derailing Democracy,* 80.

64. William Blum, *Rogue State* (Monroe, Maine: Common Courage, 2000); John Pike; "Uncloaked Daggers," *CovertAction Quarterly,* Winter 1994–95; Ralph McGehee, *Deadly Deceits* (Melbourne and New York: Ocean, 1999); "Training Abusive Militaries," editorial, *New York Times,* August 31, 1998; David Corn, "Tortured Logic from Langley's Spies (Again)," *Nation,* November 10, 1997; Lisa Haugaard, "Textbook Repression: US Training Manuals Declassified," *CovertAction Quarterly,* Summer 1997.

65. *New York Times,* March 7, 1997. The *Times* published these revelations in Jagan's obituary.

66. *New York Times,* June 29, 1996.

67. *Baltimore Sun,* June 11–18, 1995.

68. Scott Armstrong and Jeff Nason, "Company Man," *Mother Jones,* October 1988.

69. *New York Times,* December 3, 1995; June 22, 1996; and March 8, 1997.

70. <http://www.iacenter.org>, September 2000.

71. *New York Times,* April 13, 1995.

72. *Baltimore Sun,* January 27, 1997; *Vista,* Radio for Peace International, July 1977; "CIA Advocates Assassinations," *Guatemala,* Bulletin of the Guatemala Human Rights Commission/USA, Spring–Summer 1997.

73. *United States of America — Rights for All,* Amnesty International, October 1998.

74. *Washington Post,* September 16, 1977; William Schaap, "The 1981 Cuba Dengue Epidemic," *CovertAction Information Bulletin,* Summer 1982; Center for Disease Control, <http://www.cdc.gov/ncidod/dvbid/dengue.htm>; "History of CIA Biological Warfare Against Cuba, 1962–1997," *Granma International,* November 23, 1997. William Blum summarizes much of this material in his *Rogue State,* 103–12.

75. Hal Gold, *Unit 731 Testimony* (Tokyo: Yen, 1996), 125–26, 173; and Sheldon Harris, *Factories of Death* (London and New York: Routledge, 1994).

76. Howard Blum, *Wanted: The Search for Nazis in America* (New York: Quadrangle, 1977); Christopher Simpson, *Blowback: America's Recruitment of Nazis and Its Effects on the Cold War* (New York: Weidenfeld & Nicolson, 1988).

77. Russ Bellant, *Old Nazis, the New Right and the Reagan Administration* (Cambridge, Mass.: Political Research Associates, 1988).

78. Susan Lucas's report in *Peacework,* March 1995.

79. House Intelligence Committee reported in *Nation,* May 20, 1996.

80. *Washington Post,* January 4, 1978.

81. Alfred McCoy, *The Politics of Heroin* (Brooklyn, N.Y.: Lawrence Hill, 1991), passim; William Blum, *Killing Hope: U.S. Military and CIA Interventions since World War II* (Monroe, Maine: Common Courage, 1995), 351; Henrick Kruger, *The Great Heroin Coup* (Boston: South End, 1980).

82. Senate Committee on Foreign Relations, Subcommittee on Terrorism, Narcotics, and International Operations, report, *Drugs, Law Enforcement and Foreign Policy* (Washington, D.C.: U.S. Government Printing Office, 1989); McCoy, *The Politics of Heroin,* 61–62; Leslie Cockburn, *Out of Control* (New York: Atlantic Monthly Press, 1987); Peter Dale Scott and Jonathan Marshall, *Cocaine Politics* (Berkeley: University of California Press, 1991).

83. Tim Weiner, "Anti-Drug Unit of CIA Sent Ton of Cocaine to U.S. in 1990," *New York Times,* November 20, 1993; David Corn, "CIA Clears Self of Drug Charge," *Nation,* May 9, 1998; and Walter Pincus's report in *Washington Post,* November 4, 1998; "CIA Didn't Just Say No," *Nation,* November 30, 1998; Jeffrey St. Clair et al., *White-Out: The CIA, Drugs and the Press* (London and New York: Verso, 1998).

84. Dennis Dayle, quoted in Scott and Marshall, *Cocaine Politics,* x–xi.

85. Dennis Bernstein and Leslie Kean, "People of the Opiate: Burma's Dictatorship of Drugs," *Nation,* December 16, 1996.

86. Pete Brewton, *The Mafia, CIA & George Bush* (New York: Shapolsky, 1992); Rebecca Sims, "The CIA and Financial Institutions," *CovertAction Information Bulletin,* Fall 1990; Jack Colhoun, "BCCI: The Bank of the CIA," *CovertAction Quarterly,* Spring 1993.

87. Here is a small sampling of the vast research on the JFK assassination: Jim Marris, *Crossfire* (New York: Carroll & Graf, 1989); Sylvia Meagher, *Accessories after the Fact* (New York: Vintage, 1992); Jim Garrison, *On the Trail of Assassins* (New York: Sheridan Square, 1988); James Di Eugenio, *Destiny Betrayed* (New York: Sheridan Square, 1992); Michael Kurt, *Crime of the Century* (Knoxville: University of Tennessee Press, 1982); Mark Lane, *Rush to Judgment* (New York: Holt, Rinehart & Winston, 1966); Mark Lane, *Plausible Denial* (New York: Thunder's Mouth, 1991); James Fetzer (ed.), *Murder in Dealey Plaza* (Chicago: Catfeet, 2000).

88. Pratap Chatterjee, "$pying for Uncle $am," *CovertAction Quarterly,* Winter 1995–96; London *Independent,* July 2, 2000.

89. Jonathan Marshall, Peter Dale Scott, and Jane Hunter, *The Iran-Contra Connection* (Boston: South End, 1988); *Report of the Congressional Committee Investigating the Iran-Contra Affair* (Washington, D.C.: Government Printing Office, 1987).

90. Lawrence Walsh, *Firewall: The Iran-Contra Conspiracy and Cover-Up* (New York: Norton, 1997).

91. Marshall, Scott, and Hunter, *The Iran-Contra Connection,* 134–39 and passim; Baker, "CIA Out of Control," 81; Seymour Hersh, "The Iran-Contra Committees: Did They Protect Reagan?" *New York Times Magazine,* April 29, 1990.

11

Who Governs?
Elites, Labor, and
Globalization

No politico-economic system automatically maintains and re-produces itself. Constant effort must be made to fortify the existing hegemonic order. Those who control the wealth of this society, the owning class, have an influence over political life far in excess of their number. They have the power to influence policy through the control of jobs and withholding of investments. They directly influence the electoral process with their lavish campaign contributions. And they own or exercise trusteeship over social and educational institutions, foundations, think tanks, publications, and mass media, thereby greatly influencing society's ideological output, its values, and its information flow. In addition, the stewards of corporate capitalism make it their business to occupy the more important public offices or see that "reliable" persons loyal to them do so.

The Ruling Class

Not all wealthy persons are engaged in ruling; in fact most prefer to concentrate on other pursuits. The ruling class, or plutocracy, consists largely of the politically active members of the owning class. From the beginning of the Republic to modern times, the top leadership positions — including the presidency, vice-presidency, the cabinet, and Supreme Court — have rested predominantly in the hands of White males from affluent families, with most of the remainder being of upper-middle class origins (moderately successful business people, commercial farmers, and professionals). Legend has it that many U.S. presidents rose from humble origins. In fact, almost all came from families of a higher socioeconomic status than about 90 percent of the U.S. population.[1]

Most national policymakers have been drawn from the directorships of big corporations, prominent law firms, Wall Street banks, and, less frequently, from the military, elite universities, think tanks, foundations, and the scientific establishment. More than a third went to elite, Ivy League schools.[2] They carry into public life many of the class interests and values that shape their business careers. However, the crucial factor is not the class origin of leaders but the class interest they serve. A rich person who manifests markedly progressive leanings is not likely to be invited into a position of power. Conversely, persons from relatively modest background such as presidents Lyndon Johnson, Ronald Reagan, Richard Nixon, and Bill Clinton rise to the top by showing themselves to be faithful guardians of the upper circles. The question then is not only who governs, but whose interests and whose agenda are served by who governs; who benefits and who does not, questions that are the central focus of this book.

Governmental and business elites are linked by financial and social ties. Many go to the same schools, work in the same companies, intermarry, and vacation together. For almost a century, the top politco-economic elites have gathered every summer at Bohemian Grove, a luxurious male-only retreat in a California redwood forest, owned by the Bohemian Club of San Francisco. The guest list includes every Republican U.S. president and some Democratic ones, many top White House officials, and directors and CEOs of large corporate and financial institutions. Elites also meet at the Knickerbocker Club in New York and various other well-served sites.[3] These gatherings serve as a way of exchanging information, coordinating efforts, deciding what candidates to support for what openings in public life, what policies to pursue at home and abroad, how to roll back popular forces and increase profit margins, and how to manipulate money supplies, markets, and public policies. When powerful people confabulate and collude, they become even more powerful.

Policy advisory groups, with their interlocking network of corporate and political notables, play an unofficial but influential role in recruiting suitable decision makers for leadership posts during both Democratic and Republican administrations. One of the more prominent of these is the Council on Foreign Relations (CFR), started in 1918 and consisting primarily of prominent individuals drawn from finance, industry, and government. The CFR has some 1,450 members, almost half of whom come from families of inherited wealth and are listed in the *Social Register*. Over 60 percent are corporate lawyers, executives, or bankers — including representatives from the Rockefeller, Morgan, and DuPont groups. The private companies that have had the most CFR members are Morgan Guaranty Trust, Chase Manhattan

Bank, Citibank, and IBM. In recent decades, CFR members have included U.S. presidents, secretaries of state and defense and other White House cabinet members and their top officers, members of the Joint Chiefs of Staff, CIA directors, federal judges, Federal Reserve officers, scores of U.S. ambassadors, key members of Congress, executives and directors of almost all the major banks and leading corporations, numerous college and university presidents, and publishers, editors, and opinion makers from every major news organization in the United States.[4] Many of the more influential CFR members have done "revolving door" service in government and business. So, at one time or another John McCone, for instance, was a director of Standard Oil of California, ITT, and other large corporations, and alternately undersecretary of the air force, deputy to the secretary of defense, chair of the Atomic Energy Commission, and director of the CIA.

The Council on Foreign Relations has been a major force in creating the Marshall Plan, the International Monetary Fund, and the World Bank. It advocated a strategic nuclear arsenal, U.S. global interventionism after World War II, military action in Guatemala, military escalation in South Vietnam, and eventual diplomatic relations with China. In 1980, the CFR strongly recommended a sharp rise in military spending and a harder line toward the Soviets. All these positions were eventually adopted by whomever occupied the White House.[5]

Some CFR members also belong to the Trilateral Commission, an assemblage of political and business leaders from the major industrial countries, initiated by David Rockefeller for the purpose of coordinating and protecting international capitalism in a changing world. Another ruling-class organization is the Committee for Economic Development (CED), composed of about two hundred U.S. business leaders. The CED produces policy statements on a range of domestic and international issues — a number of which bear a striking similarity to government policies that are subsequently enacted. There is the Business Council, composed of representatives from such companies as Morgan Guaranty Trust, General Electric, and General Motors. Its 154 members listed in *Who's Who in America* together have held 730 directorships in 435 banks and corporations, as well as 49 foundation trusteeships and 125 trusteeships with 84 universities.[6]

The influence of these various ruling-class organizations inheres in the enormous economic power they wield, and in their capacity — unique among social groups in this country — to fill top government posts with persons directly from their corporate ranks or other persons recruited to serve their interests. President Ford appointed fourteen CFR members to positions in his administration. Seventeen top members of the Carter administration were Trilateralists, including President Carter himself and Vice-President Mondale. President Reagan's administrators included chief executives of Wall Street investment houses and directors of New York banks; at least a dozen of whom were CFR members, as were thirty-one top advisors. Most of President George H. Bush's cabinet consisted of corporate leaders who were also CFR members and some Trilateralists; Bush himself was a former Trilateralist.[7]

President Clinton's administration offered more gender and racial variety than usually found but not much class diversity. Clinton's top administrators included at least nine millionaires drawn from corporate America; many were CFR members. Clinton's first secretary of the treasury, Lloyd Bentsen, was a member of the Bilderberg Conference, an international organization that regularly brings together state leaders, financiers, military commanders, and prominent politicians from around the world. While still governor of Arkansas, Clinton himself was a member of the Council on Foreign Relations, the Trilateral Commission, and the Bilderberg Conference, having attended the latter in 1991 with David Rockefeller.[8]

How Clinton emerged as a presidential candidate itself reveals how the higher echelons of business and politics interact. At a private meeting in New York, in June 1991, top Wall Street executives, mostly linked to the Democratic party, held a series of meetings with presidential aspirants in what one organizer called "an elegant cattle show." They questioned Governor Bill Clinton of Arkansas, who was "impressing the executives with his willingness to embrace free trade and free markets."[9] Clinton became their candidate and in short order was declared by the corporate-owned media as being the "front-runner" for the Democratic nomination for president.

Ideological dominance is also fortified by conservative think tanks such as the Heritage Foundation, the American Enterprise Institute, and Hudson Institute, funded by right-wing foundations such as Coors, Olin, Scaife, and Smith Richardson to produce studies showing that America's main ailment is oppressive government regulations and bureaucracy, and the cure is laissez-faire and lower taxes for business. Richly funded right-wingers have been able to recruit and train cadres of ideologically committed writers and publicists who infiltrate government agencies, congressional and lobbying staffs, and news agencies, issuing a steady supply of materials to advance the corporate free-trade, free-market agenda.[10]

Labor Besieged

Some political science textbooks juxtapose "Big Labor" with Big Business, thereby leaving the impression that political power is pluralistically distributed among countervailing forces. In reality, government has historically been friendly to business and hostile to labor. Historically, the capitalist state's raison d'être is to secure the interests of the wealthy propertied class. State security agencies such as the Federal Bureau of Investigation (FBI) have a history of spying on unions, sometimes in cooperation with management.[11] While labor can sometimes play an effective role in support of social legislation, it usually cannot match business in material resources and political muscle. Total corporate profits are hundreds of times greater than the total income of labor unions. And few if any labor leaders are given top decision-making posts in government.

Corporate spokespersons tell us that labor unions are corrupt, unpopular, harmful, and too powerful. The truth is something else. In 1935, working people won a major victory when a federal law was passed setting up the National Labor Relations Board (NLRB) as an independent federal agency intended to protect labor's right to collective bargaining. In the years that followed, union membership increased dramatically and workers across the country made wage gains amounting to billions of dollars. Then, in 1947, a Republican-controlled Congress passed the Taft-Hartley Act, which imposed restrictions on strikes, boycotts, and labor organizing, leading to a decline in union membership from 35 percent of the workforce to about 14 percent by 2000. If we don't count public employees and consider only the private sector, union membership is only 10.2 percent, lower than it was in 1932 before the New Deal.[12]

More than a thousand consulting firms doing a $500-million yearly business teach companies how to prevent workers from organizing and how to get rid of existing unions. During union election drives, management can interfere in the organizing process, propagandizing workers as a captive audience, and plying them with gifts and promises in order to induce an anti-union vote. In contrast, union organizers are prohibited from giving gifts to workers and denied access to the worksite. Management can threaten to move the plant if a union is voted in. Workers are frequently and unlawfully fired for attempting to organize, although management always gives other reasons, such as "poor performance." The NLRB follows the rule that if there is any business reason for firing a worker unrelated to union activity then termination is legal.[13]

Bosses can use NLRB procedures to delay elections for months, even years. When unions do win recognition, management may refuse to negotiate a contract and will challenge the election results in the courts. The NLRB will sometimes spend years investigating minor or frivolous management charges. By the time the company is ordered to bargain, many union supporters may have quit or been fired, while new employees are being screened for union sympathy. And after bargaining begins, the company still can resist reaching an acceptable contract agreement.[14]

Sometimes management may refuse to renew an existing contract when it expires. It may deliberately close its doors, forcing workers out in what is known as a "lockout." Then the company brings in permanent replacements ("scabs") to break the union. The threat of scab replacement has diminished strike activity and further hampers the right to unionize.

Sometimes a climate of violence and fear is sowed by company bosses, assisted by armed thugs and complicit law officers as happened during the United Farm Workers (UFW) efforts to organize strawberry workers in 1998. It was enough to cause the UFW to boycott the union election. So the right to represent the strawberry workers went to a company union that had not existed a few weeks earlier and "had no agenda, no list of demands on behalf of the workers and no organizing strategy beyond defeating the UFW."[15]

By a margin of 60 to 23 percent, U.S. residents believe unions have been good for working people. Almost four out of five favor laws that would protect the right of workers to organize without being fired by their bosses.[16] If union membership has declined, it is not because unions are unpopular but because of the repressive, one-sided conditions under which organized labor has been forced to operate. Unions lose about half of all NLRB elections, and win contracts with only half the companies in which workers voted for union representation. Union organizers fight back by trying to build community support, mount boycotts, pursue court actions, and conduct demonstrations, sit-ins, and rallies.[17]

In recent presidential and congressional elections, business outspent labor by about eleven to one. If we add the huge sums given to lawmakers and lobbyists between elections or spent on referenda campaigns and the money from individual fat cats and wealthy candidates, the ratio is even more lopsided.[18] Far from having too much power, unions have been fighting for their lives against hostile laws, court rulings, NLRB decisions, and government witchhunts that purged the labor movement of communists. The Reds were among the most effective and dedicated organizers, including the many who performed heroically against mobsters. Meanwhile, federal authorities have done relatively little to rid unions of gangster influence.[19]

Unions and the Good Fight

To be sure, some unions are corrupt and undemocratic, and some union leaders become union dealers, voting themselves sumptuous salaries, cooperating in management speedups, and colluding with gangland thugs to intimidate the rank and file into submission. This kind of corruption tends to be concentrated in a relatively small number of locals. As noted in Chapter 9, most of the corruption comes from management's side in the form of bribes, kickbacks, tax evasion, toxic dumping, or other criminal acts. Business also plays fast and loose with labor's money, pilfering billions of dollars from employees' pension funds, putting many employees' retirement annuities at risk.[20]

Unions have been attacked for causing recessions. By driving up labor costs, they force companies to mechanize, cut back on jobs, and relocate to cheaper labor markets, the argument goes. But most downsizing and relocating in recent decades has come when labor costs were in decline. Labor has been the victim, not the cause, of recessions.

Union activity correlates with prosperity rather than with poverty. In states where unions have been traditionally weak (e.g., Alabama, South Carolina, and Mississippi), the standard of living has been lower than in states where labor has a stronger organized presence. Overall wages in the United States compare favorably to wages in Third World countries that have very weak or nonexistent unions and compare unfavorably to better-unionized nations such as Canada, Western Europe, and Scandinavia.

Unionized workers average 20 percent higher wages than nonunion workers in this country, and are far more likely to have health insurance and other benefits. Even nonunion workers benefit from the struggles of organized labor when their bosses make concessions in order to keep unions out. Criticisms and challenges from unions tend to produce better management performance. Occupational conditions and safety inspections generally are better at unionized workplaces than nonunion ones. The higher the unionization rate, the less unequal is the distribution of income. Conversely, as unions have declined, income distribution has become even more skewed in favor of the rich.[21]

The condition of labor correlates not only with prosperity but with democracy. Countries in which labor is strong and well organized enjoy more human rights than countries where unions are nonexistent. Labor unions are a vital part of whatever democracy we have. They are one of the few institutions in which ordinary working people can give an organized response to the issues affecting their lives. The rank and file participate in union elections at higher rates than in national elections. In most unions the entire membership gets to vote on a contract.

Organized labor has been at the forefront of the fight against child labor, for the eight-hour day, and for safer work conditions. Unions have played an important role in the passage of major civil-rights bills and have supported single-payer health insurance, affordable housing, mass transportation, consumer protection, public education, and progressive tax reform. They have opposed the North American Free Trade Agreement (NAFTA), the General Agreement on Tariffs and Trade (GATT), the World Trade Organization (WTO), and other circumventions of popular sovereignty. Unions have backed environmental controls and peace movements in coalitions with other organizations. Some of the more progressive unions broke with the militaristic Cold War mentality of the AFL-CIO leadership and supported nonintervention in Central America. Surveys show that 90 percent of union members want their unions involved in political and legislative action.[22]

For organized labor to reverse its long decline, it needs repeal of the anti-labor laws that hamstring its ability to organize and win decent labor contracts. The NLRB must once again become an agency that defends — rather than undermines — the right to collective bargaining. Union leaders must avoid a collaborationist policy with management. They need to invest the billions of dollars in their pension funds in housing rehabilitation, community development, and other social programs beneficial to the rank and file. And AFL-CIO leaders must stop promoting a U.S. foreign policy that supports oppressive regimes, undermines independent unions, and preserves cheap labor markets in the Third World — to which U.S. jobs are then exported.[23]

Human labor is the basis of our well-being and survival. Everywhere in the world, including the United States, it deserves far better treatment than it is getting.

Globalization, WTO, and the End of Democracy

Among the recent undertakings of global business elites and their faithful governmental servants are NAFTA and the 1993 Uruguayan round of GATT. As presented to the public, NAFTA and GATT were going to abolish irksome regulatory laws, integrate national economies into a global trade system, and create more jobs and greater prosperity.

The goal of the transnational corporation is to become truly transnational, poised above the sovereign power of any particular nation, while being serviced by the sovereign powers of all nations. Cyril Siewert, chief financial officer of Colgate Palmolive Company, could have been speaking for all transnationals when he remarked, "The United States doesn't have an automatic call on our [corporation's] resources. There is no mindset that puts this country first."[24]

With NAFTA and GATT, this becomes quite evident. The giant transnationals have been elevated above the sovereign powers of nation-states. The GATT agreements created the WTO, an international association of over 120 signatory nations. The WTO has the authority to prevent, overrule, or dilute any laws of any nation deemed to burden the investment and market prerogatives of transnational corporations. It sets up three-member panels composed of "trade specialists" who act as judges over economic issues, placing themselves above the national sovereignty and popular control of any nation, thereby insuring the supremacy of international finance capital, a process called "globalization," and treated as an inevitable natural development beneficial to all.

Elected by no one and drawn from the corporate world, these panelists meet in secret and can have investment stakes in the very issues they adjudicate, being limited by no conflict-of-interest provisions. Their function is to allow the transnational companies to do whatever they like without any restraints or regulations placed on them by any country. Not one of GATT's five hundred pages of rules and restrictions are directed against private business; all are against governments. Signatory governments must lower tariffs, end farm subsidies, treat foreign companies the same as domestic ones, honor all corporate patent claims, and obey the rulings of a permanent elite bureaucracy, the WTO. Should a country refuse to change its laws when a WTO panel so dictates, the WTO can impose fines or international trade sanctions, depriving the resistant country of needed markets and materials.[25]

Acting as the supreme global adjudicator, the WTO has ruled against laws deemed "barriers to free trade." It has forced Japan to accept greater pesticide residues in imported food. It has kept Guatemala from outlawing deceptive advertising on baby food. It has eliminated the ban in various countries on asbestos, fuel-economy, and emission standards for cars. And it has ruled against marine-life protection laws and the ban on endangered-species products. The European Union's prohibition on the import of hormone-ridden U.S. beef had overwhelming popular support throughout Europe, but a three-member WTO panel decided the ban was an illegal restraint on trade. The decision on beef put in jeopardy a host of other food-import regulations based on health concerns. The WTO overturned a portion of the U.S. Clean Air Act banning certain additives in gasoline because it interfered with imports from foreign refineries. And the WTO overturned that portion of the U.S. Endangered Species Act forbidding the import of shrimp caught with nets that failed to protect sea turtles.[26]

"Free" trade is not fair trade; it benefits strong nations at the expense of weaker ones, and rich interests at the expense of the rest of us, circumvent-

ing what little democratic sovereignty we have been able to achieve.[27] "Globalization" means turning the clock back on many twentieth-century reforms: no freedom to boycott products, no prohibitions against child labor, no guaranteed living wage or benefits, no public services that might conceivably compete with private profit-making, no health and safety protections that might cost the corporations any money.

GATT allows multinationals to impose monopoly property rights on indigenous and communal agriculture. In this way agribusiness can better penetrate locally self-sufficient communities and monopolize their resources. Ralph Nader gives the example of the neem tree, whose extracts contain naturally pesticidal and medicinal properties. Cultivated for centuries in India, the tree has attracted the attention of various pharmaceutical companies, who filed monopoly patents, causing mass protests by Indian farmers. As dictated by the WTO, the pharmaceuticals now have exclusive control over the marketing of neem tree products, a ruling that is being reluctantly enforced in India. Tens of thousands of erstwhile independent farmers must now work for the powerful pharmaceuticals on terms set by them.

In a similar vein, the WTO ruled that the U.S. corporation RiceTec has the patent rights to the many varieties of basmati rice grown for centuries by

India's farmers. It also ruled that a Japanese corporation had exclusive rights in the world to produce curry powder. In these instances, "free trade" means monopoly corporate control. Such developments caused Malaysian prime minister Mahathir Mohamad to observe:

> We now have a situation where theft of genetic resources by western biotech TNCs [transnational corporations] enables them to make huge profits by producing patented genetic mutations of these same materials. What depths have we sunk to in the global marketplace when nature's gifts to the poor may not be protected but their modifications by the rich become exclusive property?
>
> If the current behavior of the rich countries is anything to go by, globalization simply means the breaking down of the borders of countries so that those with the capital and the goods will be free to dominate the markets.[28]

Under the free-trade agreements, all public services are now at risk. A public service can be charged with causing "lost market opportunities" for business, or creating an unfair subsidy. To offer one instance: the single-payer automobile insurance program proposed by the province of Ontario, Canada, was declared "unfair competition." Ontario could have its public auto insurance only if it paid U.S. insurance companies what they estimated would be their present and *future* losses in Ontario auto insurance sales, a prohibitive cost for the province. Thus the citizens of Ontario were not allowed to exercise their democratic sovereign power to institute an alternative not-for-profit auto insurance system.

Education is a trillion-dollar industry, and private corporations want a big piece of it. If the issue is ever brought before the WTO or whatever trade council, public education and protests against corporate-run schools could be seen as a barrier to free-market investments and lost market earnings for corporations involved in privatizing schools. It is probably only the fear of a heated public outcry that keeps the forces of privatization from moving more precipitously into the "education market."

International "free trade" agreements like GATT and NAFTA have hastened the corporate acquisition of local markets, squeezing out smaller businesses and worker collectives. Under NAFTA, better-paying U.S. jobs were lost as firms closed shop and contracted out to the cheaper Mexican labor market. At the same time thousands of Mexican small companies were forced out of business. Mexico was flooded with cheap, high-tech, mass-produced corn and dairy products from giant U.S. agribusiness firms (themselves heavily subsidized by the U.S. government), driving small Mexican farmers and distributors into bankruptcy, displacing large numbers of poor peasants. The newly arrived U.S. companies in Mexico have offered extremely low-paying jobs, and highly unsafe and unhealthy work conditions.

Under NAFTA, the U.S.-based Ethyl Corporation sued the Canadian government for $250 million in "lost business opportunities" and "interference with trade" because Canada banned MMT, an Ethyl-produced gasoline additive considered carcinogenic by Canadian officials. Fearing they would lose the case, Canadian officials caved in, agreeing to lift the ban on MMT, pay Ethyl $10 million in compensation, and issue a public statement calling MMT "safe." California also banned the unhealthy additive; this time a Canadian-based Ethyl company sued California under NAFTA for placing an unfair burden on free trade.[29]

We are told that to remain competitive under GATT, we will have to increase our output while reducing our labor and production costs, in other words, work harder for less. We will have to spend less on social services and introduce more wage concessions, more restructuring, deregulation, and privatization. Only then might we cope with the impersonal forces of globalization that are sweeping us along. In fact, there is nothing impersonal about these forces. "Free trade" agreements, including new ones that have not yet been submitted to Congress, have been consciously planned by big business and its governmental minions over a period of years in pursuit of a deregulated world economy that undermines all democratic checks upon business practices, and leaves all the world's population in the merciless embrace of a global free market. The people of any one province, state, or nation are now finding it increasingly difficult to get their governments to impose protective regulations or develop new forms of public-sector production out of fear of being overruled by the WTO or some other international trade panel.[30]

NAFTA and GATT are in violation of the U.S. Constitution, the preamble of which makes clear that sovereign power rests with the people: "We the People of the United States . . . do ordain and establish this Constitution for the United States of America." Article 1, Section 1 of the Constitution reads, "All legislative Powers herein granted shall be vested in a Congress of the United States." Article 1, Section 7 gives the president (not some trade council) the power to veto a law, subject to being overridden by a two-thirds vote in Congress. And Article 3 gives adjudication and review powers to a Supreme Court and other federal courts as ordained by Congress. The Tenth Amendment to the Constitution states: "The powers not delegated to the United States by the Constitution, nor prohibited by it to the States, are reserved to the States respectively, or to the people." There is nothing in the entire Constitution that allows an international trade panel to preside as final arbiter exercising supreme review powers undermining the constitutionally mandated decisions of the legislative, executive, and judicial branches.

True, Article 7 says that the Constitution, federal laws, and treaties "shall be the supreme Law of the land," but certainly this was not intended to include treaties that overrode the laws themselves and the sovereign power of the people and their representatives. In any case, to exclude the Senate from deliberations, NAFTA and GATT were called "agreements" not treaties, a semantical ploy that enabled President Clinton to bypass the two-thirds treaty ratification vote in the Senate and avoid any treaty amendment process. The

World Trade Organization was approved by a lame-duck session of Congress held after the 1994 elections. No one running in that election uttered a word to voters about putting the U.S. government under a perpetual obligation to insure that national laws do not conflict with WTO rulings.

What is being undermined is not only a lot of good laws dealing with environment, public services, labor standards, and consumer protection, but also *the very right to legislate such laws.* Our democratic sovereignty is being surrendered to secretive plutocratic trade organizations that presume to exercise a power greater than that of the people and their courts and legislatures. What we have is an international coup d'état by finance capital over the nations of the world.

Designed to leave the world's economic destiny to the tender mercy of bankers and multinational corporations, globalization is a logical extension of imperialism, a victory of empire over republic, international finance capital over democracy. In recent times, however, given popular protests, several multilateral trade agreements have been stalled or voted down. In 1999, militant protests against free trade took place in forty-one nations from Britain and France to Thailand and India.[31] In 2000, there were the demonstrations in Seattle, Washington, Sydney, Prague, and various other locales. More and more, people throughout the world are resisting the loss of democratic accountability that masquerades under the banner of "globalization" and "free trade." Meanwhile, existing free-trade agreements need to be not "revised" but repealed.

Notes

1. Edward Pressen, *The Social Background of the Presidents* (New Haven, Conn.: Yale University Press, 1984).

2. Sidney Aronson, *Status and Kinship in the Higher Civil Service* (Cambridge, Mass.: Harvard University Press, 1964); Philip Burch, Jr., *Elites in American History*, vols. 1–3 (New York: Holmes & Meier, 1980, 1981); G. William Domhoff, *The Powers That Be* (New York: Vintage, 1979); John Schmidhauser, *The Supreme Court* (New York: Holt, Rinehart & Winston, 1960).

3. G. William Domhoff, "Politics among the Redwoods," *Progressive*, January 1981; John Roemer, "*People* Writer Kicked Out by Bohemians," *San Francisco Weekly*, August 7, 1991; Bohemian Grove Fact Sheet, Bohemian Grove Action Network, Occidental, Calif., 1992.

4. Laurence Shoup and William Minter, *Imperial Brain Trust: The Council on Foreign Relations and United States Foreign Policy* (New York: Monthly Review, 1977); G. William Domhoff, *Who Rules America Now?* (New York: Simon & Schuster, 1983); and annual reports of the Council on Foreign Relations, Pratt House, New York.

5. Shoup and Minter, *Imperial Brain Trust*, passim.

6. Stephen Gill, *American Hegemony and the Trilateral Commission* (New York: Cambridge University Press, 1991); Domhoff, *Who Rules America Now?*, 89, 134, and passim; Philip Burch Jr., "The American Establishment: Its Historical Development and Major Economic Components," *Research in Political Economy*, vol. 6 (Greenwich, Conn.: JAI, 1983), 83–156.

7. Ron Brownstein and Nina Easton, *Reagan's Ruling Class* (Washington, D.C.: Center for the Study of Responsive Law, 1982); Domhoff, *Who Rules America Now?*, 139–40.

8. *Workers World,* March 4, 1993.

9. *New York Times,* February 16, 1999.

10. Jean Stefancic and Richard Delgado, *No Mercy: How Conservative Think Tanks and Foundations Changed America's Social Agenda* (Philadelphia: Temple University Press, 1996); Sally Covington, "How Conservative Philanthropies and Think Tanks Transform US Policy," *CovertAction Quarterly,* Winter 1998.

11. Chuck Fogel, "Spying on the Union," *Solidarity,* March 1988; Tim Wheeler and Ron Johnson, "Files Reveal Four Years of FBI Spying on Unions, Peace Groups," *People's Daily World,* January 28, 1988.

12. *Economic Notes,* Labor Research Association, March 1997.

13. *New York Times,* October 24, 2000; Kate Bronfenbrenner, "'We'll Close!' Plant Closing Threats, Union Organizing and NAFTA," *Multinational Monitor,* March 1997; Michael Yates, *Power on the Job: The Legal Rights of Working People* (Boston: South End, 1995); David Bacon, "Labor Slaps the Smug New Face of Union-Busting," *CovertAction Quarterly,* Spring 1997.

14. Michael Goldfield, *The Decline of Organized Labor in the United States* (Chicago: University of Chicago Press, 1989). For a well-documented and damning report on the anti-union state of U.S. labor law, see Human Rights Watch, *Unfair Advantage: Workers' Freedom of Association Under International Human Rights Standards,* <http://www.hrw.org/reports /2000/uslabor>.

15. Don Terry quoted in *New York Times,* July 31, 1998.

16. *Economic Notes,* January/February 1992, 3.

17. Bacon, "Labor Slaps the Smug New Face of Union-Busting."

18. *Union,* Service Employees International Union, Spring 1996; *UAW Report, Region 5,* March/April 1998.

19. Dan Moldea, *Dark Victory: Ronald Reagan, MCA, and the Mob* (New York: Penguin, 1987), 66–70.

20. Michael Yates, *Why Unions Matter* (New York: Monthly Review, 1998); *New York Times,* April 22, 1993.

21. *New York Times,* August 31, 1997; *Economic Notes,* May/June 1990, 4–5; Richard Freeman and James Medoff, *What Do Unions Do?* (New York: Basic, 1984); "OSHA Enforcement," *Economic Notes,* January/February 1991.

22. *Cleveland Plain Dealer,* September 2, 1996; *Detroit News,* September 1, 1996.

23. Laurie Jo Hughes, "AIFLD: American Intervention against Free Labor Development," *Nicaragua Monitor* (Nicaragua Network Education Fund, Washington, D.C.), December 1991/January 1992.

24. Quoted in *New York Times,* May 21, 1989.

25. See Lori Wallach and Michelle Sforza, *The WTO* (New York: Seven Stories, 2000); and John R. MacArthur, *The Selling of "Free Trade": NAFTA, Washington, and the Subversion of American Democracy* (New York: Hill & Wang, 2000).

26. *New York Times,* April 30, 1996, and May 9, 1997; *Washington Post,* October 13, 1998.

27. From a report by the United Nations Development Program, *New York Times,* July 13, 1999.

28. Quoted in *People's Weekly World,* December 7, 1996.

29. MacArthur, *The Selling of "Free Trade";* John Ross, "Tortilla Wars," *Progressive,* June 1999; and Sarah Anderson and John Cavanagh, "Nafta's Unhappy Anniversary," *New York Times,* February 7, 1995.

30. For a concise but thorough treatment, see Steven Shrybman, *A Citizen's Guide to the World Trade Organization* (Ottawa and Toronto: Canadian Center for Policy Alternatives and James Lorimer, 1999).

31. *San Francisco Chronicle,* June 19, 1999.

12

Mass Media: For the Many, by the Few

The mainstream media claim to be free and independent, objective and neutral, the "watchdogs of democracy." A closer look suggests that they too often behave like the lapdogs of plutocracy.

He Who Pays the Piper

The major news media or press (the terms are used interchangeably here), consisting of newspapers, magazines, radio, films, and television, are an inherent component of corporate America, being themselves highly concentrated conglomerates. As of 2000, eight corporate conglomerates controlled most of the national media — down from twenty-three in 1989. About 80 percent of the daily newspaper circulation in the United States belongs to a few giant chains like Gannett and Knight-Ridder, and the trend in owner concentration continues unabated. Today less than 2 percent of U.S. cities have competing newspapers under separate ownership.[1]

Six major companies distribute virtually all the magazines sold on newsstands. Eight corporate conglomerates control most of the book-sales revenues, and a few bookstore chains enjoy over 70 percent of book sales. A handful of companies and banks control the movie industry. Four giant networks, ABC, CBS, NBC, and Fox, dominate the television industry, and a handful of corporations command most of the nation's radio audience.[2] NBC is owned by General Electric, Capital Cities/ABC by Disney, and CBS by Westinghouse. Jack Welch, CEO of General Electric, is a conservative who agreed to bankroll the rightist *McLaughlin Group*. Michael Jordan, head of CBS-Westinghouse, is a rightist who has spoken out against government regulations of the free market. Fox network is owned by right-wing billionaire and media mogul Rupert Murdoch, who bankrolls the *Weekly Standard,* a right-wing opinion magazine, and whose Fox News Channel reportedly quizzed journalistic applicants on whether they were registered Republicans or not.[3]

Banks such as Morgan Guaranty Trust and Citibank are among the major stockholders of networks. Representatives of powerful corporations — including IBM, Ford, General Motors, and Mobil Oil — sit on the boards of all the major networks and publications. The media conglomerates own not only television networks but other lucrative holdings such as cable companies, book publishing houses, magazines, newspapers, movie studios, satellite television, and radio stations.[4]

Over the last two decades, the broadcast industry has used its immense lobbying power to kill what few regulations were in place to protect diversity and public interest programming. It spent more than $100 million to secure passage of the 1996 Telecommunications Act, which permits a single company to own television stations serving more than one-third of the U.S. public. By lifting restrictions on the sale of media properties, the act was supposed to bring a flowing of competition that would give consumers greater choice, lower cable prices, and cheaper local phone service.

In fact, within three years, cable rates had risen 21 percent and local phone rates 10 percent. And now, one company can own up to six radio stations and two television stations in a single city (as opposed to the previous restriction of one radio and one TV outlet in any one market). Consequently, since 1996 there have been over a thousand mergers of radio companies, with over half of the nation's eleven thousand radio stations being bought up by large conglomerates. The upshot is fewer independent commentators with an alternative perspective on world affairs and community issues; and more "hate radio" types who spew their venom against feminists, ethnic minorities, the homeless, gays, labor unions, and environmentalists.[5]

Media owners do not hesitate to exercise control over news content. They frequently kill stories they dislike and in other ways inject their own preferences. As one group of investigators reported: "The owners and managers of the press determine which person, which facts, which version of the facts, and which ideas shall reach the public."[6] In recent times, media bosses have refused to run advertisements, stories, or commentaries that advocated single-payer health insurance, criticized U.S. military intervention in other countries, or opposed the North American Free Trade Agreement (NAFTA).

Corporate advertisers are another influential group who leave their political imprint on media content. They might cancel advertising accounts not only when they feel that the reporting reflects poorly on their product, but also when they disapprove of what they perceive as a "liberal" drift in news

and commentary. Network bosses are keenly aware of the control exercised by business sponsors. To quote former president of CBS Frank Stanton, "Since we are advertiser-supported we must take into account the general objective and desires of advertisers as a whole."[7] The prize-winning *Kwitney Report*, a PBS news show that revealed U.S. backing of death squads and dictators in Central America and other hot issues, went off the air because it could not procure corporate funding.[8] Lowell Bergman, former producer of *60 Minutes*, says news producers "are finding it more and more difficult to do pieces that are critical of Fortune 500 companies, or of sponsors or suppliers to the network."[9]

Journalists can sometimes slip unusually critical information into stories, but if they persist, their reports are spiked, they are reassigned, and soon their careers are at risk. The media boss controls the journalist, not the other way around. Media chiefs have canceled radio and television shows, such as Michael Moore's *TV Nation,* that contained relatively mild and flippant critiques of big companies. Jim Hightower's populist commentaries played on more than two hundred ABC radio affiliates until canceled by Disney soon after it took over ABC in 1997. (Hightower has managed to reappear on a smaller number of independent stations.)

Television journalists Steve Wilson and Jane Akre lost their jobs after doing an investigative series on the dangers of hormones fed to cows, a report that Wilson and Akre say a Fox affiliate in Tampa, Florida, refused to run because it offended Monsanto. Mike Gallagher was let go by the *Cincinnati Enquirer* after reporting that Chiquita banana company sprayed its Latin American workers with pesticides, bribed Colombian officials, and smuggled cocaine in banana boats. Controversy developed around *how* Gallagher obtained his information (he pilfered some voicemail tapes), not whether the reports were true.[10]

There are other examples: An *Atlanta Journal-Constitution* reporter was forced to resign after running stories that annoyed Coca-Cola and Atlanta banks, whose racist practices had been exposed. A consumer reporter was let go by KCBS-TV in Los Angeles after automotive advertisers repeatedly complained to his bosses about his critical reports on car safety. A writer was pressured out of his job at *Fortune* magazine after publicizing the exorbitant income received by the head of Time Warner, *Fortune*'s owner. For a series of reports on the abuses of corporate America, Frances Cerra of the *New York Times* incurred the ire of her editors and was transferred to a Long Island beat. There she wrote articles on Shorham nuclear power plant that contained some information running counter to the pronuclear editorial stance of the *Times*. Her final story was suppressed as "biased"; it reported that the plant was in serious financial trouble — which proved true. Cerra was never given a new assignment.[11]

Compare the above cases to the treatment accorded ABC correspondent John Stossel, who suddenly announced that government regulation of business led to no good and that "it is my job to explain the beauties of the free market." Instead of being reprimanded for his lack of objectivity, Stossel was given a starring role in numerous TV specials to promote his laissez-faire ideology.[12]

Working journalists are instructed to remain "neutral" when performing their tasks. Meanwhile the openly active partisan role that media *owners* play in political affairs, including attending fundraisers and state dinners, contributing to campaigns, and socializing with high-ranking officeholders, is not seen as violating journalistic standards of independence and objectivity.

Newspeople who consistently support the worldview of global capitalism and the national security state are the ones more likely to be rewarded with choice assignments, raises, bonuses, and promotions to editor and bureau chief. There are additional blandishments, such as lucrative honoraria from moneyed interests. How objective can David Broder be about Wall Street corruption after receiving $6,000 for a speech to the American Stock Exchange? How alert can William Safire be to price-gouging among utility companies after pocketing a $15,000 speaker's fee from Southern Electric? One might recall how the Shah of Iran, a dictator and torturer detested by most of his people, received glowing press in the United States for twenty-five years. More than five hundred journalists, newscasters, editors, and publishers, including such notables as Marvin Kalb and David Brinkley, were recipients of the Shah's gifts and invited to his lavish parties. Journalists who wrote critically of him did not make the gift list.[13]

On infrequent occasions, the news media will go against a strong corporate interest and give tentative exposure to consumer and environmental issues, as with the exposés on how the tobacco industry conspired to hook smokers by inserting more nicotine in cigarettes, and how smoking causes cancer. Of course, we knew about the link between smoking and cancer for over half a century. The press and policymakers took their time in giving the issue the attention it deserved, even then only after a growing public outcry and numerous class action suits against Big Tobacco.

A host of other consumer issues such as carcinogens in cosmetics, radioactive materials in products sold on the market, the use of industrial waste sludge as fertilizers, and the unsafe quality of so many prescription and over-the-counter drugs, along with manifold issues relating to the environment, still do not get the attention they deserve.

The Ideological Monopoly

Across the country, newspapers offer little variety in perspective and editorial policy, ranging mostly from moderately conservative to ultraconservative, with a smaller number that are blandly centrist. Most "independent" dailies, along with the chains, rely heavily on the wire services and on big circulation papers for stories, syndicated columns, and special features.

Despite conservative complaints about a liberal media, surveys show that Washington journalists, while more liberal on "cultural issues" such as abortion and school prayer, are decidedly more conservative on economic issues. They are more than twice as likely to support NAFTA and free trade, and far more in favor of trimming Medicare and Social Security.[14] In any case, as already noted, more important than the working journalists in shaping news content are the rich conservatives who own and control the major media.

News reports on business rely almost entirely on business sources. The workings of the capitalist political economy remain virtually unmentioned. The tendency toward chronic instability, recession, inflation, and underemployment; the transference of corporate diseconomies onto the public — these and other such problems are treated superficially, if at all, by pundits who have neither the inclination nor the freedom to offer critical observations about our capitalist paradise. Poverty remains an unexplained phenomenon in the media. Whether portraying the poor as unworthy idlers or simple unfortunates, the press seldom if ever gives critical attention to the market forces that create and victimize low-income people.

The press has failed to explain the real impact of the national debt and how it has generated an upward redistribution of income, as working people must pay back the money that government borrows from the rich. Almost nothing has been said in the mainstream media about how corporate America feeds from the public trough or how it harasses environmental activists and whistle-blowing employees; almost nothing on how the oil, gas, and nuclear interests have stalled the development of alternative and renewable energy sources such as solar power.[15]

Media coverage of electoral campaigns also leaves much to be desired, focusing mostly on the contest per se, on who will run, who will win, and what campaign ploys are effective — with relatively little if any focus on policy content. News commentators act more like theater critics, reviewing the candidate's performance and style. One study found that more than two-thirds of campaign coverage centers on insider strategy and political maneuvering rather than substantive issues.[16]

Progressive candidates who try to develop a plausible image among the electorate find themselves dependent for exposure on mass media that are owned by the same conservative interests they are attacking. They compete not only against well-financed opponents but also against the media's many frivolous and stupefying distractions. Hoping to educate the public to the issues, they discover that the media allow little or no opportunity for them to make their position understandable to voters who might be willing to listen. The sheer paucity of information can make meaningful campaign dialogue nearly impossible. By withholding coverage of minor-party candidates while bestowing it lavishly on major-party ones, the media help perpetuate the two-party monopoly.

The press has helped create the "lock-'em-up" crime craze throughout America. Between 1993 and 1996 the nationwide homicide rate dropped by 20 percent, yet coverage of murders on the ABC, CBS, and NBC evening news leaped 721 percent. As a result, the number of U.S. residents who ranked crime as the prime problem jumped sixfold.[17] Corporate crime, however, is another story, largely an unreported one. Recent surveys show that mainstream media rarely express critical editorial opinions on corporate crimes.[18]

Instead of treating affirmative action as an attempt to redress the effects of longstanding racism and sexism, the media has consistently misled the public on the issue, overlooking the persistence of racism in many walks of life, and leaving people with the impression that African Americans are enjoying special privileges at the expense of Whites.[19]

Every evening, network news studios faithfully report stock-exchange averages, but stories deemed important to organized labor are scarcely ever touched. There are no daily reports about the number of workers injured or maimed on the job. Reporters seldom enlist labor's views on national questions. On the ABC opinion show *Nightline,* corporate leaders appeared seven times more frequently than labor representatives. Workers are virtually never interviewed as knowledgeable sources regarding work issues. Unions are usually noticed only when they go on strike, but the issues behind the strike, such as occupational safety or loss of benefits, are rarely acknowledged. The misleading impression is that labor simply turns down "good contracts" because it wants too much. Unions make "demands" while management makes "offers." Most newspapers have large staffs for business news but not a single labor reporter. Strikes and demonstrations are given sympathetic and generous coverage when they occur in communist countries.

The "expert" guests appearing on newscasts are predominantly government officials (or former officials), corporate heads, and members of conservative think tanks, along with a sprinkling of conservative "New Democrats," who sound not too different from the others. Likewise, of the hundreds of mainstream editorialists, TV pundits, radio talk-show hosts, and syndicated columnists who crowd the communication universe, a small number are lukewarm "liberals." A typical example would be syndicated columnist Anthony Lewis, who accurately describes himself as "a pro-capitalist, middle-of-the-road tepid centrist" who supported George Bush's destruction of Iraq and Clinton's destruction of Yugoslavia, and who denounced unions for lobbying against NAFTA.[20] Other media "liberal" commentators and columnists who are hailed as representing the "left," such as Sam Donaldson, Cokie Roberts, Juan Williams, and Bob Beckel (a corporate lobbyist) have virtually nothing to say about progressive issues and corporate profiteering. When not chattering endlessly and superficially about insider strategies and public personalities, most "liberal" pundits boost the blessings of globalization, and support the national security state and U.S. interventionism with a hawkish fervor that sometimes outdoes their conservative counterparts.[21]

Citizens who utilize their democratic rights under the First Amendment by launching protests usually are given short shrift by the news media. For instance, the tens of thousands of people who demonstrated against the World Trade Organization (WTO) in Seattle in 1999 were characterized as misinformed zealots, violence-prone marginal figures, and "flat-earthers." Globalization is treated as a benign, equitable, and inevitable process, rather than a transnational corporate strategy to roll back the public regulations and democratic protections of every domestic economy in the world.[22]

Official Manipulation

Scores of "independent" and "objective" journalists have moved back and forth in their careers between media and government, in what has been called the "revolving door." David Gergen served in the Nixon, Ford, Reagan, and Clinton administrations, and in between was an editor at *U.S. News and World Report* and a PBS commentator. Pat Buchanan was a Nixon staff writer, a columnist and TV opinion-show host for CNN, a Reagan staffer, then a CNN host again.[23] The CEO of National Public Radio, Kevin Klose, is a former chief of all the major government propaganda agencies: Voice of America, Radio Free Europe, Radio Liberty, and Radio Marti. NPR has little to say that is critical of U.S. foreign policy and the national security state. The head of the Corporation for Public Broadcasting, Robert Coonrod, has a resumé strikingly similar to Klose's, from Voice of America to Radio Marti.[24]

Press reports about State Department and Pentagon policies rely heavily on State Department and Pentagon releases. Press coverage of the space program is regularly supportive with scarcely a word given to the program's critics. Little if any positive exposure is afforded anti-imperialist struggles throughout the world or domestic protests against U.S. overseas interventions against Third World peoples. Demonstrators and agitators who violently attack democratically elected governments in countries that resist the total embrace of the free market, such as post-communist Bulgaria and Yugoslavia, are hailed as purveyors of democracy and given lavish coverage, and are never condemned for their violence. Far from being vigilant critics of government policy, most news organizations act more like mouthpieces for officialdom's counterrevolutionary, free-market globalism.

The corporate media, along with NPR and PBS, portrayed the Vietnam War, the invasion of Grenada, the invasion of Panama, the destruction of Iraq, the destruction of Yugoslavia, and the growing U.S. intervention against revolutionary guerrillas in Colombia as arising from noble intentions, with no mention given to the underlying class interests and little attention to the horrendous devastation wreaked by U.S. forces upon the peoples of those countries.

The U.S. press ignored the slaughter of some 500,000 Indonesians by the U.S.-supported militarists of that country, and the genocidal campaign waged by those same militarists in East Timor. The media made scant mention of the massive repression of dissident peasants, workers, clergy, students, and intellectuals in Uruguay, Guatemala, El Salvador, Zaire, the Philippines, and dozens of other U.S.-supported procapitalist regimes. Ever faithful to the official line, press coverage is energetically negative toward leftist movements and governments while being supportive of right-wing procapitalist ones and having little ill to say of the Central Intelligence Agency (CIA)–supported counterrevolutionary mercenary forces, as in Angola, Mozambique, and Nicaragua, whose campaigns have taken hundreds of thousands of lives.[25]

Also unreported is the widespread U.S.-supported terrorism in scores of countries, utilizing death squads, massacres, and mass detentions. Human rights violations in noncapitalist countries like China, Tibet, and North Korea are given wide play, while longstanding bloody and repressive violations in Turkey, Honduras, Indonesia, and dozens of other U.S.-supported, free-market countries receive scant notice.[26]

The media remain largely supportive when U.S. presidents invade or bomb other countries. The press often chooses to act "responsibly" by not informing the public about U.S. covert actions and other questionable policies abroad and at home. Journalistic responsibility should mean the unearthing of truthful information no matter how troubling it be to the established powers. But the "responsibility" demanded by government officials and often agreed to by the news media means the opposite — the burying of troublesome information precisely because it is true.

Sometimes media opinionmakers are quite blatant in their partisan expressions. During the 1999 U.S./NATO bombing of Yugoslavia, which killed hundreds of innocent civilians and wrecked that country's entire economy, without the loss of a single American life, CBS Evening News Anchor Dan Rather declared: "I'm an American, and I'm an American reporter. And yes, when there's combat involving Americans, you can criticize me if you must, damn me if you must, but I'm always pulling for us to win." Is Rather saying that he supports any U.S. one-sided slaughter regardless of the costs and immoral horrors perpetrated, regardless of the actual merits of the issues involved?[27] He sounds less like a dispassionate, objective newsperson and more like a jingoistic cheerleader.

More than four hundred U.S. journalists, including nationally syndicated columnists, editors, and some major publishers, have carried out covert assignments for the CIA over the last four decades, gathering intelligence abroad or publishing the kind of stories that create a climate of opinion supportive of the CIA's interventionist objectives. Included are personnel from the *Washington Post,* CBS, NBC, ABC, *Newsweek,* the *Wall Street Journal,* the Associated Press, and prominent press moguls such as William Paley, erstwhile head of CBS; Henry Luce, late owner of Time Inc.; and Arthur Hays Sulzberger, late publisher of the *New York Times.* The CIA has owned more than 240 media operations around the world, including newspapers, magazines, publishing houses, radio and television stations, and wire services. Many Third World countries get more news from the CIA and other such Western sources than from Third World news organizations.[28]

In a series of deeply researched articles in the *San Jose Mercury News,* Gary Webb exposed the CIA's involvement in the drug traffic between the contras (U.S.-supported mercenary troops in Central America) and inner-city dealers in the United States. The series confirmed the worst suspicions of African-American community leaders and set off a firestorm of controversy. Webb was swiftly subjected to a barrage of counterattacks from the *Washington Post, New York Times, Los Angeles Times,* and the major TV networks. They accused him of saying things he had not said. They focused on a few minor speculative points not firmly established while ignoring the more damning and well-substantiated heart of the investigation. And they unquestioningly accepted the CIA's claim that it was not involved in drug trafficking. Eventually, Webb's editor caved in to the pressure, making a public self-criticism for having published the series. Webb left the *Mercury News* soon after. A subsequent report by the CIA itself largely confirmed his charges.[29]

In 1998 CNN producers April Oliver and Jack Smith ran a story accusing the U.S. military of using sarin, a highly lethal nerve gas, in an operation behind enemy lines in Laos in 1970 that killed about one hundred people, including two American defectors. An immediate and vitriolic storm of abuse came down upon Oliver and Smith from the Pentagon and the major media. CNN hastily issued a fawning retraction and fired the two producers. The story's lead reporter, distinguished newsman Peter Arnett, was reprimanded and ultimately left the network because of the controversy. Oliver and Smith put together a seventy-seven-page document showing that their story was based entirely on testimony by U.S. airmen and other military personnel, including participants in the operation who stood by their stories.[30] Oliver has sued CNN for being wrongfully fired.

Government manipulation of the press is a constant enterprise. Officials give choice leads to sympathetic journalists and withhold information from troublesome ones. They meet regularly with media bosses to discuss or complain about specific stories. And every day the White House, the Pentagon, and other agencies release thousands of self-serving reports to the media, many of which are then uncritically transmitted to the public as news from independent sources.

The Justice Department won a Supreme Court decision allowing the government to issue subpoenas requiring newspeople to disclose their sources to grand-jury investigators, in effect reducing the press to an investigative arm of the very officialdom over whom it is supposed to act as a watchdog. The *New York Times* reassured its readers that "subpoenas are rarely issued to journalists in the United States." But one study found that more than 3,500 subpoenas were served on members of the news media in one year alone.[31] Dozens of reporters who wish to protect their sources have been jailed or threatened with prison terms for trying to protect their sources by refusing to hand over materials and tapes. Such government coercion creates a chilling effect, encouraging the press to avoid trouble from officialdom by censoring itself.

Political Entertainment

The entertainment media (movies and television dramas, documentaries, and other shows) undergo a rigorous political censorship. Even the *New York Times* admits that network "production and standards" (censorship) departments have reduced their policing of sexual and other cultural taboos, but "network censors continue to be vigilant when it comes to overseeing the *political* content of television films."[32] Television shows that treat controversial, anti-establishment subjects often have trouble getting sponsors and network time. On the rare occasions a proworker or anti-imperialist film is produced, it is likely to get no financial backing from the major studios and banks and be consigned to a very limited distribution. Such was the fate of movies like *Salt of the Earth, Burn, Salvador, Reds, 1900, Matewan,* and *Romero*.[33]

What is considered a political or nonpolitical film is itself a political judgment. Movies that challenge orthodox values and stereotypes are seen as political, not movies that reinforce conventional standards. Almost all mainstream entertainment is political in one way or another. Even movies and television shows that do not promote a specifically political storyline may propagate images and themes that support militarism, imperialism, racism, sexism, authoritarianism, and other undemocratic values. In the entertainment world, adversities are caused by ill-willed individuals and cabals, never by the injustices of the socioeconomic system. Problems are solved by individual derring-do rather than by organized collective effort. Conflicts are resolved by generous applications of murder and mayhem. Nefarious violence is met with righteous violence, although it is often difficult to distinguish the two. Studies indicate that people who watch a lot of television have a higher fear of crime and of urban minorities than those who do not. Crime shows condition viewers into accepting authoritarian solutions and repressive police actions.[34]

Over the years, in response to pressures from viewers, there have been changes in gender and ethnic portrayals. Women and ethnic minorities now are sometimes depicted as intelligent and capable persons, occupying positions of authority and power. Despite these advances, gender and ethnic stereotypes still abound. Women and ethnic minorities appear in leading roles far less often than White males. They are still marketed as sexual objects in ads and storylines, often as the object of male rapacity and violence.

Years ago, African Americans predictably played servants and street criminals. Now they play police and street criminals, usually in minor roles. The Black police captain scolding the hero cop and the Black female judge admonishing the courtroom lawyers have become new African-American stock characters. African Americans abound in prime-time sitcoms, playing for laughs, but the more serious struggles faced by African Americans in almost every area of life and work are rarely afforded realistic portrayal. Black actors still experience a shortage of racially nonspecific roles about ordinary complicated people dealing with real-life problems.

There have been some notable exceptions to the dismal fare served up to mass audiences: *Bulworth* satirizes the U.S. political system; *Dead Man Walking* treats the death penalty issue; *A Civil Action* casts a revealing light on the venality of corporate polluters, as does *Erin Brokovich*. *Beloved* deals with the lingering effects of slavery; *Amistad* portrays a real-life nineteenth-century slave revolt and trial; *The Cradle Will Rock* depicts the attempt to build a people's theater during the New Deal; and *The Insider* documents the investigative efforts waged against the tobacco industry. Still, the tribulations of working-class people and their many struggles for decent treatment at work and in the community (good thematic material) are given scarce dramatic treatment in the business-owned entertainment world.[35]

The everyday worker is invisible on public TV as well. While the Public Broadcasting System (PBS) has become more sensitive to race, gender, and multiculturalism in recent years, it virtually ignores working-class concerns out of fear of alienating corporate underwriters. When labor unions have funded documentaries and dramas having a working-class perspective, public television bosses usually have refused to run them, claiming that labor (with its millions of workers) represents a "special interest."[36]

Room for Alternatives?

In sum, the media are neither objective nor honest in their portrayal of important issues. The news is a product not only of deliberate manipulation but of the ideological and economic power structure under which journalists operate and into which they are socialized.

The Fairness Law required that time be given to an opposing viewpoint after a station broadcasted an editorial opinion. But it made no requirement as to the diversity of the opposing viewpoints, so usually the range was between two only slightly different stances. The "Fairness Doctrine," as it was known, often was unfairly applied. The Federal Communications Commission (FCC) ruled that no broadcast time need be made available to "communists or the communist viewpoint" but only to "controversial issues of public importance on which persons other than communists hold contrasting views."[37] President Reagan vetoed Congress's attempt to extend the life of the Fairness Doctrine in 1987. Opponents of the law argue that it is an infringement on the freedom of the press, since it forces a private broadcaster to give time to an opposing viewpoint. Thus it also has a chilling effect on opinions, since owners will refrain from expressing their views because of the obligation to accommodate competing ones. But the airwaves are the property of the people of the United States and should be open to divergent views.

The Public Broadcasting Act of 1967 launched the Public Broadcasting System (PBS) as a public television alternative to commercial TV. Instead of being independently financed by a sales tax on television sets or by some other method, PBS was made dependent on annual appropriations from Congress and was run by a board appointed by the president. PBS and National Public Radio (NPR) are now required to match federal funds with money from other sources. Viewer or listener contributions are solicited to pay for operational costs. The programs themselves are financed by large corporations. Not surprisingly, both NPR and PBS offer public affairs shows populated by commentators and guest "experts" who are as ideologically conservative and politically safe as any found on the commercial networks.

Of the many interesting documentaries made by independent producers dealing with important and controversial political issues, few if any gain access to mainstream movie houses or major television networks. Thus, the documentary *Faces of War,* revealing the U.S.-supported counterinsurgency destruction visited upon the people of El Salvador, was denied broadcast rights in twenty-two major television markets. The award-winning *Building Bombs* and the exposé on the Iran-contra affair, *Coverup,* were denied access to PBS and all commercial channels. In 1991, *Deadly Deception,* a documentary critical of General Electric and the environmental devastation wreaked by the nuclear weapons industry, won the Academy Award, yet, with a few local exceptions, it was shut out of commercial and public television. So too with the Academy Award–winning documentary *Panama Deception,* which offered a critical exposé of the U.S. invasion of Panama.

Many areas of the country are awash in talk shows and news commentary that are outspokenly ultrarightist, procapitalist, militaristic, anti-union, anti-feminist, and anti-immigrant. Wealthy conservatives have poured millions of dollars into building the religious right's radio network, consisting of 1,300 local stations, and its television network, the Christian Broadcasting Network, which has as many affiliates as ABC. There is a significant religious left in this country, dedicated to peace and social justice issues, but it gets no substantial financial backing and therefore owns no major media outlets.

Denied access to major media, the political left has attempted to get its message across through small publications that suffer chronic financial difficulties and sometimes undergo harassment from police, the Federal Bureau of Investigation, rightist vigilantes, the Internal Revenue Service, and the U.S. Postal Service. Skyrocketing postal rates effect a real hardship on dissident publications. While defending such increases as economically necessary, the government continues to subsidize billions of pieces of junk mail sent out every year by business and advertising firms.

Pacifica network's five radio outlets and other community- and listener-sponsored stations sometimes offer alternative political perspectives (along with a great deal of cultural esoterica and conventional mainstream views). The Pacifica board of directors, as of 2000 dominated by persons unfriendly toward progressive radio, now seems determined to neutralize the few remaining dissident voices on the member stations and turn Pacifica into another NPR.[38]

A growing movement of mostly poor and inner-city individuals and communities across the country have set up unlicensed "microradio" FM stations, which have far less than one hundred watts of power and transmit in a limited radius of one to five miles. Microradio advocates argue that the are public space and their broadcast outlets are too small to interfere with the larger signals. The real threat they pose is that low-income people and other dissidents might use the airwaves to voice heterodox views. After much struggle by microradio broadcasters, the FCC reluctantly approved low-power FM signals in 2000. But the National Association of Broadcasters, the trade group representing most of the corporate media, lobbied hard to have all microstations suppressed. A measure was passed by Congress, prohibiting the FCC from licensing microstations until further study, supposedly to insure that microradio does not interfere with major broadcasting.[39]

There are sometimes limits to how the media can suppress and distort events since reality itself is radical. The Third World really is poor and exploited; the U.S. government really does side with the rich oligarchs; real wages actually have declined for many workers; corporations do wield enormous power, plunder and pollute the environment, and downsize their workforce while reaping record profits. To maintain its credibility, the press must occasionally report some of these realities. When it does, the rightists complain bitterly about a "liberal bias." Furthermore, the press is not entirely immune to more democratic and popular pressure. If, despite the media's misrepresentation and neglect, a well-organized and persistent public opinion builds around an issue, while not attacking the capitalist system as a system, it occasionally can break through the media sound barrier.

If we consider censorship to be a danger to our freedom, then we should not overlook the fact that the media are already heavily censored by those who own or advertise in them. Public television and radio should be funded by the public rather than by rich corporations and foundations who get to impose their own ideological preferences while writing off the costs as a tax deduction. Public law should require all newspapers and broadcasting stations to allot space and time to a diverse array of political opinion, including the most progressive and revolutionary. But given the interests the government serves, this is not a likely development.

Ultimately the only protection against monopoly control of the media is ownership by the people themselves, with legal provisions allowed for the inclusion of a broad spectrum of conflicting views. This is not as chimerical or radical as it sounds. In the early 1920s, before it was taken over by commercial interests, radio consisted primarily of hundreds of not-for-profit stations run mostly by colleges, universities, labor unions, and community groups.[40]

Today more community-supported radio stations and public access cable television stations are needed. The microradio station should be encouraged, for it is among the most democratic of media, requiring almost no capital while being relatively more accessible to the community in which it operates. The Internet also offers a wide range of progressive websites that provide information and opinion rarely accommodated by mainstream media.

Those who own the newspapers and networks will not relinquish their hold over private investments and public information. Ordinary citizens will have no access to the mass media until they can gain control over the material resources that could give them such access, an achievement that would take a different kind of economic and social system than the corporate "free market" we have. In the meantime, Americans should have no illusions about the "free and independent press" they are said to enjoy.

Notes

1. Dean Alger, *Megamedia: How Giant Corporations Dominate Mass Media, Distort Competition, and Endanger Democracy* (Lanham, Md.: Rowman & Littlefield, 1998); Arthur Rowse, *Drive-By Journalism* (Monroe, Maine: Common Courage, 2000); Ben Bagdikian, *The Media Monopoly*, 5th ed. (Boston: Beacon, 1997).

2. For a partial list, see *Nation*, March 17, 1997, 23–26.

3. "From the Top," *Extra!*, July/August 1998.

4. Alger, *Megamedia*, passim. *Nation*, March 17, 1997. For a detailed account of a network takeover, see Dennis Mazzocco, *Networks of Power* (Boston: South End, 1994).

5. Daniel Zoll, "Radio Rat Poison," *San Francisco Bay Guardian*, September 20, 2000; Molly Ivins, "Surprise! Telecom Act Is a Disaster," *San Francisco Chronicle*, March 16, 1999.

6. Report by the Commission on Freedom of the Press, quoted in Robert Cirino, *Don't Blame the People* (New York: Vintage, 1972), 47; also Michael Parenti, *Inventing Reality: The Politics of News Media*, 2nd ed. (New York: St. Martin's, 1993), 33–35, 47, 59.

7. Quoted in Eric Barnouw, *The Sponsor* (New York: Oxford University Press, 1978), 57.

8. Jonathan Kwitney, telephone conversation with Michael Parenti, March 1992.

9. Interview with *MediaFile*, publication of Media Alliance, January/February 2000.

10. Herb Kaye, "'Freedom of the Press' — for Publishers," *People's Weekly World*, August 22, 1998.

11. "Where's the Power: Newsroom or Boardroom?" *Extra!*, July/August 1998; *Fear and Favor in the Newsroom*, documentary film, California Newsreel, San Francisco, KQED-TV, November 12, 1998.

12. "Where's the Power: Newsroom or Boardroom?" *Extra!*, July/August 1998.

13. Burling Lowrey, "The Media's Honoraria," *Washington Post*, April 26, 1989; William Dorman, "Favors Received," *Nation*, October 11, 1980.

14. David Croteau, "Challenging the 'Liberal Media' Claim," *Extra!*, July/August 1998.

15. Carl Jensen (ed.), *America's CENSORED Newsletter*, December 1992.

16. Todd Purdum in *New York Times*, January 13, 1999.

17. According to Vincent Schiraldi, director of Justice Policy Institute, cited in David McGowan, *Derailing Democracy* (Monroe, Maine: Common Courage, 2000), 60.

18. Survey by Morton Mintz in *Nieman Reports*, July 2000.

19. Robert Entman, "The Color Game: How Media Play the Race Card," *Newswatch*, Summer 1999.

20. "Who Gets to Speak?" *Extra!*, July/August 1998; Doug Ireland, "Unfit to Print," *Nation*, July 28–August 4, 1997; Norman Solomon and Jeff Cohen, *Wizards of Media Oz: Behind the Mainstream News* (Monroe, Maine: Common Courage, 1997).

21. "Field Guide to TVs Lukewarm Liberals," *Extra!*, July/August 1998.

22. William Solomon, "More Form Than Substance: Press Coverage of the WTO Protests in Seattle," *Monthly Review*, May 2000. On how the media misrepresented NAFTA, see Edward Herman, "Mexican Meltdown," *Z Magazine*, September 1995.

23. "Journalists at Work: Who's Watching the Watchdogs?" *Alternative Press Review*, Spring/Summer 1998, and <http://www.pir.org>.

24. William Blum, *Rogue State* (Monroe, Maine: Common Courage, 2000), 10.

25. Parenti, *Inventing Reality*, passim; and Blum, *Rogue State*, passim.

26. See the discussion and citations in Chapter 7.

27. Rather quoted and criticized in Blum, *Rogue State*, 10.

28. Sean Gervasi, "CIA Covert Propaganda Capability," *CovertAction Information Bulletin*, December 1979/Janaury 1980; Daniel Brandt, "Journalism and the CIA," *Alternative Press Review*, Spring/Summer 1998; Carl Bernstein, "The CIA and the Media," *Rolling Stone*, October 20, 1977.

29. Gary Webb, *Dark Alliance: The CIA, the Contras, and the Crack Cocaine Explosion* (New York: Seven Stories, 1998); and Jeffrey St. Clair et al., *The CIA, Drugs and the Press* (New York and London: Verso, 1998).

30. "Tailwind: Rebuttal to the Abrams/Kohler Report," posted July 22, 1998, <http://www.freedomforum.org/fpfp/specialprograms/tailwind1.asp>; also April Oliver and Peter Arnett, "Did the U.S. Drop Nerve Gas?" *Time*, June 15, 1998.

31. *New York Times*, July 1, 1998; and study by Reporters Committee for Freedom of the Press, cited by Leib Dodell, letter to the editor, *New York Times*, July 8, 1998.

32. *New York Times*, November 27, 1988; italics added.

33. Michael Parenti, *Make-Believe Media: The Politics of Entertainment* (New York: St. Martin's, 1992).

34. Parenti, *Make-Believe Media,* Chapter 7 and studies cited therein.

35. Parenti, *Make-Believe Media,* Chapter 5.

36. *PBS and the American Worker,* Committee for Cultural Studies, City University of New York, June 1990; and U.S. House of Representatives, Committee on Energy and Commerce, *Public Communications Act of 1991, Report 102–363,* November 23, 1991, 13 ff.

37. Federal Communications Commission, "Applicability of the Fairness Doctrine in the Handling of Controversial Issues of Public Importance," *Federal Register* 29, July 25, 1964, 10415 ff.

38. See bimonthly publication of *KPFA Folio,* Sonoma County Peace and Justice Center, California; also <http://www.savepacifica.net/strike/>.

39. Ben Clarke, "NAB Moves to Kill Low Power FM," *San Francisco Bay Guardian,* September 20, 2000; see also <http://www.freeradio.org>.

40. Robert McChesney, *Telecommunications, Mass Media and Democracy: The Battle for the Control of U.S. Broadcasting 1928–1935* (New York: Oxford University Press, 1993).

13

Elections, Parties, and Voters

The U.S. political system, it is said, is democratic, for we get to elect our leaders, choosing between competing candidates in free and open elections. Yet, as a democratic institution, the electoral process leaves much to be desired. People complain about the quality of the candidates, the lack of real choice, the length of campaigns, the amount of mudslinging, the lack of issue discussion, and the high campaign costs. One survey found that only 23 percent agreed that "the two-party system works well," while 67 percent thought it had "real problems" or was seriously disfunctional.[1] This chapter lends support to that view.

Republicrats and Demopublicans

For generations, professional party politicians ran the "party machine," doling out little favors to little people and big favors to realty speculators, developers, business contractors, and machine leaders themselves. The party bosses were sufficiently occupied by the pursuit of office and patronage to remain untroubled by questions of social justice and "never questioned the basic distribution of resources in society."[2] Yet, concerned with winning, they were capable of responding to strong popular sentiment at times. Old-fashioned political machines can still be found in a number of cities, but they seldom exercise influence beyond the local level. Political party organizations have declined for a number of reasons:

First, campaign finance laws now allocate federal election funds directly to candidates rather than to parties, thereby weakening the influence of the party organization.

194

Second, now that so many states have adopted the direct primary, candidates no longer seek out the party organization for a place on the ticket, but independently pursue the nomination by entering the primary.

Third, since televised political ads can reach everyone's living room, the precinct captain is less needed to canvas the neighborhood and publicize the candidate. Today's candidate is more in need of moneyed backers or personal wealth to pay for costly media campaigns, complete with pollsters and public relations experts, who help select issues and shape electoral strategy, emphasizing image manipulation and catchy sound bites.

The two major parties offer a limited choice. It is not quite accurate to characterize the Republicans and Democrats as Tweedledee and Tweedledum. Were they exactly alike in image and posture, they would have even more difficulty than they do in maintaining the appearance of choice. From the perspective of those who advocate a basic change in national priorities, the question is not, "Are there differences between the parties?" but "Do the differences make a difference?"

On most fundamental economic class issues, the similarities between the parties loom so large as frequently to obscure the differences. Both the Democratic and Republican parties are committed to the preservation of the private corporate economy; huge military budgets; the use of subsidies and tax allowances to bolster business profits; the development of whole new industries at public expense; the use of repression against opponents of the existing class structure; the maximization of corporate power through global "free trade" agreements; and the defense of the multinational corporate empire with intervention against noncomplying nations and rebellious elements abroad. In short, most Republican and Democratic politicians are dedicated to strikingly similar definitions of the public interest, at great cost to the life chances of underprivileged people at home and abroad. This is especially true of the overlap between Republicans and "New Democrats" or Clinton Democrats, who have been the party of the business subsidies, tax breaks, and big military budgets almost as much as the GOP.[3] So, William Winpisinger, former president of the International Association of Machinists was moved to comment, "We don't have a 2-party system in this country. We have the Demopublicans. It's one party of the corporate class, with two wings — the Democrats and Republicans."[4]

Candidates compete vigorously for the prizes of office, expending huge sums in the doing, with campaign buttons, bumper stickers, and television and radio spots. Using every gimmick devoid of meaningful content, the candidate (usually a male) sells his image as he would a soap product to a public conditioned to such bombardments: his family and his looks; his experience in office and devotion to public service; his sincerity, sagacity, and fighting spirit; his military record and patriotism; his determination to help working families, farmers, and businesspeople, the young and old, the rich and poor, and especially those in between; his determination to improve

THE TWO PARTY SYSTEM

education, cut government waste, exercise firm leadership, strengthen our police and our national defenses, bringing us lasting peace and prosperity, and so forth. As someone once said: "You can't fool all the people all of the time, but if you can fool them once it's good for four years."

This is not to deny there are differences between — and within — the major parties. Generally, progressives and liberals are more likely to find a home in the Democratic party and conservatives in the GOP. There are discernible policy differences in Congress between conservative Republicans and the progressive wing of the Democratic party, with the latter more in favor of environmental protections, labor rights, progressive taxes, better human services, cuts in military spending, and gender and ethnic equality.

Studies show that Democratic strength has gathered increasingly at the lower end of the income scale and Republican strength increasingly at the upper end. In recent House elections, Democratic candidates got their strongest support from voters who earned under $15,000, while GOP candidates ran strongest among voters who earned over $100,000. Generally, the Democrats do best among liberals, the poor, union members and wage workers in general, women, African Americans, Jews, Latinos, city dwellers, and to a lesser extent, Catholics. Republicans do best among conservatives,

White males, White Protestants, White Southerners, rural and suburban dwellers, born-again Christians, managerial professionals, the upwardly mobile, and the wealthy.[5]

The Two-Party Monopoly

Whatever their differences, the two major parties cooperate in various stratagems to maintain their monopoly over electoral politics and discourage the growth of third parties. All fifty states have laws, written and enforced by Democratic and Republican officials, setting requirements for third-party ballot access. Various states have required that persons who sign petitions enabling independent or third-party candidates to appear on the ballot must also say they intend to vote for the candidate and agree with the party's principles. In at least eight states, the courts have ruled against such a requirement, arguing that signing a petition means only that the signers think it appropriate for the minor party to appear on the election ballot. In some states persons who sign a petition to allow a third party on the ballot were prohibited from voting in a major party primary. This law has been repeatedly challenged in various state courts, and as of 2000, Texas remained the only state where the prohibition continued. A statewide third-party candidate in Texas must collect 56,000 signatures in two months and cannot include people who voted in Democratic or Republican primaries.[6]

In some states the time to collect signatures has been cut to one week, virtually an impossible task. In 1999, West Virginia doubled the number of signatures needed to get on the ballot from 6,000 to 12,000. Ohio requires about 35,000 signatures for new parties in presidential years and about 50,000 in midterm years, and the petitions are due very early in the election year. The Ohio procedure is so daunting that it has rarely been used.[7]

In Virginia, no one may circulate a petition outside his or her congressional district or a neighboring district. In West Virginia, a petitioner must obtain "credentials" from each county clerk in every county the petitioner works. Numerous other states require that petitioners for third parties must be residents of the state in which they are soliciting signatures.[8] In Florida, an independent or third-party presidential candidate must submit 167,000 valid signatures and pay ten cents for each one, for a minimum of $16,700 in filing fees. In Louisiana, an independent candidate must pay a $5,000 filing fee just to begin the process of collecting signatures to get on the ballot.[9]

Over the years, some of the unfair restrictions against third parties have been struck down after court battles.[10] But sometimes decisions go the other way; thus, the Supreme Court upheld a Washington state law that requires minor-party candidates to win at least 1 percent of the total primary election vote in order to run in the general election, in effect depriving most of them ballot access.[11] A New Jersey state court upheld that state's ballot format, which gives the most prominent columns on the ballot to the major parties. Other parties have their candidates' names scattered about in different columns, thereby further diminishing their visibility.[12] Bills have been submitted in Congress, so far without success, that would eliminate all these various discriminatory barriers to ballot access and institute a more permissive and uniform election law throughout the fifty states.

It has been argued that restrictive ballot requirements are needed to screen out frivolous candidates. But who decides who is "frivolous"? And what is so harmful about allegedly frivolous candidates that the electorate must be protected from them by all-knowing major party officials? In any case, the few states that allow an easy access to the ballot — such as Iowa, Tennessee, and New Hampshire, where relatively few signatures are needed and plenty of time is allowed to collect them — have suffered no invasion of frivolous or kooky candidates.

The Federal Election Campaign Act provides millions of dollars in public funds to the major parties to finance their national conventions, primaries, and presidential campaigns. But public money goes to third-party candidates only *after* an election and only if they glean 5 percent of the vote, something nearly impossible to achieve without generous funds and regular media access. In sum, they cannot get the money unless they get 5 percent of the vote; but they are not likely to get 5 percent without massive amounts of money with which they could buy sufficient national exposure. While receiving nothing from the federal government, minor parties must observe all federal record-keeping and reporting requirements and are subjected to limitations on contribution and expenditure.

The Federal Election Commission, designated by law to have three Republican and three Democratic commissioners, spends most of its time looking into the accounts of smaller parties and filing suits against them and other independent candidates. Americans would balk at seeing any particular religious denomination designated the state religion, to be favored by the law over all other religions; indeed, the Constitution forbids it. Yet we have accepted laws that endow two private political parties with public authority to regulate the activities of all other parties, in effect, rigging the rules to preserve the two-party monopoly. One wonders what the electoral landscape would look like if smaller parties were granted a level playing field.

Proportional Representation: Making Every Vote Count

The system of representation itself discriminates against third parties. The single-member-district, winner-take-all plurality elections used in the United States artificially magnify the strength of major parties. A party that polls a plurality, be it 40, 50, or 60 percent, wins 100 percent of a district's representation with the election of its one candidate, while the other parties, regardless of their vote, receive zero representation. Since there are few districts in which minor parties have a plurality, they invariably have a higher percentage of wasted or unrepresented votes, and win a lower percentage of seats, if any, than their actual percentage of votes. In 1996 in Massachusetts, Republican candidates for Congress won roughly a third of the ballots cast, yet all twelve of the state's congressional seats went to the Democrats. In Kansas, Nebraska, and Oklahoma, Democratic candidates won an average of 37 percent of the votes, yet all the congressional seats were won by Republicans.[13] Across the country, those living in safe Republican or safe Democratic districts and who support the weaker party have little reason to vote, so with supporters of minor parties everywhere.

Two-party competition does not really exist in any competitive form in most districts. Usually one party dominates over the other so that the two-party system has been largely a patchwork of one-party dominances — fortified by the winner-take-all system. About one out of every ten representatives is elected to Congress with no opposition in either the primary or the general election. During the 1980s and 1990s, from 85 to 90 percent of incumbents who sought congressional office were reelected.[14] Death and voluntary retirement seem to be the important factors behind the turnover in representative assemblies.

In contrast to the single-member winner-take-all system is proportional representation, which provides a party with legislative seats roughly in accordance with the percentage of votes it wins. Let us say, ten single-member districts were joined into one ten-seat district; instead of the winner taking all, a party that gets around 50 percent of the vote would get only five seats and one that received 30 percent would get three seats, and one that received 20 percent would get two seats. Every vote would win some representation.

Some political scientists and publicists argue that proportional representation (PR) is an odd, alien, overly complicated system that encourages the proliferation of splinter parties and leads to legislative stalemate, fragmentation, polarization, and instability. They laud the two-party system because it supposedly allows for cohesion, stable majorities, and measured competition.[15] But the much lauded two-party "stability" is often just a code word for "lack of choice" and lack of coherent agendas, clear differences, and responsiveness to popular sentiment.

Furthermore, there is nothing odd or quirky about proportional representation; it is the most widespread and popular voting system in the world. Some form of PR is used in virtually every country in Europe, from Austria and Belgium to Sweden and Switzerland. Single-member, winner-take-all is used in Great Britain, Canada, and the United States. In November 1993, New Zealand adopted proportional representation in a national referendum by a vote of 85 to 15 percent. Proportional representation usually produces stable coalition governments that are consistently more representative and responsive than winner-take-all systems.[16]

Proportional representation voting systems are not unmanageably complicated. Citizens are able to cast votes for their preferred candidates and for parties that more closely reflect their interests. Nor is PR completely alien to the United States. Some local governments and school districts around the country have employed it. Between 1915 and 1960, five Ohio municipalities used PR, and it enabled ethnic and political minorities to win representation on their city councils. In 1945, in the last PR race for the New York City Council, Democrats won fifteen seats, Republicans three, Liberals and Communists two each, and the American Labor party one, and public interest in city council elections was high. Proportional representation was abolished in New York not because it didn't work but because it worked too well, giving representation to a variety of leftist views. Today under winner-take-all in New York, the Democrats have thirty-four council seats, the Republicans have one, and smaller parties are frozen out.[17]

Wedded to the unfair advantages of the current system, Democrats and Republicans in Congress passed a law in 1967 *requiring* all states to set up single-member, winner-take-all districts. In 1995, an African-American congresswoman from Georgia proposed the Voters Choice Act that would repeal the single-member requirement and allow states to run elections under some form of proportional representation. The proposal was buried in committee.

The present system deprives minority parties not only of representation but eventually of voters too, since not many citizens wish to "waste" their ballots on a minor party that seems incapable of achieving a legislative presence. Sometimes it does not even seem worth the effort to vote for one of the two major parties in districts where the other major party so predominates and will be winning the sole representation. If we had PR, however, every vote would be given some representation, and people would be more likely to vote. This partly explains why voter turnout ranges from 36 to 42 percent for congressional elections, and around 50 percent for presidential contests; while in countries that have PR, turnouts range from 70 to 90 percent.[18] With proportional representation, there is a broader and more varied choice of parties, a higher rate of participation, and a more equitable representation of ethnic minorities and women than in our two-party system.

Rigging the Game

The electoral system is rigged in other ways. A common device is *redistricting*, changing the boundaries of a constituency ostensibly to comply with population shifts but also to guarantee a preferred political outcome. U.S. House of Representative districts and state legislative districts are drawn every ten years, after the national census is taken, by the various state legislatures, subject to veto by the governors. In almost all instances of districting, political and party considerations are given prime play.

Often the purpose of redistricting is to weaken the electoral base of progressive members in Congress, state legislatures, or city councils, or dilute the electoral strength of new or potentially dissident constituencies. In Philadelphia, a Latino community of 63,000 anticipated control of at least one and possibly two seats in the Pennsylvania Assembly. Instead, their cohesive community was divided into a number of districts, none of which had more than a 15 percent Latino population. Chicago's Puerto Rican and Mexican-American community suffered a similar plight. The New York City Council split 50,000 working-class Black voters in Queens into three predominantly White districts, making them a numerical minority in all three. And in Los Angeles County and nine Texas counties, heavy concentrations of Latinos were divided into separate districts to dilute their voting power.

A common form of redistricting is the *gerrymander,* in which district lines are drawn in elaborately contorted ways so as to maximize the strength of the party that does the drawing.[19] Sometimes gerrymandering is used to deny minority representation (as in the redistricting examples just given); other times it is used to assure minority representation — by creating a district that manages to concentrate enough African-American voters so as to allow the election of an African American. Conservative opponents condemn such practices as "racial gerrymandering" and "reverse discrimination." But defendants argue that though such districts may look bizarre on a map, they are the only way to abridge a White monopoly and ensure some Black representation in states where Whites remain overrepresented even after the redistricting.

One such district was the 12th congressional in North Carolina, which elected Mel Watt, a progressive African American, in 1992. Federal courts had it redrawn three times in six years — ostensibly because of the "racial gerrymandering." By 1998 Watt found himself running in a district that was almost 70 percent White and only 55 percent Democratic. He won reelection nevertheless, but only after a difficult campaign. Representatives Eva Clayton of North Carolina and Sanford Bishop and Cynthia McKinney of Georgia, all African-American progressives, also faced redistricting, and while all three managed to win reelection in 1998, they represented districts that were no longer "safe."

In 1993 and 1996 the U.S. Supreme Court invalidated congressional district plans in North Carolina and Texas because of "racial gerrymandering."[20] But in 1999, with surprising unanimity, the Court ruled that even a conscious concentration of Black voters did not automatically make a district unconstititutional, as long as the state's primary motive was political rather than racial.[21] Federal courts generally have argued that race cannot be the primary factor in drawing a district, even in a state with a longstanding pattern of shutting out African-American representation. At the same time, the courts have accepted the *political* gerrymandering that shapes so many districts around the country. Thus, in Texas, with less than a majority of the statewide vote, the Democrats (drawing the district lines to their satisfaction) won twenty-one of the thirty congressional seats, with Republican voters being packed into the remaining districts that elected Republican incumbents.

After the 1990 census, the Republican administration of George Bush directed certain states to maximize the number of districts packed with African-American and Latino voters. Bush had an ulterior motive: by corralling minorities (who voted heavily Democratic) into electoral ghettos, the GOP would have a better chance of carrying the more numerous surrounding White districts.[22]

Proportional representation provides a more equitable form of representation. Even if districts are redrawn by a neutral computer method, under the winner-take-all method there is a kind of gerrymander effect, that is, large numbers of voters will be left without any actual representation. As one PR advocate explains: "If I'm a Democrat living in the Dallas suburbs, and they do a computer-driven map that leaves me in a 65 percent Republican district, then I've been effectively gerrymandered out of an opportunity to elect a person who represents my interests — and the shape of the district doesn't matter."[23] But with PR, the five Republican suburban districts would be made into one composite district with five representatives, and Democratic votes would count toward electing one or two of the five.

The national census taken every ten years undercounts low-income voters, missing more renters than homeowners and many poor residents in overcrowded neighborhoods and remote rural areas. Low-income people also tend to be less forthcoming with census takers. Undercounting leads to less federal aid and underrepresentation in Congress and the state legislatures. According to the Census Bureau, the 1990 census missed an estimated 8.4 million people and double-counted or improperly tallied 4.4 million, including many affluent Whites who had more than one residence.[24] To get a more accurate tally, the Census Bureau planned to supplement door-to-door counts with sampling data. But the move was squelched by a Republican-controlled Congress.

If, despite rigged rules, dissident groups prove viable, then authorities are likely to resort to more blatantly coercive measures. Radical groups that gain grassroots strength are likely to become the object of official violence. The case of the U.S. Socialist party is instructive. By 1918, the Socialist party held 1,200 offices in 340 cities including 79 mayors in 24 different states, 32 legislators, and a member of Congress. The next year, after having increased their vote dramatically, the Socialists suffered the combined attacks of state, local, and federal authorities. Their headquarters in numerous cities were sacked, their funds confiscated, their leaders jailed, their immigrant members summarily deported, their newspapers denied mailing privileges, and their elected candidates denied their seats in various state legislatures and Congress. Within a few years the party was finished as a viable political force. While confining themselves to legal and peaceful forms of political competition, the Socialists discovered that their opponents were burdened by no similar compunctions. The guiding principle of ruling elites was — and still is: When change threatens to rule, then the rules are changed.

Money: A Necessary Condition

The biggest handicap faced by third-party candidates — and progressive candidates within the major parties — is procuring the growing sums of money needed to win office. Money is the lifeblood of electoral campaigns, "the mother's milk of politics" as the old saying goes. Today, a race for a seat in the House of Representatives may cost hundreds of thousands of dollars, while senatorial and gubernatorial races can cost millions. The $2 billion spent on electoral campaigns in 1996 stood as an all-time record until the 2000 campaign, when spending reached $5 billion.[25]

Sometimes millions are expended not to win office but merely to procure the party nomination. In 1998, Al Checchi spent a record $38 million in an unsuccessful bid to win the Democratic gubernatorial primary in California, and in 2000, Jon Corzine spent over $25 million in the New Jersey Democratic primary for the Senate, his first public office, and a final total of $65 million to win the election, a record sum for a statewide office. The mere idea of competing against a rich opponent can deter challengers. When Checchi, with his fortune of $750 million, made his bid, two leading California Democrats, Senator Dianne Feinstein and former congressman and White House staffer Leon Panetta decided to bow out. And in the New Jersey race, Congressman Frank Pallone dropped out, citing Corzine's $400 million fortune as the discouraging factor.[26]

Money is also needed for the national presidential nominating conventions. In 2000, each major party received $13.5 million in federal funds to help pay for their conventions, from a Congress dominated by the two major parties. Both major-party conventions also received substantial sums from their host cities, and large cash gifts from corporations, along with fleets of cars from General Motors, software from Microsoft, and corporate-sponsored golf outings, lunches, hospitality rooms, and post-session celebrations for the delegates.[27]

Big corporations like Ford, General Motors, AT&T, and Anheuser-Busch formed the "Commission on Presidential Debates" to bankroll the televised presidential debates. This "independent bipartisan commission," financed by private corporations and staffed by Republican and Democratic party officials, decided that only the two major-party candidates should participate. The commission stipulated that candidates must appear on enough state ballots to have a chance to win an electoral college majority, and must have an average of 15 percent support in five major national polls, thus ruling out Ralph Nader, Green party presidential candidate, and Pat Buchanan, Reform party candidate in 2000.[28]

Campaign contributions are limited by law to $1000 per person. But if fifty top executives of a given company give $1000 each, that is $50,000 to a grateful candidate. A rich individual can make a host of contributions in the name of relatives, devoted staff, or whomever. In addition, there are the travel accommodations, fat speaking fees, and other free services that companies are happy to provide to needy or greedy legislators.[29]

In most national elections, business-oriented political action committees (PACs) generally outspend labor PACs by more than seven to one. When it comes to "soft money," the ratio of business over labor spending is more like 21 to 1. Personal contributions by individual businesspeople outranked individual labor contributions by a ratio of more than 700 to 1. About three-fourths of all this money finds its way into the coffers of the more conservative of the two capitalist parties, the GOP.[30]

Soft money consists of funds raised by private committees, including those run by parties, corporations, unions, and wealthy individuals. It cannot be spent directly on a candidate's campaign, but it can be used for "issue advertising" and for singing the candidate's praises — as long as the viewer is not urged to vote for or against anyone. Frequently difficult to distinguish from campaign ads, soft money ads provide an enormous loophole for circumventing federal limitations on campaign spending.

To hedge their bets, big donors often contribute to major-party candidates who are running against each other, thereby trying to ensure the cooperation of whoever wins. In the 2000 presidential election, leading industries contributed generously to both major political parties: telephone utilities gave $3 million to the Democrats and $3.6 million to the Republicans; the securities and investment industry gave a total of $7.5 million to Democrats and $7.4 million to the Republicans; casinos and gambling establishments gave $1.8 million to each of the two parties. The insurance industry and air transport industry, along with General Motors, Ford, Chrysler, Textron, Rockwell, AT&T, Microsoft, Time Warner, Exxon Mobil, Philip Morris, Walt Disney, Coca-Cola, Citigroup, Blue Cross/Blue Shield, and scores of others gave to both parties, usually substantially more to the Republicans.[31] Generous sums are even doled out to lawmakers who run unopposed, to ensure influence over the preordained victor.

In presidential contests, there is now what has become known as the "money primary." A candidate who can gather early and massive funding becomes designated as the front-runner, or at least is guaranteed survival as a candidate through much of the primary campaign. During the 2000 Republican presidential primaries, George W. Bush, the son of former president

George Bush, "won" the money primary by raising $50 million four months before the first primary in New Hampshire. That sum came from just 0.03 percent of the U.S. public.[32] Several of Bush's GOP primary opponents dropped out because of insufficient funds after they discovered that most of the big contributors they hoped to tap had already written their checks to Bush. By July 2000, at the time he was nominated as the Republican candidate for president, Bush had already spent $97.2 million — and the actual campaign against his Democratic opponent had not yet even begun. Bush also received $67.5 million in public funds for the general election.[33] In sum, well before voters have a chance to make up their minds, a handful of rich contributors are winnowing the candidate field, determining who will be chosen to run in the election. Only a select few can vote in the money primary.

Money is needed for public relations consultants, pollsters, campaign workers, campaign offices, telephones, computers, faxes, mailings, and media advertisements. Yet it is argued by some political scientists and pundits that money is not a major influence since better-financed candidates sometimes lose, as demonstrated by Steve Forbes, who spent $30 million in 2000 and still failed to gain the GOP presidential nomination. Electoral victory, the argument goes, is more likely to be determined by other factors such as party label, ideology, and incumbency; the largest sums go to entrenched incumbents who are expected to win, so money does not bring victory, it follows victory.

In response, we might note that the bigger spenders may not always win but they usually do, as has been the case over the last fifteen years in more than 80 percent of House and Senate races. In the 1996 congressional races 88 percent of the candidates who spent the most money won the election. Even in "open races," with no incumbent running, better-funded candidates won 75 percent of the time in 1996.[34]

Money influences not only who wins, but who runs, and who is taken seriously when running. Candidates sometimes are backed by party leaders explicitly because they have personal wealth and can use it to wage an effective campaign. It is true that a multimillionaire like Steve Forbes failed to gain the GOP nomination. But even though he was of lackluster personality, and had never held public office in his life, he won primaries in two states and was considered a serious contender throughout the campaign because he had enough money to pay for thousands of television ads and hundreds of campaign workers.

Candidates who win while spending less than their opponents still usually have to spend quite a lot. While not a surefire guarantor of victory, a large war chest — even if not the largest — is usually a necessary condition. Money may not ensure victory, but the lack of it usually guarantees defeat. Without large sums, there is rarely much of a campaign, as poorly funded minor-party candidates have repeatedly discovered.

The influence of money is also evident in the many state ballot initiatives from Florida to California relating to health care, transportation, environmental issues, and other vital questions. In most instances, there initially is strong voter support for the public interest position; then as the campaign progresses and big business wages a heavily financed pulverizing blitz of television ads, outspending its opponents by as much as fifty to one in some cases, the tide turns in business's favor.[35]

Some conservative pundits like George Will, mistaking wealth for virtue, think big money in politics is good for democracy. They argue that campaign spending reform would impose an unhealthy limitation on elections. But there is a growing awareness in the United States of the undue and undemocratic influence of money. In Georgia, civil rights leaders have launched a court challenge mandating the creation of publicly financed campaigns for state senate elections because winners were enjoying a more than 300-percent spending advantage over losers. In Maine, voters approved a Clean Election Act in 1996 that allows candidates to opt for full public financing of their campaigns if they agree to eschew private fundraising. In 1999, a similar law was approved by voters in Massachusetts and Vermont. Vermont Progressive party candidate for governor Anthony Pollina was the first statewide candidate in the United States to qualify for full public financing, and was being treated as an equal contender by the press. Support for full public funding of elections wins bipartisan support among voters across the nation.[36] But some legislators have challenged these laws, seeking to preserve their ability to outspend their opponents.

Electoral competition is supposed to keep political officeholders accountable to their constituents; if they wish to remain in office, they presumably must respond to the preferences of their voters. But do the conditions of electoral competition actually exist? Rigged electoral laws and moneyed forces so limit the range of alternatives as to raise serious questions about democratic accountability. The Republican and Democratic parties are loose conglomerations organized around one common purpose: the pursuit of office. For this reason, American parties have been characterized as "nonideological." In a sense they are, insofar as their profound ideological commitment to corporate capital at home and abroad and to the ongoing class structure is seldom made an explicit issue.

The major parties have a conservative effect on the consciousness of the electorate and on the performance of representative government. They operate from a commonly shared ideological perspective that is best served by the avoidance of iconoclastic politico-economic views and by the suppression or cooptation of dissenters. By evading fundamental issues, the major parties prevent class divisions from sharpening. They propagate a noisy, apolitical politics of image and personality, narrowing the scope of participation while giving a busy appearance of popular government.

The Struggle to Vote

Two centuries of struggle have brought real gains in extending the franchise, but the opportunity to vote is still not readily available to every citizen. From the early days of the Republic, rich propertied interests sought to limit popular participation. Propertyless White males, indentured servants, women, Blacks (including freed slaves), and Native Americans had no access to the ballot. In the wake of working-class turbulence during the 1820s and 1830s, formal property qualifications were abolished for White males. And after a century of agitation, women won the right to vote with the adoption of the Nineteenth Amendment in 1920. In 1961, the Twenty-third Amendment gave District of Columbia residents representation in presidential elections, but they are still denied full voting representation in Congress. In 1971, the Twenty-sixth Amendment lowered the minimum voting age from twenty-one to eighteen for all elections.

The Fifteenth Amendment, ratified in 1870, written in the blood of civil war, prohibited voter discrimination because of race. But it took another century of struggle to make this right something more than a formality. In 1944, the Supreme Court ruled that all-White party primaries were unconstitutional.[37] Decades of agitation and political pressure, augmented by the growing voting power of African Americans in Northern cities, led to the Civil Rights Acts of 1957 and 1960, the Voting Rights Acts of 1965, 1970, 1975, and 1985, and several crucial Supreme Court decisions. Taken together, these measures (a) gave the federal government and courts power to act against state officials who were discriminating against non-Whites at the polls and (b) eliminated state restrictions — such as long-term residency requirements, literacy tests, and poll taxes — that had sharply reduced the electoral participation of the poor and less educated.[38] The result was that in certain parts of the South, African Americans began voting in visible numbers for the first time since Reconstruction.

Yet low-income people, be they Black, Latino, or White, still vote at half the rate of the more affluent. One reason is that while legal restrictions have been removed, administrative barriers remain largely in place. In countries with high voter participation, such as Sweden, governments actively pursue programs to register voters. The U.S. government offers no such encouragement. If anything, federal and state officials — and officials of both major parties — have a history of making it difficult for working people to register and vote. Registration centers are usually open only during working hours. Their locations can be remote and frequently changed. A change of residence requires a change of registration. Registration forms are frequently unnecessarily complex, acting almost as a kind of literacy test. They are sometimes in short supply, maldistributed, and sluggishly processed. Elections are held on a workday (Tuesday) with polls closing by early evening.

And polling places are sometimes not situated in readily accessible places. In one Texas county, officials closed down all but one of thirteen polling places, and Black and Latino voter turnout plummeted from 2,300 to 300. In parts of Mississippi, a person might have to sign up both at the town and county courthouses, which could mean driving ninety miles. During the 1988 Democratic primary, Flint, Michigan's ninety-one polling places were reduced to nine to discourage a protest vote for Jesse Jackson, an African-American liberal Democrat.[39]

In the 1996 presidential elections, more than one in five citizens who were registered did not vote because of long work hours, school, physical disabilities, or other difficulties.[40] Early voting registrars in some counties in Northern California enable people to vote on the two days preceding election day, many of whom would not otherwise have the opportunity. Voting should be held over a three-day period, including one or two weekend days as done in some countries with beneficial effects on turnout rates.

Thirteen percent of all African-American men, nearly 1.4 million, are prohibited from casting a ballot because of past criminal records or because they are currently behind bars. Almost every state in the Union denies prisoners the right to vote. Ten states impose lifetime disfranchisement for anyone ever convicted of a felony. In seven of these states, one in four African-American men are permanently disfranchised.[41]

During the 1980s, Reagan administration officials threatened to cut off federal aid in order to discourage state and local agencies from assisting in voter registration drives. The threats were partially successful. Federal officials also urged states to prohibit registration drives at food lines; some did. Voting-rights activists who tried to register people in welfare offices were arrested. In 1986, Federal Bureau of Investigation (FBI) agents streamed into Southern counties and interrogated over two thousand African Americans about whether their ballots were fraudulently cast. While finding no evidence of fraud, the FBI did cause some voters to think twice about ever voting again. Eight voting-rights activists were indicted on 215 criminal charges; five were acquitted; two plea-bargained to misdemeanors and one was convicted of technical violations less serious than those that White registrars had long been committing with impunity.

In 1992, Congress passed a "motor voter" bill that sought to increase voter turnout among the elderly, the poor, and the infirm, by allowing citizens to register as they renew their driver's licenses, or apply for Social Security, unemployment, welfare, or disability benefits. President Bush vetoed it. The next year a bill was passed allowing registration at motor vehicle and military recruiting offices but — to avoid a Republican Senate filibuster — the bill made no provision for registration at welfare and unemployment offices.

Often presumed to have died out with old-time machine politics, crooked electoral methods are still very much with us. The computer-based punch-card systems used nowadays in most electoral jurisdictions are at least as susceptible to error, accident, and deliberate manipulation as paper ballots and mechanical-lever voting machines. Investigations reveal numerous opportunities for tabulation errors and distorted counts. In an election in St. Louis, ballots in working-class African-American wards were more than three times *less* likely to be counted as those in White wards. Computer irregularities were found in locales in at least seven other states.[42]

These irregularities are not usually of a random nature. Largely Republican-leaning counties use optical scanners that record 99.7 percent of the votes, while the punch-card systems usually in predominantly lower-income Democratic counties record only 97 percent of the votes. So approximately 3 percent of Democratic votes are discarded.[43]

In one of the closest contests in U.S. history, the 2000 presidential election between Vice President Al Gore and Texas governor George W. Bush, the final result hinged on how the vote went in Florida, which gave Bush a razor-thin margin on election night. Post-election investigations revealed serious irregularities:

- Punch-card ballots were printed in a confusing manner causing several thousand Gore supporters to mistakenly vote for another candidate; voters who realized they had made a mistake were denied a new ballot, even though the law stipulates up to three ballots in case of error.
- Punch-card ballots were nullified or disputed more often in pro-Gore precincts than in pro-Bush ones. Voting machines read nearly 4 percent of the punch cards as blank or invalid. By contrast, ballots read by modern optical scanning systems rejected only about 1.4 percent. The more modern equipment tended to be in predominantly White pro-Bush precincts.
- Some 10,000 primarily African-American voters were turned away in Seminole County and 22,000 in Duvalle County (Jacksonville) after they registered but were never added to the voter rolls.
- The telephone lines to the central registrar were continuously busy, so many voters were unable to confirm their registration status. Anticipating an unusually high turnout, Florida election officials, who operate under the command of Governor Jeb Bush, George W.'s brother, dispatched laptop computers to avoid the busy telephone lines. A *New York Times* analysis shows that computers were dispatched to counties that voted disproportionately for George Bush. Predominantly Black counties that went heavily for Gore did not get computers despite the thousands of new registrants.
- In several heavily Democratic precincts, officials closed the polls early, leaving lines of would-be voters stranded.
- Ballots were misplaced and left uncounted; at least seven ballot boxes were found in unexplained places and two bags of ballots were found in a poll worker's car trunk. An African-American church that had

served as a polling place in numerous elections was unable to get anyone to come pick up its ballot boxes at the end of the day.

- Florida state troopers, who operate under the command of Governor Jeb Bush, set up checkpoints near polling sites in predominantly Black precincts near Tallahassee. They stopped and held would-be voters for up to two hours while searching their cars.
- Many African Americans who had no police record were prevented from voting because they were incorrectly declared "convicted felons."
- Over two hundred Puerto Rican voters in Orange County were required to show two photo IDs before being permitted to vote, which many did not have. The legal requirement under Florida law was only one photo ID. This law itself, passed just before the election, posed an added difficulty for low-income or elderly voters who did not own cars or have driver's licenses or any other photo ID.
- During the recount, Bush agitators, imported from out of state, stormed the Dale County Canvassing Board, punched and kicked one of the officials, creating a climate of intimidation that caused the board to abandon its recount and accept the original pro-Bush tally. These various illegal and coercive actions, targeting areas heavily populated by Gore supporters, suppressed enough votes in Florida to give that state, the electoral college, and the presidency to George W. Bush.[44]

After the decision by the U.S. Supreme Court to halt the Florida recount in the contested counties (see Chapter 17), media organizations commissioned their own counts, gaining access to the ballots under Freedom of Information legislation. The result as of December 22, 2000, with the recounting of so-called "undervotes" in only one county, indicated that Al Gore was ahead by 140 votes.

In the 1993 New Jersey election, a Republican political consultant claimed that his party paid substantial sums to African-American ministers and Democratic campaign workers to refrain from urging their parishioners and constituents to vote on election day. "I think to a certain extent we suppressed the vote," he boasted.[45] According to the standard view, working-class people and the poor have a low turnout because they are wanting in information, education, and civic awareness. But if they are so naturally inclined to apathy, one wonders why entrenched interests find it necessary to take such stenuous measures to discourage their participation.

Another ploy for suppressing the votes of marginalized groups is the at-large elections. Instead of election by district, the at-large election gives a winner-take-all victory to a citywide slate, allowing complete White domination and freezing out minority representation, as has happened in various communities. Voter registration among low-income groups is low and declining, most notably in the northern cities where the minority poor are concentrated and where the Democratic party no longer has the organizational capacity to bring its core voters to the polls. At the same time, voter participation rates among the affluent are increasing.[46] Nonvoting has a feedback effect. As fewer among the poor and the ethnic minorities vote, the politicians pay even less attention to them, further convincing the nonparticipants that officialdom is unresponsive and that voting is a futile gesture.

Voter "Apathy" and Participation

With good reason people complain, "Politicians tell us one thing to get our votes, then do another thing once they are elected." If many politicians are half-truth artists, it is not necessarily because they are morally flawed. More often, they are caught in the contradiction of having to be both a "candidate of the people" and a servant to the desires of wealthy contributors and corporate capitalism.

Many people fail to vote because (a) as noted above, they face various kinds of official discouragement and intimidation, (b) they do not find any candidate who appeals to them, and (c) they have trouble believing that voting makes a difference. Many who do vote participate with little enthusiasm and growing cynicism. In a 1997 *New York Times*/CBS poll, 79 percent of respondents agreed that government is "pretty much run by a few big interests looking out for themselves."[47] In Reagan's "landslide" victories in the presidential elections of 1980 and 1984, less than 30 percent of eligible voters actually cast their ballots for him; almost 50 percent stayed home. In 1996, Clinton was elected by slightly less than 25 percent of the eligible electorate.

Voter turnout has been in decline since the mid-1960s. Nationwide surveys find that most nonvoters express disappointment and frustration regarding the choices available. A survey in 2000 found that some 51 percent of nonvoters feel deeply cynical and angry about politics, or disenchanted and dismayed by the incessant spin, the constant drone of campaign ads and the vast sums being spent. Another 40 percent "care little about politics and public affairs."[48]

It has been argued that since nonvoters tend to be among the less educated and more apathetic, it is just as well they do not exercise their franchise. Since they are likely to be swayed by prejudice and demagogy, their voting would constitute a potential threat to our democratic system.[49] Behind this reasoning lurks the dubious presumption that better-educated, upper-income people who vote are more rational and less compelled by self-interest and ethno-class prejudices, an impression that itself is one of those comforting prejudices upper- and middle-class people have about themselves.

Some writers argue that low voter turnout is symptomatic of a "politics of happiness": people are apathetic about voting because they are fairly content with things.[50] Certainly some people are blithely indifferent to political issues — even issues that may affect their lives in important ways. But generally speaking, the many millions of Americans outside the voting universe are not among the more contented but among the less affluent and more alienated. The "politics of happiness" is usually nothing more than a cover for the politics of discouragement. What is seen as apathy may really be antipathy. Apathy is often a psychological defense against a discouraging powerlessness. It is not contentment or lack of civic virtue that keeps people from the polls but an understandably negative response to the political frustrations they experience.

Voters who ascribe undesirable traits to one party are sometimes then induced to support the other. Thus, the suspicion that Democrats might favor the urban poor and labor unions leads some middle-class Whites to assume that the Republican party is devoted to their interests, which may not be the case. Similarly, the identification of Republicans as the party of big business suggests to some working-class voters that, in contrast, the Democrats are not for business but for the "little man," a conclusion that often may be unfounded.

Delegates to the Republican national convention in 2000 were more conservative on issues than a majority of registered Republican voters. One in five delegates put their net worth at $1 million or more. Most were White middle-aged males opposed to campaign finance reform, affirmative action, gay rights, progressive income tax, stronger environmental policies, and legal abortion. They supported a federal law to impose prayer in the schools but not federal funds for school repair programs. The chances of finding a GOP delegate with a family income under $25,000 was fifty to one. At the Democratic national convention the odds were better: fourteen to one, but still hardly representative of the wider U.S. public.[51]

When magnified by partisan rhetoric, the differences between the parties appear worrisome enough to induce millions of citizens to vote — if not for then against someone. Voters who have no great hope that one candidate will do much for them might persistently fear that the other will make things even worse. This lesser-of-two-evils appeal is the single most effective inducement to voter participation. Voters are offered a candidate who violates their interests and who is dedicated to the preservation of corporate globalism, then they are presented with another candidate who promises to be even worse. Thus, they are not so much offered a choice as forced into one, voting not so much *for* as *against* someone.

When presented with distinct issue-linked choices, voters do respond, in the main, according to their pocketbook interests and other specific preferences. Candidates who stress bread-and-butter issues like jobs, affordable health care, better services, and fairer taxes, along with clearly stated poli-

*"I'm having second thoughts about the election . . .
I'm not sure I voted against the right person."*

cies relating to peace and the environment, will win votes from constituents concerned with such matters — assuming they are able to get their message heard.[52]

The United States has one of the lowest voter participation rates in the world. Some political analysts argue low voter participation is of no great concern since the preferences of nonvoters would be much the same as the preferences of voters. They would have us believe that even though upper-income people vote at almost twice the rate as lower-income people, and vote almost three times more often for conservative candidates, it would make no difference if low-income citizens voted in greater numbers. One wonders then why Republicans launch registration drives in affluent suburbs and try to discourage voting among inner-city Blacks, blue-collar workers, and other traditionally Democratic voters with low turnout rates.

The argument is sometimes made that if deprived groups have been unable to win their demands, it is because they are numerically weak compared to White, middle-class America. In a system that responds to the democratic power of numbers, a minority poor cannot hope to have its way. The deficiency is in the limited numbers of persons advocating change and not in the representative system, which operates according to majoritarian principles.

What is curious about this argument is that it is never applied to more select minority interests — for instance, oilmen. Now oilmen are far less numerous than the poor, yet the deficiency of their numbers, or of the numbers of other tiny minorities like bankers, industrialists, and billionaire investors, does not result in any lack of government responsiveness to their wants. On most important matters, government policy is determined less by the needs of the working majority and more by the strength of moneyed interests.

Democratic Input

There are two sweeping propositions that are often mistakenly drawn from what has been said thus far: (1) it does not matter who is elected, and (2) elected officials are indifferent to voter desires and other popular pressures. Both these notions are far from being the whole picture. Having correctly observed that two-party elections are designed to blur real issues, some people incorrectly conclude that what Democrats and Republicans do once elected to office is inconsequential and farcical. In truth, major-party policies can have an important effect on our well-being — as previous chapters in this book testify.

In Western Europe, benefiting from the more democratic system of proportional representation, left-oriented parties have established a viable presence in parliaments, even ruling from time to time. So they have helped create work conditions superior to those found in the United States. Be it disposable income, paid vacations, family allowances, workplace safety, protection from speedups, the right to collective bargaining, or job security, American employees have less protection and fewer benefits than their French, German, Scandinavian, British, and Benelux counterparts. Western Europeans have lower heart and cancer rates and spend substantially less on medical care. Among industrialized capitalist nations, the United States ranks seventeenth in longevity, and possesses one of the highest unemployment rates and one of the lowest levels of social services.

There is ample indication that elected representatives are not totally indifferent to voter demands, since — along with money — votes are still the means to office and empowerment. To be sure, officeholders often respond with deceitful assurances and empty promises. For instance, the heaviest applause line in Jimmy Carter's Inaugural Address was his vow to "move this year a step towards our ultimate goal — the elimination of all nuclear weapons from this Earth." His administration then went on to build two or three more nuclear bombs a day. In an elaborate publicity campaign President Reagan pledged a war against narcotics — and then went on to cut federal funds for drug rehabilitation and drug enforcement.

Be this as it may, the pressures of public opinion and the need to maintain electoral support sometimes place limits on how singlemindedly policymakers serve the moneyed powers and how unresponsive they remain to the needs of ordinary people. Thus, in 1993 President Clinton modified his militaristic policy on Somalia because of the public outcry regarding the loss of U.S. lives in that country. And in the face of resistance from senior citizens who vote in great numbers, leaders in both parties repeatedly have had to retreat from undermining Social Security.

Generally speaking, over the long haul just about every life-affirming policy that has come out of government originated not with presidents, cabinet members, congressional leaders, or other policy elites, but with the common people. So popular struggles have won advances in women's rights, civil rights, public education, health care, the eight-hour day, workers' benefits, occupational safety, environmental protection, consumer protection, and the abolition of child labor, and mustered opposition to U.S. military attacks upon other countries.

In sum, the range of electoral choices is so structured as to raise a serious question about the representative quality of the political system. Politics has always been principally "a rich man's game." Ironically, the popular election, the one institutional arrangement ostensibly designed to overcome the advantages of wealth and register the will of ordinary people, is itself greatly dependent on wealth. The way people respond to political reality depends on the way that reality is presented to them. If large numbers have become apathetic and cynical, including many who vote, it is at least partly because the electoral system and the two-party monopoly resist the kind of creative involvement that democracy is supposed to nurture. It is one thing to say that people tend to be uninvolved and poorly informed about political life. It is quite another to maintain a system that propagates these tendencies with every known distraction and discouragement.

Still, in the face of all obstacles, third-party challenges continue to arise among people who seek a democratic alternative — bringing to mind the observation made years ago by the great American socialist Eugene Debs: "I would rather vote for what I want and not get it than vote for what I don't want and get it." These are not always the only two choices. A third-party vote is not necessarily a wasted vote. Third parties can sometimes shift the center of political gravity, affecting the major parties, forcing them to adopt stances originating outside the two-party ideological monopoly.

Finally, even within the two-party context, elections remain one of the potential soft spots in the capitalist power structure. When an issue wins broad, well-organized support and receives some attention in the media, then officeholders cannot remain supremely indifferent to it. The grassroots pressures of demonstrations, civil disobedience, strikes, boycotts, riots, and other forms of popular agitation, along with the mobilization of voters and involvement in electoral campaigns can at times have a direct effect on who is elected and how they behave once in office.

Notes

1. Vanishing Voter Project, Center on the Press, Politics, and Public Policy, Harvard University, December 1999: <http://www.vanishingvoter.org>; and *New York Times*/CBS Poll, August 12, 1995.

2. Alan Altshuler, *Community Control* (New York: Pegasus, 1970), 74–75.

3. GOP stands for "Grand Old Party," a nickname of the Republican Party. Others say it stands for "Gathering of Plutocrats."

4. *Guardian*, Special Report, Fall 1981.

5. Voter News Service exit polls, *New York Times*, November 7, 1996.

6. Newsletter, Ballot Access News, October 1 and November 1, 1999.

7. Newsletter, Ballot Access News, January 1, 2000.

8. Newsletter, Ballot Access News, February 6, 1999.

9. Newsletter, Ballot Access News, June 1, 1999, and various other issues.

10. For instance, *West Virginia Libertarian Party v. Manchin* (1982) and *Buckley v. American Constitutional Law Foundation* (1999).

11. *Munro v. Socialist Workers Party* (1986).

12. Newsletter, Ballot Access News, November 1, 1999.

13. Newsletter, Center for Voting and Democracy, Washington, D.C., December 1996.

14. Newsletter, Center for Voting and Democracy, Washington, D.C., December 1999.

15. For instance, *New York Times* editorial, "Proportional Representation Flunks," April 24, 1993.

16. David Brodsky (ed.), "Proportional Representation Handbook for Progressives: Part II," *Progressive Clearinghouse Bulletin*, no. 6, 1998, 7; Robert Richie and Steven Hill, "The Case for Proportional Representation," *Boston Review*, February/March 1988, and related commentaries therein; Douglas Amy, *Real Choice/New Voices: The Case for Proportional Representation Elections in the United States* (New York: Columbia University Press, 1993).

17. Kathleen Barber, *Proportional Representation and Election Reform in Ohio* (Columbus: Ohio State University Press, 1996); Martin Gottlieb, "The 'Golden Age' of the City Council," *New York Times*, August 11, 1991; Leon Weaver and Judith Baum, "Proportional Representation on New York City Community School Boards," in Wilma Rule and Joseph Zimmerman (eds.), *United States Electoral Systems* (New York: Praeger, 1992).

18. *Ballot Access News*, December 8, 1998; Steven Hill, "Lessons on the Mechanics of Democracy," *Los Angeles Times*, February 15, 1996.

19. Named after Governor Elbridge Gerry of Massachusetts, who employed it in 1812, and "salamander," from the odd shape of the district.

20. *Shaw v. Reno* (1993); *Bush v. Vera* (1996).

21. *Hunt v. Cromartie* (1999).

22. Barry Yeoman, "Virtual Disenfranchisement," *Nation*, September 7–14, 1998.

23. Rob Richie, quoted in William Raspberry's column, *Washington Post*, June 27, 1996.

24. *New York Times*, June 24, 1998, and August 27, 1999.

25. Center for Responsible Politics, NPR news, November 8, 2000.

26. Jennifer Steen, "Self-Financing Candidates Scare Off Competitors," *Public Affairs Report*, Institute of Government Studies, University of California, Berkeley, September 1999; and *New York Times*, November 8, 2000.

27. Micah Sifry, "How Money in Politics Hurts You," *Dollars and Sense*, July/August 2000.

28. *Nation*, October 21, 1996; and Associated Press report, September 27, 2000.

29. Laura McClure, "Corporations Are Buying the Election," *Labor Party Press*, May 2000.

30. Report by the Center for Responsive Politics, Washington, D.C., in *Anderson Valley Advertiser*, November 27, 1996; also *New York Times*, April 19, 1992.

31. *Capital Eye*, Center for Responsive Politics, Summer 2000, <http://www.opensecrets.org>; "Soft Money, Big Stakes," *Newsweek*, October 28, 1996; *Solidarity*, September 1996, 13.

32. See Sam Pizzigati, "Bored by Politics? A Primary Reason," *Too Much,* Winter 2000; Only 739 contributors provided two-thirds of the GOP's $137 million of soft money: Ellen Goodman, *Boston Globe,* August 7, 2000.

33. Associated Press, August 21, 2000; *Oakland Tribune,* August 8, 2000.

34. *Christian Science Monitor,* July 28, 1997.

35. Peter Passell, "Business Was a Big Winner, Too," *New York Times,* November 7, 1996; and *San Francisco Chronicle,* May 19, 1998.

36. *Georgia State Conference of NAACP Branches v. Massey;* see Sharon Basco, "The Color of Money," *Nation,* February 1, 1999; Deidre Davidson, "As Maine Goes . . ." *Progressive Populist,* December 15, 1999; on Vermont, see <http://www.progressiveparty.org>.

37. *Smith v. Allwright* (1944).

38. See *Harper v. Virginia State Board of Elections* (1966) on poll taxes, and *Dunn v. Blumstein* (1972) on residency requirements.

39. Frances Fox Piven and Richard Cloward, *Why Americans Don't Vote* (New York: Pantheon, 1988); Warren Mitofsky and Martin Plissner, "Low Voter Turnout? Don't Believe It," *New York Times,* November 10, 1988; *Nation,* April 9, 1988, 486.

40. Loretta Bass and Lynne Casper, *Voting and Registration in the Election of November 1996,* Census Bureau Report, Washington, D.C., 1998.

41. Report by the Sentencing Project, *New York Times,* October 23, 1998; and Human Rights Watch *World Report 1999, United States.*

42. Ronnie Dugger, "Annals of Democracy, Counting Votes," *New Yorker,* November 7, 1988; James Collier and Kenneth Collier, *Votescam: The Stealing of America* (New York: Victoria House, 1992).

43. Mark H. Levine, "Layman's Guide to the Supreme Court Decision in Bush v. Gore," unpublished ms., December 2000.

44. "The Facts on Florida," *People's Weekly World,* November 25, 2000; *New York Times,* November 30, 2000; *Boston Globe,* November 30, 2000; Jesse Jackson, "Election Train Wreck in Florida," *Progressive Populist,* January 1–15, 2001; *Observer* (UK), December 24, 2000; and <http://www.indymedia.org>, November 2000.

45. Edward Rollins quoted in *Washington Post,* November 9, 1993.

46. Frances Fox Piven and Richard Cloward, "Northern Bourbons: A Preliminary Report on the National Voter Registration Act," *PS: Political Science,* March 1996; and *New York Times,* August 11, 1999.

47. *New York Times,* August 12, 1995, and November 25, 1997.

48. Vanishing Voter Project, WashingtonPost.com highlights, <http://www.msnbc.com/news/485431.asp>, November 4, 2000.

49. For a typical example of this view, see Seymour Lipset, *Political Man* (Garden City, N.Y.: Doubleday, 1960), 215–19.

50. Heinz Eulau, "The Politics of Happiness," *Antioch Review* 16, 1956; Lipset, *Political Man,* 179–219.

51. *New York Times,* August 11, 1999.

52. On voters' ability to perceive differences in candidates, see survey in *New York Times,* July 25, 2000.

14

Congress: The Pocketing of Power

The framers of the Constitution separated governmental functions into executive, legislative, and judicial branches and installed a system of checks and balances to safeguard against abuses of power and protect property from the leveling impulses of the democratic populace. The Congress they created is a bicameral body, divided into the House of Representatives, whose seats are distributed among the states according to population, and the Senate, with two seats per state regardless of population. Thus nine states — California, New York, Florida, Texas, Pennsylvania, Illinois, Ohio, Minnesota, and New Jersey — contain more than half the nation's population but only 18 percent of the Senate's seats. Whom and what does the Congress represent?

A Congress for the Money

The people elected to Congress are not demographically representative of the nation. In 2000, women were 52 percent of our population but composed less than 13 percent of the 106th Congress; African Americans were at least 14 percent of the population but held only about 6 percent of the legislative seats. Occupational backgrounds are heavily skewed in an upper-class direction. Although they are only a small fraction of the population, lawyers (many of them corporate attorneys) compose about half of both houses. Bankers, investors, entrepreneurs, and business executives compose the next largest occupational group in Congress. More than seventy members of both houses hold commissions with one or another branch of the military, mostly as senior officers. There are almost no blue-collar persons or other ordinary working people in Congress.[1]

The people who represent us in Congress have personal incomes that put them in the top 5-percent bracket, and experience a vastly different lifestyle from the ordinary citizens they claim to represent. We get transportation policy made by lawmakers who never have to endure the suffocation of a crowded bus, agricultural policy by those who never tried keeping a family farm going, safety legislation by legislators who never worked in a factory or mine, medical policies from persons who never have to sit for hours in a crowded clinic, and minimum wage laws by people who never have to wait on tables or mop an office corridor.

Rather than slates of candidates backed by a cohesive party organization united around a common program, congressional elections are individualized district-by-district contests, fueled more by personalized candidate appeals and image manipulation than by substantive issues. As already noted, the major campaign weapon is money. "Congress is the best money can buy," said the humorist Will Rogers. The quip is truer than ever, given the skyrocketing costs of media-driven electoral campaigns.

Members of Congress go where the money is, scrambling for congressional committee assignments that deal with issues of greatest interest to big donors. In six years, members of Congress took $36.5 million in campaign donations from the banking industry. In return, bankers were granted deregulation and savings and loan bailout legislation that will cost the U.S. public $500 billion. Political action committees (PACs) with direct interest in banking gave members of House and Senate banking committees $5.8 million over a two-year period. But because he believed banks should be regulated in the public interest, Henry Gonzalez (D-Tex.), who was chair of the House Banking Committee, received but a pittance.[2] The food industry has handed out $41 million in campaign contributions over the past decade, one-third of it to members of the House and Senate Agriculture committees. Despite growing public concern about food safety, the industry has managed to block any legislation to tighten regulations on processing meat, poultry, and other foods. Lawmakers who received contributions from tobacco companies were three times more likely to have voted against increased funding to crack down on cigarette sales to minors.[3] Well-placed contributions by other wealthy interests have brought them similar legislative support.

There is an old saying, "The dollar votes more times than the man." The power of money works ceaselessly to reduce the influence of citizens who have nothing to offer but their votes. Most senators and many House representatives get the greater part of their money from outside their districts or home states. Senator Robert Dole (R-Kan.) worked hard for a billion-dollar tobacco subsidy, and received generous contributions from the

"WHAT'S IT DONE TO THE CONTENTS OF THIS BOX?"

tobacco industry. But tobacco is virtually an unknown crop in Kansas, the state that elected him, so whom was he representing?[4] Likewise, senators who received the largest sums from defense-contract PACs were almost twice as likely to support higher military spending than those who received little, regardless of how much defense industry existed in their respective states.[5]

Many legislators profess to be uninfluenced by the money they accept. Senator Durenberger (R-Minn.) maintained that the $62,775 he received from the chemical industry "hasn't had any effect on me. These people contributed in the hope that I'd be a senator, and not on the condition that I'd vote for their legislation."[6] But did the chemical industry give Durenberger money because they were just utterly taken by his personal qualities? More likely it was because he voted the way they liked on key issues. Politicians can claim that money does not influence their votes, but their votes influence the money flow. Big donors might be strung along now and then, contributing in the hope of buying a legislator's eventual support, but they do not long reward those who habitually oppose them.

Legislators themselves admit they feel obliged to accommodate big contributors. At a Senate Democratic Caucus, Senator Harold Hughes said his conscience would not allow him to continue in politics because of the way he had been forced to raise money. Senator Hubert Humphrey concurred, bemoaning the "demeaning and degrading" way he had to raise money, and "how candidates literally had to sell their souls."[7]

Lobbyists: The Other Lawmakers

Lobbyists are persons hired by interest groups to influence legislative and administrative policies. Some political scientists see lobbying as part of the "information process": the officeholder's perception of an issue is influenced primarily by the information provided him or her — and the lobbyist's job is to be the provider. But too often the arguments made on behalf of an issue are less important than who is making them and what interests he or she represents. As one congressional committee counsel explains it: "There's the 23-year-old consumer lobbyist and the businessman who gives you $5,000. Whom are you going to listen to?"[8]

Along with the slick brochures and expert testimony, corporate lobbyists offer the succulent campaign contributions, the "volunteer" campaign workers to help members of Congress get reelected, the fat lecture fees, the insider stock market tips, the easy-term loans, the high-paying corporate directorship upon retirement from public office, the lavish parties and accommodating female escorts, the prepaid vacation jaunts, luxury hotels, lavish buffets, and private jets, and the many other hustling enticements of money.

"Everyone has a price," Howard Hughes once told an associate who later recalled that the billionaire handed out about $400,000 yearly to "councilmen and county supervisors, tax assessors, sheriffs, state senators and assemblymen, district attorneys, governors, congressmen and senators, judges — yes, and vice-presidents and presidents, too."[9]

Business lobbyists outnumber legislators in Washington by more than 75 to 1.[10] Perhaps most influential of all is the Business Roundtable, the "trillion-dollar voice" of big business, composed of 190 chief executives of the nation's blue-chip corporations, one or another of whom enjoy access to key figures in the White House, the cabinet, and Congress. Credited with thwarting or watering down antitrust, environmental, prolabor, and proconsumer measures, the Roundtable exercises an influence over government eclipsing just about any other special interest group.

Some of Washington's top lobbying groups are funded by foreign governments that are among the world's worst human-rights abusers, including Turkey, Kuwait, Indonesia, Guatemala, Colombia, Saudi Arabia, Zaire, and the CIA-supported Unita rebel group in Angola.[11]

High-powered Washington lobbyists are usually corporate attorneys, business people, ex-legislators, ex-congressional aides, or former public officials with good connections in government. There exists what amounts to a revolving door between business lobbying and government service. Officials who are especially responsive to lobbying interests can be rewarded with lucrative positions in private business when they leave government service. The most effective resource lobbyists have at their command is money. Money buys access to the officeholder and, beyond that, the opportunity to shape his or her judgments with arguments of the lobbyist's choosing. Access alone does not guarantee influence. Almost a century ago, before he became president of the United States, Woodrow Wilson pointed out:

> Suppose you go to Washington and try to get at your Government. You will always find that while you are politely listened to, the men really consulted are the men who have the big stake — the big bankers, the big manufacturers, and the big masters of commerce. . . . The masters of the Government of the United States are the combined capitalists and manufacturers of the United States.[12]

When a fundraising dinner in Washington attended by President Bush netted the Republican party $9 million, with individual donations ranging up to $400,000, presidential press secretary Marlin Fitzwater defended the event: "[The donors] are buying into the political process. . . . That's what the political parties and the political operation is all about." Asked how less wealthy persons could buy into the process, Fitzwater said, "They have to demand access in other ways."[13]

Lobbyists dispense considerable sums. Professional lobbying firms like Cassidy & Associates and Patton Boggs rake in anywhere from $4 to $7 million a year serving clients like General Dynamics, NBC, Aetna, and AT&T. These figures are probably on the low side because of loopholes in reporting requirements. In addition there are six hundred corporations with full-time lobbying offices in Washington, D.C. Taken all together, lobbying is easily a $1 billion-a-year industry.[14]

In 1996, under pressure from public interest groups, Congress passed a lobbying bill that put a $100 limit on gifts and meals, except for presents from family and "longtime friends."[15] Even with these strictures, money remains a crucial factor in the influence system. Those who argue that lobbyists are effective not because of money but because they shape the "information flow" might consider that the ability to disseminate information and propagate one's cause itself presumes organization, expertise, time, and labor — things money can buy. In addition, the mere possession of great wealth and the control of industry and jobs give corporate interests an advantage unknown to ordinary working citizens, for business's claims are paraded as the "needs of the economy" and, as it were, of the nation itself.

Over forty thousand lobbyists prowl the Capitol's lobbies (hence their name) or seek favorable rulings from agencies within the vast executive bureaucracy. Members of Congress sometimes rely on lobbyists to write speeches and plant stories in the press on their behalf. Lobbyists will even draft legislation and sit next to lawmakers during subcommittee hearings. For example, a draft bill penned by a lobbying firm representing agribusiness, and designed to stifle pesticide regulation, read nearly word-for-word like the bill submitted two months later in the House by a GOP House member from California.[16]

Lobbyists enlist members of Congress to exert influence on executive agencies in order to get government contracts, government posts, and favorable administrative rulings for business clients. In this capacity, the legislator acts as little more than an extension of the lobbyist. One ex-lobbyist concludes that the lobbyist's main job is to circumvent existing laws and get preferential treatment "for clients who have no legal rights to them." To achieve this he pays cash to "one or more members of Congress — the more influential they are, the fewer he needs."[17]

During President Clinton's attempt to get a fast-track measure through Congress that would enable him to negotiate yet more pro-corporate free-trade agreements, lobbyists from Boeing, the Business Roundtable, the National Association of Manufacturers, and other firms used a congressional committee room beneath the House chamber as a command post. They used House telephones, fax machines, and other equipment in an effort to win approval of the trade bill. Some of the corporate lobbyists refused to identify themselves or explain how they got there when challenged by a group of liberal Democratic members of Congress.[18]

A favorable adjustment in rates for interstate carriers, a special tax benefit for a family oil trust, a high-interest bond issue for big investors, a special charter for a bank, the leasing of public lands to a private company, emergency funding for a faltering aeronautics plant, a helicopter carrier (that the navy did not want) for a defense contractor, a postal subsidy for advertising firms, the easing of safety standards for a food processor, the easing of pollution controls for a chemical plant, a special acreage allotment for tobacco growers, a permit for a hazardous waste incinerator — all these hundreds of bills and their thousands of special amendments and tens of thousands of administrative rulings, which mean so much to particular business interests, arouse the sympathetic efforts of legislators and administrators while going largely unnoticed by a public that pays the monetary and human costs and seldom has the means to make its case — or even to discover it has a case.

Attempting to speak for the great unorganized populace, public-interest groups do not have an easy time of it — especially when their proposals are directed against powerful economic interests. The relative sparsity of power resources (the most crucial being money) limits the efforts of citizen groups and makes problematic their very survival. Many of them are forced to devote an inordinate amount of their time foraging for funds just to pay for their offices and tiny staffs.

Despite such realities, there exists what might be called "the school of happy pluralism," which sees power as widely and democratically diffused. Thus one political scientist concludes that "nearly every vigorous push in one direction" by a lobbying interest "stimulates an opponent or coalition of opponents to push in the opposite direction. This natural self-balancing factor comes into play so often that it almost amounts to a law."[19] The evidence presented in this book does not support this cheerful view. Do the homeless, the unemployed, and most ordinary citizens really have the kind of political clout that makes them figure as near equal contestants in the influence system?

Some political scientists have theorized that the diversity of cultural, economic, regional, religious, and ethnic groups in our society creates cross-pressured allegiances that mitigate the strength of any one organized interest. While this may be true of certain broad constituencies, it does not seem to apply to the more powerful and politically active segments of the business community, whose interlocking memberships seem to compound rather than dilute their power and their class commitment. Certainly diverse business groups might clash at times, but they also can collude around common class interests, giving mutual support to each other's agendas. Special-interest legislators often achieve working majorities in Congress by "logrolling," a process of mutual support that is not the same as compromise. Rather than checking one another as in compromise situations, and thus blunting the selfish demands of each, business groups end up backing one another's claims at the expense of those who are without power in the pressure system.

Grassroots Lobbying

Pressure group efforts are directed not only at officeholders but also at the public, in what has been called "grassroots lobbying." The goal is to bombard the lawmakers with a media blitz and with messages from concerned persons, including corporate leaders of a particular industry or trade association. Among the earliest practitioners of grassroots lobbying were consumer, environmental, and other public-interest groups. It was not long before corporations and business associations also adopted this approach, the difference being that they are able to spend a hundred times more than public-interest groups. To cite one instance, in the summer of 1993, the National Association of Manufacturers launched a campaign that inundated Congress with letters and telephone calls opposing President Clinton's proposed energy tax, and as a result the plan was squashed.[20]

Corporate special interests sometimes hide behind front organizations that have uplifting, public-service sounding names. The National Wetlands Coalition is a well-financed lobby of oil and mining companies and real-estate developers with the single mission of undoing the regulations that protect our wetlands and endangered species. The Coalition on Occupational Safety and Health is actually a corporate front dedicated to watering down federal health and safety regulations. Americans for Tax Reform, a nonpartisan-sounding tax-exempt nonprofit organization, received a total of $4.6 million from the Republican National Committee, which it used to send out 19 million pieces of mail and make four million phone calls urging voters to support the GOP's campaign against Medicare.[21] These front groups can spend unlimited sums on political activities without having to disclose their donors and expenditures as long as they do not expressly advocate voting for a particular candidate.

Some grassroots lobbying is intended to build a climate of opinion favorable to the corporate giants rather than to push a particular piece of legislation. The steel, oil, and electronics companies do not urge the public to support the latest tax loophole or business handout — if anything, they would prefer that citizens not trouble themselves with such matters — but they do "educate" the public with a whole menu of false claims about the many jobs they create, the selfless services they provide the community, and the loving care they supposedly give to the environment. Rather than selling their particular products, with this kind of "institutional advertising" the corporations sell themselves and the entire business system.

Helping Themselves: The Varieties of Corruption

Members of Congress will sometimes act as pressure politicians without prodding from any pressure group, either because they are so well funded by the group or have lucrative holdings of their own in the same industry. Legislators with large agribusiness holdings sit on committees that shape agricultural programs directly benefiting them. Fully a third of the lawmakers hold outside jobs as lawyers or officers of corporations, banks, and other financial institutions that closely link them with the very industries they were elected to oversee. More than one-third of the senators have investments in firms that rank among the top defense contractors and make money every time the military budget increases. Almost half the Senate and over a hundred House members have interests in banking, including many who sit on committees that deal with banking. The only doctor in the Senate in 2000, Bill First (R-Tenn.), supposedly calls upon his medical experience when advocating "reforms" in Medicare and in Food and Drug Administration regulations, but his vast personal financial holdings in the medical industry raise questions about whether he acts as a doctor, a senator, or a wealthy investor.[22]

An analysis of congressional disclosure reports reveals that "while some lawmakers avoid buying stock in industries that coincide with their key areas of legislative responsibility — or put their assets in blind trusts — many do not."[23] What is called "conflict of interest" in the judiciary and executive branches is defined as "expertise" in Congress by those lawmakers who use their public mandate to legislate on behalf of their private fortunes.

Plutocracy — rule for the rich by the rich — prevails in Congress. With unusual candor, Senator Daniel Patrick Moynihan (D-N.Y.) remarked: "At least half of the members of the Senate today are millionaires. . . . We've become a plutocracy. . . . The Senate was meant to represent the interests of the states; instead, it represents the interests of a class."[24] The lower chamber too is going upper class, in what one critic called an "evolution from a House of Representatives to a House of Lords."[25] Many House and Senate members file financial disclosure forms that give a vague and incomplete listing of their personal wealth. For example, reactionary Senator Jesse Helms (R-N.C.) neglected to list six slum rental properties valued at over half a million dollars.[26] Because of a Supreme Court ruling that allows wealthy candidates to expend as much as they want of their own money on their own campaigns, rich individuals have an additional advantage in gaining party nominations. Recent new House members have considerably more personal wealth than previous ones.

Some senators and representatives travel for fun at government expense under the guise of conducting committee investigations ("junketing"). They place relatives on the payroll and pocket their salaries or take salary kickbacks from staff members. They charge both the government and a private client for the same expense; they use unspent travel allocations and unspent campaign contributions for personal indulgences. They keep persons on the staff payroll whose major function is to perform sexual favors. Rich companies do their share to make life more pleasant for key legislators, providing them with generous speaking honoraria, expense-paid trips to luxury resorts (spouse included), and repeated use of the company's private jets. Of course, the recipients insist that such things do not influence their votes.[27]

Several prominent House members who led a moral crusade to impeach President Clinton for committing perjury to cover up a sexual liaison he had with a female intern, were themselves guilty of illicit liaisons and other shady practices. A prime example is Representative Dan Burton (R-Ind.), an outspoken proponent of family values, a married father of three, with a 100-percent approval rating from the right-wing Christian Coalition. Burton called Clinton a "scumbag," then himself later admitted to fathering a child during an extramarital affair. Burton used campaign money and federal funds to hire women of dubious credentials. One of his ladies received about half a million dollars in payments, but it remained unclear what she did to earn her salary. Burton also paid rent on her house — which he claimed was his "campaign headquarters," though it was oddly located outside his district. He also reimbursed himself for thousands of dollars annually in travel expenses, and unexplained "campaign expenses" for gifts, flowers, golf balls, and the like.[28]

Since World War II, scores of lawmakers or their aides have been indicted or convicted of bribery, influence peddling, extortion, and other crimes. And those were only the ones unlucky enough to get caught. Numerous other members have retired from office to avoid criminal charges. The House and Senate ethics committees are charged with overseeing and enforcing ethics codes, but they lack sufficient inclination and staff to do so. The chair of the Senate Ethics Committee in the 98th Congress, Malcolm Wallop (R-Wyo.), believed that senators should not have to disclose their financial holdings and could decide their own conflict of interest. He even criticized the whole idea of a code of ethics. No wonder his colleagues picked him for the job.[29] In 1997, the House barred outside groups and individuals from lodging ethics complaints. So now it is up to congressional members to denounce their own kind, which does not happen very often, if at all.

If, as they say, power corrupts, it usually gets a helping hand from money. Members of Congress are not the only culprits. In just one six-year period, the number of public officials convicted included 3 cabinet officers, 3 governors, 34 state legislators, 20 judges, 5 state attorneys-general, 28 mayors, 11 district attorneys, 170 police officers, and a U.S. vice president, Spiro Agnew, who resigned in exchange for the dropping of charges of bribery, extortion, and income-tax evasion. A U.S. president, Richard Nixon, escaped impeachment and jail by resigning from office and being granted a pardon from his successor, Gerald Ford. In the past two decades, governors in Arizona, Arkansas, Oklahoma, Louisiana, and Alabama were charged with fraud, extortion, perjury, pocketing campaign funds, or other corrupt practices.[30]

A Government Accounting Office study found over 77,000 cases of fraud in federal agencies during a two-and-a-half-year period, nearly half in the Pentagon. Only a small portion of the individuals involved were prosecuted. In 1975, 53 federal executive officials were indicted for crimes; by 1985, the number had jumped to 563.[31] The Nixon administration was implicated in scandals involving the sale of wheat, price supports for dairy producers, an out-of-court settlement with ITT, corruption in the Federal Housing Administration, stock-market manipulations, and political espionage (the Watergate affair).

The career of Nelson Rockefeller provides an impressive example of money in action. When being considered for appointment to the U.S. vice-presidency to replace Vice President Gerald Ford, who succeeded to the presidency when Nixon resigned in disgrace, Rockefeller admitted to having given nearly $1.8 million in gifts and loans to eighteen New York and federal public officials, including $50,000 to Henry Kissinger, a former Rockefeller employee, three days before Kissinger became national security advisor to President Nixon. At a Senate hearing, Rockefeller insisted these payments were simply manifestations of his esteem for the recipients. "Sharing has always been part of my upbringing," he told the senators, none of whom doubled over with laughter. Nobody reminded him that New York law prohibits public employees from accepting any gift greater than $25. Nor did the senators wonder aloud whether a "gift" to public officials who make decisions affecting one's private fortune might not better be called a "bribe." Instead they confirmed Nelson Rockefeller as vice president of the United States.

Every administration has had its scandals but the number of high-level members of the Reagan administration accused of unethical or illegal conduct was without precedent — 110 by early 1986, with the number climbing well beyond that as the Iran-contra affair unfolded later that year.[32] These included at least three cabinet members, a Central Intelligence Agency (CIA) director, several White House staff members, several advisors and aides from the National Security Council, and numerous administrative agency heads. The charges included fraud; improper stock dealings; tax-code violations; failure to make proper financial disclosures; perjury; obstructing congressional investigations; accepting illegal or improper loans, gifts, and favors; and using public resources to aid personal interests. Only a few went to jail, many resigned, and many stayed on, including Attorney General Edwin Meese, who seemed to suffer amnesia; his memory lapsed seventy-nine times when questioned before a Senate committee regarding a host of shady financial dealings.[33]

Some observers see corruption as a more or less acceptable fact of life. Passing a little money under the table is just another way of oiling the wheels of government and getting things done.[34] But corruption has gone beyond the petty bribe to reach momentous proportions. Rather than being a violation of the rules of the game, it is the name of the game. Corruption in government promotes policies that lead to permanent public indebtedness, inefficiency, and waste; it drains the public treasure to feed the private purse; it vitiates laws and regulations that might otherwise safeguard community interests; it undermines equal protection of the law, producing favoritism for the few and injury and neglect for the many. If the powers and resources of the social order itself are used for the maximization of private greed and gain, and if the operational ethic is "looking out for number one," then corruption will be chronic rather than occasional, a systemic product rather than merely an outgrowth of the politician's flawed character.

A Special-Interest Committee System

Once elected, how do the legislators go about their work? For years, power in Congress rested with the twenty or so standing (i.e., permanent) committees in each house that determined the destiny of bills: rewriting some, approving a few, and burying most. The committees were dominated by chairpersons who rose to their positions by seniority — that is, by being repeatedly reelected, a feat best accomplished in a safe district or predominantly one-party state.

Although seniority remains the rule in both houses, in the late 1970s the House Democratic Caucus instituted a number of changes to weaken the hold of committee chairpersons, removing several from their positions and expanding the powers of subcommittees.[35] No longer can chairpersons arbitrarily select subcommittee chairpersons, nor stack a subcommittee with members of their own choice or cut its budget. Totaling 241 in the House and Senate combined, the subcommittees have staffs of their own and fixed legislative jurisdictions.

The fragmentation of power within the subcommittees simplifies the lobbyist's task of controlling legislation. It offers the special-interest group its own special-interest subcommittee. Thus, whether it be cotton, corn, wheat, peanut, tobacco, or rice producers, each major agribusiness interest is represented on a particular subcommittee of the Senate and House agricultural committees by senators and representatives ready to do battle on their behalf. To decentralize power in this way is not to democratize it. The separate units of power tend to monopolize decisions in specific areas for the benefit of specific groups. Into the interstices of these substructures fall the interests of large segments of the unorganized public. Whether Congress is organized under a committee system, a subcommittee system, or a strong centralized leadership — and it has had all three in its history — it seems unchanging in its dedication to major business interests.

Much is made of the "powerful chairmen" said to preside over this or that committee. Thus the chairman of the House Armed Services Committee (recently renamed the National Security Committee) was always considered "powerful," but it was because he served the powerful interests of corporate America and the military. Power does not adhere to a position in some mystical fashion. When a progressive Democrat, Ron Dellums, became chair of the House Armed Services Committee through seniority, and sought to roll back some military spending, he felt his position to be tenuous indeed, as most of his committee responded less to his leadership and more to the big contractors and big campaign donors from the defense industry. Suddenly the powerful committee chair was not so powerful.

Some appropriations, known as "pork barrel" or just "pork," provide funds for projects that are not the most essential or economical but are highly visible representations of the legislator's ability to bring home the federal bacon. Recent budgets suggest that pork is no longer a significant item, if ever it was. Congressional pork-barrel spending on home-town projects totals several billion dollars a year, a fraction of 1 percent of the annual budget and a relatively small sum compared to the hundreds of billions of dollars doled out for fat defense contracts annually.

When it involves the poor and the powerless, Congress knows how to save money. In recent years, it has refused to provide $9 million for a disease-control center dealing with tuberculosis. It cut five million doses out of the federal immunization program for children, for a grand savings of $10 million, and reduced venereal-disease programs by 25 percent despite increases in sexually transmitted diseases. To teach people rugged self-reliance, a Republican-controlled Congress, with assistance from conservative Clinton Democrats, cut food programs for infants and senior citizens, assistance programs for the disabled, home care and therapy programs for the infirm and handicapped, and medical care, home heating aid, and job and housing programs for low-income families and the elderly.[36]

Security, Secrecy, and Fast Track

Most members of Congress are ever responsive to the national security state and the arms industry. In 1982 a massive grassroots movement for a bilateral, verifiable freeze on nuclear weapons swept the country like few things in our history, yet the lawmakers continued to vote for major escalations in nuclear weapons systems. In 2000, over 80 percent of the U.S. public supported a ban on nuclear weapons testing, yet the Comprehensive Test Ban Treaty was defeated in the Senate by a fifty-one to forty-eight vote; all fifty-one were Republican senators. In 1986 opinion polls showed that by large majorities the public opposed aid to the Nicaraguan mercenaries who were waging war against Nicaragua from U.S.-furnished bases in Honduras, yet Congress voted $100 million in aid to the mercenaries.

Worse still is Congress's inability to rein in the national security state on the infrequent occasions it makes an attempt, and its unwillingness to force a confrontation when its strictures are violated by military and intelligence agencies. Thus when lawmakers ruled that there should be no more than fifty-five U.S. military personnel in El Salvador, the restriction was soon flouted. When Congress ruled that no military aid to El Salvador could be approved without periodic presidential certification of human rights improvement, certification was granted in blithe disregard of the facts with little complaint from Congress. No aid was to be given to mercenary forces in Nicaragua, yet funds for right-wing contra terrorists continued to be found even during the period of the most stringent congressional prohibitions.[37] More recently, in 1998 it was discovered that the Pentagon was continuing to aid Indonesian military units despite a congressional ban intended to curb the torture and murders committed by these same units. Pentagon officials claimed the aid took place under a program different from the one Congress banned, and it "enhanced our ability to positively influence Indonesia's human rights policies and behavior." No evidence was provided to showed an improvement in the military's human rights record.[38]

The Pentagon and various intelligence agencies, including the CIA, the Defense Intelligence Agency (DIA), and the National Security Agency

(NSA), sponsor fellowship programs that enable them to place their paid employees on congressional staffs for a year at a time, handling sensitive data and influencing lawmakers, who rely heavily on staff for advice and information. "[T]he mere presence of fellows from the intelligence community with their particular worldview would influence the Congress differently than would a cadre of fellows from, say, anti-poverty or environmental organizations."[39] There is little to prevent fellows from being assigned to congressional staffs for the express purpose of spying on particular senators or representatives. When DIA congressional fellows return to their agency, they serve in its legislative liaison office, applying what they learned during their stint on Capitol Hill to influence Congress in ways useful to the intelligence agency. Congressional fellowships are also awarded to employees of corporate firms with an interest in military contracts and other legislation, including General Electric, General Dynamics, and DuPont — with no provision made for possible conflict of interest.

When public opinion is aroused, Congress is likely to respond by producing legislation that appears to deal with the issue while lacking real muscle. Thus we are treated to a lobbyist registration act that does little to control lobbyists and an occupational safety act that has grossly insufficient enforcement provisions. Legislators tend to be most heedful when public sentiment is aroused and if election time is approaching. Before the 1982 and 1986 congressional elections, even under the threat of President Reagan's vetoes, the Democrat-controlled Congress pushed through a number of important human services and environmental programs.

Congressional committees hold many of their sessions behind closed doors, keeping the public in the dark while keeping influential business groups informed. "The thing that really makes me mad is the dual standard," complained a Senate committee staff member. "It's perfectly acceptable to turn over information about what's going on in committee to the auto industry or the utilities but not to the public."[40] Secrecy can envelop the entire lawmaking process. A bill cutting corporate taxes by $7.3 billion was (a) drawn up by the House Ways and Means Committee in three days of secret sessions, (b) passed by the House under a closed rule after only one hour of debate with (c) about only thirty members present who (d) passed the bill without benefit of a roll-call vote.

Legislation can have deceptive packaging and hidden contents. A bill that raised the minimum wage by 85 cents contained lesser known provisions that favored transnational corporations with tax incentives and tax shelters, and made it easier for companies to roll back worker benefits and raid retirement and pension funds. Several years later, another minimum wage bill contained a huge cut in estate taxes for the rich.[41]

After suffering public rebuke for attempting a sweeping rollback of environmental programs, the Republican leadership in Congress took a stealthier tack in 1998, inserting their anti-environmental provisions as brief "riders" in larger appropriations and other legislation. These proposals included increased logging in a rare U.S. temperate-zone rain forest in Alaska, blocking restoration of salmon habitats, and preventing government education programs on global warming.[42]

Some of the most significant legislation is drafted clandestinely. Without benefit of public hearings and public debate, a coterie of high-placed government officials and corporate executives secretly put together the North American Free Trade Agreement (NAFTA), a two-thousand-page bill that went largely unread by the lawmakers voting on it. In November 1993, the bill was given a promotional media blitz by the Clinton administration and presented to the House of Representatives with a "fast-track" proviso. Fast track requires that Congress accept or reject the agreement in toto without amending it and with only two days of debate. In 1997, the combined power of big business lobbyists and a furiously energetic president faced off against a strong mobilization of labor unions, environmentalists, and other public interest groups in an attempt to force through another fast-track free trade agreement that would give transnational corporations still more sway over governments, including state and local ones. This time Congress voted down the fast-track proposal, effectively killing the proposal — a victory for the people and a defeat for globalization.[43]

The Legislative Labyrinth

As intended by the framers of the Constitution, the very structure of Congress has a conservative effect on what the legislators do. The staggered terms of the Senate — with only one-third elected every two years — are designed to blunt any mass sentiment for a sweeping turnover. The division of the Congress into two separate houses makes legislative action all the more difficult, often giving an advantage to those who desire to prevent reforms. A typical bill before Congress might go the following route: after being introduced into, say, the House of Representatives, it is committed to a committee, where it can be pigeonholed or gutted by the chair, or parceled out to various subcommittees for hearings, where it might meet its demise. Or it might be reported out of subcommittee to full committee intact or greatly rewritten. Then it is sent to the Rules Committee, which might pigeonhole it, thus killing it. Or the Rules Committee could negotiate with the standing committee for a rewriting of certain provisions. Or the House might vote — by at least two-thirds — to bypass the Rules Committee and bring the bill directly to the House floor. The Rules Committee regulates the amount of time for debate and what provisions may or may not be open for amendment. Then the bill goes before the House, which can reject or amend the rule. The House resolves itself into the Committee of the Whole House (allowing suspension of House rules, including quorum requirements) to debate, amend, pass, or reject the bill, or recommit it to the originating committee for further study. If passed by the Committee of the Whole, the House reconstitutes itself and then decides the bill's fate.

If passed by the House, the bill is sent to the Senate, which either places it directly on its calendar for debate and vote or refers it to a standing committee to repeat the same process of hearings and amendments. It can die in committee or be sent to the Senate floor. The Senate might defeat the bill or pass the House version either unchanged or amended. If the House refuses to accept the Senate amendments, a conference committee is put together consisting of several senior members from each house. Should the conference committee be able to reach a compromise, the bill is returned to both houses for a final vote. A bill that does not make it through both houses before the next congressional election must be reintroduced and the entire process begun anew. If passed by both houses, the bill goes to the president who either signs it into law or vetoes it. The president's veto can be overridden only by two-thirds of the members of each house who are present and voting. If the president fails to sign the legislation within ten days after passage, it automatically becomes law unless Congress adjourns in that time, in which case it has been "pocket vetoed" and so dies.

The bill that survives this legislative labyrinth to become law may be only an authorization act to bring some program into existence. Congress then must repeat the entire process for an appropriations bill to finance the authorization — something the lawmakers occasionally fail to do.

Various dilatory tactics, from time-consuming quorum calls to Senate filibusters, help to thwart legislative action. Senate rules allow a small but determined number of senators to filibuster a bill to death or dilute it by exercising the threat of filibuster. This right of unlimited debate is a peculiarity the Senate has retained from its earliest days to preserve its historic role of blunting the majoritarian will of a democratic government. For seventy years, until the 1950s, the filibuster was wielded by Southern Democrats to block 257 anti-lynching bills. Today a filibuster can be broken with a cloture petition that requires sixty votes, something not easily achieved.

In the 1980s and 1990s, the Republicans used the filibuster far more frequently than did Democrats. They filibustered or threatened to filibuster bills that supported arms control, public financing of congressional campaigns, limits on private campaign spending, legal abortions at military hospitals, human rights conditions on military aid to El Salvador, a modest tax-rate increase for the rich, accessible voter registration for the poor and unemployed, outlawing the use of scabs as permanent replacements of strikers, and a $16.3 billion jobs program.[44] During 1993 alone, the first year of the Clinton administration, the Senate Republicans forced cloture votes on some sixty bills. In 1998, a bill that banned lobbyists' gifts and meals and a bill designed to end loopholes in campaign financing were killed when proponents could not achieve the sixty votes needed to overcome a filibuster threat.

About 80 percent of the bills never make their way out of the legislative labyrinth to become law. Many of these are better left buried. But the law-makers' wisdom is not the only determinant of what gets through; class power is also at work. Legislation that is intended to assist the needy moves along the slow lane: a $100-million bill to fund summer jobs for unemployed youth is debated in Congress for eight months, with dozens of attempts at crippling amendments; a pilot project supplying school breakfasts for a small number of malnourished children is debated at agonizing length. But when Continental Illinois Bank is about to go bankrupt, billions of dollars are handed out practically overnight without much deliberation. Hundreds of billions are readily channeled into the savings-and-loan bailout. Billions for new weapons systems are passed in a matter of days. NAFTA is rammed through without amendment in two days. And domestic programs that had taken many years of struggle to achieve are cut by many billions of dollars in a few weeks. The major financial interests may not always get all they want, but they usually travel the fast lane in Congress.

One Democratic senator reminded his party colleagues that they were too responsive to moneyed interests and were neglecting to keep up appearances as "the party of the people." In a speech on the Senate floor urging that the scientific patents of the $25-billion space program not be given away to private corporations but applied for public benefit, Russell Long (D-La.) candidly remarked: "Many of these [corporate] people have much influence. I, like others, have importuned some of them for campaign contributions for my party and myself. Nevertheless, we owe it to the people, now and then, to save one or two votes for them. This is one such instance. . . . We Democrats can trade on the dubious assumption that we are protector of the public interest only so long if we permit things like these patent giveaways."[45] Here Senator Long provided a perfect example of how the need to maintain democratic appearances can sometimes lead to actual democratic advocacy.

For some members of Congress, getting reelected is their major concern; for others it is their only concern. In any case, the great majority of them are quite successful at it. The turnover in Congress is rarely more than 15 or 20 percent. There are several reasons for this:

Campaign funding. By definition, incumbents are persons who have already demonstrated an ability to muster enough money and votes to win. Once in office, they have opportunities to gather additional financial support. Senate incumbents raise twice as much money as challengers, and House incumbents raise over three times more.[46]

Constituent service. Members of Congress build support by doing case-work for constituents: locating a Social Security check or getting someone into a veterans hospital. They maintain a staff in the district home office.

They do little favors for little people and big favors for big people, gathering votes from the former and campaign money from the latter.

Exposure and name recognition. Incumbents use their franking privileges (free mailing) to correspond with constituents and send out newsletters and promotional sheets that herald the officeholder's devoted efforts on behalf of his or her constituents. Members issue press releases, get their names in hometown media, and generally enjoy a long head start over potential challengers in self-advertising and name recognition.

One-party dominance. Some states and districts are demographically inclined toward one party or another, and many districts are gerrymandered to concentrate party strength in lopsided ways, so much so that it is sometimes difficult to recruit a challenger.

Earlier retirements. With the workload and fundraising tasks becoming ever more onerous, members of Congress are retiring in growing numbers. The inability to effect important changes frustrates some, while highly lucrative jobs in private industry entice others. The consolation of a generous pension is an additional inducement. Those who face tough reelection challenges and have problems raising funds usually are more inclined to quit than those who occupy comfortably safe and well-financed seats.

Term Limits

Some conservatives, most notably Presidents Nixon and Reagan, have wanted to abolish the Twenty-second Amendment, which places a two-term limit on presidential incumbents. They had no problem with limitless incumbency for Republican presidents. No conservatives have urged term limits on Supreme Court justices or federal judges; the judiciary is heavily populated with relatively young conservative ideologues. They target only Congress and those state legislatures in which the Democrats have a longstanding majority. Conservatives had nothing against limitless incumbency in Congress when conservative Southern Democrats or Republicans dominated the influential committee leadership positions. But when senior positions began going to moderately liberal and even progressive Democrats, including members of the Congressional Black Caucus, conservatives became the moving force behind term limits — along with some progressives who believed that term limits would rid the Congress of entrenched oligarchs and bring fresh infusions of new ideas and more democratic performance.

While promising to improve legislative performance, term limits will more likely do the opposite, creating a rotating amateur Congress that faces a long-entrenched national security state and professional bureaucracy. Congress would be composed largely of freshmen and sophomores who would be even more dependent on professional lobbyists. Members would also be increasingly dependent on congressional staffers who are elected by no one, including committee and subcommittee staffers who sometimes serve for decades. And when one recalls that it takes many years of struggle to pass major public-interest legislation, we might wonder who in Congress will be able to stick around long enough to see things through — especially since term limits would wipe out whatever progressive leadership now exists, which is the real objective of its major sponsors.

Term limits have been voted in for a number of state legislatures. The results are just what critics expected. In California, after voters passed a proposition limiting assembly tenure to six years and senate tenure to eight, the liberal Democratic leadership of the state legislature was forced out of office. There is weaker leadership in both the assembly and the senate, with "perpetually inexperienced legislators" being outdone by "a governor and his vast bureaucracy seizing more power than ever." Lobbyists "have become more powerful because they, like the governor, have the time and experience to manipulate information." Without benefit of an experienced assembly or senate leadership, legislators commit frequent tactical and procedural errors. Sometimes there are prolonged debates on frivolous resolutions but hardly any debate on bills of important substance. "Like herding cats, it takes hours just to get everybody in line for a single vote. . . . [M]any are distracted by new campaigns for other offices."[47] With brief term limits, the elected position is seen more than ever as a temporary career, a prelude to something else. So legislators are more inclined to depart even before their terms are finished in order to take an appointive post or run for a seat that has opened up in the state senate or the U.S. Congress.

In the Maine state legislature, the same inexperience shows. "The budget passed in record time largely because new legislators, not fully understanding what they were voting for, did not drag out debate." The majority whip of the Maine House of Representatives, a twenty-nine-year-old Democrat who has served only three years, observes, "You're beginning to see staff have stronger power in the legislature, and lobbyists too. They have real institutional memory. If you go to committee meetings, the new people are changing laws that have just been passed or reconsidering bills that were resoundingly defeated last year."[48] The same has been observed in other states with term limits. By 2008 the twenty or so state legislatures that have term limits will have undergone a complete turnover, ridding themselves of any traces of long-term legislative experience.

In 1992, highly publicized and well-financed initiatives to limit congressional terms to six or twelve years (depending on the state) won voter endorsements in fourteen states, the limits applied only to the congressional delegations of the respective states. Several years later, without judging the merits of term limits, the Supreme Court ruled that Article 1 of the constitution prohibits a state from erecting new qualifying barriers for congressional candidates, including incumbents running for reelection.[49]

A Touch of Democracy

Behind Congress there stands the entire corporate social order, with its hold over the material resources of society, its control of information and mass propaganda, its dominant influence over most cultural institutions, and its well-placed policymakers, organized pressure groups, high-paid lobbyists, influence-peddling lawyers, and big corporate contributors. Given all this, it is surprising that any democratic victories are won in Congress. Yet progressive forces do manage to get things through from time to time. The lawmakers are not entirely untouched by popular pressures. Votes still count and therefore so do voters. Hence, over the years, worthwhile laws regarding public health and safety, the environment, housing and jobs, and other such things have become law.

The legislators also perform democratic watchdog functions over administrative agencies, checking to see why a Labor Department field office is not functioning, why a Social Security office is being closed, why a cancer clinic has not received its funding, why vacancies in an agency investigating racketeering have not been filled, why a report on wage rates at rural hospitals has not been released, why compensation has not been made to injured veterans, and other such matters. The most useful watchdog of government, the General Accounting Office (GAO), created by Congress to investigate everything from military waste to environmental abuse, operates at the request of specific legislators and reports directly to Congress. This congressional watchdog function is an important democratic pressure on behalf of ordinary people, prodding a recalcitrant and often secretive federal bureaucracy.

Even during the rightist Reagan and Bush presidencies, Congress approved the expansion of Medicare, and it strengthened major civil rights statutes, federal ethics standards, and environmental programs. It bolstered programs for AIDS victims, drug addicts, and the homeless, and extended unemployment insurance and new protections for workers facing mass layoffs. The lawmakers passed a plant-closing notification bill and imposed sanctions on South Africa because of its racist apartheid policy. Congress, then, is not just a special-interest arena. It is also a place where larger critical issues are sometimes treated.

There are some ninety progressive members in the House,[50] who often respond to the needs of the many rather than the greed of the few, impelled both by their own political commitment and by popular pressure. What victories they win are almost always hard-fought, for the high ground is usually occupied by the conservative coalition, composed mostly of Republicans and conservative "New Democrats," aligned with the rather conservative Democratic Leadership Council, who frequently manage to block or seriously maul any liberal agenda for change. And when the White House also is on their side, conservatives score decisive victories against the hard-won gains of labor and public-interest groups.

In sum, Congress is still a place where democratic inputs can be registered, where progressive forces occasionally can mount attacks against a conservative status quo or maintain some (partially successful) defense against the free-market rightist rollback. A more democratic Congress would be one that is more responsive to voters and less dependent upon moneyed interests for financial support. How can that be achieved? The only money that comes with no strings attached comes from each citizen equally — from all the taxpayers, through their government — money that does not obligate the officeholder to any special interest or privileged group. What is needed is a system of public campaign financing that neutralizes the influence of private money. We need full public funding of House and Senate elections and primaries. Candidates who accept public funding would have to agree to limit their spending to the amount of the public allocation. Those who decline taxpayer money would be free of that spending limit — but their opponents would then qualify for matching funds equal to any amount spent by the privately funded candidate. Limitless private funding would be allowed — but it would be neutralized and equalized by public funding. In addition, the soft money loophole discussed in the previous chapter needs to be closed tight.

The strictest prohibitions should be placed on lobbyists' perks, the honoraria, free travel, and other gifts and services that are little more than legalized bribery. Finally, broadcast media should be required to set aside free and equal time for all candidates during campaigns. The airwaves are the property of the American people, part of the public domain. While broadcasters are granted licenses to use the airwaves, they do not own them. It is no infringement on their free speech to oblige them, as a public service, to make some portion of broadcast time available to officeseekers who want to exercise their free speech.

With public financing of campaigns, limits on private perks, and free access to media, candidates and officeholders would be liberated from the incessant task of raising money and less bound to moneyed interests. And major public office would be more accessible to others besides the rich or those supported by the rich.

Notes

1. "What Did U.S. Legislators Do for a Living before They Were Elected?" *Labor Party Press,* July 1998.

2. *PACs and Lobbies,* newsletter, Edward Zuckerman (ed.), Washington, D.C., June 1990.

3. Center for Public Integrity, reported in *USA Today,* March 24, 1998; Study by Campaign for Tobacco-Free Kids reported in Associated Press, September 2, 1997.

4. *New York Times*, April 16, 1990; Philip Stern, *The Best Congress Money Can Buy* (New York: Pantheon, 1988) 84–85.

5. Study by Military Spending Research Services, reported in *Washington Post*, January 23, 1987.

6. Quoted in *Washington Post*, November 17, 1980.

7. James Abourezk, "Clear Out PACs, Clean Up Congressional Campaigns," release by Institute for Policy Studies, Washington, D.C., March 18, 1986. Then-Senator Abourezk was himself attending the Senate Democratic Caucus.

8. Quoted in "Business Battles Back," *Environmental Action*, December 2, 1978, 14.

9. Howard Kohn, "The Hughes-Nixon-Lansky Connection," *Rolling Stone*, May 20, 1976, 44.

10. Ken Silverstein, *Washington on $10 Million a Day* (Monroe, Maine: Common Courage, 1998).

11. Center for Public Integrity, *The Torturers' Lobby* (Washington, D.C.: Center for Public Integrity, 1992); "Mobutu Money Went to Indiana Congressman," *San Francisco Examiner*, May 15, 1997.

12. Quoted in D. Gilbarg, "United States Imperialism," in Bill Slate (ed.), *Power to the People* (New York: Tower, 1970), 67.

13. *New York Times*, April 29, 1992.

14. Silverstein, *Washington on $10 Million a Day*, introduction; also *Nation*, July 19, 1999.

15. *New York Times*, June 30, 1996.

16. See Albert Hunt's column in *Wall Street Journal*, July 27, 1995; Molly Ivins's column in *San Francisco Chronicle*, August 23, 1996; and Lisa Friedman, "Ecologists Attack Source of Pombo Draft Bill," *Oakland Tribune*, September 11, 2000.

17. Robert Winter-Berger, *The Washington Pay-Off* (New York: Dell, 1972), 14 and passim for some astonishing eyewitness testimony.

18. *USA Today*, November 10, 1997.

19. Lester Milbrath, *The Washington Lobbyists* (Chicago: Rand McNally, 1963), 345.

20. Joel Brinkley, "Cultivating the Grass Roots to Reap Legislative Benefits," *New York Times*, November 1, 1993.

21. *New York Times*, March 25, 1996, and June 10, 2000; Tim Wheeler's reports in *People's Weekly World*, November 22, 1997.

22. Alice Ann Love, "Critics Question Motives of Tennessee's Doctor Senator," Associated Press report, August 23, 1997.

23. Sheila Kaplan, "Congress's Inside Traders," *Nation*, July 6, 1998.

24. Quoted in *New York Times*, November 25, 1984.

25. Mark Green quoted in Steven Roberts, "The Rich Get Richer and Elected," *New York Times*, September 24, 1985.

26. Stan Goff, "Helms Exposed as Slumlord," *People's Weekly World*, October 26, 1996.

27. Larry Sabato and Glenn Simpson, *Dirty Little Secrets: The Persistence of Corruption in American Politics* (New York: Times Books/Random House, 1996); *Washington Post*, July 20, 1998; *Oakland Tribune*, April 16, 2000.

28. Russ Baker, "The House Flunks Ethics," *Nation*, February 15, 1999. Another leading example of hypocrisy and moral turpitude is Representative Henry Hyde (R-Ill.); see Dennis Bernstein and Leslie Kean, *Henry Hyde's Moral Universe* (Monroe, Maine: Common Courage, 1999).

29. *Washington Post*, December 31, 1982.

30. *San Francisco Examiner*, September 4, 1997.

31. GAO investigation reported in *Washington Post*, October 10, 1981; on the indictments of federal executives, see U.S. Justice Department, *Report to Congress on the Activities and Operations of the Public Integrity Sector for 1986* (Washington, D.C.: Government Printing Office, 1987).

32. On corruption in the Reagan administration after 1986, see *Washington Post*, September 24, 1988; *New York Times*, July 27, 1988, and May 1, 1990.

33. *Washington Post*, February 5, 1988, and January 17, 1989.

34. An example of this apologetic approach to corruption is Peter deLeon, *Thinking about Political Corruption* (Armonk, N.Y.: M. E. Sharpe, 1993).

35. Both parties in both houses have a caucus or "conference" consisting of the entire membership of the party in that particular house. It elects the majority or minority leader and party whips. The majority-party caucus also elects the committee and subcommittee chairs.

36. "By Their Deeds," *Nation*, July 20, 1998. See John C. Berg, *Unequal Struggle: Class, Gender, Race and Power in the U.S. Congress* (Boulder, Colo.: Westview, 1994), for an analysis of how wider class forces predetermine the scope of congressional power.

37. John C. Berg, "Vietnam, Angola, Lebanon, and Central America: Limited Possibilities for Congressional Control of Military Intervention," paper given at annual meeting of the American Political Science Association, New Orleans, 1985.

38. *New York Times*, March 17, 1998.

39. Jeremy Weir Alderson, "Spooks and Brass Work the Hill," *CovertAction Quarterly*, Summer 1997.

40. Mark Green et al., *Who Runs Congress?*, 2nd ed. (New York: Bantam, 1972), 56.

41. "Goodies for the Rich Hidden in Wage Bill," *Santa Rosa Press Democrat*, October 13, 1996; "GOP Leaders' Tax Breaks for the Rich," *Solidarity*, May 2000.

42. *Sunday Oregonian*, July 12, 1998; and *New York Times*, September 1, 1998.

43. "Fast Track Backtrack," *Nation*, December 1, 1997.

44. *New York Times*, August 9, 1987, and April 8, 1993; *Washington Post*, June 17, 1987, and August 13, 1991. For instances of Democratic use of the filibuster, see *Washington Post*, November 16, 1989; *New York Times*, November 2, 1991.

45. *Washington Monthly*, April 1972, 18.

46. Some sources estimate a higher spending disparity: *Half of Senate Incumbents Seeking Election Are Financially Unopposed* (Washington, D.C.: Common Cause, 1990).

47. All the quotations above are from Robert Salladay, "Term Limits' Dark Side Coming to Light," *San Francisco Examiner*, July 26, 1998; see also B. Drummond Ayres, "Term Limit Laws Are Transforming More Legislatures," *New York Times*, April 28, 1997.

48. Ayres, "Term Limit Laws."

49. *U.S. Term Limits v. Thornton* (1995).

50. "Election Results," *Independent Politics*, Winter 1998–99.

15

The President:
Guardian of the System

In this chapter our task is to take a nonworshipful look at the presidency. The president, we are told, plays many roles: chief executive, "chief legislator," commander-in-chief, head of state, and party leader. Seldom mentioned is the president's role as promoter and guardian of corporate capitalism. The president is the embodiment of the executive-centered state system that defends American corporate interests at home and abroad.

Salesman of the System

Presidents do their share to indoctrinate the American people into the ruling-class ideology. Every modern president has had occasion to praise the "free enterprise system" and denounce collectivist alternatives. The president is the American system's top salesman. "America is standing tall. America is the greatest," exulted President Ronald Reagan to a nation with thirty-five million citizens living below the poverty level, a record trade deficit, and a runaway national debt. Prosperity, our presidents tell us, is here or not far off — but so are the nation's many wild-eyed enemies, be they communists, revolutionaries, terrorists, Islamic "fanatics," or whatever. There is no shortage of adversaries abroad supposedly waiting to pounce upon the United States, thwarted only by huge U.S. military budgets, and a strong national security state. Presidents usually downplay crises relating to the economy and emphasize the ones needed to justify arms spending, overseas military interventions, and free market "reforms."

Whether Democrat or Republican, liberal or conservative, the president tends to treat capitalist interests as synonymous with the nation's well-being. Presidents greet the accumulation of wealth as a manifestation of a healthy national economy, regardless of how that wealth is applied or distributed. America will achieve new heights spurred on "by freedom and the profit motive," President Reagan announced. "This is a free-enterprise country," said President Bill Clinton. "I want to create more millionaires in my presidency than [President] Bush and [Vice President] Quayle did."[1]

Presidents describe the overseas investments of giant corporations as "U.S. interests" abroad, to be defended at all costs — or certainly at great cost to the populace. A president's primary commitment abroad is not to democracy as such but to free-market capitalism. In an address before the United Nations, September 27, 1993, President Clinton said: "Our overriding purpose is to expand and strengthen the world's community of market-based democracies." In fact, U.S. presidents have supported any number of market-based autocracies in Latin America, the Middle East, and elsewhere. And they have helped destroy any number of popular-based governments that sought an alternative to free-market corporatism, as in Chile, Nicaragua, South Yemen, Indonesia, East Timor, Mozambique, and Yugoslavia — demonstrating that it is not the "democracies" that is of prime consideration but the "market-based."[2]

At the Constitutional Convention, the wealthy planter Charles Pinckney proposed that no one qualify for the presidency who was not worth at least $100,000 — a munificient sum in 1787. While the proposal was never written into the Constitution, it seems to have been followed in practice. Since World War II, and frequently before then, just about all presidential candidates on the Republican and Democratic tickets have been millionaires either at the time they first campaigned for the office or by the time they departed from it.

One might ponder the diverse social backgrounds of the two major candidates in the 2000 presidential election:

- Vice President Al Gore was a Democrat and a multimillionaire; his father had been a U.S. senator. Gore's opponent, Governor George W. Bush of Texas, was a Republican and a multimillionaire; his father had been a U.S. senator and U.S. president.
- Gore was a graduate of St. Albans, an elite prep school, and Harvard, an elite Ivy League university. Bush was a graduate of Phillips Academy, an elite prep school, and Yale, an elite Ivy League university.
- Gore first ran for Congress in 1976 at the age of twenty-eight; he has had an involvement with Occidental Petroleum dating back to his father's days. Bush first ran for Congress in 1978 at the age of thirty-two; he has had a long involvement with the private health care business and oil industry dating back to his father's days.

- Gore supports the North American Free Trade Agreement, the World Trade Organization, the International Monetary Fund, and other free trade agreements that serve international finance capital, and tens of billions of dollars in corporate subsidies. So does Bush.
- Gore supports a huge military establishment and U.S. global empire. So does Bush.

Presidents have drawn their top advisers and administrators primarily from industry and banking and have relied heavily on the judgments of corporate leaders. One description of President Ford could easily apply to any number of other White House occupants: He "follows the judgment of the major international oil companies on oil problems in the same way that he amiably heeds the advice of other big businesses on the problems that interest them. . . . He is . . . a solid believer in the business ideology of rugged individualism, free markets and price competition — virtues that exist more clearly in his mind than they do in the practices of the international oil industry."[3]

Whatever his class origins, it is probably not easy for a president to remain keenly aware of the travails endured by ordinary working people. He lives like an opulent potentate in the White House, a rent-free, 132-room mansion set on an eighteen-acre estate, with a domestic staff of about one hundred, including six butlers and five full-time florists, a well-stocked wine cellar, tennis courts, a private movie room, a gymnasium, a bowling alley, and a heated outdoor swimming pool. In addition, the president has the free services of a private physician, a dozen chauffeured limousines, and numerous helicopters and jets, including Air Force One. He has access to the imperial luxuries of Camp David and other country retreats, free vacations, a huge expense allowance, and — for the few things he must pay for — a $200,000 annual salary.

Journalists and political scientists have described the presidency as a "man-killing job." Yet presidents take more vacations and live far better and longer than the average American male. After leaving office they continue to feed from the public trough. Four ex-presidents (Ford, Carter, Reagan, and Bush) are multimillionaires, yet each receives from $500,000 to $700,000 in annual pensions, office space, staff, and travel expenses, along with full-time Secret Service protection costing $5 million a year for each. Some ex-presidents pick up other perks, as when a group of self-described "independently wealthy" individuals contributed $156,000 each and bought a $2.5-million home in fashionable Bel Air, California, which they gave to Reagan when he left office in appreciation for all he had done for the very rich.[4]

Big contributors to the White House may disclaim any intention of trying to buy influence, but if it should happen that after the election they find themselves or their firms burdened by a problem that only the White House can handle, they see no reason why they shouldn't be allowed to exercise their rights like other citizens and ask their elected representative, who in this case happens to be their friend, the president of the United States, for a little help.

Presidents are as capable of trading favors for money as any influence-peddling, special-interest local politician — only on a grander scale. Presidents attend major fundraisers and invite big donors to White House dinners. The Nixon administration helped settle a multibillion-dollar suit against ITT and received a $400,000 donation from that corporation. Richard Nixon ordered his staff to squeeze big contributions out of three large dairy farm groups after he promised them an increase in federal milk price supports. Reagan pushed through the deregulation of oil and gasoline prices and received huge contributions from the oil industry. President George H. Bush's Team 100, consisting of 249 wealthy financiers and corporate CEOs, put up at least $100,000 each to help elect him in 1988. In return, they enjoyed special dispensations on regulatory and legal matters.[5]

Presidents will award choice ambassadorships to big contributors. Bush received a total of $900,000 from persons he later appointed to ambassadorships; many had no political or diplomatic experience. Nixon insisted that people who were offered ambassadorships be required "to pay at least $250,000."[6]

It is said that the greatness of the office lends greatness to its occupant, so that even persons of mediocre capacity grow in response to the presidency's responsibilities and powers. Closer examination reveals that presidents have been just as readily corrupted as ennobled by high office, becoming inclined toward self-righteous assertion, tempted to demonstrate their military "toughness" against weak nations, and not above operating in unlawful ways. Thus, at least six presidents employed illegal FBI wiretaps to gather incriminating information on rival political figures. The White House tapes, which recorded Nixon's Oval Office conversations, showed him to be a self-serving, vindictive, bigoted man who manifested a shallowness of spirit and mind that the majestic office could cloak but not transform. Official audits revealed that Nixon spent over $2.4 million of taxpayers' money on improvements of his private estate and underpaid his taxes by $444,022. On occasion, he requested the Internal Revenue Service (IRS) to stop auditing the incomes of close friends and go after his political enemies.[7] President Reagan repeatedly fabricated stories and anecdotes about nonexistent events. The Iran-contra affair revealed him to be a deceptive manipulator who pretended to support one policy while pursuing another, and who felt himself to be unaccountable to Congress and the law.

The Two Faces of the President

Presidents conjure up fine-sounding labels and images to enhance their popular appeal. Roosevelt had his "New Deal," Truman his "Fair Deal," Kennedy his "New Frontier," Johnson his "Great Society," Reagan his "American Renaissance," Bush his "New World Order," and Clinton his "New Prosperity."

One of the president's many roles is that of chief liar, performed by offering the public a deceptive admixture of populist rhetoric and plutocratic policy. Consider John Kennedy, a liberal president widely celebrated for his devotion to the underdog. In foreign affairs, Kennedy spoke of international peace and self-determination, yet he invaded anticapitalist Cuba, drastically increased military expenditures, instituted new counterinsurgency programs throughout the Third World, and sent military advisors to Vietnam. In domestic matters Kennedy presented himself as a champion of civil rights, yet he refrained from taking legal action to support antidiscrimination cases and did little to prevent repeated attacks against civil rights organizers in the South. He talked as if he were a friend of working people, yet he imposed wage restraints on unions at a time workers' buying power was stagnant or declining, and he opposed introduction of the thirty-five-hour work week. He also pushed through reductions in the progressive income tax rates and deficit-spending policies that carried business profits to all-time highs without reducing unemployment.[8] (Nevertheless, Kennedy was hated by right-wingers because of his call for a reevaluation of our attitudes toward the Soviet Union, his differences with the Federal Reserve System and the steel industry, his friendliness with civil rights leaders, his atmospheric test-ban treaty with the Soviets, his attempts at bringing the Central Intelligence Agency (CIA) under White House control, and his reluctance to attempt another invasion of Cuba and unwillingness to initiate a massive land war in Vietnam.)

Presidents Richard Nixon and Gerald Ford both voiced their support for environmentalism and then opened new forest lands for commercial exploitation and strip-mining. Both gave lip service to the problems of the Vietnam veteran, the plight of the elderly, and the needs of the poor, yet cut benefits to these groups. President Jimmy Carter promised to cut the military budget and instead increased it. He promised to reduce arms sales, but under his administration arms sales rose to new levels. He talked of helping the needy, but proposed cutbacks in summer youth jobs, child nutrition programs, and other benefits, while offering lavish credits and subsidies to big business.[9]

The gap between rhetoric and policy became a virtual chasm during the Reagan years. Reagan lauded our veterans for their great sacrifices, but offered a budget that reduced veterans' health care. Before an African-American audience in Washington, D.C., he described himself as a champion of racial equality without mentioning that he advocated tax breaks for segregated private schools and had drastically cut inner-city programs while doing little to enforce existing civil rights laws. He announced that his tax cuts had benefited working folks and not the rich — though the figures said otherwise. He claimed to be a vigorous defender of the environment, while trying to gut environmental regulations. He called for the rule of law in domestic and international affairs, yet launched an unprovoked invasion of Grenada and a mercenary war against

Nicaragua, and refused to accept the lawful jurisdiction of the World Court when Nicaragua brought the case before that tribunal.[10]

Then came President George Bush, who proclaimed himself the "education president," yet slashed education funds for disadvantaged children and others. As the self-professed "environment president," he withdrew vast areas of wetlands from federal protection and opposed international measures against global warming and ozone depletion. He spoke of preserving family values, but vetoed a bill that would allow workers to take unpaid leave so they might care for an ill family member or newborn child. He invaded Panama ostensibly to arrest President Noriega for criminal dealing in drugs, but himself maintained close relations with various CIA-linked drug traffickers for years and ran an administration heavily involved in shady deals.[11]

"The courage to change" was the campaign theme that helped get Bill Clinton elected president in 1992, yet he did not seem interested in changing much. He promised labor-law reform, but for eight years did nothing to liberalize the labor laws that made union organizing so difficult. He actually decreased public service spending from what it had been under Bush, including a $3 billion reduction for low-income housing. He defended affirmative action programs when they were challenged in the courts but then conducted a sweeping reduction of these same programs. He vowed to protect the environment, then softened penalties for oil-spill polluters, and backed a plan to open ancient forest reserves to timber operations. He told a special session of the United Nations that we could not neglect the problems of global warming that were putting the entire earth at risk, yet he "stopped well short of the commitment to cutting greenhouse gases that allies have been urging," cuts that were "opposed by automobile and oil companies and other heavy industries."[12]

In foreign affairs, Clinton talked of charting a new course but tread the same path as his predecessors. He bombed Iraq on false pretexts and kept sanctions against that country in place for eight years, causing the deaths of tens of thousands. He continued Bush's armed intervention in Somalia, eventually withdrawing troops only because of the public outcry regarding the losses sustained. He bombed Yugoslavia around the clock for seventy-eight days, killing many more people and wreaking far more destruction than the "civil war" he professed to be suppressing. He called for self-determination but sent U.S. troops to occupy Bosnia, Macedonia, and Kosovo. Like numerous administrations before him, Clinton maintained a crippling embargo against Cuba. He called for peace and democracy in Haiti, yet backed the militarists and tried to undermine the democratic elections of 2000 when the more populist anti–free market party won.

Clinton signaled his intention to increase funding for intelligence operations and maintain the CIA at its ongoing level. He publicly apologized to the Guatemalan nation for the crucial role played by the United States in training and assisting the Guatemalan military in its genocidal "scorched earth" policies that between 1981 and 1983 alone killed up to 150,000 Guatemalans, mainly highlands Mayans. At the same time, his administration was quietly reinitiating full U.S. military training and aid to the Guatemalan military, even as human rights atrocities continued.[13]

Clinton was a member of the corporate-funded Democratic Leadership Council, a collection of "New Democrats" who assume many of the same positions as the Republicans in Congress: military spending kept at Cold War levels; military aid to Saudi Arabia, Turkey, Indonesia, and dozens of other right-wing states; erosion of democratic sovereignty through the passage of the North American Free Trade Agreement (NAFTA) and the General Agreement on Tariffs and Trade (GATT); corporate fast-track program to push through more "free trade" agreements; opposition to banning nuclear weapons; putting missiles into outer space ("Star Wars"); sixty new federal death penalty offenses; cuts in family assistance programs, Medicare, and aid to the disabled; privatizing a portion of Social Security; opening pristine Alaskan regions to oil exploration; outlawing gay marriages; eliminating federal programs that reserve some contracts for minority and women-owned companies; tightening the corporate grip on radio and television; increasing expenditures for prisons and police; sidetracking single-payer health care; and reducing immigrant rights.[14]

Most of Clinton's appointees were of corporate background. Some of the few liberal nominees he offered up, such as Lani Guinier, were quickly withdrawn when they met with conservative opposition. Clinton reappointed the ultraconservative Republican Alan Greenspan as chair of the powerful

Federal Reserve System, and Republicans as secretaries of defense and state and as special advisors to his staff. Yet polls indicated that most people thought of Clinton as a liberal — and they liked him for it. They correctly perceived his liberal stance on a few issues such as women's abortion rights, but they did not know about his many conservative positions. Most respondents thought he opposed GOP cuts in welfare, when in fact he strongly supported phasing out the federal welfare program. Only one in four knew that he favored an expansion of private health insurance, with nearly 60 percent incorrectly believing that he advocated universal health coverage. Most thought that labor contributed more to his campaigns than big business; only a small number knew it was the other way around. In sum, most people knew when Clinton took a liberal position, while his more conservative stances remained something of a well-kept secret. Republicans labeled him an unabashed leftist, a misleading charge that was well publicized in the corporate media. The public believed it and did not seem to mind it: "they appear to like his agenda — even if, as it turns out, they don't know what it is."[15] In this, Clinton successfully performed the role of every president in a corporate-dominated society, convincing the people he was their man when in fact he was someone else's.

The President's Systemic Role

If presidents tend to speak one way and act another, it is due less to some inborn flaw shared by the varied personalities who occupy the office than to the nature of the office itself. Like other politicians, only more so, the president is caught between the demands of democracy and the powers of plutocracy. He must satisfy the major interests of corporate America while making a show of serving the people.

He also must do for the capitalist system what individual capitalists cannot do. The president must reconcile conflicts between various business interests, usually deciding in favor of heavy industry and big finance and against light industry and small business. Sometimes he must oppose the interests of individual companies or industries, keeping them in line with the overall needs of the corporate economy. Hence he might do battle with an industry like steel, as did Kennedy, to hold prices down in order to ease the inflationary effects on other producer interests. When engaged in such conflicts the president takes on an appearance of opposing the special interests on behalf of the common interest. In fact, he might be better described as *protecting the common interests of the special interests,* keeping the free market from devouring itself. For this effort he may incur the wrath of corporate leaders who see even the palest concessions as the beginning of the end.

The success any group enjoys in winning White House intercession has less to do with the justice of its cause than with the place it occupies in the class structure. If a large group of poor migrant workers and a small group of rich aerospace executives both sought the president's assistance, it would not be difficult to predict which of them would more likely win it. Witness these events of April 1971:

- Some eighty to ninety thousand migrant farmworkers in Florida, out of work because of crop failures and exempted from unemployment compensation, were without means of feeding themselves and their families. The workers demonstrated peacefully in large numbers outside President Nixon's Florida vacation residence, hoping to get the White House to intercede. They were met only by the police, who dispersed them with swinging clubs. Eventually the farm counties were declared disaster areas. But the government emergency relief money ended up in the hands of the big commercial growers who had sustained the crop losses. Since the migrant workers had no residence in the state, they did not qualify for relief or receive a single dollar.[16]
- During the very week the farmworkers were being clubbed by police, leaders of the aerospace industry placed a few telephone calls to Washington and were invited to meet quietly with the president to discuss their companies' problems. Later that same day the White House announced a $42-million authorization to the aerospace industry to relocate, retrain, and in other ways assist its top administrators, scientists, and technicians. The spending plan, an industry creation, was immediately accepted by the Nixon administration without prior study.[17]

Was the president responding to a "national interest" or a "special interest" when helping the aerospace industry? Much depends upon how the labels are applied. If we believe the national interest requires that the profits and strength of the industrial and military establishment, of which the aerospace industry is a part, be maintained even at great cost, then the president was responding to a national interest. The president's first responsibility is to tend to the corporate economy, not to sustain farmworkers who represent a marginal group and are therefore a limited special interest. So, when workers act to disrupt and weaken the sinews of industry, as have striking coal miners, railroad operators, and steelworkers, the president may see fit to deal summarily with them.

When Ronald Reagan complained that "special interests" were resisting his attempts to serve the national interest with his budget-cutting efforts, he was using a motif long propagated by political scientists who defined "special" and "national" interests by some abstract measure (particular versus broad) and not by the class interest involved (owners versus employees and consumers). Thus, Reagan was able to portray the social needs of working people — a constituency of millions — as a narrow parochial "special" interest, while a coterie of big companies had "national," indeed international, interests.

Other people would argue that the national interest is not served when giant industries receive favored treatment at the expense of workers, taxpayers, and consumers. That the corporations have holdings that are national and often multinational in scope does not mean they represent the interests of the nation's populace. The "national interest" or "public interest" should encompass the ordinary public rather than relatively small groups of corporate elites. Contrary to an established myth, the public monies distributed to these favored few do not "trickle down" to the mass of working people at the bottom — as the hungry farmworkers can testify.

Whichever position one takes, it becomes clear that there is no neutral way of defining the national interest. Whatever policy the president pursues, he is helping some class interests rather than others. It is a matter of historical record that presidents usually have chosen a definition of the national interest that serves the giant conglomerates, at some cost to us lesser mortals.

A Loaded Electoral College

Under Article 2, Section 1 of the Constitution, presidents are directly elected not by the people but by a majority of "electors," appointed in such manner as the various state legislatures might direct. The number of electors each state has is equal to the total number of its congressional representatives and senators. When voting for the president we are actually voting for one or another slate of party-designated electors who are morally — but not in all states legally — bound to abide by the popular vote.[18] Since 1796 at least fifteen electors have failed to support their party's candidate. Thus, in 1960 a Nixon elector from Oklahoma voted for Senator Harry Byrd, as did six of the eleven Alabama electors pledged to John Kennedy. Twenty-six states, representing 268 electoral votes, have passed laws requiring electors to follow the popular vote. The Supreme Court has declared these laws constitutional.

The "electoral college," as it has come to be known, remains an undemocratic anachronism, designed by the framers of the Constitution to act as a filter of "popular passions." In keeping with their class prejudices and interests, the framers assumed that the electors would generally be propertied and educated gentlemen who supposedly would meet in their respective state capitals months after the election to deliberate and select a president, acting as a damper on popular passions. It was expected that candidates would seldom achieve a majority of the electoral college, in which case the election would be thrown into the House of Representatives, where each state would vote as a single unit.

By awarding a state's entire electoral vote on a winner-take-all basis to the candidate who wins a plurality of the popular vote, the electoral college creates artificial or exaggerated majorities. Thus, in 1984 Reagan won 58.8 percent of the votes cast but 97.5 percent of the electoral college. The *distribution* of votes sometimes becomes more important than the actual number of votes. In 1976 Gerald Ford would have won the election with a shift of a mere 5,558 votes in Ohio and 3,686 in Hawaii, giving him a majority of electoral votes (270), leaving Carter with a popular majority of 50.4 percent and over 1.5 million more votes. In 2000, Democrat Al Gore won the popular vote by over half a million ballots but lost the presidency to George W. Bush, who scraped through with a bare electoral college majority and what many observers saw as a stolen victory in Florida.

The electoral college also distorts the popular vote by giving each state, regardless of its population, two extra votes (equivalent to its seats in the U.S. Senate). Since the Republicans control a number of relatively less populated western and southern states, this gives them proportionately more electoral votes per popular votes, which helps explain how Bush was able to win the electoral college with fewer votes than Gore in 2000; he won more states. It is also nigh impossible for a third-party candidate, whose support is thinly spread around the nation rather than concentrated in one region or a few states, to carry a state and make a showing in the electoral college. This further discourages voters from considering third-party candidates.

It has been argued that by treating the large states as giant blocks of electoral votes, the electoral college enhances their importance, and since large states like New York and California tend to be liberal, this works to the advantage of liberals. But there is no set correlation between state size and ideology. Texas is a large state yet one of the most conservative. And over the last two decades California and New York have produced their share of right-wing officeholders.

With direct election of the president there would be no distortion of the popular vote. Every vote would count equally regardless of location. And there would be no possibility of someone's winning the vote but losing the election, or of having to throw an election into the House of Representatives, where further distortions can occur. An attempt to introduce a constitutional amendment through Congress for the direct election of the president failed in 1977–1978, because of the opposition of members from smaller states advantaged by the two extra electoral votes. In 1980, a Gallup poll found that 67 percent of U.S. citizens favored direct presidential elections and only 19 percent were opposed. Short of abolishing the Electoral College, a state could allocate its electoral votes to candidates in proportion to their popular vote in that state. As of now, Maine and Nebraska give two electoral votes to the statewide winner and one electoral vote for every congressional district that a candidate carries.[19]

The "New Federalism" Ploy

President Reagan sought "to curb the size and influence of the federal establishment" by giving many social programs back to the states (when not able to abolish them outright). This "New Federalism," as it was called, supposedly would revitalize state governments. In actuality, states and cities were given greater responsibility for dealing with major social problems while federal revenue sharing was cut drastically. Spending for programs like community development and mass transit dropped by over 70 percent. The remaining federal monies were allocated in block grants to the state governments instead of directly to needy urban areas, as previously done. The effect was to create new bureaucracies at the state level that shortchanged the cities and favored the relatively prosperous small towns and suburban communities.[20]

New Federalism remains a professed goal among those who dream of a marriage between Big Business and Little Government, one that allows business to play off states and communities against each other in order to extract more tax breaks and subsidies from them. It is easier for DuPont to control the small state of Delaware than deal with the federal government as a whole. More powerful and richer than Alaska, Exxon would like to see that sparsely populated state given complete control over all federal oil and natural resources within its boundaries — in effect giving Exxon easier access to those resources.

On occasions when various states impose progressive regulations upon business, conservatives discard their "New Federalism" posture and use the central government to override state powers. For instance, the Reagan administration, ever mindful of the interests of the nuclear industry, argued that the states were prohibited from establishing nuclear-plant emission standards more stringent than those imposed by federal authorities.

Since 1787, conservatives have been for a strong central government or a weak one, strong state and local governments or weak ones, depending on which arrangement served owning-class interests at any particular juncture. The moneyed class understands that abstract notions such as "states' rights" and a "revitalized federalism" are not an end unto themselves but a means of serving its interests. When a particular arrangement fails to do so, it is put aside. Now, with international trade and investment agreements and organizations like the World Trade Organization (WTO), transnational corporations have contrived a way to disempower reformist governments and circumvent popular sovereignty itself.

The Growth of Presidential Power

Relying solely on the Constitution, we might think that the legislature is a more powerful branch of government than the executive. Article 1 gives Congress the power to declare war, make the laws of the land, raise taxes, and spend money. Article 2 seems more limited; it gives the president the power to appoint ambassadors, federal judges, and senior executive officers (subject to Senate confirmation) and to make treaties (subject to ratification by two-thirds of the senators present). The president can veto laws (but the veto can be overridden by a two-thirds vote in Congress), call Congress into special session, and do a few other incidental things. The president has two more significant functions: to see that the laws are faithfully executed and to serve as commander-in-chief of the armed forces. By all appearances, it is Congress that determines policy and lays down the law and the president who does Congress's bidding.

The reality is something else. In the last century or so, with the growth of industrial capitalism at home and abroad, the role of government has grown enormously at the municipal, state, and federal levels and in the executive, legislative, and judicial branches. But the tasks of serving capitalism's vast needs and interests in war and peace have fallen disproportionately on the level of government that is national and international in scope — the federal — and on the branch most suited to carrying out the necessary technical, organizational, and military measures — the executive.

The executive branch today is a vast conglomeration of departments, agencies, commissions, and bureaus. The Executive Office of the President contains a number of administrative units to help the president formulate and coordinate overall policy. There is the Office of Management and Budget, which puts together both the president's budget and his legislative program and sometimes enforces White House policy in the bureaucracy. Also within the Executive Office is the National Security Council (NSC), created after World War II for the purpose of overall planning and coordination of military, international, and domestic policies related to national security. The NSC is the White House's instrument (along with the Defense Department and to a lesser extent the State Department) for suppressing popular insurgency throughout the Third World, and ensuring U.S. global corporate hegemony. The CIA reports directly to the NSC.

The growth of presidential powers has been so great as to have occasioned a relative decline in the powers of Congress, even though legislative activity itself has increased significantly over the years. This is especially true in international affairs. The end result is a presidency that tends to eclipse Congress — and sometimes the Constitution itself. The president commands a number of resources that give him a decided edge:

- The prestige of the office itself enables the chief executive to command the kind of media attention that most politicians can only dream of.
- The president can reward supportive lawmakers and punish uncooperative ones. The lawmaker who votes the way the president wants on crucial bills is more likely to get the Administration to build that veterans' hospital in his or her district, or receive White House

support for an emergency farm bill, or secure a federal contract for a shipyard back home.

- There being only one president but many legislators, the chief executive has the advantage of unitary initiative and action. Almost by definition, a legislature is a cacophony of voices and interests, not structured as a command post. No wonder approximately 80 percent of major laws originate in the executive branch.

- In just about every policy area — from weapons systems to management of timber lands — the executive branch controls the crucial information. Congress frequently follows the president's lead because it depends so heavily on what the executive departments have to say. At times, presidents place themselves and their associates above congressional investigation by claiming that the separation of powers gives them an inherent right of "executive privilege." Executive privilege has been used to withhold information on everything from undeclared wars to illegal campaign funds and burglaries, yet the term does not exist in the Constitution or any law. The Supreme Court collaborated in promoting "executive privilege," deciding that a "presumptive privilege" for withholding information (in noncriminal cases) belonged to the president. "Presumptive," indeed, with no basis in the Constitution.[21]

The president's claim to executive privilege is nowhere more pronounced than in regard to "national security," an area usually removed from public scrutiny and congressional oversight. Congress unknowingly funded CIA covert operations in Laos and Thailand that were in violation of congressional prohibitions. The legislature ordered a halt to expansion of a naval base in the Indian Ocean, only to discover that construction was continuing. Many members of the Senate had not heard of the automated battlefield program for which they voted secret appropriations.

By entering into "executive agreements" with foreign nations, the president can even circumvent the Senate's power to ratify treaties. The Reagan administration argued that testimony given by its officials during treaty ratification hearings need not reflect a treaty's true meaning. Some senators protested, noting that such a procedure undermined the Senate's constitutional duty to ratify a treaty, since the Senate would have no certainty about what it was actually approving.[22]

The Would-Be King

In the realm of foreign affairs, presidents have sometimes made claim to absolutist power, answerable to no one. When asked whether a U.S. military foray into Bolivia, ostensibly to catch drug traffickers, was in the national interest, President Reagan said, "Anything we do is in the national interest."[23]

President Nixon went even further, asserting an "inherent executive power" under the Constitution to commit even criminal acts when impelled by what he considered to be national security considerations. As he put it, "When the president does it, that means it is not illegal."[24] Inside every president is a divine-rights monarch trying to get out.

The president frequently issues decrees on his own, without authorization from Congress. Thus, Reagan unilaterally abrogated the treaty of commerce and friendship with Nicaragua to wage a war of attrition against that country. On another occasion he issued an executive order that authorized intelligence agencies to conduct domestic surveillance and covert operations against U.S. citizens within the United States, in violation of explicit prohibitions set forth in the National Security Act of 1947. Both Reagan and Bush used executive orders to take wetlands out of protection and grant favorable deregulations to industry. Today there are executive orders recorded in the Federal Register, and accepted by Congress, that would, upon order from the White House, deal with "national emergencies," allowing the federal government to seize all utilities, food resources, transportation, and communication media; force every individual to register; and forcibly relocate populations within the United States.[25] By using executive orders to create serious departures from the law, the president willfully concocts his own laws, something not allowed by the Constitution.

When Congress first resisted Clinton's request for a $40-billion package to bail out Mexican and Wall Street financiers, the president resorted to executive fiat, offering the financiers up to $20 billion from the Exchange Stabilization Fund (ESF). The ESF, a controversial Treasury Department account that was established by law in 1934 ostensibly to support the U.S. dollar in international markets, has since been used in various unaccountable ways. A few members of Congress have led lonely struggles to establish oversight of the fund. As Ralph Nader noted, "If the President and Treasury Secretary can singlehandedly divert billions of dollars of public funds to the Mexican government to bail out Wall Street investment firms and financiers, how can the government hope to achieve fiscal discipline? What mismanaged country and which wealthy constituency will be the next beneficiary of this 'anything-goes' fund?"[26]

The Supreme Court has long been aware that its decisions have the force of law only if other agencies of government choose to abide by them. In recent years Congress has been coming to the same realization, developing a new appreciation of the executive's power to command directly the personnel, materials, and programs needed for carrying out decisions. The peculiar danger of executive power is that it executes. The executive alone has the power of implementation, acting (or refusing to act) with the force of state, to exercise extraordinary and sometimes unlawful initiatives of its own. Some instances drawn from the last two decades illustrate how the executive can circumvent the law at home and abroad:

- The Reagan administration terminated Social Security benefits for hundreds of thousands of disabled Americans. When federal courts found the rulings to be illegal, the administration announced it would simply ignore the unfavorable court decisions.
- When a federal judge ordered the first Bush administration to make surplus federal property available to the homeless under a 1987 law, the White House ignored the order.
- Both the Reagan and Bush administrations refused to spend billions appropriated by Congress for housing and low-income programs, and impounded billions intended for improvements in mass transit and air safety.
- Congress prohibited military sales to Guatemala, yet the White House agreed to sell $14 million worth of military equipment to that government, asserting that since the sale would be a cash transaction, it would not violate the congressional ban.
- The General Accounting Office (GAO) revealed in June 1993 that the Pentagon had deliberately misled Congress about the cost, performance, and need for nuclear weapons systems.[27]

Congress itself has sometimes collaborated in the usurpation of its power, granting each president, and a widening list of executive agencies, confidential funds for which no detailed invoices are required. The growth of unaccountable executive power is nowhere more evident than in the realm of international crisis and conflict. "War is the true nurse of executive aggrandizement," wrote James Madison in 1787. It was not the intent of the framers of the Constitution to confer upon the president any power to start a war. That power was intended for Congress alone. But some two hundred years later, U.S. presidents invaded the sovereign states of Grenada and Panama, bombed Iraq and Yugoslavia, and supported proxy wars against Cuba, Angola, Mozambique, Afghanistan, Cambodia, and Nicaragua, forcibly overthrowing governments and engaging in unlawful arms sales, blockades, and other acts of war, including the arming and training of mercenary forces, without a declaration of war from Congress. While Congress debated whether to declare war on Iraq, President Bush announced, "I don't care if I get one vote in Congress. We're going in."[28] Against the expressed will of Congress, U.S. planes and bases were used to support the war against Nicaragua. Recent presidents have claimed a "constitutional and historic power" to conduct foreign affairs that could not be limited by Congress. The power of a sole ruler to make war, treating the army as his personal force, is the power of a king.

Congressional attempts to rein in unilateral presidential warmaking have proven ineffective. A case in point is the War Powers Act of 1973, which requires that the president seek congressional approval within sixty days for any military action he has launched. The War Powers Act allows the president to engage U.S. troops only in case of an attack on the United States or its territories, possessions, or armed forces. In sending "military advisors" to El Salvador and Honduras who sometimes engaged in combat, two presidents violated the act. Clinton engaged U.S. forces in combat for seventy-eight days over Yugoslavia, never bothering to get congressional approval beyond sixty days. And U.S. military advisors in Colombia will now likely be engaging in combat actions without benefit of statutory or constitutional mandate.

The Constitution does not grant the president the right to wage covert actions against other nations, yet President George H. Bush made such a claim, stating he would notify Congress of covert operations about to be launched — unless he decided not to, "based on my assertion of the authorities granted this office by the Constitution."

It would be wrong to conclude from all this that the legislative branch has been reduced to a mere rubber stamp. From time to time Congress has fought back. Both houses now have budget committees with staffs that can more effectively review the president's budgetary proposals. Along with the investigations conducted by its standing committees and subcommittees, Congress has the General Accounting Office, which, as already noted, is independent of the executive branch and reports directly to the legislature. The GAO plays an important role in uncovering executive waste, wrongdoing, mismanagement, and nonenforcement of the law.

The Conservative Context

Years ago, liberals, who saw how a conservative leadership in Congress managed to thwart the desires of liberal presidents like Truman and Kennedy, concluded that the national legislature had too much power and the executive not enough. But having witnessed conservative presidents like Nixon and Reagan impose their will on Congress, some of these same liberals concluded that the president was too powerful and Congress too weak. Actually, there was something more to these complaints than partisan inconsistency. In the first instance, liberals are talking about the president's insufficient ability to effect measures that might benefit the working populace. And in the second, they are referring to the president's ability to make overseas military commitments and thwart social welfare legislation at home.

What underlies both complaints is the realization that the president tends to be more powerful than Congress when he assumes a conservative stance and less powerful when he wants to push in a progressive direction. This reflects the entire distribution of politico-economic class power, including control of investment capital and jobs, media ownership and influence, lobbying and campaign contributions, weakened labor unions, low voter participation among working people, and other factors mentioned in this book. It is also a reflection of the way the Constitution itself structures things. As the framers intended, the system of separation of powers and checks and balances is designed to give the high ground to those who resist social change, be they presidents or legislators. Neither the executive nor the legislature can singlehandedly initiate sweeping reforms.

Small wonder conservative and liberal presidents have different kinds of experiences with Congress. Should Congress insist upon passing bills that incur his displeasure, the conservative president need control only one-third plus one of either the House or the Senate to sustain his vetoes. If bills are passed over his veto, he can still undermine legislative intent by delaying enforcement under various pretexts relating to timing, efficiency, and other operational contingencies.

The techniques of veto, decoy, and delay used by a conservative president to dismantle or hamstring domestic programs are of little help to a president who might claim an interest in progressive social change. The immense social problems he would face cannot be solved by executive sleight-of-hand. What efforts presidents do make in the field of social reform are frequently thwarted or diluted by entrenched conservative powers within and without Congress. It is in these confrontations that the Congress gives every appearance of being able to frustrate presidential initiatives.

The Reagan years lent confirmation to the above analysis, albeit with a new twist, for here was a conservative president who was not obstructionist but activist, one who sought a major transition in taxing and spending policies. The obstructionist defenses that Congress uses so well against progressive measures were less successful against Reagan, as a coalition of Republicans and conservative Democrats, backed by corporate and moneyed interests outside Congress, gave the president most of what he wanted, curtailing or diminishing in one session progressive programs developed over the previous fifty years. The same coalition gave President Clinton and corporate America their NAFTA and GATT victories in record time. Like any political officeholder, the president is more likely to enjoy a successful use of power when he moves in a direction favored by powerful interests.

During the New Deal and Fair Deal days of liberal dominance of the White House, liberals advocated a strong presidency and warned against turning the president into an ineffectual lame duck by restricting the number of terms he might serve. Having endured twenty years of Roosevelt and Truman, conservatives were convinced that their main task was to trim the power of the federal government and of the presidency in particular. So they fought successfully for the Twenty-second Amendment (1951), which limited White House occupancy to two terms.

Likewise, in the 1950s liberals were urging that the president be given a freer hand in foreign policy, while conservatives were pushing for the

Bricker amendment, a measure that would have given the states a kind of veto over the executive treaty power reminiscent of the Articles of Confederation. Liberals talked about giving the president an item veto (allowing him to veto specific items in a bill while accepting other portions of it) so that he might better resist the riders tacked on by special interests. Conservatives treated the item veto as just another example of executive usurpation.

By the 1980s we heard a different tune. Conservatives now better appreciated the uses of a strong presidency in advancing the causes of military spending and of multinational corporate capitalism at home and abroad. Furthermore, given their ability in recent times to win the presidency and their superior ability to raise the enormous sums needed for that endeavor, conservatives, including those on the Supreme Court, now favored an expanded executive power. A conservative president, Ronald Reagan, broadened the realm of unaccountable executive initiative and secrecy. He also requested an item veto. And in 1988 he and other conservatives called for repeal of the Twenty-second Amendment, so that future presidents might again enjoy an indefinite number of terms.

In contrast, liberals now railed against the "imperial president." (And, of course, some conservatives now railed against an "imperial Congress.") Liberals talked about holding firm with the War Powers Act and making the executive more accountable to Congress. Under their breaths they were thankful for the Twenty-second Amendment, and no longer insisted on an item veto. They had discovered that a powerful presidency was likely to be a powerful conservative instrument.

The failure of reform-minded leaders to deliver on their promises demonstrates the difficulty of working for major changes within a politico-economic system structured to resist change. In the case of Clinton, it was less a tactical retreat and more a quick plunge into the ranks of corporate conservatism, as he showed himself to be almost as Republican as the Republicans in both domestic and foreign affairs.

The executive has grown in power and responsibility along with the increasing concentration of monopoly capital. As already noted, a centralized nationwide capitalist economy needs a centralized nationwide state power to tend to its needs. By the same token, as U.S. corporate interests grew to international scope and were confronted with challenges from various anti-imperialist forces, so the president's involvement in international affairs grew — and so grew the military and national security establishments intended to defend "U.S. interests" abroad. The president can intervene in other countries in a variety of ways, even destroying the social support systems and ecosystems of whole nations, as in the case of Iraq and Yugoslavia. Such powers do not advance the democratic interests of the American people, nor are they so designed. The immense military power the president commands, supposedly to make us all much safer, actually gives the chief executive an increasingly destructive and undemocratic power. As the executive power grows in foreign affairs, so the president's power over the American people becomes less accountable and more dangerous. Although the president and the government are often held responsible for the economy, they do not have that much control over it. The purpose of executive economic involvement is to sustain and advance the process of "free-market" capital accumulation. There is, then, not likely to be much progressive change from the top of the social pyramid, no matter who is in the White House, unless there is also a mass social unrest and mobilization for fundamental reforms at the base.

Notes

1. Reagan quoted in *Seattle Times,* January 15, 1989; Clinton speaking on PBS News Hour, October 27, 1992. I refer to the president as "he" only because every president thus far has been male. I do not mean to imply that men should have an exclusive hold on the office.
2. See the discussion in Chapter 7.
3. William Shannon, *New York Times,* July 22, 1975.
4. Mark Shields, *Washington Post,* January 28, 1989.
5. Associated Press, "Tapes Show More Dirt in Nixon's Presidency," November 1, 1997; Juan Williams, "Reagan Is the Real King of the Special Interest Groups," *Washington Post,* April 1, 1984; "Team 100 All-Stars," *Common Cause Magazine,* April/May/June 1992.
6. Warren Lenhart, *Ambassadorial Appointments: The Congressional Debate over Qualifications and Implications for U.S. Policy,* Congressional Research Service, Report 91-385F, Washington, D.C., May 1, 1991; and Associated Press, "Tapes Show More Dirt in Nixon's Presidency," November 1, 1997.
7. *New York Times,* June 21, 22, and 25, 1973, and April 4, 1974.
8. Bruce Miroff, *Pragmatic Illusions* (New York: McKay, 1976); Richard Walton, *Cold War and Counter-Revolution: The Foreign Policy of John F. Kennedy* (Baltimore: Penguin, 1972).
9. David Wise, *The Politics of Lying* (New York: Vintage, 1973), treats patterns of manipulation and deception in the Eisenhower, Kennedy, Johnson, and Nixon administrations; Christopher Lydon, "Jimmy Carter Revealed: He's a Rockefeller Republican," *Atlantic Monthly,* July 1977; Frank Browning, "Jimmy Carter's Astounding Lies," *Inquiry,* May 5, 1980.
10. James Nathan Miller, "Ronald Reagan and the Techniques of Deception," *Atlantic Monthly,* February 1984; *Washington Post,* June 17 and 19 and July 13, 1984, and September 27, 1986; *New York Times,* December 27, 1985.
11. *New York Times,* February 20 and June 30, 1990; *Washington Post,* October 29, 1991; Peter Dale Scott and Jonathan Marshall, *Cocaine Politics* (Berkeley: University of California Press, 1991); Pete Brewton, *The Mafia, CIA & George Bush* (New York: Shapolsky, 1992).
12. *New York Times,* June 27, 1997, and March 16, 1998.
13. Susanne Jonas, "A New Guatemalan Tragedy in the Making?" *San Francisco Chronicle,* April 26, 2000.
14. *New York Times,* March 8, 1996 and July 2, 1997; James Petras, "Clinton and Volunteerism: The Poverty of American Social Policy," *New Political Science* 20, no. 2, 1998; Eric Alterman, "Clinton's Foundation," *Nation,* March 2, 1998. For one insider's disillusionment with the Clinton administration, see Robert Reich, *Locked in the Cabinet* (New York: Knopf, 1997).
15. Justin Lewis, Michael Morgan, and Sut Jhally, "Polling Clinton's Appeal," *Nation,* March 9, 1998.
16. Tom Foltz, "Florida Farmworkers Face Disaster," *Guardian,* April 3, 1971.

17. *New York Times*, April 2, 1971.

18. If no candidate gets a majority of the Electoral College, the president is chosen by the House of Representatives, with each state delegation casting only one vote. The Twenty-third Amendment gave the District of Columbia a number of electors equivalent to the least populous state (3), which in addition to the number of senators (100) and representatives (435) brings the Electoral College to 538. The Constitution prohibits any member of Congress or any other government official from serving as an elector.

19. See comments by Theodore Arrington and opposing arguments by Saul Brenner in "Should the Electoral College be Replaced by the Direct Election of the President? A Debate," *PS: Political Science*, Spring 1984; also Harvey Zeiderstein, *Direct Election of the President* (Lexington, Mass.: Heath, 1973).

20. *New York Times*, March 26, 1996; Carol O'Cleireacain, "The 'New Federalism,'" *Economic Notes*, March/April 1991; Howard Kurtz, "Hostility to 'New Federalism' Is Bipartisan among Mayors," *Washington Post*, December 10, 1984; also *Washington Post*, January 7, 1987.

21. *United States v. Nixon* (1974); see also Raoul Berger, *Executive Privilege, A Constitutional Myth* (Cambridge, Mass.: Harvard University Press, 1974).

22. *Washington Post*, February 7, 1988.

23. *Washington Post*, December 29, 1986.

24. Television interview, David Frost show, May 19, 1977.

25. *Federal Register*, vol. 59, no. 108.

26. Ralph Nader, letter to members of the House of Representatives, February 3, 1995.

27. For these various examples, see *New York Times*, March 25, 1986; *Los Angeles Times*, November 4, 1984; letter to Secretary of State George Shultz from Representative Robert Mrazek and seven other members of Congress protesting arms sales to Guatemala, October 5, 1988; General Accounting Office report B-213137, *Propriety of Funding Methods Used by the Department of Defense in Combined Exercises in Honduras*, Washington, D.C., June 22, 1984; GAO report summarized in *People's Weekly World*, August 21, 1993.

28. Quoted in *New York Times*, August 18, 1992.

16

The Political Economy of Bureaucracy

Some people would have us believe that bureaucracy is a malady peculiar to socialism or other variants of the "welfare state." In fact, bureaucracy can be found in just about every area of modern capitalist society, in big corporations, universities, religious establishments, and other private organizations as well as in government. A model bureaucracy is an organization that (a) systematically mobilizes human effort and material resources for explicitly defined projects or purposes, (b) is staffed by career personnel with specialized skills, and (c) is coordinated by a hierarchy of command accountable to some authority.[1] Bureaucracy can be used to administer a national health program or run a death camp. Much depends on the politico-economic context in which it operates.

The Myth and Reality of Inefficiency

Bureaucracies have certain bothersome characteristics that seem to inhere in the nature of the beast. For instance, the need for consistent and accountable operating procedures can create a tendency toward red tape and a limited capacity to respond to new initiatives. The need to divide responsibilities over widely dispersed areas can cause problems of coordination and accountability. And for the average citizen there are the incomprehensible forms and labyrinthine runarounds orchestrated by the petty autocrats and uncaring paper pushers who sometimes inhabit the bureaucracies of private business as well as government. Still, bureaucracies perform crucial and complex tasks — for better or worse. "The feat of landing men on the moon," observes Duane Lockard, "was not only a scientific achievement but a bureaucratic one as well."[2] The same might be said of the Vietnam War, the Social Security system, and the farm, highway, housing, and defense programs.

According to the prevailing ideology of corporate America, public bureaucracy is expensive, inefficient, and a drain on the more productive private economy. The proposed remedy is to hand over most public programs to private contractors ("privatization") or abolish them altogether. Free marketeers insist that everything works better in the hands of the private sector, and government should be "run more like a business." One might wonder how that could be possible. Government deals with complex social problems, conflicting goals, and competing constituencies. Exactly what businesses should government be run like? The fifty thousand firms that go bankrupt every year? Or the large successful corporations — themselves giant bureaucracies and recipients of generous public subsidies — that regularly skirt the law and cater only to those who have sufficient cash or credit? Do we want government run like the private companies that are controlled by nonelective directors, who answer to no one but themselves and a few banks and big investors? Indeed, that is what is happening with the establishment of an international private-sector–serving bureaucracy like the World Trade Organization (WTO), staffed by corporate representatives who can overrule the laws of our land.[3]

If we run government like a business (whatever that means), then who will take care of the costly, nonprofit public services that the public — and business itself — relies on for its existence? For instance, who will provide the hundreds of billions of dollars that government comes up with for roads and highways needed by the automobile and trucking industries, and the compensatory costs to the dislocated homeowners whose houses are in the way of new highways? In such instances, is government a burden on the auto industry, or is it the other way around?

There are inefficiencies and waste in private business as well as public administration, but they are rarely publicized. Seldom mentioned is the fact that administrative expenses are generally less in public bureaucracies than in private ones. Administrative costs for the government's Medicare program are less than 3 cents per dollar, while administrative costs for private health insurance are 26 cents per dollar. Government administrators generally work longer hours for less pay than managers in private bureaucracies. In recent decades, top federal salaries have declined in buying power (accounting for inflation) while the earnings of top corporate executives have skyrocketed.[4]

Social Security has been a more reliable and less expensive retirement program than private pension plans, which is one reason private industry hates it. A Roper poll asked people to estimate the administrative costs of Social Security as a percentage of benefits. Conditioned to think that government programs must be inefficient and costly, respondents guessed 50 percent, on average. Actually only 1 percent is spent on administration. By comparison, the administrative costs for private insurance are about 13 percent of annual payments.[5] Likewise, administrative costs average less at public hospitals than at for-profit hospitals.[6]

Corporate leaders want to eliminate social spending programs not because they don't work but because they often do. And when they do, they demonstrate the parasitic nature of an owning class. Thus, Conrail demonstrated that a government-owned rail system could give better service at less cost than the investor-owned lines it replaced. But this very success is intolerable to those who correctly see nonprofit public ownership as a threat to private-profit ownership. So, Conrail was "privatized" (sold back to private investors) at a bargain price.

Free marketeers have argued that the vast sums spent on the "war against poverty" have not reduced poverty. In fact, Supplemental Security Income, created in 1972, provides a minimum monthly income for the elderly and disabled, along with more generous Social Security payments. With all this spending, poverty among the elderly should have dropped after 1972. It did. Government spending worked. Other major poverty programs did not lift many people out of poverty — but they were never fashioned to raise anyone's income above the poverty line. They were meant to provide benefits that reduced misery, and they did. Other federal programs have worked:

- Without family assistance the number of people who live in illness and destitution would easily double, and so would the costs to society.
- In one decade, government requirements for smoke detectors, seat belts, speed limits, emergency public health facilities, and safety features on consumer products have helped produce a 21-percent drop in accidental fatalities. One dollar spent on childhood immunization saves $10 in later medical expenses.
- Federal funds to ameliorate inequality in education produced strong scholastic gains among low-income students in inner-city schools and others in the lowest performance quartile.
- Since the Occupational Safety and Health Administration (OSHA) was established — even with all of its inadequacies — the job fatality rate has been cut in half and an estimated 140,000 workers' lives have been saved.
- With the advent of food stamps, hunger and malnutrition were reduced substantially.[7]

Such programs are opposed by the business community because they expand the public sector, and shore up alternative sources of support, leaving people less desperately competing for jobs, less willing to work harder and harder for less and less. Environmental protections do save lives and benefit the public, but they can cut into profits by adding to production costs, and they place limits on industry's ability to use human labor and the environment solely as it sees fit. Public housing did dramatically reduce overcrowding between 1940 and 1980, but it also created a supply of residences that competed with the private housing industry. Rent control did keep millions of units affordable while allowing landlords to make "reasonable" profits, but it also cut into landlord profits.[8]

The efficacy of public programs can be appreciated when the programs are abolished or diminished. The cuts in public housing and rent control were accompanied by a sharp rise in homelessness. The closing of venereal disease clinics fueled an increase in VD cases. The heartless cuts in welfare and nutrition payments brought more hunger to children. Reduction in education funding increased the number of substandard, overcrowded schools. An elimination or watering down of worker-safety rules, safety information on medical devices, clean-air standards, and pesticide controls is costing the nation dearly in human life and a greatly damaged ecology.[9]

Deregulation and Privatization

As we have seen in earlier chapters, while claiming to be self-sustaining and cost-efficient, the private sector regularly feeds out of the public trough, devouring a host of tax-funded subsidies and supports. Business does not want to see an end to this bonanza, it just wants an end to any regulations that require it to waste good money on living wages, worker benefits, occupational safety, environmental protections, consumer quality controls, and regulated rates. In those policy areas, the free marketeers want deregulation.

From 1997 through 2000, the nation's $212-billion-a-year electrical power industry was undergoing deregulation in state after state, thanks to campaigns waged by corporate lobbyists. With deregulation, utility bills tripled in some locales, bringing greater profits for electric companies and much hardship for consumers, especially households of limited income that spend over 10 percent of their budgets on energy bills. "The reality behind those numbers is a lot of bent, gnarled hands trembling when they open the electric bill."[10] Those who argue that the free market will best provide for us seem to forget why utilities had their rates regulated in the first place: they are natural monopolies that provide a necessary and irreplaceable commodity to a captive market.

The deregulation of utilities can also have a deleterious effect on the environment. Deregulated hydropower facilities now achieve higher profits by producing power in quick spurts, with little thought to how these drastic fluctuations degrade water quality and harm aquatic life.[11] With deregulation, incentives provided by state regulators to develop nonpolluting energy sources have disappeared, and fatter profits are to be gleaned from fossil fuel. So today, Americans get half as much energy from wind, solar, and geothermal sources as they did in 1987.[12]

Deregulation can often be a matter of life and death. An amendment to the National Highway Safety Act passed by a Republican-controlled Congress and signed by President Clinton abolished federal safety regulations on small to medium trucks. Commercial firms like U-Haul are now solely responsible for their own safety inspection. The number of accidents and fatalities involving rental trucks is expected to rise sharply under the new law.

Along with deregulation of the private sector, corporate America has advocated privatization of the public sector, turning not-for-profit public schools, hospitals and health services, housing, postal services, transit systems, fresh water supplies, and public pension funds, into profit-making ventures. Capitalism is a jealous, restless system. It does not easily tolerate nonprofit public-sector services that could be profitably transformed into billion-dollar markets.

Advocates of privatization mount campaigns to reduce allocations for the targeted public service. With inadequate funding, the service begins to deteriorate. This in turn is treated as proof that the public sector "doesn't work" and needs to be handed over to private business, which "knows how to get the job done" and will use the taxpayers' money more efficiently.

Experience demonstrates otherwise. Privatized schools in Miami Beach, Baltimore, Hartford (Connecticut), and elsewhere found private voucher schools more costly and less serviceable and have reverted to a public school system.[13] Generally speaking, public schools are *not* a failure. High-school graduation rates have risen through most of the twentieth century. Dropout rates have been declining. Contrary to the prevailing impression that all troubled students are from inner-city districts, two-thirds of dropouts are White, two-thirds are from two-parent homes, and over 40 percent are from suburban schools. Compared to the 1970s, performance levels in reading, mathematics, and science have remained steady or have improved — and show no difference between public and private schools, or parochial and secular ones.[14]

Short of complete privatization, many functions within governments at the federal, state, and local levels have been contracted out to private business. The U.S. government spends $108 billion a year on federal workers and $120 billion on private contractors. The Clinton-Gore administration bragged about streamlining the government by letting go 300,000 federal employees, but said nothing about how it racked up the biggest private service contracting bills of all time. Be it highly skilled professional work or janitorial maintenance, the service usually ends up costing the government more when contracted out. Though private contractors spend less money on worker wages and benefits, they funnel much more into upper management

salaries and stockholder profits. In 1992, the White House acknowledged that private contractors doing government work are often left unsupervised and waste or overcharge billions of dollars.[15]

The story is the same in other countries. In Britain and Chile, government pension insurance funds were privatized. Vast fortunes were made by those who handled the accounts while the pensioners ended up with much less than before. In Bolivia, the oil refineries were privatized, leading to a 15-percent hike in gas prices. In countries throughout Eastern Europe, privatization led to poorer and vastly more expensive services, and much plundering of public resources by private profiteers.[16]

Public administration carries out tasks that private business cannot handle. Consider the much maligned postal service: what private corporation would deliver a letter three thousand miles, door to door, for the price of a postage stamp, or forward your mail to a new address at no extra cost? In recent times, however, Republican administrations attempted to put the U.S. Postal Service on a more "profit-motivated" basis. They contracted out postal jobs to low-wage nonunion workers, reduced delivery standards, paid fat bonuses to top management, and disregarded health and safety regulations for postal workers — all of which brought a marked increase in workplace stress and a deterioration in service.

This is not to make light of government waste. The General Accounting Office (GAO) found that the federal government — under a supposedly economy-minded conservative administration — lost billions of dollars because of poor management in major agencies, the most costly being the Pentagon and the National Aeronautics and Space Administration (NASA). One audit found spending abuses by NASA officials and contractors in virtually every aspect of NASA's operations. The waste, estimated at over $3.5 billion, was "only the tip of the iceberg."[17]

Nearly three years after persuading Congress to allow private developers to replace dilapidated military living quarters, the Pentagon had spent $37.5 million on consultants without breaking ground on a single new housing unit.[18] A GAO audit concluded that Pentagon management "is the worst in government," and "cannot accurately account for its more than $250 billion annual budget and over $1 trillion in assets worldwide." The same audit found that the Internal Revenue Service suffers "serious accounting and control problems," and has an inefficient collection system with a $156 billion uncollected tax debt.[19]

In cities throughout the nation, working-class neighborhoods have been razed to make way for shopping malls, industrial parks, sports arenas, and convention centers, built with public funds. Business does well with such ventures, but the public monies invested are seldom recovered; the projects incur multimillion dollar debts that drain public coffers for decades, and constitute a large part of the U.S. urban fiscal crisis. Instead of contrasting the profitability of private business with the debt-ridden costliness of government, we would do better to see the causal connection between the two. The very federal, state, and municipal governments that subsidize business "are then charged with inefficient performance by the business class."[20]

As noted earlier, government in capitalist America is not allowed to make a profit — which could then be put back into the public treasury. Unused offices in a U.S. government building may not be rented out, for it would put government in competition with private rentals. Government is allowed to operate only in the *un*profitable "markets" that business does not want. Thus, public hospitals show none of the profits of private ones because they handle the people who cannot afford the health insurance and other astronomical costs of private health care. Likewise, low-income public housing provides shelter for those financially excluded from the private housing market.

Government bureaucracies have little control over what is produced in the economy, how, where, and by whom.

Thus . . . the Department of Energy is supposed to ensure an adequate supply of gasoline, but it cannot even command accurate data from the oil companies, much less itself extract petroleum from the ground and process it. The Department of Housing and Urban Development can subsidize low-income housing, but it can neither build units itself nor divert private investment from middle-class suburban development. In each case the public bureaucracy is inefficient and ineffective. But its problems are foreordained by the conditions under which public agencies operate.[21]

Secrecy, Deception, and Corruption

Both public and private bureaucracies have a strong tendency toward secrecy. The more secrecy, the more opportunity for administrators to do what they want without having to answer for it. Most of the secrecy in public bureaucracy is on behalf of private business, the military, and the dirty operations of the Central Intelligence Agency (CIA) and other intelligence agencies. The government has suppressed information concerning bank bailouts and data on toxic waste disposal and the harmful effects of nuclear power plants, many medical drugs, and pesticides. The government withheld information regarding (a) the medical problems of thirty thousand American soldiers and thousands of Utah residents exposed to nuclear tests in the 1950s, (b) the effects of radiation on U.S. residents from nuclear weapons facilities and nuclear power plants, (c) the ill effects of defoliants upon military personnel in the Vietnam War, (d) the tens of thousands of military personnel exposed to chemical weaponry during the Gulf War in 1991, and (e) the secretly conducted germ warfare tests in U.S. urban areas and radiation tests on at least eight hundred unsuspecting subjects.[22]

President Reagan issued a presidential directive that forced some two million government workers to take a pledge of secrecy. He required almost 300,000 federal employees to agree to lifetime government censorship of their writings and speeches. Administrations have sought to undercut the Freedom of Information Act by expanding the restrictive classifications of documents, inking out more and more information on the documents that are released, imposing years of delays on releasing materials, and charging exorbitant copying fees.

In 1995, President Clinton issued an executive order ostensibly aimed at opening long-classified files and reducing the number of new documents made secret. The order called for the automatic declassification without review of most documents that are twenty-five years or older, and puts a new ten-year limit on how long documents can stay classified. However, an enormous loophole allows documents to remain classified if a review so determines. The executive branch spends at least $5.6 billion reviewing and classifying documents — and that does not count the CIA. The total number of classified documents is not known, though the figure is estimated to be well into the billions. At least 70 percent of the millions of World War II documents related to war crimes still remain secret, more than half a century later. The CIA, Federal Bureau of Investigaiton (FBI), and Pentagon are resisting any "bulk declassification" out of concern for protecting their sources and methods, leaving one to wonder what it is they have to hide.[23]

Secrecy breeds unaccountability and corruption. The Department of Agriculture has given billions of dollars worth of contracts to agribusiness firms that have been caught rigging bids, fixing prices, and defrauding government programs. Hordes of speculators and fast-buck investors, risking almost no money of their own, used mortgage loans from the Department of Housing and Urban Development, plus millions in tax credits, to acquire and rent properties at federally subsidized rates, bringing in huge profits for themselves. Housing grants and mortgage insurance, intended for affordable housing for low-income elderly, have gone to luxury and resort projects.

Top officials in the executive branch have enjoyed the free use of vacation homes, company planes, and luxury hotels; easy-term loans; artificially large honoraria for speaking appearances sponsored by corporate groups; and the opportunity to sell their assets at inflated prices or buy properties at artificially low prices.

Presidents often stand by subordinates who are accused of wrongdoing, supposedly out of "loyalty" to them. Usually they are bound to their underlings by something stronger than loyalty, namely self-interest. A subordinate abruptly cut loose might turn into a damaging source of disclosure. During the Watergate affair, the one aide President Nixon tried to throw to the wolves, John Dean, ended up singing the entire conspiracy libretto to Congress and the world. Generally, it is best for presidents who are implicated in an illegal affair, as was Nixon in Watergate and Reagan and Bush in Iran-contra, to do everything to firm up the skittish line of lieutenants who stand between them and lawful retribution.

Public servants who become "whistle-blowers" by going public about some wrongdoing risk their careers. In the federal bureaucracy, as in most other organizations — including the corporation, the police, the university, and the military — there is more concern about the bad image caused by disclosures of wrongdoing than about the wrongdoing itself.

- A federal employee who tried to warn the government that it was wasting millions on a foreign aid program had his job abolished.
- When a Census Bureau demographer reported that President Bush's war against Iraq had resulted in 158,000 Iraqi deaths, almost half of them women and children, she was informed she would be fired.
- A U.S. Attorney was dismissed for disclosing that the CIA was trying to block prosecution against a crime figure.

- After reporting that his superiors were soft on rich, influential tax-payers, a chief of an Internal Revenue Service (IRS) collection division, who had an unblemished record and several honors, was transferred to an obscure office, had his pay substantially cut, and was subjected to a criminal investigation for "unauthorized disclosures of taxpayer information."
- When several scientists announced that current radiation safety standards were at least ten times too low, the Energy Department — ever beholden to the nuclear industry — fired them, confiscated their data, and launched character assassinations.[24]

In 1995, the Energy Department announced it would protect workers who raised safety concerns at its nuclear weapons plants by refusing to cover the litigation bills of contractors who pursued legal reprisals against such whistle-blowers. But a congressional investigation discovered that the department was still paying those bills as of May 2000, sometimes without knowing it. It had not yet written a final rule on withholding funds for contractors' legal defenses.

These are not isolated instances. The special board created by the Whistleblower Protection Act to handle complaints had a backlog of 1,000 cases only four months after its creation, and in one year alone received a record 814 complaints of reprisals against whistle-blowers.[25] In private industry, whistle-blowers face harassment and job loss. Once unemployed, they find few job opportunities in either government or industry. Instead of being rewarded for their honesty, they are punished. Whistle-blowers in the U.S. military are routinely subjected to threats and reprisals; some are even railroaded into mental hospitals. In 1993, a U.S. sailor serving on an aircraft carrier could no longer tolerate the routine dumping of raw sewage and garbage into the ocean every day, including plastics, computers, and toxins. For going public he was court-martialed, demoted, and sentenced to the brig.[26]

The White House has argued in several cases that government information is government property; therefore, employees who take and release such information are guilty of theft. Thus, leaking information about crimes is itself treated as a crime. Richard Nuccio, a State Department policy advisor and White House envoy, informed his Congressman that a CIA asset was connected to two murders that the agency had covered up. The public outcry that arose when the Congressman went public with the information prompted the CIA to rid itself of a thousand informants, including more than a hundred implicated in major crimes abroad. Nuccio's reward? He was declared a security risk, had his State Department career destroyed, and faced a criminal investigation. CIA Deputy Director George Tenet, who presided over the campaign against Nuccio, soon became President Clinton's choice to head the agency.[27]

Bureaucratic Action and Inaction

Many rulings by bureaucratic agencies, published daily in the Federal Register, are as significant as major pieces of legislation, and in the absence of
precise guidelines from Congress, they often take the place of legislation.
Thus, without a word of public debate, the Price Commission approved
more than $2 billion in rate increases for utilities. Under a White House di-
rective, the Social Security Administration used "stricter eligibility" rules to
deprive 265,000 disabled persons of public assistance. By administrative
fiat, the Reagan administration shifted most Federal Emergency Management Agency funds — intended by Congress for natural disaster relief — to
secret military programs. And the Bush administration shifted billions of
dollars in Social Security funds to help cover the deficit and the savings-and-
loan bailouts.

The political process does not end with the passage of a bill but continues at the administrative level, albeit in more covert fashion, influencing
how a law is administered.

- In the 1980s and early 1990s, the Environmental Protection Agency
  (EPA) failed to enforce a program devised by Congress to ensure safe
  disposal of hazardous wastes. Enforcement of environmental laws was
  so spotty that half the nation's wetlands (valued as wildlife habitats
  and for their role in flood control) have been lost.
- The Office of Surface Mining allowed widespread mining without environmental controls, resulting in thousands of miles of landslides and
  polluted streams. More than half the mine owners who were directed
  to halt illegal operations ignored the order. Some $200 million in fines
  imposed on the owners went uncollected.
- The Clean Air Act passed by Congress was gravely weakened by administrative fiat when the EPA decided to relax national smog standards by more than 50 percent.
- The Internal Revenue Service was so lax regulating the railroad workers' retirement system that railroad owners underpaid the pension
  fund by about $73 million in three years.

There has been lax enforcement or nonenforcement of consumer protection laws, civil rights, collective bargaining rights, and protection of
public lands and parks. Most such nonenforcement is the result not of
bureaucratic inertia but political intent, perpetrated by policymakers who
are unsympathetic to the regulatory programs.

Often agencies are not sufficiently staffed to handle the enormous tasks
that confront them. The federal government has only twenty-five inspectors
to monitor the transportation of hazardous wastes over the entire country.
The EPA staff can monitor but a fraction of the one thousand new poten-

tially toxic chemicals that industry pours into the environment each year. Representatives of a farmworkers union complained that enforcement of existing laws, not enactment of new ones, was needed to alleviate the housing and safety problems faced by farmworkers.

While some laws go unenforced, others are so transformed during implementation as to subvert their intent. We have already noted how this was done to the Freedom of Information Act. Another example might suffice: a House subcommittee charged that the Merit System Protection Board created by Congress to protect whistle-blowers had been administered so as to afford even less protection than before, requiring whistle-blowers to carry the burden of proof in ways not authorized by statute.

In his 1994 State of the Union message, President Clinton boasted of his plan to reduce the federal bureaucracy by almost a quarter of a million employees. One might wonder which bureaucrats he had in mind: the highly paid Pentagon flacks who push for multibillion dollar weapons systems that feed the corporate pot of gold? Or administrative workers in the already downsized and demoralized Social Security Administration, who serve the elderly and the handicapped? While supposedly downsizing the government, Clinton proposed an increase in the military budget from $265 billion to $277 billion.

People who insist that things do not get done because that is the nature of the bureaucratic beast seem to forget that only certain kinds of things do not get done, while other things are accomplished all too well. The law to make some thirteen million children eligible for medical examination and treatment had the same legal status as the law to develop a multibillion-dollar "Star Wars" outerspace weapon system, the latter backed by the White House, giant industrial contractors, research institutes, Pentagon brass, and key members of Congress. If anything, the Star Wars program was of vastly greater technical and administrative complexity. Yet it moved full steam ahead, while the children's health program moved hardly at all. Several years later, almost 85 percent of the youngsters had been left unexamined, causing "unnecessary crippling, retardation, or even death of thousands of children," according to a House subcommittee report.

Again, the important difference between the two programs was not bureaucratic but political. The effectiveness of a law or a bureaucratic program depends on the power of the groups supporting them. Laws that serve powerful clientele are likely to enjoy a vigorous life, while laws that have only the powerless to support them are often stillborn.

The capitalist political economy is the graveyard of reform-minded administrative bodies. An agency like the Office of Economic Opportunity, which tries to represent low-income interests and invites the participation of have-nots in urban programs, runs into powerful opposition and eventually is abolished. An agency set up to regulate industry on behalf of consumers, workers, or the environment may possess a zeal for reform in its youth, but before long it is likely to be reined in.

In its youthful days after World War I, the Federal Trade Commission (FTC) moved vigorously against big business, but representatives of industry prevailed upon the president to replace some of the commissioners with others decidedly more sympathetic to business.[28] Some sixty years later, the pattern was to repeat itself. Staffed by consumer advocates, the FTC began vigorous action against shady business practices, only to find itself under fire from Congress and the business community. It was not long before the FTC had its jurisdictional powers abridged and its budget cut. In similar fashion, the EPA had its budget cut, drastically reducing its already limited capacity to regulate. The Consumer Product Safety Commission had its staff cut by more than half and was then stacked with conservatives who had no background or interest in product safety.[29]

Frequently, members of Congress demand to know why an agency is bothering their constituents or their campaign contributors. Administrators who do not want unfavorable publicity or a cut in their appropriations are likely to apply the law in ways that satisfy the legislators who control their budgets. Also the promise of a lucrative post with a private firm whose interests they favored while in office can exercise a considerable influence on the judgments of an administrator eager to pursue advancement in the private sector at some future date. Some administrative bodies, like the Army Corps of Engineers, so successfully cultivate support among powerful members of Congress and their big-business clientele that they become relatively free of supervisory control by department heads or the White House. In 1987, it was discovered that the Army Corps of Engineers was illegally overseeing more than three hundred oil and gas leases. It had failed to collect most of the royalties on these leases and could not account for the sums that had been collected.[30]

Among the few things working in favor of public interest regulations are public-interest groups. Most enforcement cases against powerful corporate polluters, for instance, are initiated by environmental and local citizens' groups. The Environmental Protection Agency rarely initiates action and usually opposes tough environmental laws, expending more effort attempting to remove companies from regulation than getting them to abide by the law. Citizen environmental groups sue to make the EPA do what the law already requires it to do. The EPA uses taxpayers' money in such cases to thwart enforcement efforts. It often takes years of struggle before the EPA will act.

Serving the "Regulated"

There are regulatory agencies that are under the command of various executive departments, such as the Labor Department's OSHA and the Justice Department's Drug Enforcement Administration (DEA). And there are independent regulatory commissions, such as the Federal Communications Commission (FCC), Federal Trade Commission (FTC), and Surface Transportation Board (STB) (successor to the Interstate Commerce Commission), which operate outside the executive branch, making quasi-judicial rulings that can only be appealed to the courts. They report directly to Congress but their personnel are appointed by the president, with Senate confirmation. For reasons just discussed, both these kinds of agencies frequently become protectors of the industries they are supposed to regulate. So the FCC serves the telephone companies and the media networks; the Securities and Exchange Commission regulates the stock market mostly for the benefit of large investors; and the Federal Energy Regulatory Commission maintains a permissive policy toward private energy producers.

So with other units of government: the Department of Transportation defers to the oil-highway-automotive combine; the Army Corps of Engineers and the Bureau of Reclamations continue to mutilate the natural environment on behalf of utilities, agribusiness, and land developers; the Department of Interior serves the oil, gas, mining, and timber companies; and, spending more than all the others combined, the Pentagon gives tireless support to the defense industry.

In 1949, with a budget of only $2 million, the Food and Drug Administration proceeded against thousands of violators. Today, with a budget a hundred times larger, the FDA rarely takes action against major food or drug companies. It has learned discretion. The result is that pharmaceutical firms can charge any price they like for drugs that may not have been reliably tested for safety and efficacy. When Monsanto marketed its bovine growth hormone (BGH), the FDA approved the drug despite a GAO study showing the harmful effects to cows and potentially to humans. When Dr. Richard Burroughs voiced his concerns about the approval of BGH, he was fired from the FDA.[31] The agency also ruled that milk producers who did not use the drug and wished to label their milk as free from BGH, would not be allowed to do so, a ruling that was rescinded after much public outcry.

A hundred or so people die every year from food poisoning and thousands of others are sickened, yet the U.S. Department of Agriculture (USDA) frequently ignores federal regulations, and turns a blind eye to health and safety violations in meat production. The USDA has little control over meat companies. All the department can do is try to persuade a company to recall a tainted product voluntarily. Proposals to give the USDA stronger enforcement powers have been opposed by powerful lobbies and influential lawmakers from meat-producing states.[32]

Over the past fifty years, intensive industrial chemical farming has damaged the quality of millions of acres of once fertile soil, enough to cause a discernible drop in the nutritional level of many grains and vegetables. The USDA is aware of the problem but shows no inclination to act on it. Ever responsive to giant agribusiness, the USDA attempted to promulgate national standards for organic foods that included irradiated and genetically modified foods, and use of sewage sludge. The move was stalled by a strong public outcry.[33]

In response to public pressure, Congress passed a food safety law in 1996 that was supposed to lower pesticide limits in food to protect children. Yet, as of 1999, not one limit was lowered as the law requires. Pesticide levels were actually increasing in fruits and vegetables heavily consumed by children.[34]

The Fair Labor Standards Act is a federal law that prohibits the employment of youth under the age of eighteen from working in hazardous occupations. Yet each year millions of minors toil long hours at hazardous jobs in sweatshops, mills, fast-food restaurants, and on agribusiness farms. Each year tens of thousands of them are injured or killed at the workplace. Employers are not too worried about their child labor violations because the laws are rarely enforced. The average business can expect to be inspected once every fifty years or so. Even when citations are issued, the maximum penalty of $10,000 per violation is rarely applied. The average fine handed down by courts and inspectors in cases involving death or permanent injury is $750 — a measure of the value placed on the life of low-income children.[35]

Rather than too much government regulation, there does not seem to be enough. Far from being overly meddlesome, federal regulators often simply do not regulate, either because their agency is too wedded to the particular industry or too intimidated by it, or because the agency's legislative mandate does not provide enough enforcement power. Even if they wished to crack down on corporate America, most federal agencies are woefully understaffed or outmanned by cadres of corporate lawyers.

The political appointees who preside over the various administrative units often are opposed to government regulation. Federal meat inspection laws have been administered by officials with a history of opposition to meat inspection. Public housing programs have been supervised by businesspeople openly hostile to public housing. Civil rights enforcement has been delegated to individuals who are opponents of civil rights. Conservation and environmental programs have been administered by people who are openly antagonistic to environmental regulations. Nuclear weapons plant cleanup has been entrusted to persons with records of notorious permissiveness toward the nuclear industry. In a recent case, Bradley Smith, who considers limits on campaign spending to be unconstitutional, was given a Republican seat on the Federal Election Commission, which enforces limits on campaign spending.[36]

Contrary to an alarmist scenario, anonymous and unaccountable bureaucrats have not usurped power for themselves. In fact, career bureaucrats pretty much do as they are told by their politically appointed agency heads. The professional ethic of most bureaucrats is: remain neutral and wait for the policy line to be set from above. "Bureaucratic failures" are usually better described as successful uses of political power to undermine regulations and laws that prove troublesome to corporate interests.

Public Authority in Private Hands

Along with its funds and services, government sometimes surrenders its very authority to big business. The private codes that trade associations develop to govern the specifications of goods produced by their respective industries are frequently written directly into statutes, thus taking on the force of law. Control of federal lands and water has been handed over to local "home rule" boards dominated by the large ranchers, who thereby successfully transform their economic power into a publicly sanctioned authority.[37]

In every significant industry, advisory committees staffed by representatives of leading firms work closely with government agencies, making most of the important recommendations. Several thousand committees and boards meet regularly with administrative leaders, costing the government many millions a year to finance. The most influential of these deal with banking, chemicals, communications, largescale commercial farming, oil, and utilities. Their reports become the basis for administrative actions and new legislation, winning them advantages over smaller competitors, workers, and consumers — advantages that would be less easily gained in open competition. The meetings of these business advisory committees are not open to the press or public.

In many state and municipal governments, as in the federal government, business associations — dominated by the biggest firms — are accorded the power to nominate their own personnel to public licensing boards and other administrative bodies. The transfer of public authority to private hands frequently is treated as a "voluntaristic" or "decentralized" form of policymaking. In fact, these measures transfer sovereign authority to favored private producers. There exists, then, unbeknownst to most Americans, a large number of private decision makers who exercise public authority to suit themselves without having to answer to the public. They are what might be called the "public-privateers."

One of the most powerful to be included under this rubric is the Federal Reserve, which controls the nation's interest rates and money supply. In 1913, at the behest of the major banks, Congress and President Woodrow Wilson created the Federal Reserve System. Its key architect was Nelson Aldrich, father-in-law of John D. Rockefeller, Jr. All federally charted banks and many state banks are members of the "Fed," as it is called. The Fed's seven-person board of governors is appointed to staggered fourteen-year terms by the president, who can make only two appointments during his four-year term. Once appointed, the board members in effect answer to no one but the banking industry. The five regional members of the Fed's top policy committee are selected not by the president but by bankers from the various regions.

The U.S. Constitution gave Congress the exclusive power to create money. But what we have today is a Federal Reserve composed entirely of private bankers exercising this sovereign power. Just check the money in your wallet; every bill is clearly labeled "Federal Reserve Note." The Fed is not a central bank of issue that serves the U.S. Treasury; it actually looms above the Treasury exercising its power to create credit and issue paper money on its own. When the Treasury needs money, it must turn to the Federal Reserve Bank. The Treasury prints interest-bearing U.S. Government Securities, an issue of, say, $10 billion face value. These securities are IOUs that are given to the Fed. The Fed then enters $10 billion as a debit which is given to the U.S. Treasury. If Treasury wants it in cash, the Fed has the cash printed at the Bureau of Engraving and Printing (the same place government securities are printed).

As with any bank loan, the Fed also enters $10 billion on its books as a credit owed to it by the U.S. Treasury. The Fed now collects interest on the $10 billion asset it created. When the reserve ratio is eight to one, the Fed can lend $8 for every $1 it has on reserve. In effect, much of the money it lends is created out of thin air. So, instead of issuing money of its own for which it would have to pay no interest, the U.S. Treasury is borrowing from a private banking source, the Fed, using its future ability to tax the U.S. public as collateral for the loan. Thus the major banks are allowed to create fiat money and collect interest on that money from the government and the taxpayers.

The Federal Reserve System is a money making machine, returning $16 to $24 billion a year in profits, an enormous source of income that goes directly into the bulging private accounts of a tiny financial class.[38] In 1963, President John Kennedy indicated that he was less than happy with this fiduciary arrangement. He began issuing silver-backed Treasury notes as currency to replace Federal Reserve Notes. Within a few months, Kennedy was assassinated and the printing of Treasury notes stopped almost immediately.

The Fed operates behind closed doors with no congressional oversight. Congress holds an agency accountable primarily by controlling its appropriations, but the Fed evades this control by drawing its operating funds from the billions it collects in interest on government securities. In 1996, in what the *New York Times* called "a rare independent examination" of "the secretive central bank," the General Accounting Office issued a report criticizing the Fed's management of its own finances. The GAO noted that the Fed's operating expenses increased three times the rate of federal discretionary spending, that the Fed did not always seek fully competitive bids for services it bought, and that it had accumulated a $3.7-billion contingency fund that should otherwise have been returned to the U.S. Treasury — all this at a time when the Fed chair Alan Greenspan repeatedly talked about how government had to reduce spending.[39]

Generally the Fed pursues a conservative, deflationary policy, making it difficult for the president and Congress to prime a sluggish economy. The Fed's autonomy supposedly demonstrates its "independence" from politics. But everything it does has a policy effect, usually favorable to banking and other moneyed interests. In sum, the big bankers have public authority to act as nonelected oligarchs who can manipulate the economy in defiance of the preferred agenda of elected officials.

Numerous *public authorities* at the federal, state, and local levels (such as the Port Authority of New York) carry out a range of activities. They all have several things in common: they are authorized by state legislatures or Congress to function outside the regular structure of government, and because of their autonomous corporate attributes, they are seldom subjected to public scrutiny and accountability. The public authorities of some states have run up debts that total more than twice the state's debt. To meet their obligations, they float new bond issues — none of which are passed by the taxpayers who will have to pay for these bonds. The public authorities are creatures that have the best of both worlds, feeding out of the public trough while remaining accountable only to themselves.

Monopoly Regulation versus Public-Service Regulation

If government is capitalism's provider and protector at home and abroad, and if government and business are so intermingled as to be often indistinguishable, why are business people so critical of "government meddling in the economy"? There are a number of explanations. First, corporate America is not against *monopolistic regulations* that limit entry into a market, subsidize select industries, set production standards that only big companies can meet, weaken smaller competitors, and encourage monopoly pricing. This kind of government regulation has long won approval from agribusiness, telecommunications, energy, oil, pharmaceuticals, and other industries.

It is *public-service regulation* that big business wants eliminated, such things as antitrust laws and worker, consumer, and environmental protections. These are anathema to business because they can cut into profits. Deregulation in the public-service realm leaves business freer to pursue profits without incurring any obligation for the social costs of that pursuit. Deregulation has given the mining companies a free hand to strip-mine and devastate the landscape without having to pay any restoration costs. Deregulation allows corporate executives to pad their paychecks with fringe benefits and perquisites without having to tell stockholders or tax collectors, an arrangement that one business journalist called "a license to steal."[40] Deregulation has enabled banks to increase customer-service fees at a time when their own computerized customer-service costs have declined. As one member of Congress observed: "It is not the customers who are clamoring for more deregulation, it is the bankers."[41]

Business is not really committed to some abstract "free-market" principle. Regulations that enhance profits are supported and those that cut into profits are denounced. It is only in the latter case that the cry for deregulation is heard throughout the nation's boardrooms. Business is concerned that public-service regulations might mobilize new constituencies, or redistribute income downward instead of upward, or increase the not-for-profit public sector of the economy.

Much of the verbal opposition to government is a manifestation of the business person's adherence to the business ideology, a belief in the virtues of rugged individualism and private competition. That individuals might violate this creed in their own corporate affairs does not mean their devotion to it is consciously hypocritical. Beliefs are no less sincerely held because they are self-serving. Quite the contrary, it is a creed's congruity with a favorable self-image and self-interest that makes it so compelling and so convincing to its proponents. Many business people, including those who have benefited in almost every way from government contracts, subsidies, and tax laws, believe their gains are the result of their own self-reliance, efforts, and talents in a highly competitive "private" market. They believe that the assistance business gets from the government benefits the national economy, while the assistance others get is a handout to parasites.

What is needed is not an endless proliferation of regulatory units but a change in the conditions that demand so much regulation — that is, a different method of ownership and a different purpose for production, one that puts people before profits.

Notes

1. See Max Weber's classic statement, "Bureaucracy," in Hans Gerth and C. Wright Mills (eds.), *From Max Weber: Essays in Sociology* (New York: Oxford University Press, 1958), 196–244.

2. Duane Lockard, *The Perverted Priorities of American Politics* (New York: Macmillan, 1971), 282.

3. See the discussion on the WTO in Chapter 11.

4. On the comparison of public and private management costs, see John Schwarz, *America's Hidden Success*, rev. ed. (New York: Norton, 1988); also Charles Goodsell, *The Case of Bureaucracy*, 2nd ed. (Chatham, N.J.: Chatham House, 1985).

5. "Don't Privatize Social Security," *Labor Party* Press, March 1999; *San Francisco Chronicle*, August 31, 1992; and Lisbeth Schorr, *Within Our Reach: Breaking the Cycle of Disadvantage* (Garden City, N.Y.: Doubleday Anchor, 1988); "Ten Excellent Reasons to Strengthen Social Security and Oppose Privatization," *Solidarity*, July/August 2000.

6. "Health Care Crisis Is Worse," *Solidarity*, April/May 1997.

7. For these various examples, see report by Mathematica Policy Research: *New York Times*, November 1, 1990; National Safety Council report, *New York Times*, October 7, 1990; Susan Mayer and Christopher Jencks, "War on Poverty: No Apologies, Please," *New York Times*, November 9, 1995.

8. Schwarz, *America's Hidden Success*, 59–69; Margery Turner, *Rent Control and the Availability of Affordable Housing in the District of Columbia* (Washington, D.C.: Urban Institute, 1988); CAP Council report, United Auto Workers, October/November 1996.

9. Christine Triano and Nancy Watzman, *Voodoo Accounting*, a report by Public Citizen and OMB Watch, Washington, D.C., 1992.

10. Molly Ivins's column, *Fort Worth Star-Telegram*, August 12, 2000; also Harvey Wasserman, "The Mega-Battle over Utility Deregulation," *Nation*, March 16, 1998.

11. "Protecting Your Water Supply," newsletter, East Bay Municipal Utility District, California, September/October 2000.

12. *New York Times*, March 9, 1997.

13. Associated Press report, January 27, 1996; Kevin Smith and Kenneth Meier, *The Case against School Choice* (Armonk, N.Y.: M. E. Sharpe, 1995).

14. Mano Singham, "The War against Public Schools," *Z Magazine*, October 1995.

15. "No, The Private Sector Doesn't Do It Better," *Labor Party Press*, September 1998; John Hanrahan, *Government by Contract* (New York: Norton, 1983); *New York Times*, December 2, 1992.

16. See Michael Parenti, *Blackshirts and Reds* (San Francisco: City Lights, 1997), 87–120.

17. *New York Times*, April 23, 1986.

18. *New York Times*, July 17, 1997; Associated Press, July 16 and August 1, 1998.

19. General Accounting Office, *High Risk Series* #GAO/HR/95-1, Washington, D.C., February 1995.

20. Susan Fainstein and Norman Fainstein, "The Political Economy of American Bureaucracy," in Carol Weiss and Allen Barton (eds.), *Making Bureaucracies Work* (Beverly Hills, Calif.: Sage, 1980), 285.

21. Fainstein and Fainstein, "The Political Economy of American Bureaucracy," 286.

22. Jay M. Gould and Benjamin A. Goldman, with Kate Millpointer, *Deadly Deceit: Low-Level Radiation, High-Level Cover-Up* (New York: Four Walls Eight Windows, 1998); Leonard Cole, *Clouds of Secrecy: The Army's Germ Warfare Tests over Populated Areas* (Totowa, N.J.: Rowman & Littlefield, 1988); *New York Times*, January 1 and 5, 1994, and October 30, 1996.

23. *Washington Post*, April 18, 1995; *New York Times*, June 28, 1996; *San Francisco Examiner*, June 28, 2000.

24. Myron Peretz Glazer and Penina Migdal Glazer, *The Whistleblowers: Exposing Corruption in Government and Industry* (New York: Basic, 1991); Scott Winokur, "Top Tax Man's Tale of Demotion," *San Francisco Examiner*, July 25, 2000; *New York Times*, May 24, 2000.

25. *San Francisco Examiner*, August 3, 1998.

26. Erik Larsen, "Sailor Court Martialled," *On Guard* (Citizen Soldier, New York), no. 14, 1993.

27. *New York Times*, November 16, 1996; and *Nation*, May 19, 1997.

28. Edwin Sutherland, *White Collar Crime* (New York: Holt, Rinehart & Winston, 1949), 232.

29. Michael Pertshuk, *Revolt against Regulation* (Berkeley: University of California Press, 1982); *Washington Post*, February 2, 1989.

30. *Washington Post,* March 27, 1987.

31. Ron Nixon, "The Corporate Assault on the FDA," *CovertAction Quarterly,* Winter 1995–96.

32. *New York Times,* August 30, 1997; Gail Eisnitz, *Slaughterhouse: The Shocking Story of Greed, Neglect, and Inhumane Treatment Inside the U.S. Meat Industry* (Amherst, N.Y.: Prometheus, 1997).

33. "As Food Quality Drops, the USDA Just Shrugs" and "National Organic Rules Revised by the USDA," both in *Organic Gardening,* May/June 2000.

34. "Something to Chew On," statement by Environmental Working Group, *New York Times,* February 23, 1999; also <http://www.foodnews.org>.

35. Ron Nixon, "Working in Harm's Way," *Southern Exposure,* Fall/Winter 1995; General Accounting Office, *Sweatshops in the U.S.* (Washington, D.C.: Government Printing Office, 1988).

36. *San Francisco Chronicle,* June 27, 2000; *New York Times,* February 5 and December 8, 1993; *In These Times,* August 7–20, 1991, 4–5; Barry Mehler, "Rightist on the Rights Panel," Nation, May 7, 1988.

37. Jack Walker, "The Origins and Maintenance of Interest Groups in America," *American Political Science Review* 77, 1983, 397; and Grant McConnell, *Private Power and American Democracy* (New York: Knopf, 1966), 210.

38. Mark Evans, "The Problem with the Fed," *North Coast Xpress,* May 1993.

39. *New York Times,* March 26, 1996.

40. Jerry Knight in the *Washington Post,* September 26, 1983.

41. Representative Fernand St. Germain, chair of the House Banking Committee, quoted in *Washington Post,* April 12, 1984.

17

The Supremely Political Court

Article 3, Section 1 of the U.S. Constitution reads: "The judicial Power of the United States shall be vested in one supreme Court, and in such inferior Courts as the Congress may from time to time ordain and establish." Supreme Court justices and all other federal judges are nominated by the president and subject to confirmation by the Senate. Federal judges have life tenure and can be removed from office only for misconduct and only through impeachment by the Senate. The size of the Supreme Court is determined by statute, fluctuating over the years from six to ten members, and being fixed at nine since 1877.

All three branches of government are sworn to uphold the Constitution, but the Supreme Court alone reviews the constitutionality of actions by the other two branches, at least in those cases brought before it. Nothing in the Constitution gives the Court this power of *judicial review,* but the proceedings of the Constitutional Convention of 1787 reveal that many delegates expected the judiciary to overturn laws it deemed inconsistent with the Constitution.[1] Of even greater significance is *judicial interpretation,* the Court's power to decide the intent and scope of laws as they are applied in actual situations. Our main concern here is with trying to understand the political role the Court has played in the struggle for and against democracy.

Who Judges?

By its nature, the Supreme Court is something of an aristocratic branch: its members are appointed rather than elected; they enjoy life tenure, are formally accountable to no one once in office, and have the final word on constitutional matters. As intended by the framers, the Court's mandate is to act as a check on the democratic majority and a protector of private property, contract, and credit.

Generally speaking, in class background and political proclivity, the justices have more commonly identified with the landed interests than with the landless, the slave owners rather than the slaves, the industrialists rather than the workers, the exponents of Herbert Spencer rather than of Karl Marx. Justice Miller, a Lincoln appointee to the Court, made note of the judiciary's class biases: "It is vain to contend with judges who have been at the bar, the advocates for forty years of railroad companies, and all the forms of associated capital. . . . All their training, all their feelings are from the start in favor of those who need no such influence."[2]

Through most of its history, "the Court's personnel were recruited mainly from the class of corporate lawyers, so there was no shortage of empathy with the desires of expanding capitalism."[3] One study finds that the American Bar Association's quasi-official Federal Judiciary Committee, whose task is to pass on the qualifications of prospective judges at all federal levels (district and appellate courts), favors those whose orientation is conservative and supportive of corporate interests.[4] With few exceptions, the acceptable range of politico-economic opinion for Supreme Court justices has been from ultraconservative to mainstream centrist.

Chief Justice Hughes once remarked, "We are under a Constitution but the Constitution is what the judges say it is."[5] And what they say is largely determined by their ideological predilections. If the justices look favorably upon an issue, then they argue, "There is nothing in the Constitution that prohibits it." If they do not like the issue, then they argue, "There is nothing in the Constitution that calls for it." Since most acts of government and social life are not specifically mentioned in the Constitution, they can be judged as either not prohibited or not granted by the Constitution, according to the political proclivities of the presiding jurists. Thus when Justice Anthony Kennedy wrote in support of a 1996 military death penalty case that there was nothing in the Constitution prohibiting Congress from delegating "implementation of the capital murder statute to the president acting as commander in chief." But one could with equal logic argue that there is nothing in the Constitution that *grants* Congress the right to delegate such power.

Occasionally a president will select someone for the Court whose behavior goes contrary to his expectations, but generally presidents have been successful in matching court appointments with their own ideological preferences. In the 1980s, President Reagan was second to none in this endeavor, systematically stocking more than half of the 744 federal judgeships with strongly ideologically committed conservatives, mostly in their thirties and forties, who would be handing down decisions and shaping the law of

"I'm happy to say that my final judgment of a case is almost always consistent with my prejudgment of the case."

the land for the next thirty to fifty years. Over 80 percent of Reagan's appointees had incomes of over $200,000, and 23 percent admitted to being millionaires.[6]

Reagan's successor, George Bush, appointed an additional 195 federal judges, all conservatives, usually youngish, including Clarence Thomas, a forty-three-year-old undistinguished archconservative to replace the great Thurgood Marshall on the Supreme Court. In the twelve years of the Reagan-Bush administrations, Republicans ransacked the nation's law schools so they could fill the federal courts with aggressively conservative jurists.

When Bill Clinton, a Democrat, became president, he had an enviable opportunity to fill more than one hundred judicial vacancies and bring a little more ideological balance to the appellate and district courts. His fellow Democrats were in control of the Senate, which confirms or rejects judicial nominees. A record number of Clinton's appointments to the district and appellate courts were women or ethnic minority members (or both), but on the whole his appointments were the least liberal of any modern Democratic president, rendering liberal decisions in only 46 percent of cases.[7] Clinton was quick to drop judicial candidates if there was serious opposition from Republicans. According to one of his aides, he was intimately involved in the selection process. When he and his staff bragged about eschewing "ideologues" for the bench, they were referring to pronounced liberals. But Clinton's avoidance of strong liberals *did* reflect his own conservative "New Democrat" ideology.

Over half the sixty-five federal judges appointed by Clinton in 1998 were millionaires. There are six admitted millionaires on the Supreme Court, and two others who gave unrealistically low estimates of their financial assets, including Chief Justice Rehnquist.[8] In the last year of Clinton's administration, the GOP-controlled Senate, hoping to take over the presidency in 2001, refused to confirm scores of qualified judicial nominees, leaving some eighty judgeships empty.

Conservative Judicial Activism

Supreme Court justices have shown an infernal agility in finding constitutional justifications for the continuation of almost every inequity and iniquity, be it slavery or segregation, child labor or the sixteen-hour workday, state sedition laws or assaults on the First Amendment.

In its early days under Chief Justice John Marshall, the Court emerged as an activist guardian of private corporate property, as in the landmark case, *Trustees of Dartmouth College v. Woodward* (1819). In response to the demands of farmers and artisans for affordable public education, the New Hampshire state legislature turned Dartmouth College, an elite private school, into a public university. The trustees opposed the move, but the state court concluded that the legislature had acted within its province, for education was "a matter of the highest public concern." Furthermore, the trustees had no property right in Dartmouth; their right of office was a public trust. The Marshall Court thought otherwise. Dartmouth's corporate charter — granted by the English Crown in 1769 — was a contract that could not be impaired by legislative enactment; Dartmouth was a private corporation and would have to remain a private school. So to this day Dartmouth has remained an elite private college, available mostly to those of relatively affluent means.

Article 1, Section 10 of the Constitution says that no state shall make any "Law impairing the Obligation of Contracts." The framers were thinking of executory contracts between individuals. In *Dartmouth College,* Marshall applied the contract clause to a corporate charter, saying that a state's responsibility to create a democratic system of education was "a power of at least doubtful utility" compared to a state's obligation to preserve contracts (made by the British crown with early colonialists) involving private corporations — even though the word "corporation" is mentioned nowhere in the Constitution. In effect, the state had no democratic sovereign power over the corporation. In *Dartmouth College,* Marshall also reasserted the Supreme Court's right of judicial review over a state law, declaring it unconstitutional.

Various justices, including Marshall himself, were slaveholders. They repeatedly protected the primacy of property rights in slaves, rejecting all slave petitions for freedom. Right up until the eve of the Civil War, in the famous *Dred Scott v. Sandford* (1857), the Court concluded that, be they slave or free, Blacks were a "subordinate and inferior class of beings" without constitutional rights, and Congress had no power to exclude slaveholders and their chattel from the territories.

Much of the debate about the Supreme Court today centers on whether (a) the Bench should act "politically" and "ideologically" by exercising a liberal "judicial activism," vigorously supporting individual rights and social needs, or (b) employ a conservative "judicial restraint" by deferring to the other two branches of government and cleaving close to the traditional intent of the Constitution. In practice, however, through most of its history the Court has engaged in a *conservative* judicial activism in defense of wealthy interests.

When the federal government wanted to establish national banks, give away half the country to private speculators, subsidize industries, set up commissions that fixed prices and interest rates for large manufacturers and banks, send Marines to secure corporate investments in Central America, imprison people who spoke out against war and capitalism, deport immigrant radicals without a trial, or use the United States Army to shoot workers and break strikes, the Court inventively found constitutional pegs to hang their decisions on.

But if the federal or state governments sought to limit workday hours, set minimum wage or occupational safety standards, ensure the safety of consumer products, or guarantee the right of collective bargaining, then the Court ruled that ours was a limited form of government that could not tamper with property rights and the "free market" by depriving owner and worker of "substantive due process" and "freedom of contract." "Substantive due process," a self-contradictory concept that exists nowhere in the Constitution, was a contrivance of conservative judicial activism. It allowed the Court to declare laws unconstitutional if they interfered with the freedom of individuals and corporations to wield their economic power as they saw fit.[9]

The Fourteenth Amendment, adopted in 1868 ostensibly to establish full citizenship for Blacks, says, "No State shall make or enforce any law which shall abridge the privileges or immunities of citizens of the United States; nor shall any State deprive any person of life, liberty, or property, without due process of law; nor deny to any person within its jurisdiction the equal protection of the laws." The Court decided that "person" included corporations and that the Fourteenth Amendment was intended to protect business conglomerates from the "vexatious regulations" of the states.[10] By 1920, federal courts had struck down roughly three hundred labor laws that had been passed by state legislatures to ease the inhumane conditions endured by working people. Between 1880 and 1931 the courts issued more than 1,800 injunctions against labor strikes.[11] (An injunction is a court order prohibiting a party from taking a specific course of action.)

When Congress outlawed child labor, the Court's conservative majority found it to be an unconstitutional usurpation of the reserved powers of the states under the Tenth Amendment, which reads: "The Powers not delegated to the United States by this Constitution, nor prohibited by it to the States, are reserved to the States respectively or to the people." But when the states passed social welfare legislation, the Court's conservative judicial activists found it in violation of "substantive due process" under the Fourteenth Amendment.[12] Thus the justices used the Tenth Amendment to stop federal reforms initiated under the Fourteenth Amendment, and the Fourteenth to stop state reforms initiated under the Tenth. Juridically speaking, it is hard to get more inventively activist than that.

In 1896, a conservative Supreme Court produced *Plessy v. Ferguson,* which rendered an inventive reading to the Fourteenth Amendment's equal protection clause. *Plessy* enunciated the "separate but equal" doctrine: that the forced separation of Blacks from Whites in public facilities did not impute inferiority as long as facilities were more or less equal (which they rarely were). This wholly novel interpretation lent constitutional legitimacy to the White supremist practice of segregation.

Convinced that they too were persons despite the treatment accorded them by a male-dominated society, women began to argue that the Fourteenth and Fifth Amendments applied to them and that the voting restrictions imposed on them by state and federal governments should be abolished. The Fifth Amendment says, among other things, that no person shall be denied "due process of law." It applies to the federal government as the Fourteenth Amendment applies to the states. But in *Minor v. Happersett* (1875), the all-male Court fashioned another tortured interpretation: women were citizens but citizenship did not *necessarily* confer the right of suffrage.[13] The Court seemingly made up its mind that "privileges and immunities of citizens," "due process," and "equal protection of the laws" applied to such "persons" as business corporations but not to women or persons of African descent.

Well into the New Deal era, the Supreme Court was the activist bastion of laissez-faire capitalism, striking down — often by only five-to-four majorities — reforms produced by the state legislatures and Congress. From 1937 onward, under pressure from the public and the White House, and with one conservative justice's move to the liberal side, the Supreme Court began to accept the constitutionality of New Deal legislation.

Circumventing the First Amendment

The Supreme Court opposed restrictions on capitalist economic power, but supported restrictions on the civil liberties of persons who agitated against that power. The First Amendment says, "Congress shall make no law . . . abridging the freedom of speech, or of the press."[14] Yet, from the Alien and Sedition Acts of 1798 to today, Congress and the state legislatures have passed numerous laws to penalize the expression of politically heretical ideas as "subversive" or "seditious." During World War I almost two thousand prosecutions were carried out, mostly against anticapitalists who expressed opposition to the war, including the U.S. socialist leader Eugene Victor Debs, who was thrown into prison. One individual who in private conversation in a relative's home opined that it was a rich man's war was fined $5,000 and sentenced to twenty years.[15]

The High Court's attitude toward the First Amendment was best expressed by Justice Oliver Wendell Holmes in *Schenck v. United States* (1919). For distributing a leaflet that urged repeal of the draft and condemning the war as a wrong perpetrated by Wall Street, Schenck was charged with attempting to cause insubordination among United States military forces and obstructing recruitment, both violations of the Espionage Act of 1917. In ordinary times, Holmes reasoned, such speech is protected by the First Amendment, but when a nation is at war, statements like Schenck's create "a clear and present danger" of bringing about "evils that Congress has a right to prevent." Free speech, Holmes argued, "does not protect a man in falsely shouting fire in a crowded theater and causing a panic." The analogy is far-fetched: Schenck was not in a theater causing a panic but was seeking a forum to voice his opposition to policies that the Court treated as beyond challenge. Holmes was summoning the same argument paraded by every ruler who has sought to abrogate a people's freedom: these are dangerous times; national security necessitates a suspension of democratic rights.[16]

More than once the Court treated the allegedly pernicious quality of a radical idea as evidence of its lethal efficacy and as justification for its suppression. When the top leadership of the Communist party was convicted in 1951 under the Smith Act, which made it a felony to teach or advocate the violent overthrow of the government, the Court upheld the convictions, arguing in *Dennis et al. v. United States* that there was no freedom under the Constitution for those who conspired to propagate revolutionary movements. Free speech was not an absolute value but one of many competing ones. Justices Black and Douglas dissented, arguing that the defendants had not been charged with any acts or even with saying anything about violent revolution, but were intending to publish and teach the classic writings of Marx, Engels, and Lenin. In any case, they argued, the First Amendment was designed to protect the very heretical views we might find offensive and fearsome; safely orthodox ideas rarely needed constitutional protection.

Six years later, fourteen more communist leaders were convicted under the Smith Act for entertaining forbidden political beliefs. This time both the political climate and the Court's political makeup had shifted, so the justices virtually reversed themselves, ruling that the Smith Act prohibited only incitement to unlawful actions and not "advocacy of abstract doctrine." The convictions were overthrown. Justice Black added the opinion that the Smith Act itself should be declared unconstitutional because "the First Amendment forbids Congress to punish people for talking about public affairs, whether or not such discussion incites to action, legal or illegal."[17] Congress repealed the Smith Act in 1977.

Communists might sometimes be denied free speech but not corporations, which the Court has determined are legal persons with First Amendment rights. Furthermore, corporate spending to influence votes during a referendum campaign "is a type of speech indispensable to decision-making in a democracy," as Justice Lewis Powell put it.[18] In a dissenting opinion, Justices White, Brennan, and Marshall argued that "corporations are artificial entities created by law for the purpose of furthering certain economic ends." Their control of "vast amounts of economic power" may "dominate not only the economy but also the very heart of our democracry, the election process."

In recent times, the First Amendment has been enlisted by the Court to block public interest reforms, just as property rights and contract rights were used in earlier times. Thus the Court's conservative activists ruled that Rhode Island's ban on advertising liquor prices violated "commercial free speech." The Supreme Court "cannot seem to distinguish between government efforts to censor speech and government efforts to regulate private power."[19]

In a seven-to-two decision, the justices found that speech on the Internet is entitled to the highest level of First Amendment protection, and that protecting children from "indecent" material must be done without an unnecessarily broad suppression of speech addressed to adults.[20] Would that the Court might give political radicals the same First Amendment protection in their jobs as pornographers are granted in theirs.

Freedom for Revolutionaries?

Some people argue that revolutionaries violate the democratic rules of the game and should not be allowed "to take advantage of the very liberties they seek to destroy"; in order to preserve our freedom, we may have to deprive some people of theirs.[21] Several rejoinders might be offered.

First, as a point of historical fact, the threat of revolution in the United States has never been as real or harmful to our liberties as the measures taken to "protect" us from revolutionary ideas. In the name of national security, first revolutionary advocacy is suppressed, then any kind of criticism that those in power find intolerable.

Second, by suppressing "harmful" thoughts, political elites are in effect making up our minds for us, depriving us of the opportunity to hear and debate heterodox ideas. An exchange with revolutionary advocates is forbidden because the advocate has been silenced — which in effect puts a limit on our own critical thoughts regarding this subject.

Third, it is not true that anticapitalists are dedicated to the destruction of freedom. Much of the working-class ferment in the United States instigated by socialists, anarchists, and communists actually widened the areas of dissent and helped extend the franchise to propertyless working people. The organized demonstrations against repressive local ordinances in the early twentieth century by the revolutionary-minded Industrial Workers of the World (the "Wobblies' free-speech fights") fortified the First Amendment against attacks by the guardians of wealth. The crucial role communists played in organizing industrial unions in the 1930s and struggling for social reforms, peace, and civil rights strengthened rather than undermined democratic forces. The militant antiwar protests against the Vietnam War challenged an immoral, illegal military action and tried to broaden the spectrum of critical opinion and information regarding U.S. foreign policy, at least for a period of time.

Fourth, instead of worrying about some future revolutionary menace, we should realize that freedom is in short supply in the present society. The construction of new socioeconomic alternatives would bring an increase in freedom, including freedom from poverty and hunger, freedom to share in the making of decisions that govern one's work and community, and freedom to experiment with new forms of production and ownership. Admittedly some freedoms enjoyed today would be lost in a revolutionary society, such as the freedom to exploit other people and get rich from their labor, the freedom to squander natural resources and treat the environment as a septic tank, the freedom to monopolize information and exercise unaccountable power.

In many countries, social revolutionary movements brought a net increase in the freedom of individuals, by advancing the conditions necessary for health and human life, by providing jobs for the unemployed and education for the illiterate, by using economic resources for social development rather than corporate profit, and by overthrowing reactionary semifeudal regimes, ending foreign exploitation, and involving large sectors of the populace in the task of economic reconstruction. Revolutions can extend a number of real freedoms without destroying those that never existed for the people of those countries.

The argument can be debated, but not if it is suppressed. In any case, the real danger to freedom in the United States is from those who would insulate us from "unacceptable" viewpoints. No idea is as dangerous as the force that would seek to repress it.

As the Court Turns

The direction the Supreme Court takes depends on (a) the pressures exerted by various advocacy groups, (b) the political climate of the times, and (c) the political composition of the Court's majority. The Court's record in the area of personal liberties, while gravely wanting, is not totally devoid of merit. Over the years it has extended portions of the Bill of Rights to cover not only the federal government but state government (via the Fourteenth Amendment). Attempts by the states to censor publications, deny individuals the right to peaceful assembly, and weaken the separation between church and state have been overturned.[22]

In the 1960s, fortified by the social activism of the wider society and a liberal majority of justices, the Court under Chief Justice Earl Warren issued a number of rulings to (a) protect civil liberties, (b) reapportion legislative districts in accordance with population distribution, and (c) extend the economic rights of the poor, deciding that they had a protected property right to the benefits they received.[23] "For the first time in the nation's history, the Court majority began to exercise initiative on behalf of the poor."[24]

The Warren Court also handed down a number of landmark decisions aimed at abolishing racial segregation. The most widely celebrated, *Brown v. Board of Education* (1954), unanimously ruled that "separate educational facilities are inherently unequal" because of the inescapable imputation of inferiority cast upon the segregated minority group. This decision overruled the "separate but equal" doctrine enunciated in 1896 in *Plessy*. In addition, the Court nullified state prohibitions against interracial marriage.[25]

In the years after the Warren Court, packed with conservative appointees, the Court moved in a decidedly rightward direction on a variety of crucial issues:[26]

Labor struggles. In decisions involving disputes between workers and owners, the Burger and Rehnquist Courts almost always have sided with the owners, weakening labor's ability to organize and bargain collectively. Thus the Court ruled that workers do not have the right to strike over safety issues if their contract provides a grievance procedure, thereby denying miners the right to walk off the job in the face of immediately dangerous safety violations that management refused to remedy. The Court ruled that employers could penalize workers for unionizing by closing down operations and denying them jobs. Companies could now unilaterally terminate a labor contract and drastically cut employees' wages by filing for "reorganization" under the bankruptcy law. In another case it was decided that nonunion members who were required by labor contracts to pay fees equivalent to union dues could demand that none of their money be used for political activity that the union supported.[27] The Court's conservative majority upheld state and federal laws denying unemployment benefits to striking workers. Companies could give preferential hiring to scabs who crossed picket lines, thereby further undermining organized labor's right to strike.[28] And they could slash health insurance for workers who develop costly illnesses. In effect, workers will have coverage only as long as they don't use it for any serious illness — which undermines the whole purpose of insurance.[29]

Economic inequality. The Court's conservative jurists gave more consideration to the preferences of the rich than the needs of the poor. By upholding laws that reduce welfare assistance, they rejected the idea that aid to the poor was protected by due process.[30] In seeming violation of the equal protection clause of the Fourteenth Amendment, the justices decided that a state may vary the quality of education in accordance with the amount of taxable wealth located in its school districts, thus allowing just about any degree of inequality short of absolute deprivation.[31]

Despite a law limiting water subsidies to farms of 160 acres or less and to farmers who "live on or near the land," the Court held that large commercial farms, including ones owned by Southern Pacific and Standard Oil, were entitled to the subsidies.[32]

California's Proposition 13 limited tax increases on property bought before 1975, so that persons with newly purchased homes carry tax burdens almost 400 percent heavier than longtime — and often big time — owners. The justices decided that the existence of a privileged class of propertyholders did not violate equal protection under the law. In a lone dissent, Justice Stevens stated that Proposition 13 "establishes a privilege of a medieval character: Two families with equal needs and equal resources are treated differently."[33]

Civil liberties. The Supreme Court allowed the U.S. Army to spy on lawful civilian political activity, but prohibited civilians from openly bringing political literature and demonstrations to military posts.[34] Reporters were denied a right to confidential news sources when subpoenaed by officials, thus limiting their ability to protect informants and conduct investigations.[35] The Court said that bans on political signs in public places were not a restriction on free speech, nor were restrictions on demonstrations and leafleting at shopping malls.[36] In *Thornburgh v. Abbott* (1989), prison officials were granted almost a free hand in deciding what publications prisoners could receive, a censorship applied mostly against politically dissident literature.

Students fared not much better when the Court ruled that high school administrators could censor student publications, run unannounced drug tests on students, and transfer faculty who dealt with materials that met with official disapproval.[37] The Court did uphold the right to criticize public figures even in objectionable ways.[38] And recently the Supreme Court did rule unanimously that state colleges and universities may assess all students an activity fee to support campus organizations even if some students dislike the politics or actions of particular groups; but fees had to be allocated so as not to prefer some viewpoints over others.[39]

The Court decided that a Michigan state worker, who had been denied a promotion because the police Red squad had a file on his politically active brother, could not sue the state, a decision that placed the state's politically repressive acts above legal challenge by its citizens.[40] In 1996, the high court ruled that the FBI could maintain files on Americans who were engaged in legal peaceful political activities protected by the First Amendment — even though Congress had passed the Privacy Act prohibiting such surveillance.[41] The federal courts have repeatedly ruled that teachers or other employees who are denied contracts or otherwise discriminated against because of their dissident political views had no grounds for legal redress unlike employees who encounter racial or gender discrimination.

Separation of church and state. The First Amendment reads in part: "Congress shall make no law respecting an establishment of religion, or prohibiting the free exercise thereof." In *support* of this constitutionally mandated separation of church and state, the Supreme Court has ruled that (a) school authorities have no business sponsoring prayer in the public schools, (b) public school districts may not allow students to lead organized prayer before football games, and (c) states have no right to require public schools teaching evolution to also teach Christian views of "creationism," which argues that evolution never occurred and the world was made by God as a perfectly finished product in six days.[42]

In *violation* of the separation of church and state, the Court has long held that religious organizations can enjoy various exemptions from taxation, in effect forcing laypersons to subsidize religious bodies. Even when religious groups have engaged actively in political issues such as abortion, the Internal Revenue Service allows them to retain their tax-exempt status.[43] In a series of five-to-four decisions, a deeply divided Court ruled that (a) federal funds given to religious groups to promote chastity did not violate separation of church and state; (b) tuition, textbook, and transportation costs for private schools (including religious ones) were tax deductible; (c) a university could not refuse to use mandatory student activity fees to subsidize a student religious publication; (d) federal money may be used to pay for special education teachers who help students on parochial school premises; and recently (e) a federal program placing computers and other "instructional equipment" in parochial school classrooms did not violate the constitutional separation between church and state.[44]

Criminal justice. Over the last two decades the Court has done little for individual rights. The Miranda rule, which forbade the use of police torture in obtaining confessions, was greatly weakened when the Court ruled in *Arizona v. Fulminante* (1991) that "the prosecutor's use of a coerced confession — no matter how vicious the police conduct may have been — may now constitute harmless error." In *Massey v. Washington* (1991) the justices decided that sentencing a mentally retarded thirteen-year-old to life imprisonment was not a violation of the Eighth Amendment's prohibition against cruel and unusual punishment; the youth's older codefendant testified that Massey "was just there" and had not killed anyone.

In *Rummel v. Estelle* (1980), the Court upheld a life sentence given to a man for three minor frauds totaling $230. Rehnquist argued that cruel and unusual punishment might be when someone is given a life sentence for "overtime parking" — an example so unlikely as to leave room for nearly any kind of unjust sentence, reducing the Eighth Amendment to virtually nothing. Three years later, a slight shift in the Court lineup produced a new five-to-four majority that overturned *Rummel* and concluded that a life sentence for a series of minor crimes *does* constitute cruel and unusual punishment.[45] Yet the Court subsequently ruled that a life sentence without parole for a first-time conviction of cocaine possession was not cruel and unusual punishment.[46]

In 1997, the Court's ever-inventive conservative activists decided that when imposing sentence, federal judges may take into account not only the crimes for which defendants were convicted but also additional charges for which juries found them *not guilty*. Thus a charge that could not be proven in court might still bring punishment. Under this rule, why bother having a trial?[47]

The prohibition against cruel and unusual punishment, the Court decided, does not protect schoolchildren from corporal punishment even if they are severely injured by school officials. And the due process clause does not impose an obligation on the government to protect an individual from abuse from another individual, not even a child from an abusive parent.[48] The Court seems to think children can fend for themselves. A law permitting minors to testify behind a screen in sexual abuse cases — to make it less traumatic for them to appear in the same venue with their molesters — was declared unconstitutional, for it deprived the accused of the right to confront their accusers.[49] (In fact, the child would still be confronted with a cross-examination.)

The Fourth Amendment protection against unreasonable searches and seizures was seriously weakened when the Court upheld the police's power to conduct sweeping searches in private homes and on buses and to arrest individuals without a warrant and hold them without a court hearing.[50] The conservative activists ruled that in order to file lawsuits against inhumane prison conditions, inmates had to show that prison officials exhibited "deliberate indifference." Bad conditions as such were not litigable, since deliberate neglect could not be ascribed to a specific official. The justices did not explain how one could demonstrate deliberate neglect if the inhumane prison conditions themselves did not.[51]

In *McNally v. United States* (1987), the Court did rein in the prosecutory power when applied to upper-class white collar offenders, making it more difficult to bring mail fraud charges against corrupt persons in private business, government, and the judiciary. Justice Stevens dissented, wondering "why a Court that has not been particularly receptive to the rights of criminal defendants" now protects "the elite class of powerful individuals who will benefit from this decision."

Death penalty. Over the last twenty-five years the Supreme Court has ruled that (a) death is an excessive penalty for the crime of rape, and only those convicted of first degree murder can be put to death;[52] (b)someone who is insane cannot be executed because a defendant must be able to comprehend the proceedings and punishment, but it is okay to execute someone who is mentally retarded;[53] (c) statistics showing that Blacks are more likely to be sentenced to death than Whites who commit similar crimes were insufficient to overturn a particular death sentence;[54] (d) persons who were sixteen when they committed a crime could be executed, but not anyone below that age.[55] The Court denied a hearing to a man on death row because his appeal was founded not on a procedural flaw but on errors of fact, specifically additional evidence proving his innocence! In a dissent, Justice Harry Blackmun bemoaned "this Court's obvious eagerness to do away with any restriction on the States' power to execute whomever and however they please" and called the ruling "perilously close to simple murder."[56]

Executive power. As part of a continuing pattern of deferring to executive power in military and foreign affairs, the federal courts refused to hear cases challenging the president on such things as the undeclared war in Vietnam, the unprovoked U.S. invasion of Grenada, the imposition of embargoes on Nicaragua, the U.S. invasion of Panama, the bombing of Iraq and Yugoslavia, and the deportation of Haitian, Guatemalan, and Salvadoran refugees. The Court struck down a Massachusetts law aimed at boycotting companies that do business with the drug-trafficking, human-rights abusing, military government of Myanmar (Burma), deeming it an interference in foreign policy and compromising the president's capacity to speak for the nation with one voice.[57] The justices ruled that the State Department could deny a passport to a former Central Intelligence Agency (CIA) employee who had written books exposing illegal CIA operations. Neither Congress nor the Constitution grants this power to the executive, but the Court's conservative activists decided that in matters of "foreign policy and national security," the president could do whatever he wanted in the absence of specific legislative prohibition.[58]

The electoral system. Several decisions nibbled away at the "one-person, one-vote" reapportionment rule and allowed for greater population disparities among state and congressional legislative districts.[59] The Court decided that states could not prohibit corporations from spending unlimited amounts of their funds to influence the outcome of public referenda or other elections because campaign expenditures were a form of "speech" and the Constitution guarantees freedom of speech to business firms, which are to be considered "persons." Nor could limits be imposed on the amount that rich candidates spend on their campaigns, the amount that "independent" political action committees (PACs) spend in presidential elections, the amount that rich individuals spend in an "independent" effort to elect or defeat any candidate, and the amount that political parties may spend to help their candidates if the expenditure is made independently of the candidate.[60] Thus the poor and the rich can both freely compete, one in a whisper and the other in a roar.

In a departure from this trend, the Supreme Court, in a six-to-three decision, recently did uphold a state's authority to impose strict limits on election campaign contributions. Justice Souter argued that preserving the public's trust in the "integrity of our electoral process" outweighs an individual's right to give large sums to a favored candidate. And Justice Stevens noted: "Money is property; it is not speech."[61]

In 1995, the Court held that states could not impose term limits on their representatives in Congress for that would add a qualification for office when the Constitution set down only three qualifications: age, residency, and citizenship.[62] In 1997, the justices ruled that states can prohibit small parties from endorsing a major-party candidate, a decision that rules out cross-endorsements or fusion tickets and diminishes the influence a minor party might exert by throwing its weight behind a candidate and building an electoral coalition.[63]

Residents of the District of Columbia (overwhelmingly Democrats) do not have a constitutional right to vote for their own representative in Congress, the justices ruled. Nor can they help choose Maryland's congressional delegation — even though persons who live in other federal enclaves, such as national parks, have a right to vote in neighboring states. (What remains of the District came entirely from Maryland.) So over 600,000 U.S. citizens who reside in Washington, D.C., and pay federal taxes continue to go without representation in Congress.[64] The Court unanimously upheld the validity of the 1990 census, deciding that the government had no constitutional obligation to adjust the results to correct an acknowledged undercount in big cities.[65]

Conservative judicial activism was nowhere more evident than in *George W. Bush v. Al Gore,* regarding the Florida vote in the 2000 presidential election. In a five-to-four decision, the conservatives overruled the Florida Supreme Court's order for a recount, arguing that since different counties might use different modes of tabulating ballots in a hand recount, this would violate the equal protection clause of the Fourteenth Amendment. The justices ignored the fact that the initial punch-card tally had worked prejudicially against those areas where the Gore vote was heaviest, and was therefore a violation of equal protection. Every indication showed that an honest recount would have given the state of Florida and the presidency to the Democratic candidate, Vice President Al Gore (see Chapter 13), who at that point was behind by only a hundred or so votes in Florida and who was gaining ground with each attempt at a recount. By preventing a complete tally, the Court handed Florida's electoral votes and the presidency to Bush — a stolen election in which the U.S. Supreme Court played a crucial role.

A dissent written by Justice John Paul Stevens in *Bush* noted that the Florida Supreme Court was completely within its rights under Article 2 to order a recount, and that the methods used by canvassing boards to count votes by hand would lead to results no less uniform than, for example, the "beyond a reasonable doubt" standard employed every day in various courtrooms across the country. The majority decision, Stevens concluded, "effectively orders the disenfranchisement of an unknown number of voters," whose legal ballots "were for some reason rejected by ballot-counting machines."

In recent years conservative justices have held that the federal government should refrain from telling the states to take action on a variety of issues; for instance, the federal government must not use the Fourteenth Amendment's equal protection clause to force states to take measures to stop violence against women, or mandate a more equitable mode of property taxes, or a more equitable distribution of funds between rich and poor school districts. But in *Bush* these same justices ruled that the equal protection clause could be used to stop a perfectly legal ballot recount. At the same time, they explicitly stated that this case could not be considered a precedent for other equal protection issues: "Our consideration is limited to the present circumstances. . . ." In other words, the Fourteenth Amendment was operative only when the conservative judicial activists said it was, as when perpetrating a judicially directed electoral coup on behalf of a right-wing presidential candidate who actually failed to get a majority of both the popular vote and the electoral college.

Abortion and gender discrimination. Abortion and sex discrimination cases have received mixed treatment. The Court has ruled that (a) sexual harassment on the job violates a person's civil rights, (b) a divorced woman cannot be denied custody of her children because of her remarriage to a man of another race, (c) victims of sexual harassment can obtain monetary damages from the institution in which the harassment occurred, and (d) schools are liable under federal law for failing to stop a student from subjecting another student to severe and continual sexual harassment.[66]

The justices ruled that a state-supported military college could not bar women candidates nor offer them a lesser program elsewhere.[67] But the Court also invalidated a six-year-old provision of federal law that permitted victims of rape, domestic violence, and other crimes "motivated by gender" to sue their attackers in federal court, thereby striking down the civil remedy provision of the Violence Against Women Act passed by Congress. The Court reasoned that rape was a local issue best left to the states.[68]

The justices declared unconstitutional a requirement that women seeking abortions notify their husbands, but underage women must obtain parental consent for an abortion.[69] The reasoning seems to be that a young woman is not mature and experienced enough to decide whether or not to get an abortion, but she is mature and experienced enough to be forced to give birth and raise a child. The justices decided that federal courts have no power to stop anti-abortion extremists from their campaigns of trespass, intimidation, and obstruction against abortion clinics.[70]

In 1994, however, the Court did uphold a law that creates a thirty-six-foot buffer zone outside entrances to abortion clinics. That same year the justices conceded that abortion clinics could invoke the federal racketeering law to sue violent anti-abortion protest groups for damages.[71] This decision leaves abortion clinics with the task of proving that specific individuals and organizations are conducting a nationwide campaign of intimidation, bombings, and other violent acts. One would think the local police and the federal government itself would take responsibility for moving against such violence. In 2000, the Court ruled by a five-to-four vote that the government could not prohibit doctors from performing what some call a "partial-birth abortion" because it might be the most medically appropriate way of terminating some pregnancies.[72]

Affirmative action and civil rights. Justice Blackmun explained in *University of California v. Bakke* that affirmative action had to be taken to correct the inequities of race relations in the United States: "In order to get beyond racism, we must first take account of race. There is no other way. And in order to treat some persons equally, we must treat them differently. We cannot . . . let the equal protection clause perpetuate racial supremacy." But by the late 1980s, the justices began to retreat, making it more difficult to establish discrimination claims against employers, giving White males increased opportunity to claim "reverse discrimination" in affirmative action cases, and sharply limiting the ability of state and local governments to set aside a fixed percentage of contracts for minority businesses.[73]

A five-to-four majority decided that if an employer asserts "business necessity" to justify a racist or sexist practice, the burden is on the worker to prove intent and show that the practice is not job-related.[74] It is often impossible to demonstrate intent. We can see the effects of an action but usually can only divine the motive. The Court continued to retreat from *Brown v. Board of Education* by refusing to act on a lower court's ruling that schools could not consider race in apportioning students, in effect reinstituting "separate but equal."[75]

Over the past fifteen years conservative judges in the federal courts have shown an indifference bordering on hostility toward African Americans and other people of color in regard to school desegregation, employment discrimination, and voting rights, invoking an ideal colorblindness that in effect accepts racist practices. When two African Americans were elected to the board of supervisors in an Alabama county, the board responded by abolishing the individual supervisor's right to make decisions regarding his or her own district and gave that power to the White-dominated board as a whole. The Supreme Court decided that this subterfuge did not constitute unfair treatment and did not violate the voting rights laws.[76]

The Court supported the rigging of the electoral process so as to freeze out all African-American representation in a Louisiana parish, arguing that if Blacks had zero representation before, a plan that keeps them at zero was acceptable.[77]

The Supreme Court's right-wing ideological bias is reflected not only in the decisions it hands down but in the cases it selects or refuses to review. Federal district courts decide almost 300,000 cases a year. Appeals made to the twelve U.S. Courts of Appeal annually number some 30,000 cases. The Supreme Court, in contrast, hands down about 170 decisions a year. During the last two decades of conservative domination, review access has been sharply curtailed for plaintiffs representing labor, minorities, consumers, and individual rights. Powerless and pauperized individuals have had a diminishing chance of getting their cases reviewed, unlike powerful and prestigious petitioners such as the government and giant corporations. State and federal prosecutors were able to gain a hearing by the high court at a rate fifty times greater than defendants. Criminal defendants who could afford the legal filing fee were twice as likely to be granted a Supreme Court review as were indigent defendants.[78]

While the number of lower-court appeals has multiplied, the amount of time the high court spends on deliberations and the number of cases they hear has diminished by one-fourth compared to the Warren Court of the 1960s. It is hard to argue that the Court is increasingly overworked when in fact its conservative majority has been reducing its caseload. Even if it were true that the Court is overburdened, this does not explain the evident class bias as to which cases are granted certiorari.

Influence of the Court

A few generalizations can be drawn about the Supreme Court's political influence. More often than not, the Court has been a conservative force. For over half a century it wielded a pro-business minority veto on the kind of reform legislation that European countries had implemented decades earlier. It prevented Congress from instituting progressive income taxes, a decision that took eighteen years and the Sixteenth Amendment to the Constitution to circumvent. It upheld the interests of slaveholders right up to the Civil War and accepted racist segregation for almost a century more. It delayed female suffrage for forty-eight years, a decision finally undone by the Nineteenth Amendment. And it has prevented Congress from placing limitations on personal campaign spending by rich candidates.

By playing a crucial role in defining what is constitutional, the Court gives encouraging cues to large sectors of the public, including the Congress itself. Unable to pass a civil rights act for seventy years, Congress enacted three in the decade after *Brown v. Board of Education*. With the law on their side, civil rights advocates throughout the nation stepped up the pressure to make desegregation a reality. Likewise, the Warren Court's decisions protecting the rights of the poor opened a whole new field of welfare reform litigation and was an inducement to various poor people's movements.

Since the Court can neither legislate nor enforce its decisions, it has been deemed the "least dangerous branch." But the Reagan and Bush years demonstrated that a militantly conservative Court bolstered by a conservative executive can exercise quite an activist influence. Again and again the Court imposed its own tortured logic to cases, blatantly violating the clear language of a law and the intent of Congress. Or it upheld administrative regulations designed to negate a statute. When Congress tried to undo the Court's right-wing activism and reinstate the law as it was intended, President Reagan or President Bush would veto or threaten to veto the new measure. Unable to muster the two-thirds vote needed to override the veto, Congress would be thwarted. Thus, a conservative president, assisted by five or more right-wing activist justices and one-third plus one member of either the House or the Senate, could rewrite many regulatory rulings and laws.[79]

The Court's right-wing jurists have been not only activist but downright adventuristic, showing no hesitation to rewrite much of the Constitution, rig the rules of the game, invent concepts and arguments out of thin air, eviscerate laws, treat congressional intent and precedence as irrelevant, bolster an authoritarian executive power, block economic and campaign reforms, roll back substantive political and economic gains, and undermine civil liberties, civil rights, and the democratic process itself (such as it is). The same is true of the jurists who preside over the lower courts — which is why conservatives on the Supreme Court are quite content to let stand without review so many lower court decisions. "Most activist, politicized judges on the federal bench today," notes one constitutional scholar, "are conservative Republicans."[80]

These highly politicized judicial activists limit the federal government's ability to protect work conditions of employees, claiming an infringement of states' rights under the Tenth Amendment. Then they restrict the ability of states to limit business's spending power in referenda, claiming federal prerogatives under the First Amendment. In such cases, one hears little complaint from conservatives about the Court's activist usurpation of policy-making powers. A consistent double standard obtains. Judicial activism that strengthens authoritarian statism and big business prerogatives is acceptable. Judicial activism that supports democratic working-class rights and socioeconomic equality invites attack.

One way to trim judicial adventurism is to end life tenure for federal judges, including the justices who sit on the Supreme Court. It would take a constitutional amendment, but it would be worth it. Today only three states provide life tenure for state judges; the other forty-seven set fixed terms ranging from four to twelve years (usually allowing for reelection). Life tenure was supposed to shield the federal judiciary from outside influences and place it above partisan politics. Experience shows that judges are as political and ideological as anyone else. A fixed term would still give a jurist significant independence, but would not allow him or her to remain unaccountable for an entire lifetime. Judges who exhibited a hostile view toward constitutional rights could be replaced. No ideologically partisan group could pack the courts for decades ahead, and there would be more responsiveness to popular needs.[81]

To be sure, judges are not impervious to the tides of opinion. The justices read not only the Constitution but also the newspapers. They talk not only to each other but also to friends and acquaintances. Few jurists remain untouched by the great tides of public opinion and by the subtler shifts in values and perceptions. The Court is always operating in a climate of opinion shaped by political forces larger than itself. The hope is that democratic forces will prove more effective in restraining the powers of an oligarchic, elitist judiciary.

Notes

1. Max Farrand, *The Framing of the Constitution of the United States* (New Haven, Conn.: Yale University Press, 1913), pp. 156–57. See Chief Justice John Marshall's argument for judicial review in the landmark case of *Marbury v. Madison* (1803).

2. Quoted in Felix Frankfurter, *Mr. Justice Holmes and the Supreme Court* (New York: Atheneum, 1965), 54.

3. Russell Galloway, *The Rich and the Poor in Supreme Court History, 1790–1982* (Greenbrae, Calif.: Paradigm, 1982), 163, and 180–81; see also Sheldon Goldman, "Johnson and Nixon Appointees to the Lower Federal Courts: Some Socio-Political Perspectives," *Journal of Politics* 34, 1972, 934–42.

4. Joel Grossman, *Lawyers and Judges: The ABA and the Politics of Judicial Selection* (New York: Wiley, 1965).

5. Dexter Perkins, *Charles Evans Hughes* (Boston: Little, Brown, 1956), 16.

6. Herman Schwartz, *Packing the Courts* (New York: Scribner, 1988); Sheldon Goldman, "Reaganizing the Judiciary," *Judicature* 68, April–May 1985, 313–29.

7. Study by Robert Carp, Donald Songer, and Ronald Stidham reported in *New York Times*, August 1, 1996.

8. *Time*, June 3, 1996; *People's Weekly World*, June 19, 1999.

9. On this and the sanctity of contract, see *Allegeyer v. Louisiana* (1897), *Lochner v. New York* (1905), *Adair v. United States* (1908).

10. *Santa Clara County v. Southern Pacific Railroad* (1886).

11. Peter Kellman, in *By What Authority*, Spring 2000, 6.

12. See *Hammer v. Dagenhart* (1918); *Carter v. Carter Coal Co.* (1936); and *Morehead v. New York* (1936).

13. In an earlier case the Court had declared that women had no right to practice law; see *Bradwell v. State* (1872).

14. Proponents of free speech allow that libel and slander might be restricted by law, although even defamatory speech — when directed against public figures — has been treated as protected under the First Amendment; see *New York Times Co. v. Sullivan* (1964) and *Time Inc. v. Hill* (1967).

15. Hearings before a subcommittee of the Senate Judiciary Committee, *Amnesty and Pardon for Political Prisoners* (Washington, D.C.: Government Printing Office, 1927), 54. See also Charles Goodell, *Political Prisoners in America* (New York: Random House, 1973), and read about the more recent incidents in Chapter 10 of this book.

16. Holmes made a similar argument in *Debs v. United States* (1919). In subsequent cases he placed himself against the Court's majority and on the side of the First Amendment: *Abrams v. United States* (1919) and *Gitlow v. New York* (1925).

17. *Yates et al. v. United States* (1957).

18. *First National Bank v. Bellotti* (1978); see also *Buckley v. Valeo* (1976).

19. Burt Neuborne, "Pushing Free Speech Too Far," *New York Times,* July 15, 1996.

20. *Reno v. American Civil Liberties Union* (1997).

21. For samples of this thinking, see the Vinson and Jackson opinions in *Dennis v. United States.*

22. See *Near v. Minnesota* (1931), *Dejonge v. Oregon* (1937), *McCollum v. Board of Education* (1948).

23. On civil liberties: *Gideon v. Wainwright* (1963), *Escobedo v. Illinois* (1964), and *Miranda v. Arizona* (1966); on reapportionment: *Baker v. Carr* (1962), *Reynolds v. Sims* (1964), *Wesberry v. Sanders* (1964); on the economic rights of the poor: *King v. Smith* (1968), *Sniadich v. Family Finance Corporation* (1969), *Shapiro v. Thompson* (1969), and *Hunter v. Erickson* (1969).

24. Galloway, *The Rich and the Poor in Supreme Court History,* 163.

25. *Loving v. Virginia* (1967).

26. For general critiques, see Tinsley Yarbrough, *The Rehnquist Court and the Constitution* (New York: Oxford University Press, 2000); David Kairys, *With Liberty and Justice for Some: A Critique of the Conservative Supreme Court* (New York: New Press, 1993); Herman Schwartz (ed.), *The Burger Years* (New York: Penguin, 1988).

27. Respectively, *Gateway Coal Co. v. United Mine Workers* (1974); *First National Maintenance Corp. v. NLRB* (1981); *Communications Workers of America v. Beck* (1988); *Lehnert v. Ferris Faculty Association* (1991).

28. *Lying v. International Union* (1988); *Public Employees Retirement System of Ohio v. Betts* (1989); *Pauley v. Bethenergy Mines* (1991); *Trans World Airlines v. Independent Federation of Flight Attendants* (1989).

29. *Frank Greenberg Executor v. H & H Music Company* (1992).

30. *Dandridge v. Williams* (1970); *Rosado v. Wyman* (1970). On the failure of federal and state courts to fulfill the promise of equality, see Charles Haar and Daniel Fessler, *The Wrong Side of the Tracks* (New York: Simon & Schuster, 1986).

31. *San Antonio Independent School District v. Rodriguez* (1973).

32. Eric Nadler, "Supreme Court Backs Agribusiness," *Guardian,* July 2, 1980.

33. *Nordlinger v. Hahn* (1992).

34. See respectively *Laird v. Tatum* (1972) and *Greer v. Spock* (1976).

35. *United States v. Caldwell* (1972); *Zurcher v. Stanford Daily* (1978).

36. *Members of the City Council of Los Angeles et al. v. Taxpayers for Vincent et al.* (1984); *Clark v. Community for Creative Non-Violence* (1984).

37. *Hazelwood School District v. Kuhlmeir* (1988); *Todd v. Rush County* (1998); and *Los Angeles Times,* October 6, 1998.

38. *Hustler Magazine v. Falwell* (1988).

39. *Board of Regents, University of Wisconsin v. Southworth* (2000).

40. *Will v. Michigan Department of State Police* (1989). On the Court's collusion with state repression, see Alexander Charns, *Cloak and Gavel: FBI Wiretaps, Bugs, Informers, and the Supreme Court* (Champaign: University of Illinois Press, 1992).

41. *J. Roderick McArthur Fund v. FBI* (1996).

42. On public school prayer: *Engels v. Vitale* (1962); *Wallace v. Jaffree* (1985); and *Santa Fe Independent School District v. Doe* (2000). On creationism: *Edwards v. Aguillard* (1987).

43. *Murray v. Curlett* (1963); *Lemon v. Kurtzman* (1971); *Walz v. Tax Commission* (1970); David Burnham, "Alter the Catholic Church's Tax Status?" *New York Times,* July 29, 1988.

44. Respectively, *Bowen v. Kendrick* (1988), *Mueller v. Allen* (1983), *Rosenberger v. University of Virginia* (1995), *Agostini v. Felton* (1997), *Mitchell v. Helms* (2000).

45. *Solem v. Helm* (1983). On some of the Supreme Court's worst decisions, see Joel Joseph, *Black Mondays* (Bethesda, Md.: National, 1987).

46. *Harmelin v. Michigan* (1991).

47. *United States v. Watts* (1997).

48. *Ingraham v. Wright* (1977), and *De Shaney v. Winnebago County Department of Social Services* (1989).

49. *Coy v. Iowa* (1988).

50. *Maryland v. Blue* (1990); *Florida v. Bostick* (1991); *County of Riverside v. McLaughlin* (1991).

51. On right to appeal: *McCleskey v. Zant* (1991) and *Keeney v. Tamayo-Reyes* (1992). On inhumane conditions: *Wilson v. Seiter* (1991).

52. *Coker v. Georgia* (1977).

53. *Ford v. Wainwright* (1986); *Penry v. Lynaugh* (1989).

54. *McClesky v. Kemp* (1987).

55. *Wilkins v. Missouri* (1989); *Standford v. Kentucky* (1989); *Thompson v. Oklahoma* (1988).

56. *Herrera v. Collins* (1993).

57. *Crosby v. National Foreign Trade Council* (2000).

58. *Haig v. Agee* (1981) and *Regan v. Wald* (1984).

59. *Mahan v. Howell* (1973) and *Davis v. Bandemer* (1986).

60. Respectively, *First National Bank of Boston v. Bellotti* (1978); *Citizens Against Rent Control et al. v. City of Berkeley et al.* (1981); *Buckley v. Valeo* (1976); *Colorado Republican Committee v. Federal Election Commission* (1996).

61. *Nixon v. Shrink Missouri Government PAC* (2000).

62. *U.S. Term Limits v. Thornton* (1995).

63. *Timmons v. Twin Cities Area New Party* (1997).

64. *Alesander v. Mineta* (2000); *Adams v. Clinton* (2000).

65. *Wisconsin v. New York* (1996).

66. See, respectively, *Mentor Savings Bank, FSB v. Vinson* (1986); *Palmore v. Sidoti* (1984); *Franklin v. Gwinnett County Public Schools* (1992); *Davis v. Monroe County Board of Education* (1999).

67. *United States v. Virginia* (1996).

68. *United States v. Morrison* (2000). The suit was brought by a Virginia Polytechnic Institute student against two varsity football players, after she learned that the college would not discipline them.

69. See, respectively, *Planned Parenthood v. Casey* (1992) and *Hodgson v. Minnesota* (1990). In *Webster v. Reproductive Health Services* (1989), the Court gave states broad powers to impose restrictions on abortions, such as barring the use of public money, medical personnel, and facilities.

70. *Jane Bray v. Alexandria Women's Clinic* (1993).

71. *Madsen v. Women's Health Clinic* (1994), and *National Organization for Women v. Scheidler* (1994).

72. *Stenberg v. Carhart* (2000).

73. *Lorance v. AT&T Technologies* (1989); *City of Richmond v. J. A. Crosson Co.* (1989); *Martin v. Wilks* (1989); *Adarand Constructors v. Pena* (1995).

74. *Ward's Cove Packing Co. v. Atonio* (1989).

75. *Missouri v. Jenkins* (1995); *Montgomery County, Md., Public Schools v. Eisenberg* (2000).

76. *Presley v. Etowah County Commission* (1992).

77. *Reno v. Bossier Parish* (2000). For an earlier example of disempowering African Americans at the ballot box, see *Shaw v. Reno* (1993).

78. Janis Judson, *The Hidden Agenda: Non-Decision-Making on the U.S. Supreme Court* (University of Maryland, Ph.D. dissertation, 1986); *Los Angeles Times,* November 9, 1989.

79. Herman Schwartz, "Second Opinion," *Nation,* June 17, 1991.

80. Garrett Epps, "Black Robe Activism," *Nation,* May 5, 1997.

81. I believe different considerations regarding term limits apply to legislators; see Chapter 14.

18

Democracy for the Few

This country contains a diverse array of interest groups. If this is what is meant by "pluralism," then the United States is a pluralistic society, as is any society of size and complexity. But those who claim that the United States is a pluralistic society presume to be saying something about how power is distributed and how democracy works. Supposedly, in a pluralistic society, the government is not controlled by corporate elites who get what they want on virtually every question. If there are elites in our society, they are specialized and checked in their demands by conflicting elites. No group can press its advantages too far and any sizable group can find a way within the political system to make its influence felt. Government stands above any one particular influence but responds to many. So say the pluralists.[1]

Pluralism for the Few

The evidence offered in the preceding chapters leaves us with reason to doubt that the United States is a pluralistic democracy as described above. To summarize and expand on previous points:

Most government policies favor large investor interests at a substantial cost to the rest of the populace. Long and hard democratic struggles have won some real benefits for the public, yet inequities and social injustices of immense proportions continue and even worsen. There is commodity glut in the private market and chronic scarcity in public services. While the rich get ever richer, possessed with more money than they know what to do with, the majority of the populace lives in a condition of economic insecurity. While defense contractors at home and military dictatorships abroad fatten on the largesse of the U.S. Treasury, human services go begging.

To think of government as nothing more than a referee amidst a vast array of "countervailing" groups (which presumably represent all the important interests within society) is to forget that government best serves those who can best serve themselves. Power in America "is plural and fluid," claimed one pluralist.[2] In reality, power is structured among entrenched, well-organized, well-financed, politico-economic conglomerates. Wealth is the most crucial power resource. It creates a pervasive political advantage, and affords ready access to most other resources. Its distribution is neither "plural" nor "fluid."

The pluralists have little to say about the pervasive role of political repression in U.S. society: the purging and exclusion of anticapitalist dissidents from government, from the labor movement, the media, academia, and the entertainment world; along with the surveillance and harassment of protest organizations and public-interest groups. Pluralists seem never to allude to the near-monopoly control of ideas and information that is the daily fare of the news and entertainment sectors of the mass media, creating a climate of opinion favorable to the owning-class ideology at home and abroad. Nor are the pluralists much troubled by the rigged rules under which the two major political parties operate, or by an electoral system that treats vast sums of money as a prerequisite for office.

The pluralists make much of the fact that wealthy interests do not always operate with clear and deliberate purpose.[3] To be sure, like everyone else, elites sometimes make mistakes and suffer confusions about tactics. But if they are not omniscient and infallible, neither are they habitual laggards and imbeciles. If they do not always calculate correctly in the pursuit of their class interests, they do so often and successfully enough.

Is the American polity ruled by a secretive, conspiratorial, omnipotent, monolithic power elite? No, the plutocracy, or ruling class, does not fit that simple caricature. First of all, no ruling class in history, no matter how autocratic, has ever achieved omnipotence. All have had to make concessions and allow for unexpected and undesired developments. In addition, ruling elites are not always secretive. The influence they exercise over governing bodies is sometimes covert but often a matter of public record, as we have seen. It is exercised through control of the top posts in business and government, control of interlocking directorates and trusteeships whose existence, while not widely advertised, is public knowledge. However, these elites do often find it desirable to plan in secret, minimize or distort the flow of information, and pursue policies that may violate the law they profess to uphold. Examples aplenty have been offered in this book.

American government is not ruled by a monolithic elite. Occasionally sharp differences arise in ruling circles about how best to mute class conflict and advance the interests of the free marketeers. Differences can arise between moderately conservative and extremely conservative capitalists, between large and small investor interests, and between domestic and international corporations. But these conflicts seldom take into account the interests of the working public. When push comes to shove, what holds the various elites together is their common interest in preserving an economic system that assures the continued accumulation of corporate wealth and the privileged lifestyles of the superrich.

Does this amount to a "conspiracy theory" of society? First, it should be noted that conspiracies do exist. A common view is that conspiracy exists only in the imaginings of kooks. But just because some people have fantasies of conspiracies does not mean that all conspiracies are fantasies. There was the secretive plan to escalate the Vietnam War as revealed in the Pentagon Papers; the Watergate break-in; the Federal Bureau of Investigation (FBI) COINTELPRO disruption of dissident groups; the several phoney but well-orchestrated "energy crises" that sharply boosted oil prices in the 1970s; the Iran-contra conspiracy; the savings and loan conspiracies; and the well-documented conspiracies (and subsequent cover-ups) to assassinate President John Kennedy, Martin Luther King, and Malcolm X.[4]

Ruling elites admit to conspiring in secret, without being held accountable to anyone; they call it "national security." But when one suggests that their plans (whether covert or overt) benefit the interests of their class and are intended to do so, one is dismissed as a "conspiracy theorist." It is allowed that farmers, steelworkers, or schoolteachers may concert to advance their interests, but it may not be suggested that moneyed elites do as much — even when they actually occupy the top decision-making posts. Instead, we are asked to believe that these estimable persons of high station walk through life indifferent to the fate of their vast holdings.

Although there is no one grand power elite, there is continual cooperation between various corporate and governmental elites in every area of the political economy. Many of the stronger corporate groups tend to predominate in their particular spheres of interest, more or less unmolested by other elites. In any case, the conflicts among plutocratic interests seldom work to the advantage of the mass of people. They are conflicts of haves versus haves. Often they are resolved not by compromise but by logrolling, involving more collusion than competition. These mutually satisfying arrangements among "competitors" usually come at the expense of the public interest. To be sure, the demands of the unfortunates may be heard occasionally as a clamor outside the gate, and now and then concessions are granted to take the edge off their restiveness.

One might better think of ours as a dual political system. First, there is the *high visibility* system centering around electoral and representative activities, including campaign contests, political personalities, public pronouncements, and certain ambiguous presentations of issues that bestir presidents, governors, mayors, and their respective legislatures. Then there is the *low visibility* system, involving multibillion-dollar contracts, tax write-offs, grants, loss compensations, subsidies, leases, and the whole vast process of budgeting, protecting, and servicing transnational companies, now ignoring or rewriting the law on behalf of the powerful, now applying it with full punitive vigor against heretics and "troublemakers." The high visibility system is taught in the schools, dissected by academicians, endlessly gossiped about by news commentators. The low visibility system is seldom acknowledged.

Big business prevails not only because it uses campaign donations and shrewd lobbyists to manipulate lawmakers and bureaucrats. Business also exerts an overall influence as a system of power, a way of organizing capital, labor, and large-scale production. Because big business controls the very economy of the nation, government perforce enters into a uniquely intimate relationship with it. The health of the economy is treated by policymakers as a necessary condition for the health of the nation, and since it happens that the economy is in the hands of large interests, then presumably government's service to the public is best accomplished by service to those interests. The goals of business (high profits and secure markets) become the goals of government, and the "national interest" becomes identified with the systemic needs of corporate capitalism.

Since policymakers must operate in and through the corporate economy, it is not long before they are operating *for* it. In order to keep the peace, business may occasionally accept reforms and regulations it does not like, but government cannot ignore business's own reason for being: the accumulation of capital. Sooner or later, business as a system must be met on its own terms or be subjected to a fundamental restructuring that goes beyond reformist tinkering.

The Limits of Reform

Government involvement in the economy represents a growth not in socialism (as that term is normally understood by socialists) but in state-supported capitalism, not the communization of private wealth but the privatization of the commonwealth. This development has brought a great deal of government involvement, but a kind that revolves largely around bolstering the profit system, not limiting it. In capitalist countries, government generally nationalizes sick and unprofitable industries and privatizes profitable public ones — in both cases for the benefit of big investors. In what amounted to a bailout of private investors, in 1986 the social democratic government in Spain nationalized vast private holdings to avert their collapse. After bringing them back to health with generous nourishment from the public treasure, they were sold back to private companies. The same was done with Conrail in the United States, as we have seen. And a conservative Greek government privatized publicly owned companies such as the telecommunications system, which had been reporting continuous profits for several years.

When a capitalist government takes over an enterprise, it gives full compensation to the previous owners, usually for a nice price. The same wealthy investors who once owned the private stocks now own public bonds and collect the interest on these bonds. "Ownership" in the form of a huge bonded debt — with all the risks and losses and none of the profits — is passed on to the public. The wealth of the enterprise remains in private hands while nominal ownership is public.

Defenders of the existing system assert that the history of "democratic capitalism" has been one of gradual reform. To be sure, important reforms have been won by working people. To the extent that the present economic order has anything humane and civil about it, it is because of the struggles of millions of people engaged in advancing their living standard and their rights as citizens. It is somewhat ironic to credit capitalism with the genius of gradual reform when (a) most economic reforms through history have been vehemently and sometimes violently resisted by the capitalist class and were won only after prolonged, bitter, and sometimes bloody popular struggle, and (b) most of the problems needing reform have been caused or intensified by capitalism.

Fundamental reform is difficult to effect because those who have the interest in change have not the power, while those who have the power have not the interest, being disinclined to commit class suicide. It is not that officeholders have been unable to figure out the steps for egalitarian change; it is that they are not willing to go that way. For them the compelling quality of any argument is determined less by its logic and evidence than by the strength of its advocates. The wants of an unorganized public with few power resources of its own seldom become marketable political demands; they seldom become imperatives to which officials find it in their own interest to respond, especially if the changes would put the officeholder on a collision course with powerful moneyed interests.

Furthermore, the reason our labor, skills, technology, and natural resources are not used for social needs is that they are used for corporate gain. The corporations cannot build low-rent houses, feed the poor, clean up the environment, or offer higher education to all qualified people regardless of their ability to pay — because their interest is not in social reconstruction but in private profit. State-supported capitalism cannot exist without state support, without passing its immense diseconomies onto the public. Our social and ecological problems are rational outcomes of a basically irrational system, a system structured not for satisfying human need but magnifying human greed.

How can we speak of the U.S. politico-economic system as being a product of the democratic will? What democratic will demanded that Washington be honeycombed with high-paid corporate lobbyists who would regularly raid the public treasury on behalf of rich clients? What democratic mandate directed the government to give away more monies every year to

the top 1 percent of the population, in interest payments on public bonds, `
than are spent on services to the bottom 20 percent? When was the public
consulted on Alaskan oil leases, interest rates, and agribusiness subsidies?
When did the public insist on having unsafe, overpriced drugs and genetically altered foods and a Food and Drug Administration (FDA) that protects rather than punishes the companies that market them? When did the
American people urge the government to go easy on polluters and allow
the utility companies to overcharge consumers? When did the voice of the
people clamor for unsafe work conditions in mines, factories, and on farms?
How often have the people demonstrated for multibillion-dollar tax breaks
for the superrich and a multibillion-dollar space shuttle that destroys the
ozone layer and leaves us more burdened by taxes and deprived of necessary
services? When did the populace insist that the laws of the land could
be overruled by a nonelective three-member World Trade Organization
(WTO) panel in service to the transnational corporations? What democratic
will decreed that we destroy the Cambodian countryside between 1969 and
1971 in a bombing campaign conducted without the consent or even the
knowledge of Congress and the public? When did public opinion demand
that we wage a mercenary war of attrition against Nicaragua; or invade
Grenada and Panama; or slaughter 100,000 Iraqis; or occupy Somalia; or
support wars against popular forces in El Salvador, Guatemala, Angola,
Mozambique, the Western Sahara, and East Timor; or subvert progressive
governments in Chile, Indonesia, Yugoslavia, and a dozen other countries?

Far from giving their assent, ordinary people have had to struggle to find
out what is going on. And when public opinion has mobilized, it is in the opposite direction, against the worst abuses and most blatant privileges of plutocracy, against the spoliation of the environment, and against bigger
military budgets and armed interventions in other lands.[5]

Democracy as Class Struggle

The ruling class has several ways of expropriating the earnings of the people.
First and foremost, as *workers,* people receive only a portion of the value
their labor power creates. The rest goes to the owners of capital. On behalf
of owners, managers continually devise methods — including speedups,
downgrading, layoffs, the threat of plant closings, and union busting — to
tame labor and intensify the process of capital accumulation.

Second, as *consumers,* people are victimized by monopoly practices that
force them to spend more for less. They are confronted with increasingly exploitative forms of involuntary consumption, as when relatively inexpensive
mass-transit systems are eliminated to create a greater dependency on automobiles; or when low-rental apartments are converted to high-priced condominiums; or a utility company doubles its prices after deregulation.

Third, over the last thirty-five years or so, working people, as *taxpayers*, have had to shoulder an ever larger portion of the tax burden, while corporate America pays less and less. Indeed, the dramatic decline in business taxes has been a major cause of growth in the federal debt. As we have seen, the national debt itself is a source of income for the moneyed class and an additional burden on taxpayers.

Fourth, as *citizens* the people get less than they pay for in government services. The lion's share of federal spending goes to large firms, defense contractors, and big financial creditors. The public endures the hidden diseconomies shifted onto them by private business, as when a chemical company contaminates a community's air or groundwater with its toxic wastes, or when there is a general deterioration in the quality of life.

The existing system of power and wealth, with its attendant abuses and injustices, activates a resistance from workers, consumers, community groups, and taxpayers — who are usually one and the same people. There exists, then, not only class oppression but class struggle, not only plutocratic dominance but popular opposition and demands for reform.

There is a tradition of popular struggle in the United States that has been downplayed and ignored. It ebbs and flows but never ceases. Moved by a combination of anger and hope, ordinary people have organized, agitated, demonstrated, and engaged in electoral challenges, civil disobedience, strikes, sit-ins, takeovers, boycotts, and sometimes violent clashes with the authorities — for better wages and work conditions, a safer environment, racial and gender justice, and peace and nonintervention abroad. Against the heaviest odds, dissenters have suffered many defeats but won some important victories, forcibly extracting concessions and imposing reforms upon resistant rulers.

In 1999–2000, massive demonstrations composed of persons from various nations and all walks of life have been directed against the International Monetary Fund (IMF), the World Bank, and the WTO in cities in the United States, Europe, India, Australia, and elsewhere. At the local level, too, people have organized against the relentless incursions of the transnationals.[6]

Democracy is something more than a set of political procedures. To be worthy of its name, democracy should produce substantive outcomes that advance the well-being of the people. Many of the struggles for political democracy — the right to vote, assemble, petition, and dissent — have been largely propelled by the struggle for economic and social democracy, by a desire to democratize the rules of the political game so as to be in a better position to fight for one's socioeconomic interests. In a word, the struggle for democracy has been part of the class struggle against plutocracy.

Through the nineteenth and twentieth centuries, the moneyed classes resisted the expansion of democratic rights, be it universal suffrage, abolition, civil liberties, or affirmative action. They knew that the growth of popular rights would only strengthen popular forces and impose limits on elite privileges. They instinctively understood, even if they seldom publicly artic-ulated it, that it is not socialism that subverts democracy, but democracy that subverts capitalism.

The conservative agenda is to return to the days before the New Deal, to a country with a small middle class and an impoverished mass, when the United States was a "Third World" nation long before the term had been coined. As Paul Volcker said, when he was chair of the Federal Reserve, "The standard of living of the average American has to decline."[7] Wages are held down by forcing people to compete more intensely for work on terms increasingly favorable to management. Historically, this is done by (a) elimi-nating jobs through mechanization, (b) bringing immigrant labor into the country, and (c) investing in countries that offer cheaper labor markets and other favorable terms. In addition, in the 1980s the Republican administra-tion eased child-labor laws, lowered the employable age for some jobs, and raised the future retirement age, thus increasing the number of workers competing for jobs.

Another way to depress wages is to eliminate alternative sources of sup-port. The historical process of creating people willing to work for subsis-tence wages entailed driving them off the land and into the factories, denying them access to farms and to the game, fuel, and fruits of the com-mons. Divorced from this sustenance, the peasant became the proletarian. Today, unemployment benefits and other forms of public assistance are re-duced in order to deny alternative sources of income. Public jobs are elimi-nated so that more workers will compete for employment in the private sector, helping to depress wages. Conservatives seek to lower the minimum wage for youth and resist attempts to equalize wages and job opportunities for women and minorities, so keeping women, youth, and minorities as the traditional underpaid "reserve army of labor" used throughout history to de-press wages.

Still another way to hold down wages and maximize profits is to keep the workforce divided and poorly organized. Racism helps to channel the eco-nomic fears and anger of Whites away from employers and toward minori-ties and immigrants, who are seen as competitors for scarce jobs, education, and housing. When large numbers of workers are underpaid because they are Black, Latino, or female, this holds down the price of labor and in-creases profits.

When democratic forces mobilize to defend their standard of living, democracy proves troublesome to capitalism. So the ruling class must attack not only the people's standard of living but the very democratic rights that help them defend that standard. Thus, the right to strike and to bargain col-lectively come under persistent attack by both the courts and legislatures. The laws against minor parties are tightened and public funding of the two-party monopoly is expanded. Federal security agencies and elaborately equipped local police, abetted by the courts, repress community activists and weaken our right to protest. And U.S. leaders enter into a series of international trade agreements to bypass our democratic sovereignty altogether and secure an unchallengeable corporate supremacy.

The Roles of the State

The capitalist state is more than a front for the economic interests it serves; it is the single most important instrument that corporate America has at its command. The power to use police and military force, the power of eminent domain, the power to tax, spend, and legislate, to use public funds for private profit, to float limitless credit, to mobilize highly emotive symbols of loyalty and legitimacy, and to suppress political dissidents — such resources of the state give corporate America a durability it could never provide for itself. The state also functions to stabilize trade arrangements among giant corporations. Historically, "firms in an oligopolistic industry often turn to the federal government to do for them what they cannot do for themselves — namely, enforce obedience to the rules of their own cartel."[8]

The state is also the place where liberal and conservative ruling-class factions struggle over how best to keep the system afloat. The more liberal elements see that by granting democratic concessions to those who make and buy its products they can keep capitalism from devouring itself. If conservative goals are too successful, if wages and buying power are cut back too far and production increased too much, then the contradictions of the free market intensify and so do its self-destructive instabilities. Profits may be maintained and even increased for a time through various financial contrivances, but overcapacity and overproduction lead to economic collapse, unemployment grows, markets shrink, discontent deepens, and small and not so small businesses perish.

As the pyramid begins to tremble from conservative victories, some of the less myopic occupants of the apex develop a new appreciation for the base that sustains them. For the rightist free marketeers, however, if demand slumps and the pie does not expand as swiftly as before but the slice that goes to the owning class continues to grow, then the economy is "doing well." Furthermore, too much already has gone to the people and into the nonprofit sector. As the common lot of the citizenry advances, so do their expectations: from adequate wages to job security, from an eight-hour day to paid vacations, from job seniority to retirement pensions, from decent housing to home ownership, from public grade schools for their kids to affordable higher education, affordable medical care, good public services, and a clean environment. Every dollar spent on such things is one less dollar to be siphoned away by the corporate owners, as they are keenly aware.

The state must act to resolve problems at the international level. One way to ease the economic competition between capitalist nations is to destroy the competing capital of other countries either by underselling and driving them out of business as in much of the Third World, or by privatization and deindustrialization as in Eastern Europe and the former Soviet Union, or by sanctions and massive bombings of a country's industrial and ecological base as in Iraq and Yugoslavia. A state that has achieved world superpower status, such as the United States, has a special advantage in such aggrandizing stratagems, and is about the only one that can realistically entertain a global agenda.

The state best protects the existing class structure by enlisting the loyalty and support of the populace. To do so, it must maintain its own legitimacy in the eyes of the people. And legitimacy is preserved by keeping an appearance of popular rule and neutrality in regard to class interests. More important than the constraints of appearances are the actual power restraints imposed by democratic forces. There is just so much the people will take before they begin to resist. Marx anticipated that class struggle would bring the overthrow of capitalism. Short of that, class struggle constrains and alters the capitalist state, so that the state itself, or portions of it, become an arena of struggle.

Having correctly discerned that "American democracy" as professed by establishment opinion makers is something of a sham, some people incorrectly dismiss the democratic rights won by popular forces as being of little account. But these democratic rights and the organized strength of democratic forces are, at present, all we have to keep some rulers from imposing a dictatorial final solution, a draconian rule to secure the unlimited dominance of capital over labor.

The vast inequality in economic power as exists in our capitalist society translates into a great inequality of social power. More than half a century ago the Supreme Court Justice Louis Brandeis commented, "We can have democracy in this country, or we can have great wealth concentrated in the hands of a few, but we can't have both." And some years earlier, the German sociologist Max Weber wrote: "The question is: How are freedom and democracy in the long run at all possible under the domination of highly developed capitalism?"[9] That question is still with us. As the crisis of capitalism deepens, as the contradiction between the egalitarian expectations of democracy and the demoralizing thievery of the free market sharpens, the state must act more repressively to hold together the existing class system.

Why doesn't the capitalist class in the United States resort to fascist rule? It would make things easier: no organized dissent, no environmental or occupational protections to worry about, no elections or labor unions. In a country like the United States, the success of a dictatorial solution to the crisis of capitalism would depend on whether the ruling class could stuff the democratic genie back into the bottle. Ruling elites are restrained in their autocratic impulses by the fear that they could not get away with it, that the people and the enlisted ranks of the armed forces would not go along. A state that relies solely on its bayonets to rule is exposed as an instrument of class domination. It loses credibility, generates resistance rather than compliance, and ignites a rebellious and even revolutionary consciousness. Given secure profit margins, elites generally prefer a "democracy for the few" to an outright dictatorship.

Representative government is a serviceable form of governance for corporate America, even if often a troublesome one, for it offers a modicum of liberty and self-rule while masking the class nature of the state. Rather than relying exclusively on the club and the gun, bourgeois democracy employs a cooptive, legitimating power — which is ruling-class power at its most hypocritical and most effective. By playing these contradictory roles of protector of capital and "servant of the people," the state best fulfills its fundamental class role.

What is said of the state is true of the law, the bureaucracy, the political parties, the legislators, the universities, the professions, and the media. In order to best fulfill their class-control functions yet keep their social legitimacy, these institutions must maintain the appearance of neutrality and autonomy. To foster that appearance, they must occasionally exercise some critical independence and autonomy from the state and from capitalism. They must save a few decisions for the people, and take minimally corrective measures to counter some of the many egregious transgressions against democratic interests.

What Is to Be Done?

Here are some of the things that need to be done to bring us to a more equitable and democratic society:

Reform the electoral system. To curb the power of the moneyed interests and lobbyists, minor-party as well as major-party candidates should be provided with public financing. In addition, a strict cap should be placed on campaign spending by all candidates and supporters, with no loopholes allowed. The various states should institute proportional representation so that every vote will count and major parties will no longer dominate the legislature with artificially inflated majorities. Also needed is a standard federal electoral law allowing uniform and easy ballot access for third parties and independents. We should also abolish the electoral college to avoid artificially inflated majorities that favor the two-party monopoly and undermine the popular vote.

Encourage voter participation by having (a) more accessible polling and registration sites in low-income areas; (b) an election on an entire weekend instead of a workday (now usually Tuesday) so that persons who travel long distances and work long hours will have sufficient opportunity to get to a polling place; (c) ballots that do not confuse voters or lead to fraudulent counts; (d) federal protection against attempts by local authorities to suppress or intimidate voters, as was done by Republican officials in Florida during the stolen election of 2000.

The District of Columbia should be granted statehood by Congress. As of now its 607,000 citizens are denied full representation in Congress and genuine self-rule. They elect a mayor and city council but Congress and the president retain the power to overrule all the city's laws and budgets. Washington, D.C., remains one of the U.S. government's internal colonies.

Democratize the judiciary. Do away with oligarchic court power and lifetime judgeships, and wage a vigorous criticism of conservative judicial activism. According to one poll, 91 percent of the citizenry want the terms of all federal judges to be limited.[10]

Democratize the media. The airwaves are the property of the U.S. people. As part of their public-service licensing requirements, television and radio stations should be required to give — free of charge — public air time to all political viewpoints, including dissident and radical ones. The media should be required to give equal time to all candidates, not just Democrats and Republicans. Free air time, say, an hour a week for each party in the month before election day, as was done in Nicaragua, helps level the playing field and greatly diminishes the need to raise large sums to *buy* air time. In campaign debates, the candidates should be questioned by representatives from labor, peace, consumer, environmental, feminist, civil rights, and gay rights groups, instead of just fatuous media pundits who are dedicated to limiting the universe of discourse so as not to give offense to their corporate employers.

Cut military spending and accelerate peacetime conversion. The military spending binge of the last two decades is the major cause of the enormous national debt, the decaying infrastructure, and crushing tax burden. Military spending has transformed the United States from the world's biggest lender into the world's biggest debtor nation. To save hundreds of billions of dollars each year, we should cut the bloated, wasteful, and destructive "defense" budget by two-thirds over a period of a few years. The Pentagon now maintains a massive nuclear arsenal and other strike forces designed to fight a total war against another superpower, the Soviet Union, that no longer exists. To save additional billions each year and cut down on the damage done to the environment, the United States should stop all nuclear tests, including underground ones, and wage a diplomatic offensive for a nuclear-free world.

Washington also could save tens of billions of dollars if it stopped pursuing armed foreign interventions. "Power Projection" forces and most of the navy's carrier battle groups could be eliminated with no loss of national security, along with the U.S. Central Command (formerly the Rapid Deployment Force).

The depressive economic effects of ridding ourselves of a war economy could be mitigated by embarking upon a massive conversion to a peace economy, putting the monies saved from the military budget into human services and domestic needs. The shift away from war spending would improve our quality of life and lead to a healthier overall economy.

Abolish the CIA and the national security state. Congress should eliminate all national security agencies, since they do little to enhance our national security, their goal being to make the world safe for the Fortune 500. Prohibit covert actions against anticapitalist social movements. End U.S.-sponsored counterinsurgency wars against the poor of the world. Eliminate all foreign aid to regimes engaged in oppressing their own peoples. The billions of U.S. tax dollars that flow into the Swiss bank accounts of foreign autocrats and militarists could be better spent on human services at home. Lift the trade sanctions imposed on Cuba, Iraq, and other countries that have dared to deviate from the free-market orthodoxy.

The Freedom of Information Act should be enforced instead of undermined by those national security flacks who say they have nothing to hide, then try to hide almost everything they do.

Economic reform. Reintroduce a steeper progressive income tax for rich individuals and corporations — without the many loopholes and deductions that still exist. Strengthen the inheritance tax instead of eliminating it, but with dispensations for small farmers and other small propertyholders. Give tax relief to the working poor and other low-income employees. At present, corporations have more rights than do citizens. They should be rechartered to limit their powers and make them subordinate to popular sovereignty. As was the case in the nineteenth century, corporations should be reduced to smaller units with employee and community control panels to protect the public's interests. They should be prohibited from owning stock in other corporations, and granted charters only for limited times, such as twenty or thirty years, and for specific business purposes, charters that can be revoked by the government for cause. Company directors should be held criminally liable for corporate malfeasance and for violations of occupational safety, consumer, and environmental laws.

Reform labor law. Abolish anti-labor laws like Taft-Hartley. Provide government protections to workers who now risk their jobs when they try to organize. Prohibit management's use of permanent replacement scabs for striking workers. Penalize employers who refuse to negotiate a contract after certification has been won. Repeal the restrictive "right to work" and "open shop" laws that undermine collective bargaining. Lift the minimum wage to a livable level. In California, Minnesota, and several other states, there are "living wage movements" that seek to deny contracts and public subsidies to companies that do not pay their workers a living wage.[11] Repeal the North American Free Trade Agreement (NAFTA) and the General Agreement on Tariffs and Trade (GATT), which place national sovereignty in the hands of nonelective, secretive, international tribunals that can over-

rule the pro-labor, environmental, and consumer laws of any federal or state government, and further undermine living standards throughout the world.

Reform Social Security. But do it in a progressive direction by cutting 2 percent from the current 12.4 percent Social Security flat tax rate, and offset that lost revenue by eliminating the cap on how much income can be taxed. At present, earnings of more than $76,200 are exempt from FICA withholding tax. This change would give an average working family a $700 tax relief and would reverse the trend that has been reducing taxes for the wealthy while raising FICA payroll taxes for the rest of us. Eliminate offshore tax shelters and foreign tax credits for transnational corporations, thereby bringing in over $100 billion in additional revenues. And put a cap on corporate tax write-offs for advertising, equipment, and CEO stock options and perks.[12]

Improve agriculture and ecology. Distribute to almost two million needy farmers the billions of federal dollars now handed out to rich agribusiness firms. Encourage organic farming and phase out the use of pesticides, chemical fertilizers, hormone-saturated meat products, and genetically modified crops. Stop the agribusiness merger mania that now controls almost all of the world's food supply. Agribusiness conglomerates like Cargill and Continental should be broken up or nationalized.

Engage in a concerted effort at conservation and ecological restoration, including water and waste recycling and large-scale composting of garbage. Phase out dams and nuclear plants, and initiate a crash program to develop thermal, tidal, and solar-energy sources, along with a massive cleanup of the land, air, and water, and programs to protect wildlife and restore damaged coastal areas. Decentralized production of solar energy should be subsidized by federal, state, and local governments. It would bring thousands of new jobs to communities that would no longer have to pay out hundreds of millions of dollars every year to transnational oil and gas cartels.[13]

Develop rapid mass transit systems within and between cities for safe, economical transportation, and develop zero-emission vehicles to minimize the disastrous ecological effects of fossil fuels. Ford had electric cars as early as the 1920s. If research and development had continued, by now we would have affordable and proficient electric vehicles. As it is, Stanford Ovshinsky, president of Energy Conversion Devices, claims that a newly developed electric car now has a long driving range on a battery that lasts a lifetime, uses environmentally safe materials, is easily manufactured, with operational costs that are far less than a gas-driven car — all reasons why the oil and auto industries are not supportive of electric cars.[14]

Improve health care and safety. Institute a "Universal Medicare" that would allow all Americans to receive coverage similar to the Medicare now enjoyed by seniors, but a coverage that includes alternative medicines such as herbal treatments, acupuncture, homeopathy, and chiropractic. People of working age would contribute a sliding scale portion of the premium through payroll deductions or estimated tax payments for the self-employed, and employers would match those payments dollar for dollar. Or funding might come from the general budget as in the single-payer plan used in Canada and elsewhere, providing comprehensive service to all. There is no reason to spend tens of billions more on health-care insurance (as proposed by President Clinton) when we already expend vastly more per capita than any other nation. Under single-payer health care, the billions of dollars that go as profits to health maintenance organization (HMO) executives and stockholders would be used for medical treatment.

Thousands of additional federal inspectors are needed for the various agencies responsible for the enforcement of occupational safety and consumer protection laws. "Where are we going to get the money to pay for all this?" one hears. The question is never asked in regard to the gargantuan defense budget or enormous corporate subsidies. As already noted, we can get the additional funds from a more progressive tax system and from major cuts in big business subsidies and military spending.

Revise fiscal policy. The national debt is a transfer payment from taxpayers to bondholders, from labor to capital, from have-nots and have-littles to have-it-alls. Government could end deficit spending by taxing the financial class from whom it now borrows. It must stop bribing the rich with investment subsidies and other guarantees, and redirect capital investments toward not-for-profit public goals. The U.S. Treasury should create and control its own money supply instead of allowing the Federal Reserve and its private bankers to pocket billions every year while creating a privatized money supply.

Eliminate gender, racial, and political injustice. End racial and gender discriminatory practices in all institutional settings, including the law and the courts themselves. Vigorously enforce the law to protect abortion clinics from vigilante violence, women from male abuse, children from adult abuse, homosexuals and minorities from police brutality and hate crimes. Release the hundreds of dissenters who are serving long prison terms on trumped-up charges and whose major offense is their anticapitalism. And release the thousands who are enduring astronomical incarceration sentences for relatively minor drug offenses.

Improve employment conditions. Americans are working harder and longer for less, often without any job security. In 1960, a man who graduated from college with a C average could earn enough to buy a three-bedroom house and support a wife and three children. Today in many parts of the country it takes two childless adults working full time to afford rent on a one-bedroom apartment.[15] We should initiate a thirty-six-hour work week with no cut in pay. Many important vital services are needed, and many people need work. A Works Progress Administration (WPA), more encompassing than the one created during the New Deal, could employ people to reclaim the environment, build affordable housing and mass transit systems, rebuild a crumbling infrastructure, and provide services for the aged and infirm and for the public in general.

People could be put to work producing goods and services in competition with the private market. The New Deal's WPA engaged in the production of goods, manufacturing clothes and mattresses for relief clients, surgical gowns for hospitals, and canned foods for the jobless poor. This kind of not-for-profit public production to meet human needs brings in revenues to the government both in the sales of the goods and in taxes on the incomes of the new jobs created. Eliminated from the picture is private profit for those who live off the labor of others — which explains their fierce hostility toward government attempts at direct production.

The Reality of Public Production

None of the measures listed above will prevail unless the structural problems of capitalism are themselves resolved. What is needed then is public ownership of the major means of production and public ownership of the moneyed power itself — in a word, socialism.

But can socialism work? Is it not just a dream in theory and a nightmare in practice? Can the government produce anything of worth? As mentioned in an earlier chapter, various private industries (defense, railroads, satellite communication, aeronautics, the Internet, and nuclear power, to name some) exist today only because the government funded the research and development and provided most of the risk capital. Market forces are not a necessary basis for scientific and technological development. The great achievements of numerous U.S. university and government laboratories during and after World War II were conducted under conditions of central federal planning and not-for-profit public funding. We already have some socialized services and they work quite well when sufficiently funded. Our roads and some utilities are publicly owned, as are our bridges, ports, and airports. In some states so are liquor stores, which yearly generate hundreds of millions of dollars in state revenues.

There are credit unions and a few privately owned banks, like the Community Bank of the Bay (Northern California), whose primary purpose is to make loans to low- and middle-income communities. We need public banks that can be capitalized with state funds and with labor union pensions that are now in private banks. The Bank of North Dakota is the only bank wholly owned by a state. In earlier times it helped farmers who were being taken advantage of by grain monopolies and private banks. Today, the Bank of North Dakota is one of the leading lenders of student loans in the nation and an important source of credit for farmers, small businesses, and local governments. Other states have considered creating state banks, but private banking interests have blocked enactment.

Often unnoticed is the "third sector" of the economy, consisting of more than 30,000 worker-run producer cooperatives and thousands of consumer cooperatives, 13,000 credit unions, nearly 100 cooperative banks, and more than 100 cooperative insurance companies, plus about 5,000 housing co-ops, 1,200 rural utility co-ops, and 115 telecommunication and cable co-ops. Employees own a majority of the stock in at least 1,000 companies.[16] Labor unions have used pension funds to build low-cost housing and to start unionized, employee-owned contracting firms.

There are also the examples of "lemon socialism," in which governments in capitalist countries have taken over ailing private industries and nursed them back to health, testimony to the comparative capacities of private and public capital. In France immediately after World War II, the government nationalized banks, railways, and natural resources in a successful attempt to speed up reconstruction. The French telephone, gas, and electric companies were also public monopolies. Public ownership in France brought such marvels as the high-speed TGV train, superior to trains provided by U.S. capitalism, and the Minitel telephone computer, a communication-information service far in advance of anything offered by AT&T or other private U.S. companies. The publicly owned railroads in France and Italy work much better than the privately owned ones in the United States (which work as well as they do because of public subsidies). The state and municipal universities in the United States are public and therefore "socialist" (shocking news to some of the students who attend them), and some of them are among the very best institutions of higher learning in the country. Publicly owned utilities in this country are better managed than investor-owned ones; and since they do not have to produce huge salaries for their CEOs and big profits for stockholders, their rates are lower and they put millions in profits back into the public budget.[17] Then there is the British National Health Service, which costs 50 percent less than our private system yet guarantees more basic care for the medically needy. Even though a Tory government during the 1980s imposed budget stringencies on British health care "in order to squeeze economies from the system at the expense of quality," a majority of Britons still want to keep their socialized health service.[18]

Free marketeers in various countries do what they can to undermine public services by depriving them of funds and imposing various restrictions. As the quality of the service deteriorates, they then claim that it "doesn't work" and they impose further cutbacks and eventually privatization.[19] Privatization usually is a bonanza for rich stockholders but a misfortune for workers and consumers. The 1987 privatization of postal services in New Zealand brought a tidy profit for investors, wage and benefit cuts for postal workers, and a closing of more than a third of the country's post offices. Likewise, the privatization of the telephone and gas industries in Great Britain resulted in dramatically higher management salaries, soaring rates, and inferior service.

A growing public sector is potentially a great danger to the free marketeers. Rightist governments rush to privatize because public ownership *does* work. Were the not-for-profit public sector to provide an ever expanding array of goods and services, what would be left for the private investor who profits from other people's labor?

Most socialists are not against personal-use property, such as a home, a plot of land, and private possessions, nor even small businesses if they are not used to exploit others. Nor are most against modest income differentials or special rewards to persons who make special contributions to society. Nor are they against having an industry produce a profit, as long as it is used for the needs of society. The benefits as well as the costs of the economy should be socialized.

There is no guarantee that a socialized economy will always succeed. The state-owned economies of Eastern Europe and the former Soviet Union suffered ultimately fatal distortions in their development because of (a) the backlog of poverty and want in the societies they inherited; (b) years of capitalist encirclement, embargo, invasion, devastating wars, and costly arms buildup; (c) excessive bureaucratization and poor incentive systems; (d) lack of administrative initiative and technological innovation; and (e) a repressive political rule that allowed little critical expression and feedback. At the same time, it should be acknowledged that the former communist states transformed impoverished countries into relatively advanced societies. Whatever else may be said about them, they achieved what capitalism cannot and has no intention of accomplishing: adequate food, housing, and clothing for all; economic security in old age; free medical care; free education at all levels; and a guaranteed income in countries that were never as rich as ours.

As the peoples in these former communist countries are now discovering, the "free market" means freedom mostly for those who have money and a drastic decline in living standards for most everyone else. With the advent of "free-market reforms," inflation diminished workers' real wages and dissolved their savings. Health and education systems deteriorated. Unemployment, poverty, beggary, homelessness, crime, violence, suicide, mental depression, and prostitution skyrocketed. By 70- and 80-percent majorities, the people in these newly-arrived free-market countries testify that life was better under the Communists. The breakup of farm collectives and cooperatives and the reversion to private farming has caused a 40-percent decline in agricultural productivity in countries like Hungary and East Germany — where collective farming actually had performed as well and often better than the heavily subsidized private farming in the West.[20]

Whether socialism can be brought about within the framework of the existing modern capitalist state or by a revolutionary overthrow of that state is a question unresolved by history. So far there have been no examples of either road to socialism in modern industrial society. The question of what kind of public ownership we should struggle for deserves more extensive treatment than can be given here. American socialism cannot be modeled on the former Soviet Union, China, Cuba, or other countries with different historical, economic, and cultural developments. But these countries ought to be examined so that we might learn from their accomplishments, problems, failures, and crimes. Our goal should be an egalitarian, communitarian, environmentally conscious socialism, with a variety of participatory and productive forms, offering both security and democracy.

What is needed to bring about fundamental change is widespread organizing not only around particular issues but for a movement that can project both the desirability of an alternative system and the possibility and indeed the great necessity for democratic change. There is much evidence — some of it presented in this book — indicating that Americans are well ahead of political leaders in their willingness to embrace new alternatives, including public ownership of the major corporations and worker control of production. With time and struggle, as the possibility for progressive change becomes more evident and the longing for a better life grows stronger, we might hope that people will become increasingly intolerant of the monumental injustices of the existing free-market system and will move toward a profoundly democratic solution. Perhaps then the day will come, as it came in social orders of the past, when those who seem invincible will be shaken from their pinnacles.

There is nothing sacred about the existing system. All economic and political institutions are contrivances that should serve the interests of the people. When they fail to do so, they should be replaced by something more responsive, more just, and more democratic. Marx said this, and so did Jefferson. It is a revolutionary doctrine, and very much an American one.

Notes

1. For classic pluralist statements, see Earl Latham, *The Group Basis of Politics* (Ithaca, N.Y.: Cornell University Press, 1952); Robert Dahl, *Who Governs?* (New Haven, Conn.: Yale University Press, 1961).

2. Max Lerner, *America as a Civilization* (New York: Simon & Schuster, 1957), 398.

3. Dahl, *Who Governs?*, 272. Also see Robert Dahl, *Modern Political Analysis* (Englewood Cliffs, N.J.: Prentice Hall, 1970).

4. On the murder of John Kennedy, see the citations in Chapter 10. See also Philip Melanson, *The Martin Luther King Assassination* (New York: Shapolsky, 1991); Mark Lane and Dick Gregory, *Murder in Memphis: The FBI and the Assassination of Martin Luther King* (New York: Thunder Mouth, 1993); Baba Zak A. Kondo, *Conspiracys: Unravelling the Assassination of Malcolm X* (Washington, D.C.: Nubia, 1993); Karl Evanzz, *The Judas Factor: The Plot to Kill Malcolm X* (New York: Thunder Mouth, 1992); George Breitman et al., *The Assassination of Malcolm X* (New York: Pathfinder, 1976).

5. The Gulf War against Iraq did stir jingo fervor once it began. But up to the eve of hostilities, despite the relentless interventionist propaganda hype of the major media, a majority of the U.S. public favored a diplomatic settlement rather than military engagement.

6. Makani Themba, *Making Policy, Making Change: How Communities Are Taking the Law into Their Own Hands* (Oakland: Chardon, 1999); Center for Public Integrity, *Citizen Muckraking: How to Investigate and Right Wrongs in Your Community* (Monroe, Maine: Common Courage, 2000); *Not for Sale!*, newsletter of Center for Commercial-Free Public Education, Spring 2000.

7. *Washington Post*, March 9, 1980.

8. Frank Kofsky, *Harry S. Truman and the War Scare of 1948* (New York: St. Martin's, 1993), 190.

9. Brandeis quoted in David McGowan, *Derailing Democracy* (Monroe, Maine: Common Courage, 2000), 42; also H. H. Gerth and C. Wright Mills (eds.), *From Max Weber: Essays in Sociology* (New York: Oxford University Press, 1958).

10. Survey by the *National Law Journal*, reported in *People's Daily World*, September 12, 1986.

11. James Ridgeway, "Mondo Washington," *Village Voice*, June 27, 2000.

12. Bernard Sanders, *Outsider in the House* (New York and London: Verso, 1997), 207–9.

13. See Daniel M. Berman and John T. O'Connor, *Who Owns the Sun? Preparing for the New Solar Economy* (White River Junction, Vt.: Chelsea Green, 1996).

14. Correspondence, *New York Times*, July 20, 1993.

15. *Nation*, January 17, 1994.

16. Christopher Gunn and Hazel Dayton Gunn, *Reclaiming Capital: Democratic Initiatives and Community Development* (Ithaca, N.Y.: Cornell University Press, 1991); PBS brochure for *Livelyhood*, documentary series on work in America with Will Durst, 1999.

17. Martin Espinoza, "The Public Power Advantage," *San Francisco Bay Guardian*, August 19, 1992, 19–23.

18. *New York Times*, June 3, 1987.

19. See, for instance, Tor Wennerberg, "Undermining the Welfare State in Sweden," *Z Magazine*, June 1995.

20. See Michael Parenti, *Blackshirts and Reds: Rational Fascism and the Overthrow of Communism* (San Francisco: City Lights, 1997), chapters 6 and 7; and Parenti, *To Kill a Nation: The Attack on Yugoslavia* (New York and London: Verso, 2000), chapters 18 and 19.

Cartoon Acknowledgments

Page 10: Dana Fradon. Copyright © The New Yorker Collection, 1979. Dana Fradon from <cartoonbank.com>. All rights reserved. Originally published in *The New Yorker,* February 9, 1979, p. 32. Reprinted by permission.

Page 18: Fred Wright. Copyright © Wright/UE News Service. Reprinted by permission.

Page 22: Jeff MacNelly. Copyright © Tribune Media Services, Inc. All rights reserved. Reprinted with permission.

Page 30: Andrew B. Singer. Copyright © 1995 Andrew B. Singer. From *Z Magazine,* July/August 1997, p. 61. Reprinted by permission.

Page 34: Donald Reilly. Copyright © The New Yorker Collection, 1974. Donald Reilly from <cartoonbank.com>. All rights reserved. Originally published in *The New Yorker,* June 3, 1974, p. 46. Reprinted by permission.

Page 50: Tom Meyer. Copyright © San Francisco Chronicle. Reprinted by permission.

Page 56: Clay Bennett. From *Extra!,* November–December 1995, p. 6. Copyright © 1995 Bennett/North America Syndicate. Reprinted by permission.

Page 69: Herblock. From the *Washington Post.* Copyright © 1985 Herblock. Reprinted by permission.

Page 78: Charles Barsotti. Copyright © The New Yorker Collection, 1998. Charles Barsotti from <cartoonbank.com>. All rights reserved. Originally published in *The New Yorker,* April 27–May 4, 1998. Reprinted by permission of United Media.

Page 87: Johnny Hart. "B.C." By permission of Johnny Hart and Creators Syndicate, Inc. All rights reserved.

Page 99: Etta Hulme. From the *Fort Worth Star-Telegram.* Copyright © 1995 by Etta Hulme/*Fort Worth Star Telegram.* Reprinted by permission of Newspaper Enterprise Association, Inc.

Page 107: Jawn Kloss. Copyright © 1991 by Kloss. Reprinted by permission.

Page 111: Bill Schorr. From the *New York Daily News.* Copyright © 1998 by Bill Schorr. Reprinted by permission of United Features Syndicate, Inc.

Page 120: Carol Simpson. From *The People* (December 1997). Copyright © 1986 by Carol Simpson <carolsim@mos.com>. Reprinted by permission.

Page 128: Bruce Beattie. From *USA Today,* June 16, 2000. Copyright © 2000 by John Beattie/ Copley News Service. Reprinted by permission.

Page 144: Herblock. From the *Washington Post.* Copyright © 1976 Herblock. Reprinted by permission.

Page 153: Gary Huck. Copyright © huck/ue/huck-konopacki: cartoons. Reprinted by permission.

Index

Abbott, Dwight Edgar, 137 n. 57
abortion, 34–35, 129–30, 298–99,
    304 n. 69, 321
Abourezk, James, 239 n. 7
Abu-Jamal, Mumia, 145
Adams, Frank T., 65 n. 10
Adler, Ron, 115 n. 20
AFDC. *See* Aid to Families with
    Dependent Children (AFDC)
affirmative action, 299–300
African Americans
    in Congress, 218
    death penalty and, 127
    gerrymandering and, 201–2
    mass media portrayal of, 188
    New Deal and, 64
    poverty rates, 22–23
    racist law enforcement and, 132–34
    redistricting and, 201–2
    repression of, 143–45
    separate but equal doctrine and, 288
    Supreme Court and, 299–300,
        305 n. 77
    toxic waste near communities of,
        106–7
    voting and, 207–8
    welfare and, 96
African Peoples Socialist Party, 145
Agency for International Development
    (AID), 68
Agnew, Spiro, 227
agribusiness, 13, 26 n. 16, 112–13, 270,
    320
Agriculture (USDA), Department of,
    106, 114, 270, 275–76
Aid to Families with Dependent
    Children (AFDC), 96
Akre, Jane, 180
Albrecht, W. S., 135 n. 1
Alderman, Clifford Lindsey, 54 n. 10
Alderson, Jeremy Weir, 240 n. 39
Aldrich, Nelson, 277
Alger, Dean, 191 n. 1, 192 n. 4

Alien and Sedition Acts, 60–61, 289
Allen, James S., 65 n. 14
Alterman, Eric, 260 n. 14
alternative energy, 113
Altshuler, Alan, 216 n. 2
American Bar Association, 284
American Enterprise Institute, 168
American Express, 22
American Indian Movement, 147
American Renaissance, 244
Americans for Tax Reform, 225
Amnesty International, 125
Amy, Douglas, 216 n. 16
Anderson, Jack, 156
Anderson, Sarah, 26 n. 14, 177 n. 29
Andrews, Charles, 115 n. 20
Andrews, Louise, 160 n. 32, 160 n. 33
Anheuser-Busch, 203
Anti-Terrorism and Effective Death
    Penalty Act, 127
Antoine, Darlene, 133
Antoine, Max, 133
Appalachia, coal-mining companies in,
    17, 95
Aptheker, Herbert, 53 n. 3, 54 n. 9,
    54 n. 25
Arizona v. Fulminante, 294
Armstrong, Louise, 137 n. 57
Armstrong, Scott, 161 n. 68
Army Corps of Engineers, 112, 274, 275
Arnett, Peter, 186, 192 n. 30
Arnold, Michael William, 133
Aronson, Sidney, 53 n. 1, 53 n. 2, 176 n. 2
Arrington, Theodore, 261 n. 19
Ashley, Jane, 137 n. 61
Ashy, Joseph, 81
AT&T, 70, 203
Ayres, B. Drummond, 240 n. 47,
    240 n. 48

Bacon, David, 177 n. 13, 177 n. 17
Baez, Anthony, 133
Bailey, Britt, 26 n. 19, 117 n. 76

bailouts, 70–71
Baird, Sandra, 160 n. 32, 160 n. 33
Baker, Russ, 161 n. 55, 163 n. 91,
    239 n. 28
Bamford, James, 161 n. 56
Banc One Corp., 11
Banisar, David, 161 n. 58
Bank of America, 11
Bank of North Dakota, 322
Baraldini, Silvia, 146
Baran, Paul, 26 n. 29
Barber, Kathleen, 216 n. 17
Bari, Judi, 150
Barile, Pat, 25 n. 4
Barnouw, Eric, 192 n. 7
Bartlett, Donald, 79 n. 2, 79 n. 10
Basco, Sharon, 217 n. 36
Bass, Jack, 160 n. 37
Bass, Loretta, 217 n. 40
Bates, Eric, 115 n. 18
Baum, Judith, 216 n. 17
Beard, Charles, 49, 53 n. 4, 54 n. 9
Beck, Allen, 135 n. 21
Becker, Theodore Becker, 160 n. 21
Bedau, Hugo Adam, 136 n. 41
Begich, Nick, 92 n. 8
Bell, Herman, 145
Bellant, Russ, 41 n. 14, 162 n. 77
Benjamin, Phil, 115 n. 19
Bentsen, Lloyd, 167
Berg, Alan, 148
Berg, John C., 240 n. 36
Berger, Raoul, 261 n. 21
Bergman, Lowell, 180
Berman, Daniel M., 325 n. 13
Bernstein, Barton, 66 n. 30, 66 n. 31,
    66 n. 36
Bernstein, Carl, 192 n. 28
Bernstein, Dennis, 161 n. 52, 162 n. 85,
    239 n. 28
Bernstein, Irving, 66 n. 29
Bettmann, Otto L., 65 n. 3
BGH. *See* bovine growth hormone
    (BGH)
Bielski, Vince, 161 n. 52
Bilderberg Conference, 167
bill of attainder, 52
Bill of Rights, 51, 53

bioengineering, 112–13
biological warfare, 155
Bishop, Sanford, 201
Black, Don, 149
Black, Hugo, 62, 122, 289, 290
Black Liberation Army, 145
Black Men's Movement Against Crack,
    143
Blackmun, Harry, 296
Black Panther Party, 144–45, 147
Blackstock, Nelson, 159 n. 12
Blackwell, Savannah, 79 n. 13
Blau, Joel, 116 n. 38
Bleifuss, Joel, 115 n. 25
Blighton, Frank Harris, 66 n. 17
Blum, Howard, 162 n. 76
Blum, William, 93 n. 33, 94 n. 34, 160 n.
    20, 161 n. 64, 162 n. 74, 162 n. 81,
    192 n. 24, 192 n. 27
Blunk, Tim, 145–46
Boeing Aircraft, 83, 119, 223
Boesky, Ivan, 121–22
Bohemian Grove, 165
Bolles, Don, 148
Bomse, Audrey, 136 n. 33
Bonner, Robert, 156
Bottom, Anthony, 145
bovine growth hormone (BGH), 101–2,
    275
Boyer, Richard, 65 n. 4, 65 n. 5, 65 n. 6,
    65 n. 7, 66 n. 18, 66 n. 20, 66 n. 27,
    66 n. 29, 79 n. 1
Brady, Nicholas, 14
Brandeis, Louis, 315, 325 n. 9
Brandt, Daniel, 192 n. 28
Breggin, Peter, 137 n. 58
Brennan, William, 290
Brenner, M. Harvey, 27 n. 56
Brenner, Saul, 261 n. 19
Brewton, Peter, 79 n. 8, 162 n. 86
Bricker amendment, 259
Brinkley, David, 181
Brinkley, Joel, 239 n. 20
Broder, David, 181
Brodsky, David, 216 n. 16
Brody, Reed, 93 n. 34
Bronfenbrenner, Kate, 177 n. 13
Brower, Michael, 116 n. 46

Brown, Robert, 54 n. 10
Browning, Frank, 260 n. 9
Brownstein, Ron, 176 n. 7
Brown v. Board of Education, 292, 299,
  300
Bruno, Kenny, 116 n. 53
Buchanan, Pat, 184, 204
Buck, Marilyn, 146
budget, 76–77, 81
Burch, Philip, Jr., 176 n. 2, 176 n. 6
bureaucracy, 262–82
  action and inaction of, 272–74
  inefficiency, myth and reality of,
    262–65
  public authority given to private
    interests, 277–79
  secrecy and unaccountability of,
    269–71
  whistle-blowers in, 270–71
  See also government regulation
Bureau of Engraving and Printing, 278
Bureau of Indian Affairs, 147
Bureau of Intelligence and Research,
  151
Bureau of Reclamations, 275
Burger and Rehnquist Court rulings,
  292–93
Burnham, David, 135 n. 16, 159 n. 1,
  303 n. 43
Burroughs, Richard, 275
Burton, Dan, 124, 226–27
Bush, George H., 33, 76, 103, 155, 205,
  255
  appointment of corporate leaders to
    government posts, 167
  covert actions authorized by, 257
  on ecological safeguards, 108
  federal court orders ignored by, 256
  gerrymandering and, 202
  image of, 246
  Iran-contra scandal and, 158
  motor voter bill veto, 208
  New World Order, 244
  Supreme Court appointments, 285
  Team 100, 244
Bush, George W., 48, 204–5, 209–10,
  251, 297–98
Bush, Jeb, 209, 210

Business Roundtable, 221, 223
Byrd, Harry, 250

Cagan, Joanna, 79 n. 10
Cahill, Tom, 136 n. 29
campaign finance, 203–6
  contribution limits, 204
  laws, 194
  in presidential elections, 204–5
  third parties and, 203
  See also elections
Camus, Albert, 5
Canada
  ban on MMT, 175
  communists in, 140
  single-payer automobile insurance
    program, 174
  single-payer health care program, 100
Canham-Clyne, John, 79 n. 4
capitalism
  democracy and, 39–40
  nature of, 25 n. 3
  owning class versus employee class,
    6–8
  pursuit of profits, 8–9
  states' role in, 314–16
  unemployment and, 19–20
  See also corporations
Carp, Robert, 302 n. 7
Carter, Jack, 137 n. 57
Carter, Jimmy, 3, 167, 214, 245, 251
Carthan, Eddie, 143
Carvajal, Doreen, 26 n. 40
Casolaro, Danny, 149
Casper, Lynn, 217 n. 40
caucus, 240 n. 35
Caute, David, 159 n. 18
Cavanaugh, John, 26 n. 14, 177 n. 29
caveat emptor, 58
CCC. *See* Civilian Conservation Corps
  (CCC)
CED. *See* Committee for Economic
  Development (CED)
census, 202
Center for Cuban Studies, 147
Central Intelligence Agency (CIA), 12,
  70, 93 n. 32, 139, 151, 230–31
  biological warfare program, 155

Central Intelligence Agency (CIA)
(continued)
crimes of, 152–57
domestic surveillance by, 152
drug trafficking and, 156
elimination of, 318
infiltration of dissenting
organizations, 152
mass media and, 152, 186
mind-control projects of, 152
savings-and-loan swindles, 156
centrists, ideology of, 35
CFCs. See chlorofluorocarbons (CFCs)
CFR. See Council on Foreign Relations
(CFR)
Charns, Alexander, 303 n. 40
Chase Manhattan Bank, 11, 22, 165–6
Chatterjee, Pratap, 116 n. 42, 162 n. 88
Checchi, Al, 203
Cheney, Dick, 34
Cherney, Darryl, 150
Chevron, 71
children
confined to psychiatric wards, 131
crime and, 130–31
physical abuse of, 130
sexual abuse of, 131
victimization of, 130–31
chlorofluorocarbons (CFCs), 109
Chong Choe, 137 n. 62
Chossudovsky, Michel, 135 n. 4
Christian Coalition, 226
Christopher, Neil, 115 n. 31
Chrysler, 20, 70
church and state, separation of, 294
Churchill, Ward, 159 n. 12, 160 n. 27,
160 n. 38, 161 n. 53
CIA. See Central Intelligence Agency
(CIA)
CIO. See Congress of Industrial
Organizations (CIO)
Cirino, Robert, 192 n. 6
Cisco Systems, 73
Citibank, 166, 179
Civilian Conservation Corps (CCC), 63
civil rights, 299–300
Civil Rights Act of 1957 and 1960, 207
Clark, Charles, 26 n. 40

Clark, Ramsey, 94 n. 37
Clarke, Ben, 193
class
bigotry, 32
interests upheld by Supreme Court,
286–88
states' role in protecting structure,
315
wealth and, 6–8
Clayton, Eva, 201
Clean Air Act, 110, 172, 272
Clean Election Act, 206
Clinton, Bill, 19, 75, 76, 89, 90, 126,
226, 255, 259, 266
appointment of corporate leaders to
government posts, 167
automatic declassification of
documents, 269–70
on creating millionaires, 242
crime bill, 123
emergence as presidential candidate,
167–68
expansion of FISA, 140
image of, 246–48
lobbyists and, 223
mass transit funding, 105
military spending, 81, 82
modest background of, 165
New Prosperity, 244
pesticide laws, 110
public opinion and policy on Somalia,
215
reduction of federal bureaucracy,
273
Supreme Court appointments,
285–86
cloture petition, 233
Cloward, Richard, 66 n. 31, 66 n. 32,
217 n. 39, 217 n. 46
CNN, 186
Coalition on Occupational Safety and
Health, 225
Coast Guard, U.S., 111
Cobella, Nicholas, 135 n. 15
Coca-Cola, 12, 180
Cockburn, Leslie, 162 n. 82
code authorities, 62
Cohen, Jeff, 192 n. 20

Cointelpro. *See* counterintelligence program (Cointelpro)
Colangelo, Philip, 159 n. 8
Colburn, Theodore, 116 n. 47
Cole, Leonard, 281 n. 22
Coles, Robert, 41 n. 8
Colhoun, Jack, 162 n. 86
Collier, James, 217 n. 42
Collier, Kenneth, 217 n. 42
Collingsworth, Terry, 93 n. 27
Collins, Chuck, 25 n. 5, 25 n. 10, 25 n. 14
Colliver, Victoria, 25 n. 12
Colombia, 91
Committee for Economic Development (CED), 167
communism, 36, 140, 324
Communist party, 139
Communist Workers Party, 149
Community Bank of the Bay, 322
Comprehensive Test Ban Treaty, 230
Congress, 218–40
  campaign contributions for members of, 219
  changes needed for democracy in, 238
  Constitutional powers of, 43, 47
  corruption and, 225–28
  demographic representation of, 218–19
  ethics committees, 227
  fast-track legislation, 231–32
  fragmentation of power in, 229
  intelligence agencies and, 230–31
  legislative process in, 232–35
  lobbyists and, 221–25
  logrolling, 224
  national security state and, 230–31
  PACs and, 219–21
  as plutocracy, 226
  pork barrel appropriations, 229
  president and, 254–58
  progressive legislation and, 237–38
  public opinion and, 231
  seniority in, 229
  special interests, 228–30
  term limits, 235–36
  turnover in, 234–35

See also House of Representatives, U.S.; Senate, U.S.
Congress of Industrial Organizations (CIO), 62
Conkin, Paul, 66 n. 32
Conrail, 264, 309
conservatives, 33–35, 135
conspiracy theory of society, 308
Constant, Emmanuel, 154
Constitution
  amendments, 47, 54 n. 17, 60
  class interests of framers of, 49–52
  class power in early America and, 42–44
  as conservative document, 51
  containment of democracy and, 44–47
  fragmenting of majority power by, 47–49
  interests of property and, 45–46
  NAFTA and GATT violations of, 175–76
  progressive features of, 52–53
  slavery and, 46–47
Constitutional Convention, 42–43
Consumer Price Index (CPI), 21
Consumer Product Safety Commission, 274
Cook, Christopher, 115 n. 30
Coonrod, Robert, 184
cooperatives, 322
Cooperman, Edward, 148
Cordes, Helen, 117 n. 75
Corn, David, 116 n. 56, 161 n. 64, 162 n. 83
corporate state
  capitalism, 70
  early years, 55–56
  law in, 58–59
  New Deal and, 61–65
  in Progressive Era, 59–60
  Red Scares and, 61
  rise of, 55–66
  taxation in, 72–74
  World War I and, 60–61
corporate welfare, 67–70
corporations
  bailouts, 70–71
  concentration of, 11–12

corporations *(continued)*
environmental impact of, 106–8, 109,
111–14
government subsidies for, 67–70
interests upheld by Supreme Court,
286–88
purpose of, 8
repression by, 140
taxation of, 72–74
Third World labor markets and, 85–88
transnational, 171–72
See also capitalism
Corzine, Jon, 203
Council on Foreign Relations (CFR),
12, 165–67
counterintelligence program
(Cointelpro), 141
Countryman, Edward, 54 n. 20
Covington, Sally, 177 n. 10
Cox, John Stuart, 159 n. 16
CPI. *See* Consumer Price Index (CPI)
creationism, 294, 303 n. 42
Creaven, Jim, 93 n. 21
creeping socialism, 67
crime, 118–38
children and, 130–31
class law and, 122–23
corporate, 118–22, 134
domestic violence, 128–29
homosexuals and, 131–32
mass media coverage of, 183
penalties for corporations, 121–22
prisons, 125–26
racism and, 132–34
rate, 124
street, 118–22, 134
tough on crime craze, 123–24
violent, 124
war on drugs, 124
women and, 130
wrongful convictions, 126–28
See also legal system
Criner, Roy, 126
Croteau, David, 192 n. 14
Cummins, Eric, 136 n. 30
Cuomo, Mario, 143
Curry, Richard, 159 n. 6
Curzi-Laaman, Barbara, 145, 146

Dahl, Robert, 325 n. 1, 325 n. 3
Davidson, Deidre, 217 n. 36
Davis, James Kirkpatrick, 159 n. 9
Davis, L. J., 115 n. 17, 115 n. 22
Dayle, Dennis, 162 n. 84
DEA. *See* Drug Enforcement Agency
(DEA)
dead zones, 106
death penalty, 127–28, 296
Debs, Eugene Victor, 142, 215, 289
De Dios, Manuel, 148
Defense, Department of. *See* Pentagon
Defense Intelligence Agency (DIA),
151, 230–31
deficit spending, 76–77, 320–21
deLeon, Peter, 240 n. 34
Delgado, Richard, 177 n. 10
Dellums, Ron, 229
Del Monte, 13
deMause, Neil, 79 n. 10
democracy
capitalism and, 39–40
as class struggle, 311–14
Constitution and containment of,
44–47
defined, 39
as system of power, 40
Democratic party, 194–97
Dennis et al. v. United States, 289,
303 n. 21
deregulation, 265–69, 280
DIA. *See* Defense Intelligence Agency
(DIA)
Diallo, Amadou, 133
Diamond, Sara, 41 n. 13
Diamond, Sigmund, 161 n. 59
Dickerson, James, 159 n. 9
Dicks, Shirley, 136 n. 44
Dieter, Richard, 136 n. 40
Di Eugenio, James, 162 n. 87
DiGrazia, Robert, 134
Dillon, John, 161 n. 58
discretionary spending, 81
Disney, 71, 83, 86, 178, 180
Dodell, Leib, 192 n. 31
Dole, Robert, 219–20
Doman, Chaquita, 131
domestic violence, 128–29

Domhoff, G. William, 176 n. 2, 176 n. 3, 176 n. 4
Donner, Frank, 159 n. 10
Dor, Fritz, 160 n. 39
Dorman, William, 192 n. 13
Douglas, William, 289
Downgrading, 14–15
Downsizing, 14–15
Dred Scott v. Sandford, 287
Drexler, Millard, 12
Drug Enforcement Agency (DEA), 156, 274
Dugger, Ronnie, 217 n. 42
Duke, David, 35
Dumanoski, Dianne, 116 n. 47
Dunlea, Mark, 114 n. 7
DuPont corporation, 119, 231, 252
DuPont family, 12
Durenberger, David, 220
Durst, Will, 325 n. 16
Dushoff, Jonathan, 79 n. 4
Dusky, Lorraine, 136 n. 45
Dwyer, Jim, 136 n. 37

Easton, Nina, 176 n. 7
Eckert, Charles, 66 n. 25
economic sanctions, 31
education, 29–31, 102–3, 174, 266
Eighth Amendment, 294, 295
Eisenhower administration, 67
Eisner, Michael, 12
Eisnitz, Gail, 282 n. 32
Elderly, poverty and, 24
elections, 194–217, 296
    at-large, 210–11
    direct primary, 195
    Florida electoral controversy in 2000
        presidential, 48, 209–10
    gerrymandering, 201–2
    influence of money on, 205–6
    media campaigns, 195
    presidential, 48, 204–5
    proportional representation versus
        winner-take-all, 198–200
    punch-card voting systems, 208–9
    redistricting, 200–203
    reform, 206, 316–17
    third parties, 197–98, 203, 215

two-party monopoly, 194–98
voting rights, 207–11
voting turnout, 207–8, 211–14
See also campaign finance
electoral college, 261 n. 18
    2000 presidential election and, 48, 209–10
    as undemocratic anachronism, 250–51
Eli Lilly, 120
eminent domain, 58
employee class. *See* working class
Endangered Species Act, 110, 172
Energy, Department of, 85, 110, 112, 271
Energy Conversion Devices, 320
Ensign, Tod, 93 n. 24
Entman, Robert, 192 n. 19
environment
    air pollution, 107
    chemical farming and, 107–8
    conservation and ecological
        restoration, 320
    global warming, 108–9
    greenhouse effect, 108–9
    industry's impact on, 106–8
    ozone layer, 109
    population growth and, 106
    regulations, 108, 110–14
    water pollution, 107
Environmental Protection Agency
    (EPA), 112, 272–73, 274
EPA. *See* Environmental Protection
    Agency (EPA)
Epps, Garrett, 305 n. 80
ESF. *See* Exchange Stabilization Fund
    (ESF)
Espinoza, Martin, 136 n. 46, 326 n. 17
Espionage Act of 1917, 289
estate tax, 75
Estes, Ralph, 26 n. 14
Ethyl Corporation, 174–75
EU. *See* European Union (EU)
Eulau, Heinz, 217 n. 50
European Union (EU), 89
Evans, Linda, 145, 146, 149
Evans, Mark, 282 n. 38
Exchange Stabilization Fund (ESF), 255

excise tax, 79 n. 27
Exxon, 7, 17, 71, 73, 121, 252

factory farms, 102
Fainstein, Norman, 281 n. 20, 281 n. 21
Fainstein, Susan, 281 n. 20, 281 n. 21
Fair Deal, 244
Fair Labor Standards Act, 276
Fairness Doctrine, 189
Fairness Law, 189
Farm Credit System, 77
farming, 13, 107–8, 114, 275–76
Farrand, Max, 54 n. 13, 54 n. 19,
    54 n. 22, 302 n. 1
fast-track legislation, 231–32
FBI. *See* Federal Bureau of
    Investigation (FBI)
FCC. *See* Federal Communications
    Commission (FCC)
FDA. *See* Food and Drug
    Administration (FDA)
Federal Bureau of Investigation (FBI),
    149–50
Federal Communications Commission
    (FCC), 119, 189, 275
Federal Election Campaign Act, 198
Federal Election Commission, 198, 276
Federal Emergency Management
    Agency, 272
Federal Energy Regulatory
    Commission, 275
Federal Judiciary Committee, 284
Federal Reserve Bank, 278
Federal Reserve Board, 12
Federal Reserve System, 277–79
Federal Trade Commission (FTC), 274,
    275
feed efficiency, 102
Feinstein, Dianne, 203
fertilizer, recycled toxic waste as,
    111–12
Fessler, Daniel, 303 n. 30
Fetzer, James, 162 n. 87
Fifield, Adam, 114 n. 7
Fifteenth Amendment, 207
Fifth Amendment, 288
filibuster, 233
Financing Corporation, 77

Fine, Sidney, 65 n. 6
Finkelman, Paul, 54 n. 16
Firestone, 121
First, Bill, 225
First Amendment, 140, 286, 289–90,
    294, 302 n. 14, 303 n. 16
First Chicago, 11
First Nation People. *See* Native
    Americans
FISA. *See* Foreign Intelligence
    Surveillance Act (FISA)
Fitzwater, Marlin, 222
Fix, Michael, 27 n. 46
flat tax, 74–75
Florida, 2000 presidential election
    controversy, 48, 209–10
Flynn, Elisabeth, 137 n. 62
Fo, Dario, 140
Fogel, Chuck, 177 n. 11
Folkes, Lebert, 133
Foltz, Tom, 260 n. 16
Foner, Philip, 65 n. 5, 65 n. 7
Food and Drug Administration (FDA),
    101–2, 120, 225, 275, 311
food disparagement laws, 112–13
food stamps, 96
Forbes, Steve, 33, 205
Ford, Gerald, 158, 167, 227, 243, 245,
    251
Ford, Henry, 57
Ford Motor Company, 22, 119, 179,
    203
Foreign Intelligence Surveillance Act
    (FISA), 140
Form, William, 41 n. 8
Forster, Cindy, 161 n. 52
Fourteenth Amendment, 287–88, 293
Fourth Amendment, 140, 295
Fowles, Richard, 27 n. 56
France, Anatole, 39
France, socialism in, 322–23
François, Joseph Michel, 154
Frankenfood, 113
Frankfurter, Felix, 302 n. 2
FRAPH, 154
Freedom of Information Act, 273, 318
freedom of speech. *See* First
    Amendment

Freeman, Richard, 177 n. 21
free trade, 171, 172–76
Friedenberg, Daniel M., 53 n. 1
Friedman, George, 92 n. 7
Friedman, Lisa, 239 n. 16
Friedman, Meredith, 92 n. 7
Friedrichs, David, 135 n. 7
FTC. *See* Federal Trade Commission
   (FTC)

Gagnon, Bruce, 92 n. 7
Gallagher, Carole, 117 n. 67
Gallagher, Mike, 180
Galloway, Russell, 302 n. 3, 303 n. 24
Ganesan, Arvind, 94 n. 50
Gannett, 178
GAO. *See* General Accounting Office
   (GAO)
Garcia Marquez, Gabriel, 140
Garrison, Jim, 162 n. 87
Gates, Bill, 12
GATT. *See* General Agreement on
   Tariffs and Trade (GATT)
GDP. *See* gross domestic product
   (GDP)
Gelbspan, Ross, 116 n. 56, 117 n. 59,
   159 n. 17
General Accounting Office (GAO), 69,
   82, 237, 247, 256, 257, 268
General Agreement on Tariffs and
   Trade (GATT), 171–75, 258, 318
General Dynamics, 231
General Electric, 17, 112, 119, 178, 231
General Motors, 7, 71, 73, 104–5, 119,
   120, 179, 203
George, Susan, 93 n. 31
George W. Bush v. Al Gore, 297–98
Gergen, David, 184
Gerry, Elbridge, 45, 216 n. 19
gerrymandering, 201–2
Gerstner, Louis, 12
Gerth, Hans, 280 n. 1, 325 n. 9
Gervasi, Sean, 192 n. 28
Gervasi, Tom, 92 n. 1
Gettleman, Marvin, 94 n. 46
Gibbs, Lois Marie, 116 n. 42
Gilbarg, D., 239 n. 12
Gill, Stephen, 176 n. 6

Gillespie, Michael, 54 n. 24
Gilliard, Darrell, 135 n. 21
Gingrich, Newt, 34
Glazer, Myron Peretz, 281 n. 24
Glazer, Penina Migdal, 281 n. 24
Glendinning, Chellis, 117 n. 64
Glick, Brian, 159 n. 15
globalization, of trade, 171–76
global warming, 108–9
Goff, Stan, 239 n. 26
Gold, Hal, 162 n. 75
golden parachutes, 25 n. 12
Goldfield, Michael, 66 n. 35, 177 n. 14
Goldman, Benjamin A., 281 n. 22
Goldman, Ivan, 159 n. 11
Goldman, Sheldon, 302 n. 3, 302 n. 6
Goldstein, Robert J., 159 n. 18
Goldwin, Robert, 54 n. 6, 54 n. 21
Gonnerman, Jennifer, 136 n. 46,
   137 n. 48
Gonzalez, Henry, 219
Goodell, Charles, 302 n. 15
Goodman, Ellen, 217 n. 32
Goodsell, Charles, 280 n. 4
Goodstein, Eban, 116 n. 54
Gordon, David, 26 n. 22
Gore, Al, 48, 209–10, 242–43, 251,
   297
Gottlieb, Martin, 216 n. 17
Gould, Jay M., 281 n. 22
Gould, Robert, 117 n. 60
government
   corporate welfare and, 67–70
   deficit spending, 76–77
   as dual political system, 308–9
   efficient programs of, 263–65
   growing involvement in economic
      affairs, 64–65
   idealized version of, 1–2
   local, 71
   operating like a business, 263
   reform, limits of, 309–11
   as representative of privileged few, 2
   repression by agencies of, 139–42
   state, 71
   streamlining of, 266–67
   See also specific branches and
      agencies

government regulation
  agencies of, 274–77
  business opposition to, 280
  lack of, 276
  monopoly versus public-service,
    279–80
  See also bureaucracy
Grace, W. R., 120
Gramajo, Héctor, 154
grassroots lobbying, 224–25
Great Britain, nationalized health-care
  system in, 100, 323
Great Depression of 1930s, 61
Great Society, 244
Green, Mark, 240 n. 40
Greenhouse, Steven, 26 n. 22
greenhouse effect, 108–9
Greenspan, Alan, 247–48, 279
Greer, Jed, 116 n. 53
Gregory, Dick, 325 n. 4
Gregory, Thomas, 61
Grim, Anabel, 156
Griswold, Belinda, 138 n. 74
gross domestic product (GDP), 17
Grossman, Joel, 302 n. 4
Grossman, Karl, 92 n. 6, 117 n. 65
Grossman, Richard, 25 n. 7, 65 n. 10
Grossman, Steve, 160 n. 41, 160 n. 42
Gruber, Donald, 26 n. 18
Guinier, Lani, 247
Gunn, Christopher, 325 n. 16
Gunn, Hazel Dayton, 325 n. 16

Haar, Charles, 303 n. 30
Haddigan, Michael, 79 n. 14
Hall, Gus, 142
Hamilton, Alexander, 4, 45
Hampton, Fred, 147
Hampton, Fred, Jr., 144
Hancock, Graham, 93 n. 30
Hanrahan, John, 281 n. 15
Harris, Sheldon, 162 n. 75
Hartman, Chris, 25 n. 10, 25 n. 14
Hartung, William, 93 n. 29
hate crimes, 38
Hauck, Flannery, 41 n. 3
Haugaard, Lisa, 161 n. 64
Hayes, Ace, 161 n. 44

health care, 98–101, 320
health insurance, 99–101
Health Maintenance Organizations
  (HMOs), 100–101, 320
hedge funds, 71
Heineman, Kenneth, 160 n. 19
Held, Richard, 124
Helms, Jesse, 226
Helsinki accords, 140
Henwood, Doug, 26 n. 21, 114 n. 10
Herbert, Bob, 138 n. 73
Heritage Foundation, 168
Herman, Bernard, 54 n. 8
Herman, Edward, 26 n. 31, 92 n. 11,
  94 n. 51, 94 n. 52, 192 n. 22
Herrera, Leonel Torres, 127
Hersh, Seymour, 163 n. 91
Hetherly, Marian, 116 n. 49
Higham, Charles, 135 n. 2
Higham, John, 66 n. 21
Hightower, Jim, 180
Hill, Joe, 142
Hill, Steven, 216 n. 16, 216 n. 18
Himmelstein, David, 115 n. 13
Hispanics. *See* Latinos
Hitchens, Christopher, 92 n. 5
HMOs. *See* Health Maintenance
  Organizations (HMOs)
Hobbes, Thomas, 4
Hoffman, William, 94 n. 46
Holmes, Oliver Wendell, 289, 303 n.16
homelessness, 24, 104
homosexuals, crimes against, 131–32
Honey, Martha, 92 n. 4
Honeywell, 120
Hooper, John, 94 n. 42
Hoover, Herbert, 63
Hoover, J. Edgar, 141
Hope, Barbara Jean, 160 n. 35
Horowitz, David, 66 n. 23
Horowitz, Morton, 65 n. 11
House of Representatives, U.S., 12, 45,
  47, 48–49
  See also Congress; Senate, U.S.
housing, economic inequality in, 103–4
Housing and Urban Development
  (HUD), Department of, 103,
  270

HUD. *See* Housing and Urban
    Development (HUD), Department
    of
Hudson, Michael, 27 n. 44
Hudson Institute, 168
Huffington, Arianna, 137 n. 51
Hughes, Charles Evans, 284
Hughes, Harold, 221
Hughes, Howard, 221
Hughes, Laurie Jo, 177 n. 23
Hulin, Rodney, 125
human rights abuses, 91, 185
human services, 32, 95–98
Humphrey, Hubert, 221
hunger, 23–24
Hunt, Albert, 239 n. 16
Hunter, Jane, 163 n. 89, 163 n. 91
Hwang, Lucia, 114 n. 8
Hyde, Henry, 239 n. 28

IBM, 166, 179
ICBMs. *See* Inter-Continental Ballistic
    Missiles (ICBMs)
IMF. *See* International Monetary Fund
    (IMF)
Immigration and Naturalization Service
    (INS), 139, 140
imperialism, 91–92
individualism, 31–32
Industrial Workers of the World, 291
Industrial Workers of the World
    (IWW), 57
inflation, 15–16
inheritance tax, 75
INS. *See* Immigration and
    Naturalization Service (INS)
Intel, 7
Intelligence Oversight Board, 153
Inter-Continental Ballistic Missiles
    (ICBMs), 80
Interior, Department of, 112, 119
Internal Revenue Code, 73
Internal Revenue Service (IRS), 72,
    139, 268, 272
International Criminal Court, 90
International Monetary Fund (IMF),
    37, 70, 87–88, 146, 166, 312
Internet, 191

Iran-contra scandal, 158
Iraq, 89, 325 n. 5
IRS. *See* Internal Revenue Service
    (IRS)
Isuzu Motors, 122
ITT, 119
Ivins, Molly, 135 n. 15, 192 n. 5,
    239 n. 16, 281 n. 10

J. C. Penney, 86
J. P. Morgan, 11
Jackson, Andrew, 55
Jackson, Jesse, 208, 217 n. 44
Jagan, Cheddi, 153
Jamison, Kay Redfield, 27 n. 58
Janofsky, Michael, 27 n. 53
Javier Giraldo, S.J., 94 n. 49
Jay, John, 4
Jazz Age, 61
Jefferson, Thomas, 55, 325
Jencks, Christopher, 116 n. 36,
    281 n. 7
Jensen, Carl, 192 n. 15
Jensen, Merrill, 54 n. 7
Joffe, Josef, 92 n. 5
Johns-Manville Corporation, 120
Johnson, Becky, 116 n. 39
Johnson, Lyndon, 165, 244
Johnson, Ron, 177 n. 11
Johnston, David Cay, 79 n. 22
Jolly, Richard, 93 n. 25
Jonas, Susanne, 260 n. 13
Jones, Allen, 137 n. 57
Jones, Jacqueline, 41 n. 9
Jones, Michael A., 137 n. 67
Jordan, Michael, 178–79
Joseph, Joel, 304 n. 45
Josephson, Matthew, 65 n. 8, 65 n. 12,
    65 n. 13
Judson, Janis, 305 n. 78
junketing, 226
Justice, Department of, 118

Kairys, David, 303 n. 26
Kalb, Marvin, 181
Kaplan, Fred, 92 n. 1
Kaplan, Sheila, 239 n. 23
Katel, Peter, 160 n. 40

Kay, Jane Holtz, 116 n. 40, 116 n. 41
Kaye, Herb, 192 n. 10
Kazdin, Carolyn, 161 n. 46
Kean, Leslie, 162 n. 85, 239 n. 28
Keeran, Roger, 66 n. 35
Kellman, Peter, 302 n. 11
Kennedy, Anthony, 284
Kennedy, John F., 157, 244, 245, 250, 257, 278, 325 n. 4
Kiernan, Ben, 94 n. 47
King, Martin Luther, Jr., 141
Kinney, Joseph, 115 n. 29
Kirsh, David, 94 n. 43
Kissinger, Henry, 227
Klose, Kevin, 184
Knickerbocker Club, 165
Knight, Jerry, 282 n. 40
Knight-Ridder, 178
Kofsky, Frank, 79 n. 6, 325 n. 8
Kohn, Howard, 239 n. 9
Kohn, Stephen, 41 n. 17
Koistinen, Paul, 66 n. 19
Kolko, Gabriel, 66 n. 15, 66 n. 16, 66 n. 17, 66 n. 34
Koogle, Timothy, 12
Kozol, Jonathan, 41 n. 9, 115 n. 31
Krebs, A. V., 26 n. 17, 26 n. 18, 26 n. 19
Kruger, Henrick, 162 n. 81
Ku Klux Klan, 35, 149
Kurkeu, Ertugrul, 94 n. 39
Kurshan, Nancy, 137 n. 51
Kurt, Michael, 162 n. 87
Kurtz, Howard, 261 n. 20
Kutler, Stanley, 159 n. 6
Kuwait, 89
Kwitney, Jonathan, 192 n. 8

labor
  big business versus, 168–70
  condition of, 170–71
  law reform, 318–19
  mass media coverage of, 183
  New Deal and, 61–65
  strikes and law enforcement, 123
  war against, 56–57
  See also working class
Labor, Department of, 119

labor unions, 57, 168–70, 322
  benefits of, 170–71
  corporate view of, 168
  corruption in, 170
  prosperity and, 170–71
  recessions and, 170
  U.S. residents' view of, 169
La Guardia, Fiorello, 61
Lam Van Minh, 148
Lane, Mark, 162 n. 87, 325 n. 4
Lansing, Robert, 61
Lapham, Lewis H., 26 n. 24
Lappé, Marc, 26 n. 19, 117 n. 76
Larsen, Erik, 281 n. 26
Latham, Earl, 325 n. 1
Latinos
  poverty rates, 22–23
  racist law enforcement and, 132–34
  redistricting and, 201
  toxic waste near communities of, 106–7
  voting and, 207–8
  welfare and, 96
Lawrence, Ken, 161 n. 47
Lazare, Donald, 66 n. 25
leftists. *See* progressives
legal system
  class and, 122–23
  class-control function of police, 134
  corporate crime versus street crime, 118–22
  racism and, 132–34
  sexism and, 128–30
  wrongful convictions, 126–28
  See also crime
Legion of Justice, 149
legislative process, 232–35
Lehtinen, Ulla, 116 n. 47
lemon socialism, 322–23
Lenhart, Warren, 260 n. 6
Lens, Sidney, 65 n. 7
Lerner, Max, 325 n. 2
Levin, Jack, 41 n. 18
Levine, Mark H., 217 n. 43
Levine, Rhonda, 66 n. 26, 66 n. 30
Lewis, Anthony, 41 n. 15
Lewis, Jake, 25 n. 11
Lewis, Justin, 260 n. 15

Lieberman, Trudy, 27 n. 55, 114 n. 2
Lienesch, Michael, 54 n. 24
Lincoln, Abraham, 8
Lipscomb, Andrew, 65 n. 1
Lipset, Seymour, 217 n. 49
literacy, 24
lobbyists, 72–73, 221–25, 236
  corporate, 221
  foreign government-funded, 221
  grassroots, 224–25
  legislators as extensions of, 223
  lobbying bill and, 222–23
  money and, 222
  professional, 222
Lockard, Duane, 262–63, 280 n. 2
Locke, John, 4, 5 n. 1
Lockheed, 70
lockout, 169
Lofquist, William, 136 n. 41
logrolling, 224
Long, Russell, 234
Loory, Stuart, 161 n. 59
Louima, Abner, 133
Love, Alice Ann, 239 n. 22
Lowrey, Burling, 192 n. 13
Lozano, Rudy, 148
Lucas, Susan, 162 n. 78
Luce, Henry, 186
Ludlow Massacre of 1914, 57
Lugar, Richard, 75
Lumpe, Lora, 93 n. 16
Lutsky, Julia, 136 n. 28
Lydon, Christopher, 260 n. 9
Lynd, Staughton, 50, 54 n. 20

MacArthur, John R., 177 n. 25,
  177 n. 29
MacEwan, Arthur, 26 n. 28
Mackenzie, Angus, 161 n. 59
Madison, James, 4, 7, 44–45, 47, 51, 256
Main, Jackson Turner, 54 n. 24
Makover, Michael, 115 n. 20
Managers, 8
mandatory spending, 81
Manning, Jeane, 92 n. 8
Marathon Oil, 19
Marcos, Ferdinand, 150
market demand, versus need, 16

Marks, John, 161 n. 61
Marquez, Myriam, 114 n. 5
Marris, Jim, 162 n. 87
Marshall, John, 286, 302 n. 1
Marshall, Jonathan, 162 n. 82, 162 n. 84,
  163 n. 89, 163 n. 91, 260 n. 11
Marshall, Thurgood, 285
Marshall Plan, 166
Marx, Karl, 4, 7, 25 n. 3, 77, 284, 325
Mason, Colonel, 51
Massey v. Washington, 294–95
mass media, 178–93
  advertisers' influence on, 179–81
  alternatives, 189–91
  censorship of, 187–88, 191
  CIA and, 186
  consumer issues and, 181–82
  control of journalists, 180–81
  crime coverage, 183
  democratization of, 317
  electoral campaign coverage, 182–83
  entertainment sector of, 187–88
  expert guests, 183–84
  gender and ethnic portrayals in, 188
  government manipulation of, 184–87
  as ideological monopoly, 182–84
  journalistic responsibility of, 185
  labor coverage, 183
  lobbying power of, 179
  ownership of, 178–79, 191
  racism and sexism coverage, 183
  subpoenas issued to journalists, 187
mass transit, 105
May, Christopher, 66 n. 22
Mayer, Susan, 281 n. 7
Mazzocco, Dennis, 192 n. 4
McCarthy era, 142
McChesney, Robert, 193 n. 40
McClure, Laura, 115 n. 21, 216 n. 29
McCone, John, 166
McConnell, Grant, 282 n. 37
McCoy, Alfred, 162 n. 81, 162 n. 82
McDevitt, Jack, 41 n. 18
McDonald, Forrest, 53 n. 4
McDonald's, 15
McDonnell Douglas, 83
McGee, Joyce A., 135 n. 18
McGehee, Ralph, 161 n. 64

McGowan, David, 92 n. 4, 92 n. 7,
  136 n. 35, 137 n. 55, 137 n. 68,
  138 n. 71, 161 n. 63, 192 n. 17,
  325 n. 9
McHenry, James, 53
MCI WorldCom, 119
McKenzie, Richard, 117 n. 62
McKinley, A. E., 53 n. 2
McKinney, Cynthia, 201
McNally v. United States, 295–96
Meagher, Sylvia, 162 n. 87
meat industry, 122
Medicaid, 100, 101
medical industry, 100–101
Medicare, 100, 101, 225, 263, 320
medication, overpricing of, 101
Medoff, James, 177 n. 21
Meese, Edwin, 228
Mehler, Barry, 282 n. 36
Meier, Kenneth, 281 n. 13
Meiksins, Peter, 26 n. 35
Melanson, Philip, 325 n. 4
Mellon, Margaret, 115 n. 28, 117 n. 79
Mellon family, 12
mental illness, 24
Mercedes-Benz, 71
Mercer, John, 49
mergers, 11–12
Merit System Protection Board, 273
Merrill Lynch, 71
Merva, Mary, 27 n. 56
Messick, Hank, 159 n. 16
Meyers, John Peterson, 116 n. 47
microradio stations, 190, 191
Microsoft, 73, 203
middle class, 6–7, 9, 20–21
Mifflin, James, 161 n. 56
Mihelick, Stanley, 26 n. 33
Milan, Michael, 159 n. 16
military, the
  environmental impact of, 85, 110, 111
  global kill capacity of, 80–82
  interventionism and, 88–92
  occupational safety of personnel, 85
military spending
  compared to other government
    spending, 84
  creation of jobs and, 84

defense contractors and, 82, 83–84
  expansion of, 81
  inflation and, 16
  military pensions and, 83
  peacetime conversion and cuts in,
    317–18
  U.S. military aid, 86
  waste and fraud, 82–83
Milken, Michael, 121
Miller, James Nathan, 260 n. 10
Miller, John, 25 n. 8
Miller, Samuel F., 284
Miller, Tyisha, 133
Millpointer, Kate, 281 n. 22
Mills, C. Wright, 280 n. 1, 325 n. 9
Minor v. Happersett, 288
Minter, William, 176 n. 4, 176 n. 5
Mintz, Morton, 192 n. 18
Miranda rule, 294
Miroff, Bruce, 260 n. 8
Mitgang, Herbert, 159 n. 16
Mitofsky, Warren, 217 n. 39
Mittal, Anuradha, 114 n. 1
MMT (gasoline additive), 175
Mobil Oil, 71, 73, 179
Moix, Bridget, 93 n. 29
Mokhiber, Russell, 135 n. 10
Moldea, Dan, 177 n. 19
Mondale, Walter, 167
money primary, 204–5
monopolistic regulation, 279–80
Monsanto, 101–2, 112–13, 114, 180,
  275
Montgomery, David, 65 n. 5
Moore, Michael, 180
Morais, Herbert, 65 n. 4, 65 n. 5,
  65 n. 6, 65 n. 7, 66 n. 18, 66 n. 20,
  66 n. 27, 66 n. 29, 79 n. 1
Moran, Richard, 136 n. 27
Morgan family, 12
Morgan Guaranty Trust, 165, 179
Morris, Gouverneur, 43–44, 49
motor vehicles, environmental impact
  of, 105
motor voter bill, 208
Moynihan, Daniel Patrick, 226
Munro, Richard, 12
murder, 24

Murdoch, Rupert, 73, 179
Murray, Robert, 66 n. 22
Murray, Vernon, 160 n. 21
Myerson, Allen, 115 n. 15

Nadel, David, 149
Nader, Ralph, 29, 79 n. 4, 135 n. 14,
  173, 204, 255, 261 n. 26
Nadler, Eric, 303 n. 32
NAFTA. *See* North American Free
  Trade Agreement (NAFTA)
Naiman, Arthur, 79 n. 2, 79 n. 3, 79 n. 5,
  79 n. 11
NASA. *See* National Aeronautics and
  Space Administration (NASA)
Nason, Jeff, 161 n. 68
Nathan, Debbie, 137 n. 63
National Aeronautics and Space
  Administration (NASA), 268
National Association of Broadcasters,
  190
National Association of Manufacturers,
  223, 224
national debt, 76–77, 78, 320–21
National Highway Safety Act, 266
National Labor Relations Act (1935),
  64
National Labor Relations Board
  (NLRB), 64, 168–70
National Lawyers Guild, 142
National Public Radio (NPR), 189
National Reconnaissance Office (NRO),
  151
National Recovery Administration
  (NRA), 62
national sales tax, 75
National Security Act of 1947, 255
National Security Agency (NSA), 140,
  151, 230–31, 318
National Security Council (NSC), 151,
  228, 253
National Wetlands Coalition, 225
NationsBank, 11, 22
Native Americans, 30, 56, 58
  repression of, 147
  toxic waste near communities of,
    106–7
  voting and, 207

NATO. *See* North Atlantic Treaty
  Organization (NATO)
Navarro, Vicente, 26 n. 34
Nedelsky, Jennifer, 54 n. 17
need, versus market demand, 16
Nelson, Jack, 160 n. 37
Nelson, Sandy, 137 n. 63
Neruda, Pablo, 140
Neuborne, Burt, 303 n. 19
Neufeld, Peter, 136 n. 37
New Deal, 61–65, 244
New Federalism, 252
New Frontier, 244
New Prosperity, 244
New World Order, 244
New Zealand, privatization of postal
  service in, 323
Nineteenth Amendment, 207, 300
Nixon, Richard M., 157–58, 165, 227,
  235, 244, 245, 249, 255, 257
Nixon, Ron, 282 n. 31, 282 n. 35
Noriega, Manuel, 246
Norman, Carlos, 160 n. 32
Norris-La Guardia Act, 64
Norse, Robert, 116 n. 39
North American Free Trade Agreement
  (NAFTA), 171–72, 174–75, 232,
  247, 258, 318
North Atlantic Treaty Organization
  (NATO), 89
Norton, Augustus Richard, 94 n. 34
Novak, Robert, 34
NPR. *See* National Public Radio (NPR)
NRA. *See* National Recovery
  Administration (NRA)
NSA. *See* National Security Agency
  (NSA)
NSC. *See* National Security Council
  (NSC)
Nuccio, Richard, 271
nuclear power, 110–11
nursing homes, 100

O'Brien, Lawrence J., 115 n. 12
occupational safety, 102, 320
Occupational Safety and Health
  Administration (OSHA), 102, 264,
  274

O'Cleireacain, Carol, 261 n. 20
O'Connor, John T., 325 n. 13
off-budget deficit, 77
Office of Economic Opportunity, 273
Office of Management and Budget, 253
Office of Surface Mining, 272
Oklahoma City bombing, 150–51
Oliver, April, 186, 192 n. 30
Olivier, Jean-Claude, 160 n. 39
O'Melveny, Mary, 160 n. 33
Oraflex, 120
O'Reilly, Kenneth, 159 n. 9
Orphan Drug Act of 1983, 101
OSHA. *See* Occupational Safety and
    Health Administration (OSHA)
Ovshinsky, Stanford, 320
owning class, 6–8, 77
    See also ruling class
ozone layer, depletion of, 109

Pacifica network, 190
PACs. *See* political action committees
    (PACs)
Paley, William, 186
Pallone, Frank, 203
Panetta, Leon, 203
Parenti, Christian, 117 n. 61, 138 n. 71
Parenti, Michael, 25 n. 9, 41 n. 1, 41 n. 5,
    41 n. 6, 94 n. 35, 94 n. 40, 94 n. 41,
    94 n. 51, 94 n. 52, 160 n. 19,
    161 n. 46, 192 n. 25, 193 n. 33,
    193 n. 34, 193 n. 35, 281 n. 16,
    326 n. 20
Passell, Peter, 217 n. 35
Patterson, E. F., 135 n. 2
PBS. *See* Public Broadcasting System
    (PBS)
Peltason, Jack, 29
Peltier, Leonard, 145
Pentagon, 82, 83, 112, 151, 230–31
Pepper, William, 161 n. 60
Perkins, Dexter, 302 n. 5
Perlo, Victor, 25 n. 2
Pertshuk, Michael, 281 n. 29
Pessen, Edward, 65 n. 3
pesticides, 108, 110, 116 n. 51
Petras, James, 260 n. 14
PG&E, 71

pharmaceutical industry, 7, 70, 101, 173
Phillips, Michael, 79 n. 18
Pike, John, 161 n. 64
Pilger, John, 94 n. 47
Pinckney, Charles, 242
Pincus, Walter, 162 n. 83
Piven, Frances Fox, 66 n. 31, 66 n. 32,
    217 n. 39, 217 n. 46
Pizzigati, Sam, 25 n. 10, 217 n. 32
Plessy v. Ferguson, 288, 292
Plissner, Martin, 217 n. 39
Plowshares, 145
pluralism, 306–9
plutocratic culture, 28–41, 307
    in Congress, 226
    corporate aspects of, 28–29
    democracy in, 39–40
    ideological orthodoxy in, 29–33
    individualism and, 31–32
    political socialization, 29–31, 38
    public opinion and, 37–39
pocket veto, 233
Podhoretz, Norman, 33
Poe-Yamagata, Eileen, 137 n. 67
police, racism and, 133–34
political action committees (PACs), 204,
    219–21
political parties
    conservative effect on electorate, 206
    similarities between, 195–97
    third parties, 197–98, 203, 215
    two-party monopoly, 194–98
political prisoners, 142–47
political system, 2
politician, defined, 3
politico-economic system, 3–5
politics of happiness, 212
Pollina, Anthony, 206
pork barrel appropriations, 229
Porter, Kathryn, 27 n. 49
postal service, 267
Potomac Electric Power Co., 120–21
poverty, 21–24
    African Americans, 22–23
    children, 23
    elderly, 24
    Latinos, 22–23
    women, 23

Powell, Lewis, 290
power
defined, 4
democracy as system of, 40
fragmenting of majority, 47–49
wealth as, 11
PR. *See* proportional representation (PR)
Pratt, Geronimo, 145
Preis, Art, 66 n. 35
president, 241–61
administrative units to assist, 253
background of, 242–43
Congress and, 254–58
conservative context of, 257–60
corporate influence on, 243–44
corruption and, 244
direct election of, 251
dual role of serving corporate and
public interests, 248–50
electoral college and, 250–51, 261 n. 18
executive orders, 254–55
executive privilege and, 254
life of, 243
loyalty to subordinates, 270
national interest and, 249–50
New Federalism ploy, 252
powers of, 252–54, 259–60
as promoter and guardian of
capitalism, 241–44
resources of, 253–54
rhetoric versus action of, 244–48
salary and pension, 243
special interests and, 249–50
Supreme Court appointments and,
284–86
war-making powers of, 256–57
Pressen, Edward, 176 n. 1
Preston, William, Jr., 65 n. 9
Price Commission, 272
Priest, Dana, 94 n. 43
Primus, Wendell, 27 n. 49
Prison Litigation Reform Act, 126
prisons, 125–26
privatization of, 126
rape in, 125
suspicious deaths in, 125–26
treatment of prisoners, 125
waste and pilfering in, 126

Privacy Act, 294
private enterprise system, 29, 67–70
privatization, 97–98, 126, 263, 265–69
productivity, 17–19
human value of, 16
low, 18–19
worker, 17–18
profits, 8–9, 83–84
Progressive Era, 59–60
progressive income tax, 74
Progressive party, 206
progressives
entering the U.S., 140
ideology of, 35–36
proportional representation (PR),
198–200, 202
proportionate income tax, 74–75
Public Broadcasting Act of 1967, 189
Public Broadcasting System (PBS), 188,
189
public money, to subsidize private
enterprise, 67–70
public opinion, 37–39
public policy, 2
public-service regulation, 279–80
Purdum, Todd, 192 n. 16
Putnam, Constance, 136 n. 41

Quayle, Dan, 34

R. J. Reynolds, 13
racial profiling, 133
racism
economy and, 313
elimination of, 321
in law enforcement, 132–34
mass media coverage of, 183
Radelet, Michael, 136 n. 41
radioactive waste, 110
Radio Free Europe, 184
Radio Liberty, 184
Radio Marti, 184
Rainwater, L., 27 n. 43
Rampton, Sheldon, 117 n. 75
Randolph, Edmund, 45
Raspberry, William, 27 n. 52,
216 n. 23
Rather, Dan, 185–86

Reagan, Ronald, 33, 76, 214, 251, 254, 255, 257, 259
  American Renaissance, 244
  as America's salesman, 241, 242
  appointment of corporate leaders to government posts, 167
  authorization to infiltrate progressive organizations, 141–42
  Fairness Doctrine and, 189
  federal court orders ignored by, 256
  image of, 245–46
  Iran-contra scandal and, 158
  modest background of, 165
  secrecy pledge for government workers, 269
  Supreme Court appointments, 284–85
  term limits and, 235
Reconstruction Finance Corporation, 62
redistricting, 200–203
Red Scares, 61
Red squads, 141, 149
regressive income tax, 75
Rehnquist and Burger Court rulings, 292–93
Reich, Robert B., 15, 26 n. 25, 260 n. 14
Reisner, Marc, 117 n. 74
repression, 139–63, 307
  of African Americans, 143–45
  of anticapitalist activists, 145–46
  of antiwar activists, 142, 145, 146, 147
  by corporations, 140
  of dissenters, 139–42, 147–49
  by government agencies, 139–42, 149–57
  of labor leaders, 142
  of Native Americans, 147
  of prisoners, 144
  right-wing violence and, 149–51
Republican party, 194–97, 216 n. 3
Republic of New Afrika, 145
Reuben, William, 160 n. 32
Rhoads, Heather, 159 n. 17
RiceTec, 173–74
Richie, Robert, 216 n. 16, 216 n. 23
Ridgeway, James, 161 n. 49, 325 n. 11
rightists. *See* conservatives

Ritalin, 131
Robertson, Pat, 35
Rocawich, Linda, 41 n. 7
Rockefeller, David, 167
Rockefeller, John D., Jr., 277
Rockefeller, Nelson, 227, 228
Rockefeller family, 12
Rockwell International, 121
Roderick, David, 8
Roemer, John, 176 n. 3
Rogers, Will, 32, 219
Rollins, Edward, 217 n. 45
Roosevelt, Franklin D., 62, 244
Roosevelt, Theodore, 59
Rose, Stephen, 25 n. 10
Rosenberg, Daniel, 117 n. 71
Rosenberg, Ethel, 142
Rosenberg, Julius, 142
Rosenberg, Susan, 145–46
Ross, John, 177 n. 29
Roth, Hank, 93 n. 24
Rothmiller, Mike, 159 n. 11
Roundup, 112
Rowse, Arthur, 191 n. 1
Rule, Wilma, 216 n. 17
Rules Committee, 232–33
ruling class, 164–68, 307–8, 311, 312–13
  See also owning class
Rummel v. Estelle, 295
Russian Revolution, 61
Ryan, George, 127
Rytina, Joan, 41 n. 8

Sabato, Larry, 239 n. 27
Sabelli, Fabrizio, 93 n. 31
Sabow, James, 149
Safe Drinking Water Act, 110
Safire, William, 181
Sale, Kirkpatrick, 117 n. 76
sales tax, 79 n. 27
Salladay, Robert, 240 n. 47
Samuelson, Paul, 25 n. 10
Sanders, Bernard, 325 n. 12
SAP. *See* structural adjustment program (SAP)
Savimbi, Jonas, 154
savings and loan (S&L) associations, 70, 121, 122

Schaap, William, 162 n. 74
Schambra, William, 54 n. 6, 54 n. 21
Scheck, Barry, 136 n. 37
Scheer, Robert, 93 n. 19
Schenck v. United States, 289
Schiraldi, Vincent, 135 n. 21, 137 n. 56,
   192 n. 17
Schlesinger, Jacob, 26 n. 30
Schlosser, Eric, 136 n. 25
Schmidhauser, John, 176 n. 2
school of happy pluralism, 224
school prayer, 35, 294, 303 n. 42
Schorr, Lisbeth, 281 n. 5
Schrecker, Ellen, 159 n. 6, 159 n. 18
Schwartz, Herman, 302 n. 6, 303 n. 26,
   305 n. 79
Schwarz, John, 27 n. 41, 27 n. 42,
   280 n. 4
Scott, Frank, 41 n. 11
Scott, Peter Dale, 162 n. 82, 162 n. 84,
   163 n. 89, 163 n. 91, 260 n. 11
scrip, 46
Sea-Launched Ballistic Missiles, 80
Sears, 86
Secret Army Organization, 149
Selective Service System, 37
Senate, U.S., 12, 45, 47
   See also Congress; House of
   Representatives, U.S.
separate but equal doctrine, 288
Seventeenth Amendment, 48, 60
Sforza, Michelle, 177 n. 25
Shannon, William, 260 n. 3
Shapiro, Bruce, 138 n. 71
sharecroppers, 7–8
Shays, Daniel, 44
Shays' Rebellion, 44
Shell, 17, 71
Sherman, Roger, 45
Sherrill, Robert, 135 n. 8
Shields, Janice, 79 n. 2
Shields, mark, 260 n. 4
Shoup, Laurence, 176 n. 4, 176 n. 5
Shrybman, Steven, 177 n. 30
Shuford, Frank, 143
Shulman, Seth, 93 n. 22
Shultz, George, 261 n. 27
Shweder, Richard, 27 n. 56

Siegal, Nina, 136 n. 46
Sifry, Micah, 216 n. 27
Silkwood, Karen, 148–49
Silverstein, Ken, 79 n. 16, 115 n. 23,
   239 n. 10
Simpson, Christopher, 162 n. 76
Simpson, Glenn, 239 n. 27
Sims, Rebecca, 162 n. 86
Singham, Mano, 281 n. 14
Sixteenth Amendment, 60, 300
Sklar, Holly, 25 n. 10, 25 n. 14, 93 n. 34
SLAPP suits (Strategic Lawsuit Against
   Public Participation), 122
slavery, 46–47, 59
Sloan, Allan, 26 n. 21
Sloan, Don, 115 n. 23
Smeeding, T. M., 27 n. 43
Smith, Adam, 4, 5 n. 1, 7, 25 n. 1
Smith, David G., 54 n. 21
Smith, Gar, 92 n. 8
Smith, Jack, 186
Smith, Kevin, 281 n. 13
Smith, Wesley, 135 n. 14
Smith Act of 1940, 142, 289–90
SmithKline Beckman, 120
socialism, 35–37, 321–25
Socialist party, 202–3
Social Security, 77–78, 97–98, 263–64,
   272, 319
Social Security Act of 1935, 63
soft money, 204
solar power, 113
Soley, Lawrence, 41 n. 3
Solomon, Norman, 192 n. 20
Solomon, William, 192 n. 22
Songer, Donald, 302 n. 7
Son of Star Wars project, 81
Sostre, Martin, 143
Special Supplemental Food Program
   for Women, Infants, and Children
   (WIC), 95–96
Spencer, Herbert, 284
Spillance, Margaret, 159 n. 2
Spofford, Tim, 160 n. 37
SSI. *See* Supplemental Security Income
   (SSI)
St. Clair, Jeffrey, 162 n. 83, 192 n. 29
St. Germain, Fernand, 282 n. 41

St. Plite, Dona, 160 n. 39
standard of living, in democracy,
313–14
Standard Oil, 104–5
Stanton, Frank, 180
Star Wars outerspace weapon system,
273
State, Department of, 139, 140, 151
state, role in capitalism, 314–16
Stauber, John, 117 n. 75
STB. *See* Surface Transportation Board
(STB)
Steele, James, 79 n. 2
Steen, Jennifer, 216 n. 26
Stefancic, Jean, 177 n. 10
Stein, Benjamin J., 135 n. 13
Stein, Bobbie, 137 n. 50
Stein, Jeff, 160 n. 40
Steingraber, Sandra, 116 n. 50
Stern, Philip, 239 n. 4
Stevens, John Paul, 293, 295, 297,
298
Stewart, James, 135 n. 13
Stewart, Jean, 136 n. 32
Stidham, Ronald, 302 n. 7
Stone, I.F., 160 n. 37
Stossel, John, 181
strikes, 56–57, 123, 168
structural adjustment program (SAP),
87
Struyk, Raymond, 27 n. 46
substantive due process, 288
suicide, 24
Sullivan, Kathleen, 93 n. 24
Sulzberger, Arthur Hays, 186
Summers, Anthony, 159 n. 16
Superfund toxic waste cleanup
program, 112
Supplemental Security Income (SSI),
96, 264
Supreme Court, 48, 255, 283–305
abortion, 298–99
affirmative action, 299–300
Burger and Rehnquist Court rulings,
292–93
church and state, separation of,
294
civil liberties, 293–94

civil rights, 299–300
class background and biases of
justices, 283–86
conservative activism, 286–88, 301
corporate and class interests upheld
by, 286–88
criminal justice and, 294–95
death penalty, 296
democratization of, 317
economic inequality and, 293
electoral system and, 296–98
executive power and, 296
First Amendment and, 289–90
Florida vote recount decision in 2000
election, 210
gender discrimination, 298–99
influence of, 300–302
labor struggles, 292–93
powers of, 283
president and, 284–86
revolutionaries and, 290–91
separate but equal doctrine, 288
substantive due process, 288
term limits for justices of, 301–2
Surface Transportation Board (STB),
275
surplus value, 7
Sutherland, Edwin, 281 n. 28
Swearingen, M. Wesley, 159 n. 12,
159 n. 14
Sweeny, Paul, 26 n. 29, 79 n. 21
Symms, Steve, 109
Szatmary, David, 54 n. 12

Taft, William Howard, 59
Taft-Hartley Act, 168, 318
Talbot, Karen, 93 n. 22
taxes, 72–74
estate, 75
excise, 79 n. 27
flat, 74–75
inheritance, 75
national sales, 75
progressive income, 74
proportionate income, 74–75
reform, 318
regressive income, 75
sales, 79 n. 27

state and local, 75
value added, 75
Taxpayer Relief Act of 1997, 74
technology, obsolescence and low
    productivity, 18
Tenet, George, 271
Tenth Amendment, 175, 301
term limits, 235–36, 301–2
terrorism, coverage of, 185
Terry, Don, 26 n. 40, 177 n. 15
textbooks, biases of, 30, 41 n. 6
Themba, Makani, 325 n. 6
Theoharis, Athan, 159 n. 16
third parties, 197–98, 203, 215
Third World, 18, 20, 29, 85–88
Thomas, Clarence, 285
Thompson, A. Clay, 137 n. 56
Thornburgh v. Abbott, 293
Three Mile Island, Pennsylvania, 110
Time Warner, 181
tobacco industry, 7, 181, 220
Toobin, Jeffrey, 135 n. 20
Torres, Alejandrina, 146
torture, as American export, 154–55
Transportation, Department of, 275
transportation system, 104–5
Treasury, U.S., 278
treasury bonds, 76–77
Triano, Christine, 281 n. 9
Trilateral Commission, 167
Truman, Harry S, 244, 257
*Trustees of Dartmouth College v.
    Woodward*, 286
Turner, James C., 135 n. 18
Turner, Margery, 281 n. 8
Turner, Marjorie, 27 n. 46
Twenty-second Amendment, 258, 259
Twenty-sixth Amendment, 207
Twenty-third Amendment, 207

UFW. *See* United Farm Workers
    (UFW)
ultraviolet radiation, 109
Underemployment, 19–20
Unemployment, 19–20
unions. *See* labor unions
United Brands, 12
United Farm Workers (UFW), 169

United Nations, 87
universities, as corporate plutocracies,
    28–29, 31
University of California v. Bakke, 299
U.S. Forest Service, 68
U.S. Space Command, 81–82
U.S. Steel, 19
USDA. *See* Agriculture (USDA), U.S.
    Department of
Usher, Graham, 92 n. 11
utilities, deregulation of, 265–66

value added in manufacture, 7
value added tax, 75
Van Den Bosch, Robert, 116 n. 52
Vanderlip, Frank, 62
Verhoogen, Eric, 93 n. 26
Vietnam, 90–91
Vietnamese Organization to
    Exterminate Communists and
    Restore the Nation (VOECRN),
    148
Violence Against Women Act, 298
Vipers, 149
VOECRN. *See* Vietnamese
    Organization to Exterminate
    Communists and Restore the
    Nation (VOECRN)
Voice of America, 184
Volcker, Paul, 313
Volgy, Thomas, 27 n. 41, 27 n. 42
voting
    apathy, 212
    in early America, 42–43
    issues and, 212–13
    proportional representation, 198–200
    racial discrimination in, 207
    reasons for, 212
    struggle for rights, 207–11
    suppression of, in Florida 2000
        campaign, 209–10
    turnout, 207–8, 211–14
    women's suffrage movement, 59
Voting Rights Act of 1965, 1970, 1975,
    and 1985, 207

Wagner, Janet, 117 n. 62
Waldman, Michael, 135 n. 14

Walker, Jack, 282 n. 37
Wall, Jim Vander, 159 n. 12, 160 n. 27, 160 n. 38
Wallach, Lori, 177 n. 25
Wallop, Malcolm, 227
Wal-Mart, 86
Walsh, Lawrence, 163 n. 90
War Powers Act of 1973, 256–57, 259
Warren, Earl, 292
Warren, Leon, 116 n. 46
Warriors of God, 129
Washington, Albert, 145
Washington, George, 43, 45
Wasserman, Harvey, 281 n. 10
Watergate affair, 157–58
Watt, James, 121
Watt, Mel, 201
Watzman, Nancy, 281 n. 9
wealth
    accumulation of, 8–9
    class and, 6–8
    distribution of, 9–11
    as power, 11
Weaver, Leon, 216 n. 17
Webb, Gary, 186, 192 n. 29
Weber, Max, 280 n. 1, 315
Webster, William, 129
Weiner, Tim, 162 n. 83
Weinstein, Corey, 136 n. 30
Weisbord, Merrily, 159 n. 3
Weissman, Robert, 135 n. 10
Welch, Jack, 178
welfare. *See* Aid to Families with Dependent Children (AFDC)
Wennerberg, Tor, 326 n. 19
Westinghouse, 178
Wheeler, Tim, 177 n. 11, 239 n. 21
Whistleblower Protection Act, 271
White, Geoffry, 41 n. 3
Whitney, Craig, 115 n. 19
WIC. *See* Special Supplemental Food Program for Women, Infants, and Children (WIC)
Will, George, 206
Williams, Hayes, 126
Williams, Juan, 260 n. 5

Williams, William Appleman, 5 n. 2, 66 n. 23
Wilson, James, 51
Wilson, Steve, 180
Wilson, Woodrow, 22, 59–60, 277
wind power, 113
Winerip, Michael, 116 n. 36
Winfrey, Oprah, 122
Winner, Karen, 137 n. 47
Winokur, Scott, 281 n. 24
Winpisinger, William, 195
Winter-Berger, Robert, 239 n. 17
Wise, David, 161 n. 57, 260 n. 9
Wisely, Willie, 136 n. 34
Witanek, Robert, 161 n. 59
Wojcik, John, 160 n. 24
women
    in Congress, 218
    domestic violence and, 128–29
    elimination of discrimination against, 321
    mass media portrayal of, 188
    poverty rates, 23
    in prison, 130
    sexism in legal system and, 128–30
    suffrage, 59
    Supreme Court and discrimination against, 298–99, 302 n. 13
    voting and, 207
Wooden, Kenneth, 137 n. 57
Woolhandler, Steffie, 115 n. 13
worker compensation laws, 102
working class, 6–8
    depressed wages for, 313
    exploitation of, 7–8
    expropriation of earnings, 311–12
    hardships of, 20–23
    improvements needed for, 321
    taxation of, 73
    unemployment and, 19–20
    See also labor
working poor, 21
Works Progress Administration (WPA), 63, 321
World Bank, 37, 87–88, 146, 166, 312
World Trade Organization (WTO), 37, 146, 171, 172–76, 263, 311, 312

World War I, 60–61
World War II, 63, 67, 119
WPA. *See* Works Progress
   Administration (WPA)
WTO. *See* World Trade Organization
   (WTO)

Yarbrough, Tinsley, 303 n. 26
Yates, Michael, 41 n. 3, 177 n. 13,
   177 n. 20
Yeoman, Barry, 216 n. 22
Yeskel, Felice, 25 n. 5
Young, Alfred, 54 n. 20
Yugoslavia, 89–90

Zeiderstein, Harvey, 261 n. 19
Zepezauer, Mark, 79 n. 2, 79 n. 3,
   79 n. 5, 79 n. 11
zero emission vehicles (ZEVs), 113–14
ZEVs. *See* zero emission vehicles (ZEVs)
Zichuhr, Clare, 92 n. 8
Zimmerman, Joseph, 216 n. 17
Zimring, Franklin, 137 n. 54
Zinko, Carolyne, 27 n. 52
Zinn, Howard, 65 n. 2, 65 n. 4, 66 n. 24,
   66 n. 28
Zoll, Daniel, 192 n. 5
Zuckerman, Edward, 238 n. 2
Zuckerman, Mortimer, 21, 26 n. 37